the book of
modern Scandal

By the same author

India: A Literary Companion

the book of
modern Scandal

From Byron to the Present Day

edited by Bruce Palling

Weidenfeld & Nicolson
London

First published in Great Britain in 1995
by Weidenfeld & Nicolson

The Orion Publishing Group Ltd
Orion House
5 Upper Saint Martin's Lane
London WC2H 9EA

A catalogue record for this book is available
from the British Library

ISBN 0 297 81298 X

Printed in Great Britain by
Butler & Tanner Limited,
Frome and London

To Lucinda, with love

Contents

Acknowledgements

The inspiration for this book really belongs to Tejbir Singh, with whom I first discussed the concept while we were travelling to the Kulu Dussehra in the Himalayas. One night we started listing all of the most significant scandals we could think of and within no time had reached 100. I am also indebted to various libraries and librarians, especially the London Library, the British Library Newspaper Library at Colindale, the Age Library in Melbourne and Allan Bell and Linda Williams at Rhodes House Library for their invaluable assistance on American material. Helen Simpson was extraordinarily enterprising in digging out obscure material for me while my editors Ion Trewin and Benjamin Buchan performed miracles in order to meet numerous deadlines.

I would also like to thank Rachel Cusk, Christopher Silvester, Phillip Knightley, Ron Hall, Anne McDermid, Nicholas Coleridge, Chris Mullin MP, Michael Cockerell, Maddie Mogford, Judy Stowe, Auberon Waugh, Dorothy Bredin, Phillip Marsden, Hugh Bredin, Robert Milliken, Victor Sebasteyn, Richard Addis, Lucy Hughes-Hallett, Carol Livingston, John Hatt, Nigel Dempster, Ian Buruma, James Fenton, Jamie Fergusson, Godfrey Hodgson, Jeremy Paxman, Raghubir Singh, William Shawcross, Patrice de Beer, Robert Cottrell, Anna Craven, Ian Hamilton, Francis Wheen, James Fox, Anthony Gardner, Christopher Hitchens, Bridget Beck and Peter Levi.

I am grateful to the sources indicated for permission to reproduce the excerpted material.

But my greatest debt is to my wife Lucinda, for providing numerous ideas for scandals that I had not thought of and for tolerating my behaviour during the book's compilation.

Introduction

Despite having researched the subject of scandal extensively for the past few years, I find that it is extraordinarily difficult to define what makes a 'good' scandal. There are so many variables that it is perfectly possible for individuals to be equally scandalised by an incident for diametrically different reasons. The best recent example of this is the Salman Rushdie affair. For many Islamic fundamentalists, what he wrote about the Prophet was an utter scandal and blasphemy, while members of the liberal intelligentsia were equally outraged by the notion that a foreign zealot thought he could pass a death sentence on a British writer. This is doubly interesting because the original meaning of the word scandal was a stumbling block to faith or something that brought discredit upon religion.

More often, though, scandal can be defined as some act or behaviour which is socially shocking and could cause a serious erosion of a person's reputation if made public. While it is true that standards vary enormously and change with time, it is interesting how consistent are the values which we hold sacrosanct. The adulterous affair of David and Bathsheba would cause just as much trouble now as it did then, while Alcibiades manifested many of the attributes of a contemporary politician.

A key ingredient for a scandal to be memorable is the extent of hypocrisy that is exposed by the revelations. John Profumo has always been remembered in a sympathetic light for his affair with a call girl partly because he never tried to lecture anybody about their morals. By contrast, Jim Bakker, the American preacher, deserves utter contempt for his trumpeting of moral values which he completely ignored in his personal behaviour.

Another important factor in our abiding interest in scandal is that it can be such spectacularly gripping entertainment. The case of failed American presidential contender Gary Hart is a good example. No sooner did he deny any hanky-panky and even invite journalists to follow him around, than he was discovered in the arms of a blonde. Or the extraordinary case of David Mellor lecturing the press about their behaviour while carrying on an adulterous affair with an out-of-work actress. A scandal does not have to involve sexual peccadilloes to arouse our interest, as anybody who lived through the Watergate affair can vouch. The sheer amount of wrongdoing and malfeasance that was uncovered made it a serious alternative to a soap opera for many people.

There are, however, serious limits on scandal when it comes to exposing horrendous criminal behaviour or the foulness of war. It is not possible to encompass the wickedness or evil of Hitler, Stalin or Pol Pot simply by highlighting their personal peccadilloes. And even though they were both guilty of scandalous behaviour, there is also a world of difference between the private goings-on of President John Kennedy and the public behaviour of President Richard Nixon. The shortcoming of scandals is that they tend to emphasize the trivial at the expense of far more serious affairs which do not involve prominent personalities or public figures.

One of the most interesting aspects of my research was the discovery of how standards have changed when it comes to royal scandals. Charles II went so far as to attend Easter church services with three of his bastards and received hardly any social opprobrium while his descendant and namesake has been subjected to ridicule on the basis of a single recorded telephone conversation made three years earlier with a woman said to be his mistress.

When it comes to modern scandals, no society comes close to the United States of America. This is not so much due to the fact that behaviour in America is more outrageous than in other nations as to the freedoms the American people enjoy to expose such behaviour. If one goes through contemporary indexes to either *The Washington Post* or *The New York Times*, one will find between 1,000 to 1,600 stories listed each year as scandals.

Howard Kurtz of *The Washington Post* has produced a succinct guide to the basic rules of the Washington journalist's scandal game: 'Personalize scandal: Advance three spaces. Spice up scandal with sex angle or famous person: Advance five spaces. Pin scandal on someone who's bad at damage control: Win a free trip to Page 1. Unearth scandal in a slow news month: Collect 100 bylines. Discover scandal that fuels the political wars: Proceed directly to journalistic heaven.'*

Britain is not so different except that the most readable scandals tend to be found in the tabloid papers rather than the broadsheets, with the notable exception of page three of *The Daily Telegraph*. Even so, there were obvious changes in attitude by the early part of this decade. For instance, one Tory minister was exposed in the press as having a string of jilted mistresses and girlfriends and managed to survive politically. There is a dearth of examples of scandals from other countries with the partial exception of Australia, chiefly because of the difficulty in finding original accounts in translation.

There are some scandals that I had to decline to print – particularly one that I unearthed in the Public Records Office involving a serving monarch that Lord Mountbatten accused of murder. There was another involving

* *The Washington Post*, 22 September, 1991.

the writings of Sir Edmund Backhouse, the fraudulent sinologist that Sir Hugh Trevor-Roper so brilliantly exposed in his *Hermit of Peking*. After tracking down his memoirs in a section of the Bodleian Library at Oxford and signing for them (just below an earlier signature of Bruce Chatwin) they were so obscene rather than scandalous that I couldn't personally justify republishing them. I apologize in advance for any scandals that I have overlooked – there is admittedly a bias in favour of readable scandals. Far too many involving businessmen and politicians are so turgid that I would not risk including any more than I have already. My present selection is shaped more by entertainment than educational motives, but I hope that anybody who manages to read through the entire book will emerge with a broader understanding of the human condition. For future editions, I will obviously add stories that with hindsight should have been included, so if any readers think they know of a good contemporary account of any scandals that I have missed, please do write to me.

Mad, Bad and Dangerous to Know

Lord Byron and Lady Caroline Lamb

Lord Byron was involved in numerous incidents, which could more accurately be called scandals, but managed to handle them with a combination of luck, bravado and, ultimately, egress after he was accused of sodomy and incest with his half-sister. Lady Caroline Lamb, wife of Lord Melbourne, the future prime minister, was infatuated with Byron. She dispatched some of her pubic hairs to him as a memento and disguised herself as a pageboy in his carriage. He called her 'the cleverest, most agreeable, absurd, amiable, perplexing, dangerous, fascinating little being that lives'. However, the following letter shows that he was bored by her enthusiasm and was more than happy to contemplate the prospect of her being unmasked in public.

4 Bennet Street April 29th, 1813

If you still persist in your intention of meeting me in opposition to the wishes of your own friends & of mine – it must even be so – I regret it & acquiesce with reluctance. I am not ignorant of the very extraordinary language you have held not only to me but others – & your avowal of your determination to obtain what you are pleased to call 'revenge' – nor have I now to learn that an incensed woman is a dangerous enemy. Undoubtedly those against whom we can make no defence – whatever they say or do – must be formidable – your words & actions have lately been tolerably portentous – & might justify me in avoiding the demanded interview – more especially as I believe you fully capable of performing all your menaces – but as I once hazarded every thing *for* you – I will not shrink *from* you – perhaps I deserve punishment – if so – you are quite as proper a person to inflict it as any other. You say you will '*ruin me*' – I thank you – but I have done that for myself already – you say you will 'destroy me' perhaps you will only save me the trouble. It is useless to reason with you – to repeat what you already know – that I have in reality saved you from utter & impending destruction. Every one who knows you – knows this also – but they do not know as yet what you may & will tell them as I now tell you – that it is in a great measure owing to this persecution – to the accursed things you have said – to the extravagances you have committed – that I again adopt the resolution of quitting this country – In your assertions – you have either *belied* or *betrayed* me – take your choice – in your actions – you have hurt only yourself – but is that nothing to one who wished you well? – I have only one request to make – which is not to attempt to see Lady O[xford] – on her you have no claim. You will settle – as you please – the arrangement of this conference – I do not leave England till June – but the sooner it is over the better – I once wished for your own sake Lady M[elbourne] to be present – but if you are to fulfil any of your threats in word or deed – we had better be alone.

yrs. ever

Byron's Letters and Journals (John Murray, 1974), vol. 3, p. 43.

Difference of Opinion over a Lady's Affections

Duel between Lord Buckingham and Sir Thomas Hardy

Thomas Creevey, a minor Whig politician who kept a lengthy diary during the early nineteenth century, reported the following incident from Holland House in May 1816.

The town has been much occupied by a very strange affair which led to a duel between Lord Buckingham and Sir Thomas Hardy. It is a mysterious business, but I sincerely hope quite over for ever. It was the charge of Lord Buckingham being the author of some very scandalous, offensive anonymous letters to, and about, Lady Hardy. You would naturally suppose that the character of a gentleman, which Lord Buckingham has never forfeited, would have been a sufficient guard to have repelled such a charge; but the Lady was angry. There are various conjectures about the writer of these letters; but, except just the angry parties, the world gen-erally does justice to Lord Buckingham, from the impossibility of a man of character and in his station of life being capable of such an abominable proceeding. It is not the mode of revenge which a man takes, however he may have been jilted, or believed himself as so.

John Gore (ed.), *Creevey* (John Murray, 1948), p. 154.

The Indiscretions of the Princess of Wales

Queen Caroline when Princess of Wales

Queen Caroline (1768–1821), the ugly, smelly, overweight wife of George IV, was considered by Lady Hester Stanhope to be 'a downright whore'. She was offered the colossal sum of £50,000 p.a. by the government if she agreed to stay abroad and not to seek to be crowned as Queen. She refused, so the House of Lords began proceedings against her for adultery. The trial in 1820 was the sensation of the year, with the Attorney-General, Sir Robert Gifford, offering the following account of her adventures abroad a few years earlier. She began her travels in 1814 with a sizeable group of aristocratic English ladies-in-waiting, maids of honour, equerries and a chamberlain. Three weeks after arriving in Milan she took on a handsome local servant called Bartolomeo Bergami as her footman. In a matter of weeks his stature amongst the royal party grew considerably, especially after he suffered a minor injury in Naples. At the same time, the English contingent of the princess rapidly departed only to be replaced by members of Bergami's family.

During her majesty's stay at Naples this person [Bergami] received an injury by a kick from a horse, and this was one of the circumstances which tended to shew the influence he had acquired over his royal mistress. He had obtained such an ascendancy, that he had it in his power to introduce into the house a servant to wait upon himself. This man slept in a room close to that allotted to Bergami, and during the time that he was in attendance he observed her majesty two or three different times advancing, after all the other domestics were retired to rest, with great care and caution from her own apartment to Bergami's room. Into that room she entered, and each time remained in it for a considerable period; and he had further to state, that on one occasion after she had entered a sound was heard, which convinced the person who observed this proceeding that her majesty and Bergami were kissing each other. He was aware of the reluctance with which their lordships must listen to these disgusting details; they were such, he was sensible, as must excite disgust in a certain measure even towards the person stating them, but that consideration would not prevent him from performing his duty. The painful duty of stating them was cast upon him, and the no less painful duty of hearing and considering them was cast upon their lordships. He was bound to describe the circumstances which formed the case, but he was sure their lordships would not censure him for stating, in the way he was doing, those facts which it was necessary he should lay before them.

By now, all of the English ladies of rank had left Caroline, except for Lady Colin Campbell, who had only briefly joined the entourage at Genoa. In their place, had come a large number of Bergami's extended family.

When Lady C. Campbell left her majesty at Milan, no English lady remained in her suite. One would have thought that, considering the high rank which she occupied – considering that she was in the situation of expecting soon to become queen consort of this country – one would have thought that she would have been anxious to have had constantly about her person some English ladies of distinction, or, at least, that she would have looked out for ladies of a similar rank in her native country of Brunswick, or in that part of the continent in which she resided. But, quite the contrary; she received here into her service and confidence a person whom she had never seen before, a person of vulgar manners and totally uneducated; and (was it credible?) this person was another sister of Bergami's. Such was the power of this man over her, that this person, dignified by the title of Countess of Oldi, was received into her house as her principal attendant. Thus their lordships had now under the same roof with her majesty, two sisters, the mother, the brother, and the child of Bergami; one sister sitting at table with the queen as her lady of honour, while the other dined with the servants.

After a series of incidents which culminated in the departure of Mr Burrell, the last remaining English member of her entourage, new outrages were reported back to London by the large number of spies which had been inserted into her party by the Prince of Wales.

Her majesty then proceeded to Bellinzone, and here the intimacy between her and Bergami continued, and his influence was carried to such a height that he now sat at table with her. He had never before attempted this publically, though they had often breakfasted together privately; he had never before sat down to dine with her majesty, but now at this place that step was for the first time taken, and he was admitted to dine with her majesty in his courier's dress. ... Was such conduct ever before heard of, he would not say amongst the highest ranks of life, but amongst the middle classes of society? If it was not the custom among them to admit menial servants to the same table – if it was considered improper by private individuals – it must in the case of her royal highness be viewed as most indecorous and disgusting. It could be accounted for only by that unfortunate attachment which she had formed, and to that criminal intercourse, the usual effect of which was to throw down all distinctions between the parties to it, to raise the obscure to a level with the high, and induce the one to claim equal privileges and attention to the other. On this occasion they visited Lugano, where their lordships would find decisive evidence that the same adulterous intercourse which had taken place elsewhere was renewed. The same arrangements with regard to the occupation of rooms were made, and the chamber of the courier Bergami adjoined to that of the Princess of Wales. If these facts should be supported in evidence, no doubt could remain in the minds of their lordships that a criminal intercourse was regularly carried on.

The Princess of Wales occasionally travelled in southern Italy on English frigates, including one where the Captain refused to allow her to dine at table with him if she insisted on being accompanied by Bergami.

It would appear, too, that her majesty had conceived an extraordinary fondness for an infant child of Bergami, between two and three years old, which slept in the same room, and often in the same bed with her. She treated it with every mark of parental affection, sometimes calling it 'princess'; and the child, on the other hand, would cry, and was with difficulty pacified when she happened to quit the room. The child called her 'mamma'; and these circumstances altogether persuaded the servants at Catania that it was not the first occasion on which an adulterous intercourse had been carried on. Having conferred so many honours on Bergami, she now procured for him the dignity of a knight of Malta, and always addressed him as chevalier. What necessity was there for this, or what reason but that guilty attachment which had been so often indicated could be assigned for it? Whilst at Catania, the nobility tendered to her their respects, and she enjoyed at first the society of the first persons there; but, after a short residence, she became indifferent to all society but that of her paramour, and they gradually withdrew...

The Trial at Large of Her Majesty Caroline Amelia Elizabeth in the
House of Lords, 1821, vol. 1, pp. 124–33.

Despite the conclusive evidence presented to the Lords, the Princess of Wales was acquitted of the charges thanks to the brilliance of her defence, led by Lord Brougham. She maintained the affections of a large portion of London society. When George IV was being crowned, she attempted to accompany him at Westminster Abbey but was barred at the door. A short time after she took ill and died two days later.

....

'Publish and be Damned'

The Duke of Wellington and Harriette Wilson

In the 1820s, numerous members of the British aristocracy were confronted with lurid details of their exploits with Harriette Wilson, a charming courtesan of French descent who decided to increase her income by publishing her highly salacious memoirs concerning her adventures in Mayfair. It is hard to imagine a more alluring opening paragraph for a sensational book than the following...

I shall not say why and how I became, at the age of fifteen, the mistress of the Earl of Craven. Whether it was love, or the severity of my father, the depravity of my own heart, or the winning arts of the noble Lord, which induced me to leave my paternal roof and place myself under his protection, does not now much signify: or if it does, I am not in the humour to gratify curiosity in this matter.

What made her case more sensational is that she offered various of her customers the opportunity to literally purchase her silence by first submitting the chapters concerning her former admirers. This led to the purported response of the Duke of Wellington to 'Publish and be damned.' According to the Dictionary of National Biography, *'Among the well known names that figure prominently in the narrative are those of the Duke of Wellington, the Duke of Leinster, Lord Hertford, Marquis Wellesley, the Earl of Fife, Prince Esterhazy, Lord Granville Leveson-Gower, Lord Ebrington, Beau Brummell, Henry Luttrell and "his impossibly fat Nugent", Viscount Ponsonby, Richard Meyler, Lord Frederick Bentinck, Lord Byron, and Henry Brougham...'*

The following extract takes up the story from her first encounter with the Duke of Wellington.

I was getting into debt, as well as my sister Amy, when it so came to pass, as I have since heard say, that the – immortal!!! No: that's common; a very outlandish distinction, fitter for a lady in a balloon. The terrific!!! that will do better. I have seen His Grace in his cotton night-cap. Well, then, the terrific Duke of Wellington!! the wonder of the world!!! Having six feet from the tail to the head, and – but there is a certain technicality in the expressions of the gentleman at Exeter 'Change, when he has occasion to show off a wild beast, which it would be vanity in me to presume to imitate; so leaving out his dimensions, etc. etc., it was even the Duke of Wellington, whose laurels, like those of the giant in the *Vicar of Wakefield*, had been hardly earned by the sweat of his little dwarfs' brows, and the loss of their little legs, arms, and eyes; who, feeling himself amorously given – it was in summer – one sultry evening, ordered his coachman to set him down at the White Horse Cellar, in Piccadilly, whence he sallied forth, on foot, to No. 2 or 3, in Berkeley St, and rapped hastily at the door, which was immediately opened by the tawdry, well-roughed house-keeper of Mrs Porter, who, with a significant nod of recognition, led him into her mistress's boudoir, and then hurried away, simpering, to acquaint the good Mrs Porter with the arrival of one of her oldest customers.

The Duke wished to meet Harriette at the earliest opportunity so Mrs Porter went to see her the next morning.

'I am now come to inform you, that you have made the conquest of a very fine, noble, most unexceptionable man.'

'Delightful!' said I. 'Who is he?'

'I dare not tell you his name,' interrupted Mrs Porter; 'but you may rest assured that he is a man of fashion and rank.'

'It will not do,' reiterated I, striking my head. 'Tell your friend that I have no money, that I do not know how to take care of myself, and Argyle [the Duke of Argyll] takes no care of me. Tell him that nobody wants a real steady friend more than I do; but I cannot meet a stranger as a lover. Tell him all this, if he is really handsome, that is to say (for the stranger I had twice met, riding down Sloane St, accompanied by his large dog, had lately run often in my head) and let me know what he says, tomorrow.'

. . .

The next morning I received another visit from Mrs Porter, who informed me that she had just had an interview with my new lover, and had reported to him all I had desired her to say.

'Since you object to meet a stranger,' continued Mrs Porter, 'His Grace desires me to say, he hopes you can keep a secret, and to inform you, that it is the Duke of Wellington who so anxiously desires to make your acquaintance.'

'I have heard of His Grace often,' said I, in a tone of disappointment; for I had been indulging a kind of hope about the stranger with the great Newfoundland dog, with whose appearance I had been so unusually struck as to have sought for him every day, and I thought of him every hour.

'His Grace,' Mrs Porter proceeded, 'only entreats to be allowed to make your acquaintance. His situation, you know, prevents the possibility of his getting regularly introduced to you.'

'It will never do,' said I, shaking my head.

'Be assured,' said Mrs Porter, 'he is a remarkably fine-looking man, and, if you are afraid of my house, promise to receive him in your own, at any hour when he may be certain to find you alone.'

Well, thought I, with a sigh; I suppose he must come. I do not understand economy, and am frightened to death at debts. Argyle is going to Scotland; and I shall want a steady sort of friend, of some kind, in case a bailiff should get hold of me.

'What shall I say to His Grace?' Mrs Porter inquired, growing impatient.

'Well, then,' said I, 'since it must be so, tell His Grace that I will receive him tomorrow at three; but mind, only as a common acquaintance!'

Away winged Wellington's Mercury, as an old woman wings it at sixty; and most punctual to my appointment, at three on the following day, Wellington made his appearance. He bowed first, then said –

'How do you do?' then thanked me for having given him permission to call on me; and then wanted to take hold of my hand.

'Really,' said I, withdrawing my hand, 'for such a renowned hero you have very little to say for yourself.'

'Beautiful creature!' uttered Wellington. 'Where is Lorne [the Duke of Argyll]?'

'Good gracious,' said I, out of all patience with his stupidity – 'What come you here for, Duke?'

'Beautiful eyes, yours!' reiterated Wellington.

'Aye, man! they are greater conquerors than ever Wellington shall be; but, to be serious, I understand that you came here to try to make yourself agreeable?'

'What, child! do you think that I have nothing better to do than make speeches to please ladies?' said Wellington.

'*Après avoir dépeuplé la terre, vous devez faire tout pour la repeupler,*' I replied.
'You should see where I shine,' Wellington observed, laughing.
'Where's that, in God's name?'
'In a field of battle,' answered the hero.
'*Battez-vous, donc, et qu'un autre me fasse la cour!*' said I.
But love scenes, or even love quarrels, seldom tend to amuse the reader, so, to be brief, what was a mere man, even though it were the handsome Duke of Argyle, to a Wellington!!!!

Lesley Blanch (ed.), *Harriette Wilson's Memoirs* (Folio Society, 1964), pp. 51–9

The book was originally produced in four volumes and after the first one appeared, special barricades had to be put up in front of the publisher's office to control the crowds of eager purchasers. It eventually went into twenty editions in the first year alone. According to Sir Walter Scott, 'The gay world has been kept in hot water lately by this impudent publication ... the wit is poor, but the style of the interlocutors exactly imitated ...' Further volumes of the memoirs failed to appear after a discreet whip around by her admirers which enabled her to retire to France, where she died in 1855.

....

Queen Victoria and a Phantom Pregnancy

Lady Flora Hastings

Very early in her reign, Queen Victoria was booed during a performance at Drury Lane and hissed at Ascot because of the accurate public perception that the monarch and her courtiers were persecuting Lady Flora Hastings, the thirty-three-year-old lady-in-waiting to the Duchess of Kent, Queen Victoria's mother. Lady Flora was the unmarried daughter of the first Marquess of Hastings, the Governor-General of India who later secured the cession of Singapore. When Lady Flora returned from a trip in 1839 complaining of a pain in her abdomen, palace rivals were quick to accuse her of being pregnant by Sir John Conroy, a

*senior courtier who had travelled on the same ship as Lady Flora. Her error was
to confide in the Queen's physician, Sir James Clark, who was a poor diag-
nostician and an enemy of Sir John.*

*After a cursory examination, he concluded she was pregnant, which meant
that Lady Flora was banned from any contact with the Queen, who took the
side of Lady Flora's detractors. When Lady Flora protested, another physician
was called and, along with Sir James, submitted her to a humiliating inspection
which showed that in fact she was still a virgin.*

*The rumours, however, continued, as shown in this extract from Lord Greville's
diaries in 1839.*

March 2nd. – The whole town has been engrossed for some days with a
scandalous story at Court, and although of course great exaggerations and
falsehoods are grafted upon the real case, and it is not easy to ascertain
what and how much is true, enough is known and indubitable to show that
it is a very discreditable transaction. It appears that Lady Flora Hastings, the
Duchess of Kent's lady, has been accused of being with child. It was at first
whispered about, and at last swelled into a report, and finally into a charge.
With whom it originated is not clear; but the Queen appears to have been
apprised of the rumour, and so far to have entered into it as to sanction
an intimation to the lady that she must not appear at Court till she could
clear herself of the imputation. Medical examination was either demanded
by her or submitted to, and the result was satisfactory to the virtue of the
accused damsel. Then naturally exploded the just indignation of insulted
honour. Her brother, Lord Hastings, came up to town, saw Melbourne,
who is said to have endeavoured to smother the affair, and to have tried
to persuade Lord Hastings to do so; but he was not at all so inclined, and
if he had been, it was too late, as all the world had begun to talk of it, and
he demanded and obtained an audience of the Queen. I abstain from
noticing the various reports of what this or that person did or said, for the
truth of which I could not vouch; but it is certain that the Court is plunged
in shame and mortification at the exposure, that the palace is full of
bickerings and heart-burnings, while the whole proceeding is looked upon
by society at large as to the last degree disgusting and disgraceful. It is
really an exemplification of the saying that 'Les Rois et les Valets' are made
of the refuse clay of creation, for though such things sometimes happen
in the servants' hall, and housekeepers charge still-room and kitchen-
maids with frailty, they are unprecedented and unheard of in good society,
and among people in high or even respectable stations. It is inconceivable
how Melbourne can have permitted this disgraceful and mischievous

scandal, which cannot fail to lower the character of the Court in the eyes of the world.

Philip Morrell (ed.), *Leaves from the Greville Diary* (Heinemann, 1929), pp. 366–7.

However, the scandal refused to disappear, especially after Hamilton FitzGerald, Lady Flora's uncle, published the following letter in The Examiner *just a fortnight later.*

Statement in Vindication of Lady Flora Hastings

[It is not our practice to notice matters of private scandal, but, called upon to publish a statement corrective of certain injurious impressions, and in vindication of a lady's reputation, we have only to comply: –]

Sir, – Many false and contradictory reports of the deplorable insult which has lately been offered to my niece, Lady Flora Hastings, at Buckingham Palace, having appeared in the public papers, I, as her Ladyship's nearest connection, feel it my duty to request of you to publish the following account of the transaction, for the correctness of which I vouch. An imperfect knowledge of this odious affair has produced various false conclusions. In well-informed circles, where Lady Flora is known, the idea of her guilt was never entertained for a moment; but in other quarters, where, in the absence of positive information, a judgement is formed by what oozes out in the public papers, I find an injurious idea exists 'that she had been spared, or let off easy.' The facts are briefly these:–

Lady Flora arrived some weeks since from Scotland, very unwell. She immediately consulted Sir James Clark, the physician to both her Majesty and the Duchess of Kent. One symptom of her complaint was a swelling of her stomach. By dint of exercise and medical treatment she was getting better, the swelling had considerably subsided, and she had every hope of a speedy recovery, when, on or about the 1st of March, Sir James Clark went to her room and announced to her the conviction of the Ladies of the Palace that she was pregnant.

In answer to all his exhortations to confession, 'as the only means of saving her character', Lady Flora returned an indignant but steady denial that there was anything to confess. Upon which Sir James Clark told her 'that nothing but her submitting to a medical examination would ever satisfy them, or remove the stigma from her name'. Lady Flora found that the subject had been brought to the Queen's notice, and that all this had been discussed, arranged, and denounced to her without one word having been said on the subject to her own mistress, the Duchess of Kent, who had no suspicion of what was going on, and whose sanction was not sought for the humiliating proposition which had been made to Lady Flora.

On leaving Lady Flora's room, Sir James Clark went to the Duchess of Kent, and announced his conviction that Lady Flora was with child; and was followed by Lady Portman, who conveyed a message from her Majesty to her mother to say that the Queen would not permit Lady Flora to appear till the examination had taken place. Lady Portman (who with Lady Tavistock are those whose names are mentioned as most active against Lady Flora) expressed to the Duchess of Kent her conviction of Lady Flora's guilt. 'Her beloved mistress' never for a moment doubted Lady Flora's innocence. She said that she knew her, her principles, and her family too well to listen to such a charge. However, the edict was given; and the next day, Lady Flora having obtained the Duchess of Kent's very reluctant consent – 'for her Royal Highness could not bear the idea of her being exposed to such a humiliation' – but Lady Flora 'feeling it her duty to her Royal Highness, to her family, and to herself, that a point blank refutation should be instantly given to the lie', submitted herself to the most rigid examination; and now possesses a certificate, signed by Sir James Clark, and also by Sir Charles Clark, stating, as strongly as language can state it, that 'there are no grounds for believing that pregnancy does exist, or ever has existed.' Lord Hastings, though at the time very ill from influenza, went to London instantly, and demanded and obtained from Lord Melbourne, a distinct disavowal of his participation in the affair, and demanded and obtained an audience of her Majesty, in which, while he disclaimed all idea that the Queen had any wish to injure his sister, he plainly, though respectfully, stated his opinion of those who had coun-selled her, and his resolution to find out the originator of the slander, and bring him or her to punishment. Lady Flora is convinced that the Queen was surprised into the order which was given, and that her Majesty did not understand what she was betrayed into – for ever since the horrid event her Majesty has showed her regret by the most gracious kindness to Lady Flora, and 'expressed it warmly with tears in her eyes'. The Duchess of Kent's conduct was perfect; 'a mother could not have been kinder.' 'She immediately dismissed Sir James Clark from her service, and refused to see Lady Portman'; and has crowned her goodness by a most beautiful letter she has written to the Dowager Lady Hastings, from whom the accounts were kept till all hope of avoiding publicity was impossible.

I am, Sir, your very obedient servant,

Hamilton FitzGerald

The Examiner, 21 March 1839, p. 179.

However, there were still those who thought that the Queen acted badly in not rushing to Lady Flora's defence earlier. Although Lady Flora remained in service, her condition deteriorated and she died in June 1839. She had insisted that after her death a post mortem be held to dispel the continuing rumours still emanating from rival court ladies that she had a stillborn child within her. There was no foetus – she had died of a badly swollen liver. The papers carried stories of the scandal for months after her death and Queen Victoria continued to be wary of public engagements because of popular anger at her behaviour.

....

Russian Flogger

The flogging of Russian servant girls

Alexander Herzen (1812–70), the Russian writer and revolutionary, was exiled from St Petersburg in the 1830s due to a trifling political offence. Because of his family connections, he was able to take a position in 1840 as a clerk in the provincial government of Novgorod, where he ended up in charge of the department dealing with people under police supervision. This led to the Kafkaesque situation where every quarter he had to countersign the police report confirming his own continuing good behaviour. While in this role he uncovered the following accounts of servants' fates at the hands of their employers.

Unfortunately the 'attributes' of brutality, debauchery, and violence with house-serfs and peasants are more 'invariable' than those of 'honour' and 'truthfulness' among our nobility. Of course there is a small group of cultured landowners who do not knock their servants about from morning to night, do not thrash them every day ... but the rest of them have not yet advanced beyond the stage of the American planters.

Rummaging about in the files, I found the correspondence of the provincial government of Pskov concerning a certain Madame Yaryzhkin, a landed lady. She had flogged two of her maids to death, was tried on account of a third, and was almost completely acquitted by the Criminal Court, who based their verdict among other things on the fact that the

third maid did not die. This woman invented the most amazing punishments, hitting with a flat iron, with gnarled sticks or with a
beetle.

I do not know what the girl in question had done, but her mistress
surpassed herself. She made the girl kneel in filth, or on boards into which
nails had been driven; in this position she beat her about the back and
the head with a beetle [heavy wooden hand-tool] and, when she had
exhausted herself, called the coachman to take her place; luckily he was
not in the servants' quarters, and she went out to find him, while the girl,
half frantic with pain and covered with blood, rushed out into the street
with nothing on but her smock and ran to the police-station. The police-
inspector took her evidence and the case went its regular course. The
police busied themselves and the Criminal Court busied itself over it for
a year; at last the court, obviously bribed, very sagaciously decided to
summon the lady's husband and suggest to him that he should restrain
his wife from such punishments, and they obliged her, while leaving her
under suspicion of having brought about the death of two servants,
to sign an undertaking not to inflict punishments in future. On this
understanding the unfortunate girl, who had been kept somewhere else
while the case was going on, was handed over to her mistress again.

The girl, terrified by what lay before her, began writing one petition
after another; the matter reached the ears of the Tsar; he ordered it to
be investigated, and sent an official from Petersburg. Probably Madame
Yaryzhkin's means were not equal to bribing the Petersburg, the ministerial
and the political police investigators, and the case took a different turn.
The lady was relegated to Siberia and her husband was put under ward.
All the members of the Criminal Court were tried; how their cases ended
I do not know . . .

I will add one more story of a lady. The maid of the wife of a colonel of
gendarmes at Penza was carrying a tea-pot full of boiling water. Her
mistress's child ran against the servant, who spilt the boiling water, and
the child was scalded. The mistress, to exact her vengeance in the same
coin, ordered the servant's child to be brought and scalded its hand from
the samovar . . .

Panchulidzev, the governor, hearing of this monstrous proceeding,
expressed his heartfelt regret that his relations with the colonel of the
gendarmes were somewhat fragile, and that consequently he felt it
improper to start proceedings which might be thought to be instigated by
personal motives!

And then sensitive hearts wonder at peasants murdering landowners
with their whole families, or at the soldiers of the military settlements at

Staraya Russa massacring all the Russian Germans and all the German Russians.

In halls and maids' rooms, in villages and the torture-chambers of the police, are buried whole martyrologies of frightful villainies; the memory of them works in the soul and in the course of generations matures into bloody, merciless vengeance *which it is easy to prevent*, but will hardly be possible to stop once it has begun.

Humphrey Higgins (ed.), *The Memoirs of Alexander Herzen*, Constance Garnett (trans.) (Chatto & Windus, 1968), vol. 2, pp. 463–4.

....

The Cost of Diplomacy

The extravagance of ambassadors

John Wade (1788–1875), a former wool sorter, was a leader writer on The Spectator *and a harsh critic of sinecures of all kinds. His books exposing corruption and hypocrisy in high places were best sellers from the 1820s onwards. A keen advocate of universal suffrage, he was partly financed by Jeremy Bentham. In his book,* Unreformed Abuses in Church and State *(1849), he attacked the practice of handing over enormous sums of money to various fortunate Ambassadors and Consuls.*

Next to the game of war, the game of diplomacy is the most dazzling of kingly pastimes; and the fine gentlemen who are periodically launched forth, without liability to travelling expenses, and with sumptuous outfits, to bask in this enviable region, enjoy much of the pomp, circumstance, and immunities of majesty – clothed with inviolability of person, and disporting themselves rent-free in gorgeous palaces. Like the exalted personage they personate, their chief vocation is a pageant or ceremony; and no other branch of the public service accords so well with the taste and acquirements of the aristocracy as this vice-regal mimicry and ostentation.

According to the late Earl of Malmesbury, who was long an adept in the craft, the most indispensable requisites of an ambassador are, that he should be a good, but cautious gossip; be able to listen and learn – to keep his own secrets, and find out those of other people; have an open, but inscrutable countenance; if, in addition, he be six feet high, bow gracefully, and have a portly presence, with a disposition to keep a good table, for the entertainment of absentee lords and ladies, he is esteemed perfect in all his parts. As to substantive duties and business, these are despatched by the secretary or *attaché*; or, if anything extra is required to be done, there is a special mission for the purpose. Some of the most famous jobs in the past history of corruption have been achieved under the pretext of an embassy. Witness the mission of the late Mr Canning to Lisbon. This gentleman had a son in bad health, who required a milder atmosphere, when the father was sent out in splendid style, in an admiralty yacht, as ambassador to Lisbon, where there was actually no court, at an expense to the country of eighteen thousand pounds. On another occasion the co-operation of the Grenvilles was required, when it was stipulated that a member of the family, Mr Henry Wynn, should be sent on a mission to Switzerland, with a salary of 4,000*l.*, and this large salary was justified on the pretext that it was necessary to enable the minister to maintain a liberal hospitality towards his countrymen, who in their autumnal flights for German baths and wash-houses, or in quest of the picturesque, and the sublimities of Mont Blanc, might need a house-of-call for refection and entertainment. Such hospitality for wayfarers in this instance was soon called into exercise, for Mr Wynn had scarcely arrived at his destination before his brother, Sir Watkin Williams Wynn, Lady Harriet Williams Wynn, and eight more Wynns, repaired to Berne, to join the free table spread out of English taxes.

But these jobs were outdone by others, perpetrated under the pretext of missions to South America. Some of these were experimental trips, undertaken for the purpose of ascertaining what the expense of a resident in the transatlantic states might be. Almost the first sent out on this kind of exploratory voyage was Mr Ward to Mexico, the present admiralty-secretary and tenacious MP for Sheffield, who, though not answering the expectations of his constituents, has intimated his resolve to serve out his septennial lease.

Mr Ward was absent, partly occupied in collecting the materials of a future literary speculation, twenty-five months, during which he ran up a charge against the public for salary, outfit, and passage-money to the amount of 19,808*l*. This was pretty well for a beginning; it opened the way on a liberal scale for his successors, some of whom received enormous sums for mere attempts, or preparations for departure, without ever reaching their place of destination. This was the case with a Mr Cockburn, who twice crossed the Atlantic at the public expense without ever penetrating to the capital of Columbia, to which he was officially appointed. He was the first year three weeks in America, and the second nine weeks, receiving for his services 13,000*l.*, and had the modesty, on his return, to apply for a further remuneration, and actually received 1,660*l.* to complete his allowances, when this highly-efficient envoy-extraordinary rested from his labours on a pension of 1,500*l.* a year.

On this same mission to Bogota Mr Chad was next appointed, and received large sums of money, but never left London, and still sticks, along with Mr Cockburn, in the diplomatic pension-list. The present Lord Holland shared freely in these windfalls. He was in Italy receiving a large salary as minister, and then obtained an outfit of 1,500*l.* for Buenos Ayres, but whether he ever left the banks of the Arno for the banks of the Plate we forget.

> John Wade, *Unreformed Abuses in Church and State*
> (Effingham Wilson, Royal Exchange, 1849), pp. 85–8.

....

'I Know a Clergyman of Eminence in Brooklyn Who Lives in Concubinage'

The Revd H. W. Beecher and his best friend's wife

Henry Ward Beecher (1813–87), brother of Harriet Beecher Stowe, the author of Uncle Tom's Cabin, *had the status of the American Evangelist Billy Graham in nineteenth-century America. He believed that a sermon was only effective if it changed the moral character of the congregation. Beecher, who was unconventional in his dress and manner, was against slavery and in favour of women's suffrage but was unfortunately flawed in his passion for Elizabeth Tilton, his best friend's wife. The details were first revealed by Victoria Claflin Woodhull in her journal,* Woodhull and Claflin's Weekly, *a lively radical magazine that advocated equal rights for women and free love. Woodhull, who was married three times, was the leader of the New York section of Marx's Second International and published the first English translation of the* Communist Manifesto. *What made her publication of the Beecher scandal even more fascinating was that she was doing it in order to defend him, believing that 'The immense physical potency of Mr Beecher and the indomitable urgency of his great nature for the intimacy and the embrace of the noble and cultured women about him, instead of being a bad thing as the world thinks, or thinks that it thinks, or professes to think that it thinks, is one of the noblest and grandest of the endowments of this truly great and representative man.'*

The Beecher–Tilton Scandal
The detailed statement of the whole matter by Mrs Woodhull

I propose, as the commencement of a series of aggressive moral warfare on the social question, to begin in this article with ventilation of one of the most stupendous scandals which has ever occurred in any community. I refer to that which has been whispered broad-cast for the last two or three years through the cities of New York and Brooklyn, touching the character and conduct of the Rev. Henry Ward Beecher in his relations with the family of Theodore Tilton. I intend that this article shall burst like a bomb shell into the ranks of the moralistic social camp . . .

More than two years ago the cities of New York and Brooklyn were rife with rumours of an awful scandal in Plymouth Church. These rumours were whispered and covertly alluded to in almost every circle. But the very enormity of the facts, as the world views such matters, hushed the agitation and prevented exposure. The press, warned by the laws of libel, and in a tacit and in the main honourable *consensus* to ignore all such rumours until they enter the courts, or become otherwise matters of irrepressible notoriety, abstained from any direct notice of the subject, and the rumours themselves were finally stifled or forgotten. A few persons only knew something directly of the facts, but among them, situated as I was, I happened to be one. Already the question pressed on me whether I ought not to use the event to forward the cause of social freedom, but I only saw clear in the matter to the limited extent of throwing out some feelers to the public on the subject. It was often a matter of long and anxious consultation between me and my cabinet of confidential advisers.

Under the pretext of reproducing her comments to a reporter about the scandal, Woodhull repeats the crux of her case for exposing Beecher.

Reporter: 'I confess, then, I cannot understand why you of all persons should have any fault to find with Mr Beecher, even assuming everything to be true of him which I have hitherto heard only vaguely hinted at.'

Mrs Woodhull: 'I have no fault to find with him in any such sense as you mean, nor in any such sense as that in which the world will condemn him. I have no doubt that he has done the very best which he could do under all the circumstances – with his demanding physical nature, and with the terrible restrictions upon a clergyman's life, imposed by that ignorant public opinion about physiological laws, which they, nevertheless, more, perhaps, than any other class, do their best to perpetuate. The fault I find with Mr Beecher is of a wholly different character, as I have told him repeatedly and frankly, and as he knows very well. It is, indeed, the exact opposite to that which the world will condemn him. I condemn him because I know, and have had every opportunity to know, that he entertains, on conviction, substantially the same views which I entertain on the social question; that, under the influence of these convictions, he has lived for many years, perhaps for his whole adult life, in a manner which the religious and moralistic public ostensibly, and to some extent really, condemn; that he has permitted himself, nevertheless, to be over-awed by public opinion, to profess to believe otherwise than as he does believe, to have helped to maintain for these many years that very social slavery under which he was chafing, and against which he was secretly revolting both in thought and in practice; and that he has, in a word, consented, and still consents to be a hypocrite. The fault with which I, therefore, charge him is not infidelity to the old ideas, but unfaithfulness to the new. He is in heart, and in conviction and in life, an ultra socialist reformer; while in seeming and in pretension he is the upholder of the old social slavery, and, therefore, does what he can to crush out and oppose me and those who act and believe with me in forwarding the great social revolution. I know, myself, so little of the sentiment of fear, I have so little respect for an ignorant and prejudiced public opinion, I am so accustomed to say the thing that I think and do the thing that I believe to be right, that I doubt not I am in danger of having far too little sympathy with the real difficulties of a man situated as Mr Beecher has been, and is, when he contemplates the idea of facing social opprobrium. Speaking from my feelings, I am prone to denounce him as a poltroon, a coward and a sneak; not, as I tell you, for anything that he has done, and for which the world would condemn him, but for failing to do what it seems to me so clear he ought to do; for failing, in a word, to stand shoulder to shoulder with me and others who are endeavouring to hasten a social regeneration which he believes in.

He was charged with adultery but was acquitted after a lengthy court case in 1875.

Victoria Claflin Woodhull, *Woodhull and Claflin's Weekly*
(19th-century magazine).

....

The Court Case of the Decade

Colonel Valentine Baker seduces girl on train

Colonel Baker became one of the most talked-about officers during the Victorian reign, not because of any exploits on the battlefield but because he was found guilty in 1875 of molesting a respectable girl in a railway carriage en route to Waterloo. The brother of the explorer Sir Samuel Baker, Valentine was friendly with the Prince of Wales and was well connected in court circles. After serving his sentence he emigrated to the Ottoman Empire. There, he was created a general and later became commissioner of police in Egypt, where he died after contracting typhoid. Despite repeated efforts to be reinstated in the British Army, Queen Victoria adamantly refused any such move but did finally agree that he could be buried with full military honours. The following account appeared in The Times *on 3 August 1875.*

Home Circuit
Croydon, 2 August
Crown Court – (*Before Mr Justice Brett*)

Colonel Baker appeared to take his trial on the threefold charge of attempt to ravish, indecent assault, and common assault on Miss Dickinson, and has been convicted on the minor but acquitted on the graver charge, and sentenced to 12 months' imprisonment, without hard labour, and a fine of £500.

From as early as 8 o'clock in the morning people had begun to assemble around the doors of the court, and long before the time for opening them a dense crowd had congregated before the court-house, and not only obstructed the entrances, but completely blocked up the roadway before and for some distance on each side of the court-house. No case has ever been tried within living memory which appears to have caused such excitement. It is hardly necessary to say that the court was densely crowded in every part . . .

Colonel Baker, with his attorney, appeared long before the time appointed for the sitting of the court, and was soon followed by his counsel, Mr Hawkins and Mr Serjeant Ballantine.

Mr Serjeant Parry and Mr Poland appeared on the part of the prosecution; Mr Hawkins, QC, Mr Serjeant Ballantine, and Mr Lillie appeared for the defence . . . On being arraigned, he [Colonel Baker] pleaded in a firm voice 'Not Guilty' . . .

Mr Serjeant PARRY rose to state the case for the prosecution . . . I regret the position in which the defendant stands. He is an officer of distinction, he is a married man, he is 50 years of age, and he stands at the bar charged with a cowardly and unmanly assault upon a young lady whom he met in a railway carriage on the 17th of June last. The charge is stated in a threefold way – attempt at rape, indecent assault, and common assault. The young lady is 22 years of age, residing with her mother and two sisters at Durnford, near Midhurst, where she had been residing since her father died.

. . .

Miss Dickinson was then called, and was with great difficulty brought into court by her mother and her brothers and placed in the witness-box . . . On the Thursday the 17th of June I went to the Midhurst station with my sisters, who saw me into the train. I went to Petersfield to join the Portsmouth train, and there I had to change carriages. I got into a first-class carriage, which was empty, with my luggage, which was labelled 'Dr Bagshawe, Dover.' I sat in a corner, with my face to the engine, and I travelled so alone to Liphook. There the defendant got into the carriage, and sat on the other seat. The window was down, and he asked me if I felt the draught. I said, 'No, thank you; I like it.' He said nothing more to me then . . . Until we left Woking there was nothing in the conduct of the defendant which at all alarmed me. After leaving Woking he said 'I suppose you don't often travel alone?' I said 'Never.' He said 'Could you fix a time when you will be on the line again?' I said 'No.' He said 'You won't?' I said nothing. He said 'Will you give me your name?' I said 'I shan't.' He said 'Give me your name that I may know when I hear.' I said 'I shan't.' 'Why not?' he said. 'Because,' I said, 'I don't choose; I don't see any reason why I should.' He then got up and put up the window. He said 'Give me your Christian name.' I said nothing. He then sat beside me – that is, he came after he had put up the window. There was no division or arm on the seat between us. He sat beside me and took hold of my hand, still asking for my name. I said, 'Get away, I won't have you so near,' and pushed him off. He said, 'You're cross; don't be cross.' He put his arm round my waist and held me by the other and kissed me on my cheek – once, I think – and said, 'You must kiss me, darling.' He held me in front of him. I pushed him off. He put one arm round my waist and held me in front. He was sitting beside me at the time. I pushed him off, and got up and tried to ring the bell to warn the guard. I tried the dial in the centre of the compartment, but it would not act. He said, 'Don't ring; don't alarm the guard.' He forced me back into the corner where I was before. He pushed me back, and pressed me back against the cushions of the carriage, he himself being on me – that is, he was in front of me, standing up. He kissed me on the lips many times. His body was on me at the time. I was quite powerless; I could not move at all. I said nothing, but as soon as I could speak I said, 'If I tell you my name will you get off?' I don't think he said anything. He was kissing me on my lips; so that I could not speak before. Then he stooped down close in front of me, and I felt his hand underneath my dress; on my stocking, above my boot . . . I got up instantly, and pushed the window with my elbow to see if I could break the glass, but I could not. I got the window down and put my head out and screamed. I 'propped' myself out with my elbows. He pulled me back. I felt quite strangled; I can't tell how. I kept up and screamed once more, fearing it might be the last time I should be able to do so, and at the same time I twisted round the handle of the door and stepped out backwards, on the footboard, I think, holding on with my left hand to the outside handle of the door, the door opening towards the engine – that is, the back; the hinge of the door was towards the engine. I held on by the outside handle; with my right hand I held on to his arm. I think he had caught hold of mine. He held firmly to me – that is, to my arm. He said, 'Get in, dear, get in; you get in, and I'll get out at the other door!' I said, 'If you let me go I shall fall.' I had seen the other door locked at Guildford. I recollect nothing more said, and travelled on in that way some distance. I spoke to two gentlemen in the next compartment, and asked 'How long is it before the train stops?' The wind was so strong that I could not hear what they said, but I fancy one of them said, 'I don't know.' The train stopped close to Esher station. My hat had blown away as soon as I got out. When the train stopped persons came to my assistance. He spoke to me and said, 'Don't say anything – you don't know what trouble you'll get me into.

Say you were frightened. I'll give you my name or anything.' I said nothing; I was nearly exhausted. I was helped down from the carriage, and the defendant got out as soon as it was stopped. They said, 'What is the matter?' I said, 'That man will not leave me alone.' He said nothing. He was put into another compartment. They said, 'He is removed, get in again.' I said, 'I can't go alone,' and the Rev. Mr Brown got in, and I travelled to Waterloo Station, and the defendant was brought there, and I gave my name and address; indeed, I had previously given it to the guard. He said, as we travelled along, 'I know your brother very well indeed. Give me his address, and I'll write to him.' I said, 'You may do what you choose,' and did not give him the address. Mr Brown saw me to the house of my brother, Dr Dickinson, in Chesterfield-street, and I told him what had occurred. Next day I went to Guildford, and obtained a warrant. Some of the railway officers were with me.

. . .

Mr HAWKINS, in beginning his address to the jury, said that they must feel he had never had a more painful task before him and one of more than ordinary difficulty . . . In his address to them on behalf of the defence he desired to assist them in their discharge of their duty, and he not only had the complete concurrence of his client, but he acted on his original instructions . . . Upon his express instructions he declared that he had no desire to make the slightest reflection upon the young lady. He would now proceed to tell them how far he felt able to make a defence. How could he – how could any man – in the face of the evidence given to-day, how could he say that Colonel Baker had not been guilty of an assault, and of an indecent assault?

He could not so far stultify himself as to dispute that. He had no means of calling any witnesses to state the view which Colonel Baker would have given of the case, for he could not call Colonel Baker to explain how he had come to be guilty of these improprieties. But as Colonel Baker could not be called it was very hard that the counsel for the prosecution should suggest that he had formed the design of seducing this young lady . . . The learned JUDGE observed that the defendant had been committed for the attempt to violate. The magistrates had taken that view of the case, and had committed him upon that charge.

Mr HAWKINS said that was so, no doubt, but, after all, the question would be whether, on the direction of the learned Judge, the evidence sustained that view. His friend had quite mistaken the view with which he had cross- examined the young lady – it was with no idea of imputing levity, but only to explain the circumstances of the case on which the jury were asked to find the defendant guilty on this serious charge ... Up to the time of the young lady getting up to ring the bell there surely was nothing to show such an intention. But, finding that she was about to ring the bell and alarm the guard, it was natural that he would rise to prevent her; it was natural that he should lay hold of her and try to pull her back. No doubt, she said that he pushed her on her seat and pressed against her; but, even if she was right in all this, though there would be an aggravated assault, it did not show an intention to ravish. Let the jury consider the circumstances and judge whether it was possible that he could have had that intention, for of a surety she would have been powerless to prevent him ... Surely the circumstances rather negatived the attempt to commit a rape! ... He could not raise any defence against the minor charges; he had endeavoured to make a defence against the more serious charge. Colonel Baker stood in a most lamentable position. Lowered from such a pinnacle of honour to such a depth of shame! To say that he felt remorse for his act was saying nothing. To say that he wished to make reparation – any reparation in his power – was saying little, though it was all he could say. He offered the deepest expression of his remorse, his regret, and his self-reproach; he awaited with terrible anxiety the verdict on the more serious parts of the charge; and he looked with sorrow and bitter regret to his clouded future and ruined prospects...

The jury then retired to consider their verdict. After being absent about a quarter of an hour they returned into court with a verdict acquitting the defendant upon the first, the graver charge, but convicting him upon the minor charge of an indecent assault...

The learned JUDGE then, addressing the defendant, proceeded to pass sentence as follows:– When, he said, the story of this case was first published, a thrill of dishonour went through the country. When it was heard that a young and innocent girl, travelling by the ordinary conveyance, had been obliged to risk her life in order to save herself from gross outrage, every part of society, every household, felt as if it had received a personal injury; and, when the country heard that her assailant was a gentleman, and a soldier, and an officer, and an officer high in command, it felt fear, and horror, and, I think I may add, disgust. Nevertheless, you have had what everybody must admit to have been a calm and dispassionate trial; and that jury of whom some fear was expressed have known how to discriminate between the charges made against you. They have most honestly, most fearlessly, most properly absolved you from the heaviest part of the charge, though they have found you guilty of that of which no one can doubt you to be guilty. As to the young lady, I have heard it said that she ought not to have remained so long in a railway carriage alone with a man; but it seems to me that this suggests a state of society in this country which, happily, does not exist in any part of it. It seems to suggest that a defenceless woman in a public conveyance in this country, if she is alone in a railway carriage with a man, may expect to suffer some outrage from him. It is not true of any part of society, from the highest to the lowest. There may be now and then a man who gives way to passion, but it is not characteristic of this country, and I wholly deny that there is anything wrong in a woman, however young, being alone in a railway carriage with a man who appears to be respectable and treats her with respect. But if it were otherwise, the arm of the law would be outstretched with vigour to put down such a state of things. It is in general true that a woman, however unprotected, is safe. It has been further suggested that the young lady was wrong in entering into prolonged conversation with one who was a stranger to her. But I cannot agree to that, and it seems to me that it suggests rather a prurient fear than a feeling of self-respect and safety which every innocent woman in this country possesses. It may be suggested that the libertine outrage which you have committed upon her has defiled her, but I say it has not, and that she walks out of this court as pure and as innocent as ever she was, and as undefiled as she was – nay, more, that the courage and spirit she displayed have added a new ray of glory to her youth, her innocence, and her beauty! (A burst of applause.) With regard to you, when I say that you were not only in the rank of a gentleman, but an officer high in command, it implies that, of all who were in that train, you were the last who might have been expected to assail her; and it might rather have been expected that you would do anything to defend a defenceless woman. And I say it advisedly, that even if a girl so young had conducted herself with imprudence and indiscretion, it was for you, as so much older, to have protected her, if necessary, against herself. But there is nothing from the first to the last in her conduct which can palliate or excuse in the slightest degree that dishonourable thing which you have committed. For the crime itself there is no palliation. It is, when I think of her and think of you – think of all the circumstances – the crime itself appears as bad as such a crime could possibly be. But there are circumstances which I am bound to take into consideration in the discharge of my duty, and these are the high character you have received and the probability that this was a sudden outbreak of wickedness in you. You have attained a high rank and a high reputation. I cannot forget that for your brilliant services your country is indebted to you. I therefore have to treat this case as one of a wicked outrage which I must call cowardly and dishonourable, and which you must all your life feel to have been so, but as a sudden outbreak of wickedness in a man who has up to this time borne a high character, and has served his country well. In those circumstances I wish to spare you the physical degradation, which would probably be to you a torture, which would prevent you hereafter retrieving your character, in the hope that at some distant day you may be allowed, by some brilliant service of which you are so well capable, to wipe out the injury you have done to yourself and the dishonour you have done to your country. Yet I must pass a severe sentence upon you, and that sentence is that you be imprisoned for 12 months in the common gaol, that you pay a fine of £500 and be imprisoned until you have paid it, and that you also pay all the costs of this prosecution and be further imprisoned for three months until they are paid.

Colonel Baker was then removed in custody and the trial terminated, the vast audience slowly dispersing.

The Times, 3 August 1875.

The Downfall of a Future Prime Minister

Sir Charles Dilke

Sir Charles Wentworth Dilke (1843–1911), the radical politician, seemed destined to succeed Gladstone as Prime Minister until 1885, when he was accused of adultery by a Mrs Crawford. Sir Charles fought back in court and was indirectly found guilty which was catastrophic for his political career. The following editorial in The Times *on 24 July 1884, reports the verdict with glee and priggish satisfaction.*

It is very painful to comment upon a verdict which pronounces the fall, irretrievable and complete, of a statesman who has played a distinguished part, and for whom a great career seemed assured. It would have been preferable to pass over the matter in silence. But that cannot be; things have travelled much too far. The verdict leaves him in a position very different from that which he occupied – unsatisfactory though it was – at the close of proceedings of the last trial. On that occasion he did not go into the witness box, although, if his story were true, he knew that the Court was being grossly deceived, and that his name was linked with an infamous falsehood. But every man is the judge of what is due to his honour, and he could plead the advice of his counsel, who told him that there was nothing to answer. Since that time he seemed hurried down a steep declivity to his fall. He proclaimed at public meetings his entire innocence, and challenged an inquiry into the whole story. He was taken at his word, and the decision is against him.

Nor is the result much to be wondered at. It has been expected and predicted ever since the evidence for Mrs Crawford was heard. True, there was oath against oath, but there was not probability against probability. Some of the witnesses who were called by the Queen's proctor were not in such a position that one could dismiss all thought of bias. Others who were above all suspicion merely stated that they did not observe the relations said to have existed between Sir Charles Dilke and Mrs Crawford; at most, they raised doubts whether the visits of the latter to his house could have been made without their knowledge. On the other hand, Mrs Crawford's clear statement was corroborated as to material points by Mrs Ashton Dilke, by Ellen Drake, and by the three Helliers, husband, wife, and daughter, all of whom spoke of visits to Warren St, which Sir Charles has denied...

It is well to pass over the story of brutish profligacy disclosed in the case without much comment. We feel, indeed, that it is incurring no small responsibility to do more than refer to the passionless nastiness, worthy of Yahoos, which has been the subject of inquiry. Silence in the circumstances is best. It is a miserable close of the public career of a statesman who has performed considerable public services, who possessed many qualifications for the conduct of affairs, and who, while the friend of democratic movements, was saved by his knowledge from espousing crude, visionary schemes. He has published a letter in which he says, 'as far as public life goes, I have no option but to accept the verdict' and in the natural course of things his name will be struck off the list of Privy Councillors and he will pass for ever out of the sight of the world in which he has played so conspicuous a part. But the public aspect of the case cannot be lost sight of – the letter addressed by Sir Charles to his former constituents forbids this. If the jury be right in their view of the evidence, there has been no ordinary perjury; it has been deliberate, systematic, and renewed; it is even possible that there has been insubordination of perjury and conspiracy on a scale rarely witnessed.

It is incumbent on those who in the last resort are responsible for the administration of the criminal law to consider carefully and honestly what is their duty in the circumstances.

The question is far from simple. They will be bound to reflect on the possible serious harm which might be done by another trial, in which, for the third time, a mass of garbage should be exposed to public gaze. This is a weighty consideration. On the other hand, the magnitude and persistency of the offence, if the jury are right, must be remembered. What would have happened to Mrs Crawford if her evidence had been stamped as false? It would be unfortunate if there were any pretext given to the notion that there was one law for the poor and another for the rich, and if it were supposed that its terrors are only for people who lie and conspire in an obscure fashion. The question is not simple, but it ought to be examined honestly, dispassionately and fearlessly. Of Sir Charles Dilke's address bidding farewell to his old constituents and to public life it is unnecessary to say much. He complains that he has not had a fair trial, that he was not represented by counsel, that he was not able to present the case as he desired, and that he was placed at a great disadvantage. Giving these criticisms what weight they have, can it be suggested that any particular portion of the evidence against his account could have been overthrown? Can it be said that the representative of the Queen's Proctor was unlacking in zeal for Sir Charles Dilke? The letter in the circumstances is marked by effrontery which we need not characterise. Perhaps the result most to be desired is that he should spare the public another demoralising inquiry by at once betaking himself out of the country.

The Times, 24 July 1886.

The Trade in Vamped-up Virgins

W. T. Stead reveals child prostitution

W. T. Stead (1849–1912), editor of the Pall Mall Gazette, *was the greatest crusading journalist of his generation. His most notorious case was a splendid series of articles published in 1885 under the title* The Maiden Tribute of Modern Babylon *which exposed the evils of child prostitution in London. Stead was himself imprisoned for three months for assisting in the procuring of a teenage girl to prove his point. Later in his career, he became obsessed with spiritualism and drowned on the* Titanic.

Although many of the great and the good, including Cardinal Manning and Lord Shaftesbury, praised Stead's campaign, which led to the raising of the age of consent to sixteen, the sentencing judge said Stead's articles had 'greatly lowered the English people in the eyes of foreign nations'.

The following extract deals with his questioning of some madams and their victims.

'I was told the other day,' said I, by way of opening the conversation, 'that the demand for maidenheads has rather fallen away of late, owing to the frauds of the procurers. The market has been glutted with vamped-up virgins, of which the supply is always in excess of the demand, and there are fewer inquiries for the genuine article.'

'That is not our experience,' said the senior partner, a remarkable woman, attractive by the force of her character in spite of the ghastliness of her calling, compared to which that of the common hangman is more honourable.' With genuine maids to be had for the taking, I do not think it worth while to manufacture virgins. I should say the market was looking up and the demand increasing. Prices may perhaps have fallen, but that is because our customers give larger orders. For instance, Dr —, one of my friends, who used to take a maid a week at £10, now takes three a fortnight at from £5 to £7 each.'

'What!' I exclaimed; 'do you actually supply one gentleman with seventy fresh maids every year?'

'Certainly,' said she; 'and he would take a hundred if we could get them. But he is so very particular. He will not take a shop-girl, and he always must have a maid over sixteen.'

The Procuress Learned in the Law

'Why over sixteen?' said I.

'Because of the law,' she replied; 'no one is allowed to take away from her home, or from her proper guardians, a girl who is under sixteen. She can assent to be seduced after she is thirteen, but even if she assented to go, both the keeper of the house where we took her, and my partner and I, would be liable to punishment if she was not over sixteen. Hence my old gentleman, who is very careful, will not look at a girl under sixteen. That diminishes the area from which maids can be drawn. The easiest age to pick them up is fourteen or fifteen. At thirteen they are just out of school, and still more or less babies under the influence of their mothers. But at fourteen and fifteen they begin to get more liberty without getting much more sense; they begin to want clothes and things which money can buy, and they do not understand the value of what they are parting with in order to get it. After a girl gets past sixteen she gets wise, and is more difficult to secure.'

'You seem to know the law,' said I, 'better than I know it myself.'

'Have to,' said she promptly. 'It's my business. It would never do for me not to know what was safe and what was not. We might get both ourselves and our friends into no end of trouble, if we did not know the law.'

'But how do you get to know all these points?' I inquired.

'From the newspapers,' she replied. 'Always read the newspapers, they are useful. Every week I take in two, Lloyd's and *The Weekly Dispatch*, and I spend the great part of Sunday in reading all the cases in the courts which relate to this subject. There is a case now going on at Walworth, where a man is charged with abducting a girl, fifteen, and it was laid down in court that if she could be proved to be one day over sixteen he was safe. I am watching that case with great interest. All these cases when reported I cut out and put in a book for reference, so that I know pretty well where I am going.'

The Speciality of their Business

'Then do you do anything in the foreign trade?' I asked.

'Oh, no,' she said. 'Our business is in maidenheads, not in maids. My friends take the girls to be seduced and take them back to their situations after they have been seduced, and that is an end of it so far as we are concerned. We do only with first seductions, a girl passes only once through our hands, and she is done with. Our gentlemen want maids, not damaged articles, and as a rule they only see them once.'

'What comes of the damaged articles?'

'They all go back to their situations or their places. But,' said the procuress reflectively, 'they all go to the streets after a time. When once a girl has been bad she goes again and again, and finally she ends like the rest. There are scarcely any exceptions. Do you remember any, Z.?' The junior partner remembered one or two, but agreed that it was very rare girls ever went straight after once they had been seduced.

'Do they ever have children?'

'Not very often the first time. Of course we tell them that it never happens. Girls are so silly, they will believe anything. That silly little child we brought you, for instance, thought she had been seduced when the midwife touched her. But of course sometimes they get in the family way the first time.'

'And then,' said I, 'I suppose they affiliate the child?'

'On whom, pray?' said the senior partner, laughing. 'We make it a special feature of our business that the maid never knows who is her seducer, and in most cases they never know our address. How can she get to know? . . . Even if she noticed the house, which is doubtful, she does not know the name of its owner, and in many cases the house is merely a brothel. What can she do?'

The Profits of a Procuress

'It pays, I suppose?'

'Oh yes, there is no need for me to go to work. It is only for appearance sake and opportunities. I can leave when I like,' said Miss Z., 'after I get them started in the morning. We are paid by commission.'

'Fifty per cent?' I asked.

'That depends,' said the senior partner. 'Taking the average price of a maid at £5, we sometimes take £1; but sometimes we take it all, and merely make the girl a present. It depends upon the trouble which we have, and the character of the girl. Some girls are such sillies.'

'How do you mean?'

'We'll take Nance, for instance. She was a light-headed girl who had never fancied money. We got £10 for Nance. If she had got half that, or quarter, it would have turned her head. She would have gone and bought no end of clothes, and her mistress and her mother would have found it out, and Nance would have got into no end of a row. So for Nance's own sake we only gave her a pound, and as we made her stand treat out of that, she had very little left out of her money to play the fool with. But we have been good to Nance, afterwards. I gave her a bonnet, a dress, and a pair of shoes. I should think we have spent £2 over her.'

'So that she had altogether £3, and you had £7.'

'Just so,' said Miss X., 'and girls are often like that; we have to save them from themselves by keeping most of the money out of their reach'; and the good lady evidently contemplated herself with the admiration due to a virtue so careful of the interests of the young sillies who place themselves in her experienced hands.

'Tell me,' said I, reverting to a previous subject, 'when these maids scream so fearfully does no one ever interfere?'

'No; we take them to a quiet place, and the people of the house know us and would not interfere, no matter what noise went on. Often we take them to private houses, and there of course all is safe. The time for screaming is not long. As soon as it is over the girl sees it is no use howling. She gets her money and goes away. We do not need any specially prepared room. Any quiet room in a house where you are known will do. I have never known one case of interference in the four years I have been in the business.'

Delivered for Seduction

The firm of Mesdames X. and Z. had, however, no intention of allowing me to call up my virgins without their intervention. They had carefully instructed all the girls to give false addresses, in order that I might be compelled to obtain them through the firm ... The reason for this breach of faith was, they allege, that if I had communicated directly with the girls I might have alarmed their parents or employers, and that it was necessary to do it through them. The real reason was the desire of the firm to make quite sure that they received the fifty per cent commission which they charged the unfortunate victims of their benevolent intervention. Finding that I could not help myself, I ordered the delivery of two of those whose agreements I held on Saturday night last. They only had six instead of forty-eight hours' notice, but they were punctually brought to Mdme Tussaud's at seven o'clock. Mdmes X. and Z. were both in attendance, and at first insisted upon accompanying their charges to the place of seduction. This, however, for obvious reasons I would not permit, but I had to pay another pound a head before I could get the girls out of their clutches. My friend drove off rapidly in a cab in an opposite direction to the house in which I awaited them, and then doubled back when the procuresses were out of sight. They stipulated, however, that they had to be returned to Mdme Tussaud's at nine o'clock.

The two virgins, both certified, were among the older girls. One, Bessie, the cook, had been destined for Dr — who takes three maids a fortnight. He was out of town, however, and she was brought on to me, to be handed over to an imaginary friend, to whom I was supposed to have resold her. She was eighteen years old. Her father was dead. Her mother was given to drink, and she was in a good situation as under-cook at a first-class hotel. She came perfectly prepared to be seduced, apparently believing it was the proper thing to do, although her ideas were somewhat hazy. I told her before I could take the responsibility of handing her over to my friend I wished to be quite sure, first, that she knew what she was going to experience, and, secondly, that she had calculated the consequences.

'I suppose I must go through with it now,' she said, 'whatever it is.'

'Oh, no,' I replied; 'that would be the case in most places; but here you have only to say you would rather not, and you are free to go at once.' In conversation I found that the idea of being seduced never occurred to her until a month or two before, when it was proposed by Miss X. as a thing every one did, and a convenient method of raising a little ready money. At first she was indignant and somewhat frightened; but an old school friend who had gone through the ordeal assured her that it was not so very dreadful and the procuress, to use her own phrase, 'so poisoned her mind that she felt she must go through with it,' and she consented. She was to have £2 10s. as her share, the rest would go to the firm. She did not mind the pain, and she would chance the baby, for Miss X. had told her that girls never had babies the first time. She knew it was wrong, her mother would not like it, and if she had a baby she would either get it put away or she would drown herself. But, on the whole, except for one trivial detail, she thought she would prefer to be seduced. 'There are very few virtuous girls about now, they say,' was the remark by which she apparently soothed her conscience. But the triviality appearing to weigh with her, I sent her into another room to a lady friend, and turned my attention to the second maid, who had been waiting below.

She was a nice, simple, and affectionate girl of sixteen, very different from the other, but even more utterly incapable of understanding the consequences of her act. Her father is 'afflicted' – that is, touched in his wits; her mother is a charwoman. She herself works at some kind of millinery, for which she receives 5s. a week. Until a month or two ago she had attended Sunday school, and to all appearance she was a girl decidedly above the average. She was to have £4, of which the firm were to have £2. The poor child was nervous and timid, and it was touching to see the way in which she bit her lips to restrain her tears. I talked to her as kindly as possible, and endeavoured to deter her from taking the fatal step, by setting forth the possible consequences that might follow. She was very frank and I believe perfectly straightforward and sincere. The one thing she dreaded about being seduced was having to be undressed. Poor child, it was the only thing she could realise. Her lips quivered and her eyes filled with tears as she pleaded to be allowed to escape that ordeal. What being seduced meant beyond the formula that she would 'lose her maid' she had not the remotest idea. When I asked her what she would do if she had a baby, she started, and then said, 'But having a baby doesn't come of being seduced, does it? I had no idea of that.'

'Of course it does,' I replied; 'they ought to have told you so.'

'But they did not,' she said; 'indeed, they said babies never came from a first seduction.'

Nevertheless, to my astonishment, the child persisted that she was ready to be seduced. 'We are very poor,' she said. 'Mother does not know anything of this: she will think a lady friend of Miss Z.'s has given me the money; but she does need it so much.'

'But,' I said, 'it is only £2.'

'Yes,' she said, 'but I would not like to disappoint Miss Z., who was also to have £2.' By questioning I found out that the artful procuress had for months past been actually advancing money to the poor girl and her mother when they were in distress, in order to get hold of her when the time came! She persisted that Miss Z. had been such a good friend of hers; she wanted to get her something. She would not disappoint her for anything.

'How much do you think she has given you first and last?'

'About 10s. I should think, but she gave mother much more.'

'How much more?'

'Perhaps 20s. would cover it.'

'That is to say, that for a year past Miss Z. has been giving you a shilling here and a shilling there; and why? Listen to me. She has already got £3 from me for you, and you will give her £2 – that is to say, she will make £5 out of you in return for 30s., and in the meantime she will have sold you to destruction.'

'Oh, but Miss Z. is so kind!'

Poor, trusting little thing, what damnable art the procuress must have used to attach her victim to her in this fashion! But the girl was quite incapable of forming any calculation as to the consequences of her own action. This will appear from the following conversation.

'Now,' said I, 'if you are seduced you will get £2 for yourself; but you will lose your maidenhood; you will do wrong, your character will be gone, and you may have a baby which it will cost all your wages to keep. Now I will give you £1 if you will not be seduced; which will you have?'

'Please sir,' she said, 'I will be seduced.'

'And face the pain, and the wrong-doing, and the shame, and the possible ruin and ending your days on the streets, all for the difference of one pound?'

'Yes, sir,' and she burst into tears, 'we are so poor.'

Could any proof be more conclusive as to the absolute inability of this girl of sixteen to form an estimate of the value of the only commodity with which the law considers her amply able to deal the day after she is thirteen?

W. T. Stead, *Pall Mall Gazette*, 7 July 1885.

....

The Cleveland Street Scandal

Aristocracy and homosexuality

A decade before Oscar Wilde's name became synonymous with scandal and buggery, another case involving the aristocracy and homosexuality was played out at length. Known as the Cleveland Street Scandal, it involved a number of fashionable homosexuals going to a house in Cleveland Street which was inhabited by a number of boy prostitutes. Although there were rumours that Prince Eddy – later the Duke of Clarence and fanciful suspect of being Jack the Ripper – had also frequented the house, there was never any convincing evidence that he did. Lord Arthur Somerset, younger son of the Duke of Beaufort, was someone who did regularly go there but managed to avoid prosecution for a long time, and he was tipped off so that he was able to flee to France before papers could actually be served on him. He remained in exile for the remainder of his life, dying in the South of France in 1926. Despite considerable evidence of his involvement in the Cleveland Street Scandal, the Salisbury Government was reluctant to prosecute him because of the public scandal that would ensue. In response to this cover-up, the Director of Public Prosecutions, Sir Augustus Stephenson, wrote a strong letter to the Attorney-General, Sir Richard Webster.

I have no apprehension that either the Secretary of State or that you as

Attorney General will allow the responsibility of not proceeding against Lord Arthur Somerset, Ripley or Captain Barber to rest upon myself whether with the public or in Parliament; but there is one responsibility of which you cannot relieve me nor can I relieve myself except by distinctly disclaiming, as I now do most respectfully and most decidedly, any agreement with *the opinion* that the evidence in our possession does not justify nor call for the prosecution of Lord Arthur Somerset.

My opinion is that Lord Arthur Somerset ought to be charged and proceeded against by warrant for conspiring with Hammond with respect to the boy Allies, as Newlove, Veck and Hammond have been charged with respect to the boy Wright.

I think in the interest of public justice this charge ought to be preferred, for if it is not, the evidence of Allies as to the statement made by Hammond to him, when he took the letter written by Lord Arthur Somerset at 19 Hill Street to 19 Cleveland Street and Hammond admitted him 'as a friend of Mr Brown's', would be excluded.

In my opinion there is at present direct and overwhelming moral evidence against Lord Arthur Somerset for conspiring to procure and incite young Allies to commit the felony in addition to the offences under the Criminal Law Amendment Act. There is at present some evidence of the same description against Ripley and Captain M. Barber, and it is my duty as Director of Public Prosecutions (unless otherwise directed by the Attorney General) having undertaken at the direction of the Secretary of State the prosecution of Newlove and Hammond on the charge of conspiracy, to include in that prosecution any other person or persons to whom the evidence already obtained points, as it clearly does to Ripley and Captain M. Barber as co-conspirators with Newlove and Hammond.

I am also of the opinion that excepting as to the 6 persons above mentioned there is no evidence – nothing beyond the uncorroborated statements of accomplices – which would justify criminal proceedings against any others who have been referred to either by name or description as frequenting No. 19 Cleveland Street, but I think it extremely probable that further inquiries would furnish corroboration of those statements with respect of some of such persons.

Whether or not such inquiries should be made depends upon considerations of public policy or expediency. In my judgement much can be said both for and against prosecuting such inquiries – but unless and until further evidence should come to light in the prosecution of such inquiries re: the 6 persons above mentioned I do not consider it my duty to prosecute such inquiries.

But I do consider it my duty either as Director of Public Prosecutions or as Solicitor to the War Office, unless I am expressly prohibited from doing so by the Home Secretary or the Attorney General, to furnish the War Department with all the information which has come to my knowledge affecting persons under War Office control.

Although no criminal charge could be preferred or conviction obtained in a criminal court against a commissioned officer for shaking hands with a private soldier at the door of a house known to be frequented by sodomites, or against private soldiers for entering such a house, I cannot think that a public official can be justified in withholding information which he believes to be worthy of credit of such occurrences from another public Department responsible for the observance of the Articles of War.

The question of public policy is not for me, assuming as I do that the entire responsibility for *not* preferring a charge – if no charge is to be preferred – or of not communicating with the War Office is taken from me by the Home Secretary or by yourself. Nor do I discuss again the sufficiency or otherwise of the evidence. The Secretary of State and you know all that I know and, although some of it may be technically inadmissible on the particular charge, in my opinion the moral effect of it leaves no reasonable doubt that Lord Arthur Somerset was a frequent visitor at 19 Cleveland Street *for immoral purposes*.

The public scandal involved in a criminal charge against a man in his position in Society is undoubted. But in my opinion the public scandal in declining to prefer such a charge and in permitting such a man to hold Her Majesty's Commission and remain in English society is much greater.

In my opinion the attempt to avoid such publicity – even if such attempt were justifiable which in my judgement it is not – must absolutely fail and the public scandal will then be infinitely aggravated.

Whatever may be said – and much may be said – as to the public policy of allowing *private* persons being full grown men to indulge their unnatural taste in private or in such a way as not necessarily to come to public knowledge, in my judgement the circumstances of this case demand the intervention of those whose *duty* it is to enforce the law and to protect the children of respectable parents taken in the service of the public, as these unfortunate boys have been, from being made the victims of the unnatural lust of full grown men – and no consideration of public scandal owing the position in society or sympathy with the family of the offender should in my judgement militate against *this paramount duty*. (Stephenson's italics)

The Attorney-General ignored his advice but three years after the initial court case, Ernest Parke, editor of the North London Press, *published Lord Arthur's name. By then, however, he had fled the country.*

The West-End Scandals
Names of Some of the Distinguished Criminals who have Escaped

In an issue of the 28 September we stated that among the number of aristocrats who were mixed up in an indescribably loathsome scandal in Cleveland Street, Tottenham Court Road, were the heir to a duke and the younger son of a duke. The men to whom we thus referred were the Earl of Euston, eldest son of the Duke of Grafton, and Lord H. Arthur G. Somerset, a younger son of the Duke of Beaufort. The former, we believe, has departed for Peru. The latter, having resigned his commission and his office of Assistant Equerry to the Prince of Wales, has gone too.

These men have been allowed to leave the country, and thus defeat the ends of justice, because their prosecution would disclose the fact that a far more distinguished and more highly placed personage than themselves was inculpated in these disgusting crimes. The criminals in this case are to be numbered by the score. They include two or three Members of Parliament, one of them a popular Liberal.

> H. Montgomery Hyde, *The Cleveland Street Scandal* (W. H. Allen, 1976),
> pp. 62–4, 106.

Lord Euston sued for libel and won despite one boy saying in evidence, 'He is not an actual sodomite. He likes to play with you and then "spend" on your belly.' Although he had definitely been sighted at Cleveland Street, Lord Euston claimed this was merely on an invitation to view some poses plastiques, *a euphemism for naked maidens posing as Grecian statues. However, he had never been to Peru in his life and Parke went down for a year with hard labour.*

....

She was not Amused

Prince of Wales named in divorce proceedings

Queen Victoria's reaction on being informed that her son, the profligate Prince of Wales, was subpoenaed as a respondent in the divorce proceedings concerning Sir Charles and Lady Mordaunt – Britain's lengthiest and costliest divorce scandal – is revealed in a letter from her to Lord Hatherly, the Lord Chancellor:

The fact of the Prince of Wales's intimate acquaintanceship with a young married woman being publically proclaimed will show an amount of imprudence, which cannot but damage him in the eyes of the middle and lower classes, which is to be deeply lamented, in these days when the higher classes, in their frivolous, selfish and pleasure-seeking lives, do more to increase the spirit of democracy than anything else.

The following rhyme was popular at the time of the scandal, when Lady Mordaunt became rather overweight and a lonely figure socially.

> This lady's appetite
> It really is enormous,
> But whether right or wrong,
> The papers will inform us.
> She is fond of veal and ham,
> To feed she is a glutton.
> She got tired of Charley's lamb,
> And longed for royal mutton.

H. Montgomery Hyde, *A Tangled Web*
(Constable, 1986), p. 97.

The Mayerling Affair

Double suicide of Archduke Rudolf and lover

Archduke Rudolf, the dissolute son and heir of Emperor Franz Joseph of the Austro-Hungarian Empire, was said to have died of heart failure at his hunting lodge in Mayerling in 1889. Three days later it was finally revealed that he had first shot his eighteen-year-old lover, Baroness Marie Vetsera, before shooting himself. The double suicide was for a long time considered the greatest modern royal scandal. Franz Joseph tried to maintain the fiction that his son had died of heart failure and when that failed, that he had been poisoned by his lover, who then shot herself. Her naked body lay in a woodshed at Mayerling for two days and her mother was forbidden to see the corpse. Franz Joseph then threatened her with deportation if she did not immediately leave the country, which she did.

For a long time the killings were portrayed as a lovers' pact, as Rudolf was married at the time. However, contemporary historians believe it had more to do with Rudolf's cowardice at facing death alone and of Baroness Marie's desire to make a grand exit.

Count Josef Hoyos, a courtier, was present at Mayerling when the shootings occurred and he wrote the following confidential account for palace officials.

His Imperial Highness had told me the previous evening that he had ordered breakfast for the following day, Wednesday, the 30th, to be served for us all immediately upon the arrival of the Prince of Coburg from Vienna. As I knew that the Prince would be travelling by the same train we had arrived by the previous day, it was obvious that he would arrive at the same time, namely ten minutes past eight. Therefore, I decided to go to the castle at eight. It was still a few minutes before this hour, and I was quite ready, when my valet announced the castle guard, Zwerger. When the latter entered he informed me that the Crown Prince's personal servant, Loschek, wished to let me know that he had been unable to wake the Crown Prince. When I said that he must be sleeping very well and soundly, I was informed that the Crown Prince had been up at half-past six, and had gone into the ante-room, to waken him again at half-past seven, and to order his breakfast, and the hackney-cab driver, Bratfisch, with the carriage for the same time. Then, whistling to himself, he had gone back to his room. Loschek had now been knocking uninterrupted since half-past seven on the bedroom door, first with his knuckles and then with a piece of wood, without evoking a sign of life. The bedroom door leading into the ante-chamber and the door leading from the spiral staircase from the first floor to the bedroom were both locked and keys were missing.

There were obvious reasons for suspecting a disaster. I hastened with the guard, Zwerger, to the castle. On the way, Loschek repeated his account. After I myself had knocked and called the Crown Prince loudly, I asked quickly if the place were heated with coal. I was told that it was not. As Loschek would not undertake the responsibility of finally breaking down the doors, I ordered that they should be broken down on my own responsibility. Now Loschek explained for the first time that the Crown Prince was not alone, and added that a Baroness Vecsera (sic) was with him. This news naturally caused me the greatest embarrassment, all the more as I had neither suspected the presence of the Baroness at Mayerling, nor had I known of her relations with the Crown Prince. Indeed there was not the remotest reason for me to suspect the existence of any such relations. Now the worst was to be feared, on account of the deathlike silence in the bedroom. It was hardly possible to think that one could render effectual assistance, as almost an hour and three quarters had passed since half-past six. The responsibility which I would have to assume was overwhelming. By my watch it was nine minutes past eight. Prince Coburg should be arriving at any moment. When I remarked upon this a servant ran out and returned saying that the Prince was just driving up.

In the billiard-room I briefly explained things to the Prince, and after a short deliberation we decided to have the doors burst open on our own responsibility. On account of the exceptionally delicate circumstances, Loschek was to go in alone and see how matters stood. The nomination of other witnesses was to be left – unless such postponement were dangerous – to His August Majesty.

As the door leading to the outer part of the house was locked, Loschek, in the presence of Prince Coburg and myself, tried to break the lock with a hatchet, but the door itself had to be crashed in. Loschek looked into the room and told us that both occupants were dead in bed. Our horror and grief were beyond words. But we had to decide whether a doctor should be called. As there were no signs of life, this was not desirable. The chief thing was to find out whether help would be in vain. Loschek must convince himself of this. When the door had been unlocked from the inside, through the broken panel, Loschek entered the room. He came back a few minutes later, explaining that there was not a sign of life in the bodies. The Crown Prince was lying bent over the edge of the bed, with a great pool of blood in front of him. Death from cyanide of potassium, as

was indicated by the haemorrhage, was presumed. It was only later that
death from a bullet wound was proved.

Count Carl Lónyay, *Rudolf: The Tragedy of Mayerling*
(Hamish Hamilton, 1950), pp. 150–2.

....

Tranby Croft Affair or the Baccarat Scandal

Card-cheating scandal

*In the 1890s, London Society was thrilled by the prospect of hearing the Prince
of Wales give evidence in court about his gambling in the country with some
racing friends. His evidence was quite bland although it did tell against Lieutenant-Colonel Sir William Gordon-Cumming, Bt, who had been accused of one of
the foulest crimes then imaginable amongst friends – cheating at cards. Sir
William was once described in* The Sporting Times *as 'possibly the handsomest
man in London, and certainly the rudest'. Claiming descent from Charlemagne,
not to mention the ducal families of Northumberland and Sutherland, he was a
close friend of the Prince and had in the past put his London house at his
disposal for his dalliances.*

*The Prince of Wales and a number of his friends, including Sir William, were
staying during the Doncaster races at Tranby Croft, the house of Arthur Wilson,
a wealthy Hull shipowner. Several of the other players noticed that while playing
baccarat, Sir William would surreptitiously push betting chips into play after he
had first checked that he had the winning hand. Such sharp practices netted him
£228 in winnings, which was a relatively trivial sum, but the real shock was
that he was there as a guest of the Prince of Wales. Although Gordon-Cumming
always insisted he was innocent of the cheating charges, his downfall was to
sign the following statement at the behest of the other players, including the
Prince of Wales, in a vain attempt to cover up the scandal:*

In consideration of the promise made by the gentlemen whose names are subscribed to preserve silence with reference to an accusation which has been made with regard to my conduct at baccarat on the nights of Monday and Tuesday, the 8th and 9th September 1890, at Tranby Croft, I will on my part solemnly undertake never to play cards again as long as I live.

By the next day, it was the talk of the Doncaster races and Sir William decided rather unwisely a few months later to sue some of the signatories (but not the Prince of Wales) for slander. That was the beginning of his downfall.

The case was heard in front of Lord Coleridge, the Lord Chief Justice of England. The evidence of the following three players was sufficient for Sir William to lose his case and become a social outcast.

Sir Charles Russell was the lawyer for the defendants and Arthur Stanley Wilson, the son of the owner of Tranby Croft and the first of the players to notice something rum about Sir William's tactics.

ARTHUR STANLEY WILSON: 'As I looked across at Lord Edward Somerset ... I noticed Sir William was sitting with his hands in front of him ... and there was one five-pound counter on top of his sheet of note-paper...'

SIR CHARLES RUSSELL: 'Well?'

WILSON: 'Then, I turned around. Lord Edward Somerset picked up the cards, and the plaintiff (Sir William) leaned over like this to see what cards he had got. As I looked, at the same time I saw something red in the palm of his hands, and this I immediately knew could be nothing less than one of the five-pound counters.

He looked, as I said, over Lord Edward's hand to see what card he had. Lord Edward had a natural. Immediately the plaintiff saw this, he opened his hands and let drop three more five-pound counters, and he was paid twenty pounds on that coup.'

SIR CHARLES: 'You were sitting next to Mr Berkeley Levett and you knew him to be a brother office of the plaintiff?'

WILSON: 'Yes.'

SIR CHARLES: 'Did you say anything to Mr Berkeley Levett?'

WILSON: 'Yes. Directly I saw this, I turned around to him and whispered "My God, Berkeley, this is too hot!"'

SIR CHARLES: 'Explain what you meant by this.'

WILSON: 'The incident I have described ... Mr Levett said, "What on earth do you mean?" I said to him "This man next to me is cheating." He said, "My dear chap, you must be mistaken. It is absolutely impossible." I said, "Just look for yourself." He looked and said "It is too hot. It is just too hot!"'

The next witness was Lieutenant Levett.

LEVETT: 'He (Gordon-Cumming) had five pounds staked and when the banker declared his own cards and our tableau won he added one more counter to his stakes. It was dropped on the paper before him. He was paid ten pounds.'

SIR CHARLES: 'Having seen these two coups, do you remember turning to Mr Wilson?'

LEVETT: 'I do. I said, "It is too hot!" The game continued for some time after this, but not very long – I should think about half an hour, or a little more. I remember going to my own room that night. Mr Stanley Wilson went in with me. I flung myself down on the bed, but I cannot remember what I said. We had a conversation which lasted, I should think, about an hour. I was so horrified at what had happened that I cannot remember exactly what the conversation was, but I can remember the gist of it . . .'

SIR CHARLES: 'Do you remember making any entreaty to young Mr Wilson?'

LEVETT: 'I said, "For God's sake, don't say anything about it." '

SIR CHARLES: 'Did you say why?'

LEVETT: 'For the sake of the man and of the regiment.'

In an attempt to make it more difficult for Sir William to cheat the following night, Wilson extended the line in front of the players so that it would be more obvious if anyone was attempting to surreptitiously push counters into play. This did not stop Sir William from doing the same thing the following night as witnessed by Lycett Green, a thirty-one-year-old master of hounds from Yorkshire, who when asked what his profession was, told the court he was fond of 'staking a counter or two'.

SIR CHARLES: 'I want you to tell us what you noticed as to the plaintiff's play.'

GREEN: 'I saw him push a blue counter over the line with his hands after the cards had been declared favourable to him . . . On the next occasion, I saw Lady Coventry holding the cards. She did not take a card and Sir William Gordon-Cumming was looking over her hand. She was making no effort to conceal her hand. I then saw him first of all look round to see if anyone was looking, and he gradually got up a counter, covering it with his hands close to the line.

'When the stakes were paid, Sir William Gordon-Cumming said, "There is ten pounds more to come here," and I think His Royal Highness said to General Williams, "Owen, give him another tenner," or something to that effect. He was paid that stake, making altogether fifteen pounds that he was paid.'

SIR CHARLES: 'You have no doubt that the counter was pushed over the line after the card was seen to be favourable?'

GREEN: 'I have no doubt of it.'

SIR CHARLES: 'When you saw this, what did you do?'

GREEN: 'At first I was horrified. I cannot precisely express my feelings. My first impulse was, I must say, to jump up and expose him, and say, "Sir William Gordon-Cumming, you are cheating at cards!" But I did not do so. On second thought, I felt it would be a horrible thing in the presence of ladies and His Royal Highness to jump up and make a scene; therefore I got up from the table and left the room.'

The jury took less than a quarter of an hour to find against Gordon-Cumming. He was immediately dismissed from the Army, expelled from his clubs and placed in social quarantine. The Prince of Wales wrote a letter to his son George: 'Thank God! the Army and Society are now well rid of such a damned blackguard.'

Gordon-Cumming quickly married an American heiress, and the couple remained out of polite Society for the rest of their lives. Sir Gordon devoted himself to collecting postmarks while the Prince of Wales thought it prudent to give up baccarat and concentrate on bridge.

W. Teignmouth Shore (ed.), *The Baccarat Case* (William Hodge & Co., 1922).

'I Will Furnish War' – William Randolph Hearst

Hearst foments war in Cuba

William Randolph Hearst, the American newspaper baron, can be accused of many outrageous acts. None, however, came close to his role in fomenting the 1898 war between Spain and the United States in Cuba. It was not a question of patriotism – rather the fact that a war would be good for the circulation of his ailing New York World. *There was an exchange of telegrams between Hearst and one of his employees who found the situation rather anti-climactic. He sent the following cable to Hearst:*

EVERYTHING IS QUIET STOP THERE IS NO TROUBLE HERE STOP THERE WILL BE NO WAR STOP I WISH TO RETURN STOP

Hearst's response was:

PLEASE REMAIN STOP YOU FURNISH PICTURES STOP I WILL FURNISH WAR STOP

He was as good as his word.

Phillip Knightley, *The First Casualty*
(Harcourt Brace Jovanovich, 1975), pp. 55–6.

The Fall of Oscar Wilde

Wilde, Queensberry and Lord Alfred Douglas

Playwright Oscar Wilde (1854–1900) helped to bring about his own destruction by suing the Marquess of Queensberry, the father of Lord Alfred Douglas – Wilde's unstable lover – for libel. The Marquess, who was responsible for the 'Queensberry Rules' which govern boxing, was outraged at his son's passion for Wilde and wrote the following letter to him:

1 April 1894

Alfred, – It is extremely painful for me to have to write to you in the strain I must, but please understand that I decline to receive any answers from you in writing in return. After your recent hysterical impertinent ones I refuse to be annoyed with such, and I decline to read any more letters. If you have anything to say do come here and say it in person. Firstly, am I to understand that, having left Oxford as you did, with discredit to yourself, the reasons of which were fully explained to me by your tutor, you now intend to loaf and loll about and do nothing? All the time you were wasting at Oxford I was put off with an assurance that you were eventually to go into the Civil Service or to the Foreign Office, and then I was put off with an assurance that you were going to the Bar. It appears to me that you intend to do nothing. I utterly decline, however, to just supply you with sufficient funds to enable you to loaf about. You are preparing a wretched future for yourself, and it would be most cruel and wrong for me to encourage you in this. Secondly, I come to the more painful part of this letter – your intimacy with this man Wilde. It must either cease or I will disown you and stop all money supplies. I am not going to try and analyse this intimacy, and I make no charge; but to my mind to pose as a thing is as bad as to be it. With my own eyes I saw you both in the most loathsome and disgusting relationship as expressed by your manner and expression. Never in my experience have I ever seen such a sight as that in your horrible features. No wonder people are talking as they are. Also I now hear on good authority, but this may be false, that his wife is petitioning to divorce him for sodomy and other crimes. Is this true, or do you not know of it? If I thought the actual thing was true, and it became public property, I should be quite justified in shooting him at sight. These christian English cowards and men, as they call themselves, want waking up.

> Your disgusted so-called father,
>
> QUEENSBERRY

Lord Alfred responded by sending a telegram to his father which stated:

WHAT A FUNNY LITTLE MAN YOU ARE

The Marquess, at five foot eight inches, an inch shorter than his son, replied by letter:

You impertinent young jackanapes. I request that you will not send such messages to me by telegraph. If you send me any more such telegrams, or come with any impertinence, I will give you the thrashing that you deserve. Your only excuse is that you must be crazy. I hear from a man at Oxford that you were thought crazy there, and that accounts for a good deal that has happened. If I catch you again with that man I will make a public scandal in a way you little dream of; it is already a suppressed one. I prefer an open one, and at any rate I shall not be blamed for allowing such a state of things to go on. Unless this acquaintance ceases I shall carry out my threat and stop all supplies, and if you are not going to make any attempt to do something I shall certainly cut you down to a mere pittance, so you know what to expect.

The final straw that led Wilde to sue the Marquess was receiving a card in his club from him which stated: 'To Oscar Wilde posing Somdomite' (although Wilde thought it said 'To Oscar Wilde, ponce and Somdomite').

Wilde lost his libel case and was himself prosecuted twice in succession and convicted for 'immoral homosexual activity'. He was sentenced along with Alfred Taylor, a friend of his who was charged with being involved in various homosexual acts with male prostitutes. The judge showed little sympathy for the defendants when he came to pass sentence:

Oscar Wilde and Alfred Taylor, the crime of which you have been convicted is so bad that one has to put stern restraint upon one's self to prevent one's self from describing, in language which I would rather not use, the sentiments which must rise to the breast of every man of honour who has heard the details of these two terrible trials. That the jury have arrived at a correct verdict in this case I cannot persuade myself to entertain the shadow of a doubt; and I hope, at all events that those who sometimes imagine that a judge is half-hearted in the cause of decency and morality because he takes care no prejudice shall enter into the case, may see that this is consistent at least with the common sense of indignation at the horrible charges brought home to both of you.

It is no use for me to address you. People who can do these things must be dead to all sense of shame, and one cannot hope to produce any effect upon them. It is the worst case I have ever tried. That you, Taylor, kept a kind of male brothel it is impossible to doubt. And that you, Wilde, have been the centre of a circle of extensive corruption of the most hideous kind among young men, it is equally impossible to doubt.

I shall, under the circumstances, be expected to pass the severest sentence that the law allows. In my judgement it is totally inadequate for such a case as this. The sentence of the Court is that each of you be imprisoned and kept to hard labour for two years.

Wilde, once renowned throughout the civilised world for his wit and insouciance, quickly changed in prison and sensed a further scandal if Douglas published any of his letters or said anything more about the case. Douglas wished to reprint a letter from Wilde to him which stated: 'This is to assure you of my immortal, my eternal love for you.' In an article he wished to publish, Douglas continued:

I do not hope to gain any sympathy by lies, so I shall not pretend that the friendship between Mr Wilde and myself was an ordinary friendship nor simply an intellectual friendship, nor even that it was like the feeling which an older brother might have for his younger brother. No, I say now frankly (let my enemies interpret it as they will!) that our friendship was love, real love – love, it is true, completely pure but extremely passionate. Its origin was, in Mr Wilde, a purely physical admiration for beauty and grace (*my* beauty and *my* grace); it matters little whether they are real or whether they exist only in the imagination of my friend; what must be remarked is that it was a perfect love, more spiritual than sensual, a truly Platonic love, the love of an artist for a beautiful mind and a beautiful body.

Wilde was appalled at the prospect of Douglas publishing any of his poems or printing any such claptrap about him. He was also concerned at the scandal being prolonged by his letters being reproduced. From his prison cell, he wrote to his old friend Robert Ross. Such was his disgust with his former lover that he no longer referred to him by his nickname, 'Bosie', but simply by his surname.

30 May 1896

You said that Douglas was going to dedicate a volume of poems to me. Will you write at once to him and say he must not do anything of the kind. I could not accept or allow such a dedication. The proposal is revolting and grotesque. Also, he has unfortunately in his possession a number of letters of mine. I wish him to at once hand all these without exception over to you; I will ask you to seal them up. In case I die here you will destroy them. In case I survive I will destroy them myself. They must not be in existence. The thought that they are in his hands is horrible to me, and though my unfortunate children will never of course bear my name, still they know whose sons they are and I must try and shield them from the possibility of any further revolting disclosure or scandal.

Also, Douglas has some things I gave him: books and jewellery. I wish those to be also handed over to you – for me. Some of the jewellery I know has passed out of his possession under circumstances unnecessary to detail, but he has still some, such as the gold cigarette-case, pearl chain and enamelled locket I gave him last Christmas. I wish to be certain that he has in his possession nothing that I ever gave him. All these are to be sealed up and left with you. The idea that he is wearing or in possession of anything I gave him is peculiarly repugnant to me. I cannot of course get rid of the revolting memories of the two years I was unlucky enough to have him with me, or of the mode by which he thrust me into the abyss of ruin and disgrace to gratify his hatred of his father and other ignoble passions. But I will not have him in possession of my letters or gifts. Even if I get out of this loathsome place I know that there is nothing before me but a life of a pariah – of disgrace and penury and contempt – but at least I will have nothing to do with him nor allow him to come near me. In writing to Douglas you had better quote my letter fully and frankly, so that he should have no loophole of escape. Indeed he cannot possibly refuse. He has ruined my life – that should content him.

Richard Ellmann, *Oscar Wilde* (Jonathan Cape, 1987),
pp. 394–5, 448–9, 458–9, 469–70.

Wilde was released exactly two years after his sentence and went into self-imposed exile in Paris, where he was frequently spotted by curious Londoners. He effected an uneasy reconciliation with Douglas before dying in 1900.

L'Affaire

The Dreyfus affair

The Dreyfus case, or L'Affaire, as it became known, was a scandal that had the most far-reaching effects on a country and its ruling elite. It ultimately led to the separation of the Church and State in France and gave an enormous boost to the credibility of the Left.

Alfred Dreyfus, an artillery captain on the French General Staff, was wrongly accused in 1894 of passing on military documents to the German Military Attaché in Paris. The case whipped up a fury of anti-Semitism against Dreyfus and the entire French press from both the left and right, warmly approved of the verdict of life banishment to Devil's Island. But, because of growing criticism of the conviction, which was based solely on the assertion that the handwriting of the spy and of Dreyfus were identical, Lieutenant Colonel Georges Picquard was asked by the General Staff to search for further evidence of Dreyfus's guilt. Instead, Picquard discovered that Dreyfus had been framed and that the real culprit was Commandant Count Walsin-Esterhazy, an Austrian by birth but a naturalised Frenchman.

The General Staff's response was to sack Picquard – who was later imprisoned – and to exonerate Esterhazy, who in 1898 demanded to be court-martialled so he could prove his innocence. His request was granted and after three minutes, the judges acquitted him. Three days later, Emile Zola, the distinguished novelist, published a lengthy attack on the entire case, which became known as J'Accuse. It was addressed to Félix Faure, the French President (who deserves further mention in this book for the manner of his death – he suffered a stroke while in the arms of his mistress in the Elysée Palace a year later).

I accuse Lieutenant-Colonel du Paty de Clam of having been the diabolical artisan of judicial error, without knowing it, I am willing to believe, and then of having defended his nefarious work for three years through the most grotesque and culpable machinations.

I accuse General Mercier of having become an accomplice, out of mental weakness at the least, in one of the greatest iniquities of the century.

I accuse General Billot of having had in his hands the definitive evidence of Dreyfus's innocence and of having stifled it, of being guilty of an outrage against humanity and outrage against justice for a political end and in order to save the compromised General Staff.

I accuse General de Boisdeffre and General Conse of being guilty of the same crime, one, no doubt, out of clerical passion, the other, perhaps, out of that esprit de corps that makes the offices of War an impregnable holy ark.

I accuse General de Pellieux and Commandant Ravary of having conducted an inquest which is vile, by which I mean an inquest of the most monstrous partiality, of which we have, in the latter's report, an imperishable monument of naive audacity.

I accuse the three handwriting experts, Mssrs. Belhomme, Varinard, and Couard, of having composed deceitful and fraudulent reports, unless a medical examination declares them to be stricken with an impairment of vision or judgement.

I accuse the offices of War of having conducted in the press, particularly in *L'Eclair* and in *L'Echo de Paris*, an abominable campaign designed to mislead public opinion and to conceal their wrongdoing.

Finally, I accuse the first Court Martial of having violated the law in convicting a defendant on the basis of a document kept secret, and I accuse the second Court Martial of having covered up that illegality on command by committing, in turn, the juridical crime of knowingly acquitting a guilty man.

In bringing these accusations, I am not without realising that I expose myself in the process to Articles 30 and 31 of the press law of July 29 1881, which punishes offences of slander. And it is quite willingly that I so expose myself.

As for those whom I accuse, I do not know them, I have never seen them, I have neither rancour nor hatred for them. They are for me no more than entities, spirits of social malfeasance. And the act that I hereby accomplish is but a revolutionary means of hastening the explosion of truth and justice.

I have but one passion, one for seeing the light, in the name of humanity which has so suffered and which is entitled to happiness. My fiery protest is but the cry of my soul. Let me be brought then before a criminal court and let the investigation be conducted in the light of day!

I am waiting.

Rest assured, Mister President, of my deepest respect.

> Jean-Denis Bredin, *The Affair* (George Braziller, 1986), pp. 248–9.

Zola was tried and sentenced to 12 months' imprisonment, but he fled to England. It took a further eight years before Dreyfus was finally exonerated and taken back into the army, where he was awarded the Legion of Honour.

....

Monkey Business

Big-game hunter Richard Meinertzhagen

Colonel Richard Meinertzhagen (1878–1967), soldier, spy and ornithologist, was one of the most famous big-game hunters in East Africa at the turn of the century. While he was happy to shoot animals in their natural environment, he was outraged at any untoward cruelty towards them.

Meinertzhagen returned home in disgrace from Kenya in 1906 after the suspicious shooting of a Laibon or Nandi medicine man during an anti-poaching expedition that he headed.

Although there were allegations that his party had deliberately provoked the tribesmen into attacking them first, he was exonerated after three courts of inquiry. However, one official later remarked that:

There was never such an unsuccessful ambuscade in the history of warfare. The men who are taken in the ambuscade escape without a scratch, while the 50 or more ambuscaders lose 23 killed. These facts appear to testify stronger than any evidence that treachery was not intended by the Laibon.

Meinertzhagen Papers, Appendix B, British East Africa 1902–6, No. 4c,
Rhodes House Library, Oxford.

After the First World War, Meinertzhagen told Colonel T. E. Lawrence that he had enjoyed 'spattering the brains of a cornered mob of Germans one by one with his African knob-kerri'. He maintained his affection for lower primates though, having his divorce papers served on him outside the monkey house in Regent's Park Zoo.

During a voyage between Rangoon and Mombasa in 1902, the German crew of the boat discovered his wrath for their maltreatment of a pet monkey, whose buttocks were burnt with cigarettes for their enjoyment, plus other horrors.

They made the poor creature comatose with drink and to cure him they decided to tie a line round his waist and let him dangle in the sea for a bit. I protested but was politely told to mind my own business ... I could stand it no longer and taking out a knife, I cut the line. I trust he quickly drowned he was so drunk that he cannot have lived long in the water. The Germans all jabbered with rage, gesticulated and were, I thought, at one time about to lay hands on me. But they decided not to. I told them they were a lot of cowardly savages and left them livid with rage on deck. I should dearly have loved to throw them all after the monkey and I told them so. In consequence I am by no means popular on board.

Richard Meinertzhagen, *Kenya Diaries* (Eland Books, 1983), p. 2.

Australia's Noblest Son

Ezra Norton

The following letter was composed by Ezra Norton, perhaps the biggest scoundrel in Australia to have edited a newspaper, which was called, of all things, The Truth. *A New South Wales Supreme Court Justice accurately described Norton as 'an habitual drunkard of the worst type'. Norton, who was also a blackmailer, published this extraordinary letter in 1902 addressed to Edmund Barton, Australia's first prime minister. It was generally believed that the intemperate tone of the letter was prompted by Norton's own self-loathing as an alcoholic and also his failure to be elected to the House of Representatives.*

OPEN LETTER TO EDMUND BARTON, PRIME MINISTER OF THE COM-
MONWEALTH, CONCERNING HIS DISGUSTING DRINKING HABITS
Sir – Presuming that you are now as I am, thank God, sober, I hasten to address to you yet another Open Letter, before you relapse into that 'shikkery' state in which you have been so often of late. I am aware that you have an utter detestation of 'the scurrilous writings of that scoundrel Norton' especially when they are directly addressed to yourself. You and the whole of the cronk crew with whom you consort and carouse, hate and curse at the mere mention of my humble but notorious name. Why? Simply because I have done with you and them in the past what I am now about to do with you again, exposed and denounced your Political truculency and treachery, your Professional dishonour and your Personal dishonesty.

The hatred with which the push of panderers, parasites, and pimps who surround you bear me, is so bitter and sincere, that when it was recently rumoured that I was either dead or dying in Brisbane, they drank the Devil's health for taking me off before my time. This toast of 'Prosperity to Satan and Hell to Norton', was proposed and enthusiastically drunk here in Melbourne a few weeks ago by a select circle of those hangers-on who have either already received at your hands federal favours in the form of federal billets, or expect to receive them later on. But here I am back from the gates of that hell to which you and yours so wantonly consigned to me, to serve you up about the hottest dish of 'hell-broth', in the shape of straight talk and candid criticism, ever yet prepared for a perverted patriotic(?) politician's pampered palate.

. . .

Before coming to the point, permit me to premise that, in view of your hopes of seeing me in perdition having been blighted, I am going to give you the opportunity of revenge by sending me to prison – if you can. I intend telling something of the truth about you and your doings here in Melbourne in your dual capacity of 'Australia's Noblest Son' and 'First Federal Premier of Australia'. What I have to say is, if possible, worse than anything I have yet spoken and printed about you. I have already categorically charged you with political poltroonery as a politician, professional dishonour as a Cabinet Minister, and personal dishonesty as a citizen. The capacity and digestive power of your moral stomach seem even more abnormal than that of your physical 'corporation'. You have 'stomached' these outrageous charges, reiterated in the press and on the platform, with the same complacency with which you would swallow an elephantine repast, and wind up with a gargantuan guzzle. To these charges I now add another, and in view of the onerous responsibilities of the position you hold, a much more serious charge than any I have yet brought against you. Hitherto I have been content to depict you merely as a genial but withal gluttonous guzzler and gorger. *I now charge you with being not only a disgusting drunkard, but also a most decidedly dangerous one from a public point of view.* This is an accusation which no decent citizen could ignore; much less can a public man in your position be permitted to brush it aside as a matter of no serious concern, either to you or the public. Either it is true or false. If true, you ought to be compelled, with as little scandal as possible, to retire into private life; if false, you ought to prosecute me and get me sent to prison. You know whether you are a drunkard or not. Beware of the attitude you assume in this matter. The public, acting on the popular maxim 'Silence gives consent', will condemn you should you not seek to clear your character of this serious charge in a Court of Law.

. . .

You and others will, perhaps, ask what right has John Norton, above all other men, to bring forward such a charge against Edmund Barton? Even if it were true, Norton should be the last man in the world to make such a charge against such a man. That is, of course, a matter of opinion; but I am free here to repeat, with a clear conscience, what I have said before, that, whatever my faults – and, like most other men's, they are many and heinous – whatever I am now, and have been in the past, I am a soberer, honester, and in every way a more honourable man than Barton. Besides, these questions now to be considered, it is not the personality of the individual making the charge, but, rather, the personality of the person against whom it is made, and the *prima facie* probability of the charge itself. The best services to mankind have not always been rendered by the best of men. Indeed, some of the worst of men have rendered the highest services. In ancient Athens, Alcibiades, the prototype of the modern dema-gogue, rendered immortal services to Greece; even as that more morally worthless and meanest of modern mercenary mountebanks, John Wilkes, was the means of establishing the illegality of General Warrants, of widen-ing the Liberty of the Press, and of arresting from present, and possibly future, corrupt Parliaments the assumed prerogative to override the free choice of the constituents in electing their representatives. So much for my present position as Barton's public accuser. To this you might and may reply, that some of the world's greatest statesmen, orators, poets and soldiers, have been drunkards.

. . .

You could plead that Philip of Macedon and his still greater son, Alex-ander the Great, were drunkards; that Ben Jonson and Shakespeare were hard drinkers; and that Pitt, Fox, and Sheridan were the same. But such a plea would not absolve you; and the fact that the brilliant Brinsley Sher-idan was at his best and his worst when positively drunk, would not make you comparatively sober. What British self-governing communities today desire and demand in their public men is sobriety and integrity.

. . .

As I have said before, I myself have seen you drunk in the Legislative Assembly of New South Wales, and in the ante-rooms of the Chamber. I have seen you snoring drunk on several occasions within the last three years. You have addressed audiences while under the influence of drink at the New Masonic Hall, and at the Town Hall, in Sydney. So, too, have you done at West Maitland, and in Brisbane and Adelaide. When in Brisbane about a year ago you got so disgracefully drunk and incapable that medical aid had to be called in so that you could be 'toned up' in time to address a big public meeting. On that occasion your condition and demeanour, the result of your drinking, so shocked some of the audience nearest to the platform that they left in shame and disgust. In Brisbane the bladder of 'Australia's Noblest Son' has burst.

. . .

But let me be a little more explicit with you. I charge you with being very frequently under the influence of drink ever since the meeting of the Federal Parliament, with one short interim of comparative sobriety; and with being absolutely drunk on more than one occasion on the floor of the House of Representatives, and within the precincts of the House while Parliament was sitting, and when you were supposed to be discharging the duties of your high constitutional office of Prime Minister. Quite recently you came into the Chamber so drunk that you were scarcely able to stand; and when, on this occasion, you rose to move the adjournment of the House, you were so shaky on your pins, that you stood leaning on the table, swaying to and fro, positively unable to articulate distinctly. The spectacle you then presented was, so I am informed by several spectators, at once disgusting and degrading. On another occasion, seeing your drunken, helpless state, the Speaker generously put an end to the painful scene by abruptly putting the motion for adjournment without its having been formally moved, which he saw you were incapable of properly doing. During the Federal celebrations you had found your way into the Government Press Club-room – a room reserved for the use of the representatives of the Australian and European press, who attended to report the proceedings in connection with the visit of the Duke of York. On this particular occasion you behaved like the drunken fool that you were. Whether of your own volition or at the prompting of others, I know not, you mounted the table, and, amid the derisive applause of the interstate and international pressmen present, attempted to harangue them like some drunken Demosthenes. You wound up this edifying performance by falling on the necks of some of these jocular journalists, slobbering, snivelling and sighing on their sympathetic bosoms. 'Australia's Noblest Son', quotha!

. . .

Your drinking habits are too well known here to be ignored. Instead of being a pattern of propriety and sobriety to the Federal Parliament, you are an example and a warning of the awful effects of indulgence in alcoholic drink ... I've said all I intend to say just now concerning your virtuous and patriotic self. None but you will deny that sufficient has been said to compel any ordinary, decent, sober and honourable man to seek to vindicate his character and career in the Courts of Law. If you cannot afford to take that course, why don't you hop off the pedestal of 'Australia's Noblest Son', and retire to the privacy of a pub parlour, which would seem to be the most congenial retreat for so confirmed a soaker as you have shown yourself to be? There is not much hope of your adopting such a course until public opinion or poverty, the ultimate fate of all sluggards and boozers, force you into an unwelcome but well merited oblivion.

Yours in all sobriety,

JOHN NORTON

Cyril Pearl, *Wild Men of Sydney* (W. H. Allen, 1958), pp. 217–21.

Norton failed to get a response, drunk or sober, from Prime Minister Barton.

....

The Man with the Muckrake

Teddy Roosevelt attacks the press

In 1860, there were estimated to be only three American millionaires but three decades later, there were nearly 4,000. The rapacious behaviour of the large oil and gas cartels prompted a new approach to journalism, which coincided with a growing middle-class market and cheaper printing costs. William Randolph Hearst and Joseph Pulitzer both encouraged investigative articles which initially won the endorsement of President Theodore Roosevelt but later caused him to condemn such an approach, especially after the appearance of an article entitled 'The Treason of the Senate'. Shortly afterwards, Roosevelt spoke to the Gridiron Club in Washington off the record about the phenomenon, which he called 'Muckraking'. Such was the reaction amongst the press to the speech that he soon repeated it on the record when he dedicated the cornerstone of the House of Representatives office building on 14 April 1906.

In Bunyan's *Pilgrim's Progress* you may recall the description of the Man with the Muckrake, the man who could look no way but downward, with a muckrake in his hands; who was offered a celestial crown for his muckrake, but who would neither look up nor regard the crown he was offered, but continued to rake to himself the filth of the floor.

In *Pilgrim's Progress* the Man with the Muckrake is set forth as the example of him whose vision is fixed on carnal instead of on spiritual things. Yet he also typifies the man who in this life consistently refuses to see sight that is lofty, and fixes his eyes with solemn intentness only on that which is vile and debasing. Now, it is very necessary that we should not flinch from seeing what is vile and debasing. There is filth on the floor, and it must be scraped up with the muckrake; and there are times and places where this service is the most needed of all the services that can be performed. But the man who never does anything else, who never thinks or speaks or writes save of his feats with the muckrake, speedily becomes, not a help to society, not an incitement to good, but one of the most potent forces of evil.

There are in the body politic, economic and social, many and grave evils, and there is urgent necessity for the sternest war upon them. There should be relentless exposure of and attack upon every evil man, whether politician or businessman, every evil practice, whether in politics, in business or in social life. I hail as a benefactor every writer or speaker, every man who, on the platform or in book, magazine or newspaper, with merciless severity makes such attacks, provided always that he in his turn remembers that the attack is of use only if it is absolutely truthful. The liar is no whit better than the thief, and if his mendacity takes the form of slander he may be worse than most thieves. It puts a premium upon knavery untruthfully to attack an honest man, or even with hysterical exaggeration to assail a bad man with untruth. An epidemic of indiscriminate assault upon character does not good but very great harm. The soul of every scoundrel is gladdened whenever an honest man is assailed, or even when a scoundrel is untruthfully assailed.

Now, it is easy to twist out of shape what I have just said, easy to affect to misunderstand it, and, if it is slurred over in repetition, not difficult really to misunderstand it. Some persons are sincerely incapable of understanding that to denounce mudslinging does not mean the endorsement of whitewashing; and both the interested individuals who need whitewashing and those others who practice mudslinging like to encourage such confusion of ideas. One of the chief counts against those who make indiscriminate assault upon men in business or men in public life is that they invite a reaction which is sure to tell powerfully in favour of the unscrupulous scoundrel who really ought to be exposed, who ought, if possible, to be put in the penitentiary. If Aristides is praised overmuch as just, people get tired of hearing it; and overcensure of the unjust finally and from similar reasons results in their favour.

Any excess is almost sure to invite a reaction; and, unfortunately, the reaction, instead of taking the form of punishment of those guilty of the excess, is very apt to take the form either of punishment of the unoffending or of giving immunity, and even strength, to offenders. The effort to make financial or political profit out of the destruction of character can only result in public calamity. Gross and reckless assaults on character – whether on the stump or in newspaper, magazine or book – create a morbid and vicious public sentiment, and at the same time act as a profound deterrent to able men of normal sensitiveness and tend to prevent them from entering the public service at any price. As an instance in point, I may mention that one serious difficulty encountered in getting the right kind of men to dig the Panama Canal is the certainty that they will be exposed, both without, and, I am sorry to say, sometimes within, Congress, to utterly reckless assaults on their character and capacity.

At the risk of repetition let me say again that my plea is, not for immunity to, but for the most unsparing exposure of, the politician who betrays his trust, of the big businessman who makes or spends his fortune in illegitimate or corrupt ways. There should be a resolute effort to hunt every such man out of the position he has disgraced. Expose the crime and hunt down the criminal; but remember that even in the case of crime, if it is attacked in sensational, lurid and untruthful fashion, the attack may do more damage to the public mind than the crime itself. It is because I feel that there should not be rest in the endless war against the forces of evil that I ask that the war be conducted with sanity as well as with resolution. The men with the muckrakes are often indispensable to the well-being of society, but only if they know when to stop raking the muck, and to look upward to the celestial crown above them, to the crown of worthy endeavour. There are beautiful things above and around them; and if they gradually grow to feel that the whole world is nothing but muck their power of usefulness is gone. If the whole picture is painted black there remains no hue whereby to single out the rascals for distinction from their fellows. Such painting finally induces a kind of moral colour blindness, and people affected by it come to the conclusion that no man is really black and no man really white, but they are all gray. In other words, they neither believe in the truth of the attack nor in the honesty of the man who is attacked; they grow as suspicious of the accusation as of the offence; it becomes well-nigh hopeless to stir them either to wrath against wrongdoing or to enthusiasm for what is right; and such a mental attitude in the public gives hope to every knave, and is the despair of honest men.

To assail the great and admitted evils of our political and industrial life with such crude and sweeping generalisations as to include decent men in the general condemnation means the searing of the public conscience. There results a general attitude either of cynical belief in and indifference to public corruption or else of a distrustful inability to discriminate between the good and the bad. Either attitude is fraught with untold damage to the country as a whole. The fool who has not sense to discriminate between what is good and what is bad is well-nigh as dangerous as the man who does discriminate and yet chooses the bad. There is nothing more distressful to every good patriot, to every good American, than the hard, scoffing spirit which treats the allegation of dishonesty in a public man as a cause for laughter. Such laughter is worse than the crackling of thorns under a pot, for it denotes not merely the vacant mind, but the heart in which high emotions have been choked before they can grow to fruition.

There is any amount of good in the world, and there never was a time when loftier and more disinterested work for the betterment of mankind was being done than now. The forces that tend for evil are great and terrible, but the forces of truth and love and courage and honesty and generosity and sympathy are also stronger than ever before. It is a foolish and timid, no less than a wicked thing to blink the fact that the forces for evil are strong, but it is even worse to fail to take into account the strength of the forces that tell for good. Hysterical sensationalism is the very poorest weapon wherewith to fight for lasting righteousness. The men who with stern sobriety and truth assail the many evils of our time, whether in the public press, or in magazines, or in books, are the leaders and allies of all engaged in the work for social and political betterment. But if they give good reason for distrust of what they say, if they chill the ardour of those who demand truth as a primary virtue, they thereby betray the good cause and play into the hands of the very men against whom they are nominally at war.

New York Tribune, 15 April 1906.

Chicago's First Ward Ball

Protectionism and racketeering in Chicago

The First Ward Ball was run by two seedy Chicago politicians – Michael 'Hinky-Dink' Kenna and John 'Bathhouse John' Coughlin – every year for nearly half a century as a political fund-raising event. As Will Irwin, the author of the following piece for Collier's magazine later reported, 'I went to Chicago, established that the collectors for the First Ward machine were shaking down the department stores, the office buildings, the saloons, the gamblers, the madams of the bawdy houses, even the small prostitutes of the cribs – everyone who needed influence or "protection" – for from two to five hundred tickets apiece.' Only one more ball was held after this article appeared in 1909 and that was a mere shadow of the one described below.

'Bathhouse John' Coughlin stood on the center floor of the great Coliseum, swept his eye over the outpouring of the moral sewers of Chicago, and waved his hand to the two bands, one in either gallery, as a signal that the Grand March of the First Ward Ball was to begin.

'Bathhouse John' is a large, bull-necked Irishman of the John L. Sullivan type, the kind of Celt whose spirit responds, as a flower in rain, to polite public ceremonial. Over the white shirt-front, which clothed his well-provisioned torso, he wore a red sash, with the inscription: 'Grand Marshal'. Eight and forty floor managers, selected either from the powers which rule in Chicago or the powers which rob Chicago – one does not know in which division to place many of them – scattered through the dancing floor, arranging the couples into line. The band masters flourished their staves, and brass and wind struck into the key tune of the evening:

> Hail, Hail, the Gang's all right —
> What the hell do we care;
> What the hell do we care —

A movement surged through the tawdry masters on the floor – they were singing. From end to end of the great hall ran the refrain – women of the half-world and of no world, all the cheapest, dirtiest and most abbreviated costumes, hired, for two dollars and deposit from professional costumiers; scrubby little boys of the slums, patching out their Sunday clothes with five cent masks that they might obey the rules of the floor; pickpockets, refraining, by the truce of the devil which reigned that night, from plying their trade; scarlet women and yellow men who live from and by them; bartenders; professional repeaters; small politicians; prosperous beggars; saloon bouncers; prize- fight promoters; liquor salesmen; police captains; runners for gambling houses – all united in this hymn to the power that is in the First Ward of Chicago:

> Hail, Hail, the gang's all right —
> What the hell do we care now?

It was just striking midnight when 'Bathhouse John' strode out before the assembled couples to lead the grand march. For two hours the sweepings and scourings had crowded into the Coliseum, the largest assembly hall in the United States. At that very moment the police were raiding the crowd without and closing the doors, for the hall was packed to danger point. That overflow crowd, shoving and rioting to express their disappointment, filled the streets for a block either way. Within, floor, gallery, passageways and boxes were choked. Those boxes ran all the way about the dancing floor and only a step above it, like the boxes at the horse show. They were reserved, mainly, either for rich slummers or for the aristocracy of the ministers of dissipation. The galleries held those who came not to revel but to look on. Along the passage way, behind the boxes, moved a crowd which jammed into knots at intervals, and untied itself with much mauling of women and many fights. A policeman skated across the floor just as 'Bathhouse John' set off the grand march. He was shoving before him a young man who lagged back and who threw out his knees very far in front as he walked. The first serious fight of the evening was being bounced. As Bathhouse John pranced down the floor at the head of the march, beating time to the music with his outstretched hands, the tables in the boxes began to blossom with the white and bronze seals of the brands of champagne whose agents were the most liberal buyers that night. One, it appeared, had anticipated the blossoming of the tables. From an end box resounded a feminine shriek which rose above the bands, the singings, and the shuffling feet. The woman who shrieked had risen and was pouring Tenderloin billingsgate at some enemy on the floor. Her man hauled her back and carried her away. The first drunk of the evening had passed out.

They are not here strictly for the joy of it, these greasy revellers; let me make that plain before I go further. Strictly, 'Bathhouse John' Coughlin and 'Hinky-Dink' Kenna, aldermen of the First Ward, need money to pay repeaters, colonisers, district leaders, and hellers – money for all the expenses of keeping in line this, the richest graft district in the United States. The annual ball is their way of collecting that money.

A month before, certain collectors, known for their works in the Tenderloin, have visited every saloon, every brothel, every opium joint, every dance hall, and certain favoured business houses. They carry sheaves of tickets – and lists. 'A hundred and fifty tickets for yours this year,' says the collector to the saloonkeeper. 'What are youse giving us?' says the saloonkeeper. 'It was only a hundred last year.' 'Yes, but look at all the business you done last year – things is coming the way of this corner.' And a hundred and fifty it is – unless the saloonkeeper wishes to add a fourth fifty as a token of his esteem. 'Mercy, a hundred tickets!' says the fat, marcelled woman in the mirrored room. 'Why, it was only seventy-five last year – and my girls don't go anymore, it is getting that common!' 'You've got two more girls here than you had last winter, ain't you? Well, then.' And a hundred it is. 'Seventy-five tickets?' says the man at the roll-top desk. 'Your ball is getting pretty tough and the newspapers —' 'You got a permit for a sign last year, didn't you? Huh?' And seventy-five it is. Lower and higher elements than these pay their tribute of fifty, a hundred, two hundred tickets – the dens from which footpads for their periodical raids on Chicago, the legitimate business houses which furnish supplies or service to the dark end of the First Ward. This bit of business conversation floated into my box from the door: 'Say, the — Carriage Company only took thirty tickets. Think of all the business they get hauling souses out of Twenty-second Street!' 'Oh, well, they're a new concern – and the Bathhouse knows his business.' Still other ways there are of making the First Ward profitable.

Let us push the hands of the clock ahead for an hour, during which times the piles of empty champagne bottles in the boxes have grown and grown, during which the great Annex, where the common herd is served, has become a dump of empty beer bottles. In a box over by the Northeast corner sits a little man, swaying gently under his load of champagne. Everything about him is slight – his legs, his shoulders, the lines of his drawn face. His skin is as white as his hair, and that is the colour of fresh paper. He appears like a man who is struggling with a great hidden grief. You look a second time before you perceive that the mere mechanics of his face produce this effect. For his eyebrows are set slantwise, so that they rise at the inner corner above the nose, giving what actors call the 'grief forehead'. His large violet eyes are never still, even when the champagne has clouded them a little. One bejewelled hand rests on the edge of the box. Slender as it is, the soft, white flesh conceals every knuckle – it is a hand that has never been clenched.

The maskers on the floor, promenading between the crowded dancers, nudge each other as they pass, and halt to stare. The ribboned committeemen, as police captains, police-court lawyers, popular saloonkeepers and ward heelers, all stop to exchange the time of night. He answers them in a flat voice, devoid of inflection, and in flat words devoid of individual turns of expression: 'Sure. More here than there ever was before. Those damn reformers tried to blow the place up, and look what they got for it. Every big business house is represented here; all my friends are out.' Where he sits is the royal box, for this is Hinky-Dink Kenna; and it is his ball. He will run for re-election next Spring; so that the profits tonight – the guesses at these profits run from $60,000 up – all go to his campaign fund. Next year, 'Bathhouse John', on the eve of his own re-election, will get the profits.

Drinking is in full swing now; the effects of it show not in any special joyousness, but in a sodden and dirty aspect of the whole place – floor, boxes and Annex, and especially that cellar cafe, where one drunk has already tried to undress a woman in a scarlet costume, and succeeded to the point of attracting police attention. No Latin verve and gaiety about it; not Mardi Gras, but Gin Lane. In passing, these public debaucheries with the English-speaking peoples seem always to accompany a bad conscience ... Ten thousand 'revellers' in floor and boxes and cafes getting joylessly drunk on champagne; five thousand spectators, come to see how the other half thinks that it lives, looking joylessly on! ...

So it goes on, more and more noisy, more and more unsteady, more and more noisome, until half-past two. The early comers have left, but there is no diminution of the crowd. The people whose business keeps them until midnight in the Tenderloin have finished their work. They are sweeping in to take the vacant places, and to increase the sales of the white foil and the bronze. This year the reformers have threatened to make arrests if the sale of drinks does not stop promptly at three o'clock, according to law and licence. The waiters pass from box to box with the admonition: 'Order all the wine you want now; bar closes at three!' Later, they come back with sheaves of bottles for the grand, final alcoholic burst of the evening. By half-past three, even the provident are drinking their last glasses; and 'Bathhouse John', waving to the musicians in the gallery, shouts: 'Give 'em "Home, Sweet Home." ' There is a flurry about the royal box. Hinky-Dink is going away. He steadies himself as he rises by the little hand without knuckles which moves all these dirty puppets of First Ward politics. Five thousand drunken people at this hour of half-past three doing everything that a drunk does! In the box next to that of the most popular wine agent a woman has gone clean mad with liquor, as women do. She wears an extreme Directoire costume, with a large hat. The hat has fallen back on her shoulders, and her hair has tumbled down over it. As she stands on the table with outstretched arms, shouting loud obscenities to the crowd which collects to watch her, she bears a fearful resemblance to one of those furies of the French Revolution. Before her box lies a little flashily dressed man, dead drunk, grovelling in the lees of the floor. No one pays more than passing attention to him. A telegraph messenger boy sways in the corner, very sick from free champagne. A woman in a bedraggled white evening dress hangs draped head down over the edge of her box, like clothes on a line. The two men and the other woman in her box are drinking a standing toast, oblivious of her. A woman in a page's costume passes another similarly dressed. She hurls a vivid insult as she passes; the other turns, spitting like a cat, and lays hold on her hair. The drunkards in the vicinity gather about them and cheer until the police break through and 'bounce' them to the ladies' dressing room. An old-time wrestler, now a saloon bouncer, lolls over the edge of a box talking to a woman who sprawls across the table, regarding him with fishy eyes. A little scrubby boy, a pick-pocket from the look of him, comes along in the blazing, nervous stage of drunkenness. He lurches against the rail and begins to address the woman. The bouncer wheels and hits him just once in the middle of the body. The scrubby boy shoots back like a cannon ball and brings up sprawling on the floor, where he lies kicking. The bouncer, taking no further look at him, goes on with the conversation. Four fat women sit in a corner box, drinking stupidly. Dressed gaudily in evening clothes, their laces, their white gloves, even their powdered complexions, are becoming grimy with the soot of drunkenness which falls over the great hall. Between them, on the table, stand seven empty champagne bottles and a monumental bouquet of wilting pink roses. They have been taking their pleasures very, very sadly. One nods drowsily; the others watch with eyes as hard and dead as pebbles the crowd which pays tribute to notoriety by stopping to stare. The pickpocket has recovered now; he picks himself up, reviles the bouncer at a safe distance, and staggers over to his box. Worming his way through the crowd, he halts at the rail and lays hold of the lace sleeve of the nearest woman. Expertly, she gets the lace out of his clutch; calmly, she puts her white-gloved hand in his face, sends him spinning back by a motion like the straight-arm in football, and goes on talking with her neighbour. An old man, blind drunk, comes down the hall brandishing a champagne bottle. A woman gets in his way; he hurls the bottle and strikes her on the shoulder. One spectator, more sober than the rest, complains to a policeman who stands grinning at the spectacle. 'Oh, that's all right,' says the policeman. 'Can't you see he's drunk?'

At four o'clock some merry drunkard, on his way out, smashes the box at the door and rings in a fire alarm. The engines and the hook and ladder, ploughing through the cabs and automobiles parked on the street, finish off the First Ward Ball for the year 1908.

I who had watched this for five hours, jostled to the door over drunken men, past drunken women, got clear of the crowd which still swayed and fought outside, clear of the parasites upon parasites who waited beyond, clear of the shouting newsboys with their early editions, clear of the soliciting nighthawk cabmen. The first breath of clean air struck me; I raised my face to it.

And suddenly, I realised there were stars.

Will Irwin, *Collier's*, 6 February 1909.

....

Family at the End of its Tether

H. G. Wells's seduction of his friends' children

H. G. Wells, the utopian socialist, was a notorious cuckolder who made a habit of seducing the children of his Fabian contemporaries. Later in life the problem became so bad that he had to plead to Lords Beaverbrook and Northcliffe to keep various stories about his unfortunate liaisons out of the press. The following account of the problems involved in such promiscuous behaviour is provided by Beatrice Webb in her diary for 1909.

Early August [Brynlerion, Llanfair, Harlech]

The end of our friendship with H. G. Wells. A sordid intrigue with poor little Amber Reeves – the coming of a baby, and the run to cover of marriage with another man, a clever and charming young Fabian (Blanco White), who married her, knowing the facts, out of devoted chivalry. The story got about owing to Amber's own confidence to a Cambridge don's wife, and owing to H. G. Wells's own indiscretions. Moreover, after the hurried marriage, without the Reeveses' knowledge, of Amber and Blanco, Amber and H. G. Wells insist on remaining friends – a sort of *Days of the*

*Comet** affair. We hear of it late in the day and feel ourselves obliged to
warn Sydney Olivier, who was over on holiday, against letting his four
handsome daughters run about with H. G. Wells. (Apparently H. G. tried
to seduce Rosamund Bland. If the Reeveses had only known of that, they
would not have allowed Amber to stay with him [at his Sandgate home]
for a month at a time.) So I think we were right to tell Sydney Olivier. But
as a matter of fact H. G. had already told him that Amber was going to
have a baby, that he was supplying the rent of the house, and that he had
been madly in love with Amber and that 'we were much too timid about
these things'.

For some reason that we do not understand, Sydney Olivier quoted us
as his authority, and so we got these letters from H. G. Wells as well as a
pathetic one from Reeves. It is a horrid affair and has cost us much. If
Amber will let us, we shall stand by her as Blanco's wife and drop H. G.
Wells, once and for all, as he no doubt will drop us. He will doubtless drift
into other circles – probably the only person of his own *ménage* who will
suffer is his patient and all-enduring little wife, who, having entered
into that position illicitly herself at the cost of another woman, cannot
complain.

But the whole case, and the misery that seems likely to follow, is a
striking example of the tangle into which we have got on the sex question.
We accepted Wells, in spite of his earlier divorce case, on grounds of
tolerance. He and his wife were happy – the other wife had married again –
and there seemed no reason, on ordinary enlightened principles, for us to
hold back or object. The Reeves knowing all these facts, and Mrs Reeves
claiming to be 'advanced' in her opinions (she did not object to *In the
Days of the Comet*), were very intimate with him and allowed him to
become Amber's guide, philosopher and friend. Amber being a little
heathen, and H. G. being a sensualist, they both let themselves go, and
start a surreptitious liaison. At first, both of them think that they will
stand it out. But Amber gets into a panic, and marries the first faithful
swain, who will let himself be married to a lady with a 'past' of an
imminent character. But apparently there is no breach; and the household
goes on being of a very mixed sort – the Reeves parents looking on in
tragic sorrow, and Reeves calling H. G. a 'vile impudent blackguard'.

And all this arises because we none of us know what exactly is the sexual
code we believe in, approving of many things on paper which we violently
object to when they are practised by those we care about. Of course,
the inevitable condition today of any 'sexual experiments' is deceit and

---

* A novel he wrote in 1906.

secrecy – it is this that makes any divergence from the conventional morality so sordid and lowering. That is why upright minds are careful not to experiment, except in the 'accustomed way' (i.e. with prostitutes). It is hardly fair to become intimate with a young girl, fresh from college, on the assumption that you believe in monogamy, and then suddenly to propose a polygamous relationship without giving her guardians and friends any kind of notice. That is not playing the game of sexual irregularity even according to the rules of a game full of hazards, at any rate, for the woman.

Norman and Jeanne MacKenzie (eds),
The Diary of Beatrice Webb (Virago, 1984), pp. 120–6.

....

The Dreadnought Affair

Bloomsbury Group hoax on HMS Dreadnought

This was the most amazing hoax ever perpetrated by the Bloomsbury Group. Virginia Woolf, her brother Adrian Stephen, Duncan Grant, Anthony Buxton, Guy Ridley and Horace Cole thought it would be fun to impersonate a group of Abyssinian princes and be royally entertained on Britain's flagship, HMS Dreadnought in 1910. Nobody noticed anything extraordinary about the party, even though Virginia Woolf was dressed up as a man. It infuriated certain elements in the Establishment and led to several parliamentary questions. The following account appeared on the front page of The Daily Express.

Five young men and one young woman, all of them extremely well connected, and all of them well-to-do, have perpetrated a most amazing and somewhat reprehensible practical joke on the Admiralty, the British Navy, and H.M.S. *Dreadnought* in particular.

It is a joke of such colossal proportions, and so audacious – Theodore Hook, that master of practical jokes might himself have been proud of it – that it is a little hard to put it in a nutshell.

Briefly, however, it may be said that on Monday last three of the young men and the girl, fully disguised as Abyssinian princes, travelled down to Portland, and were there received with princely honours on board the flagship. The two other young men played the parts respectively of attaché to the Foreign Office and interpreter.

From start to finish they were forty minutes on board H.M.S. *Dreadnought*, and from the point of view of the perpetrators of the joke, the escapade was entirely successful. In fact, on the following day, the battleship in question put to sea without one single officer or man on board being aware of the manner in which they had been hoaxed.

Pertinent Inquiries

That the matter could have remained a secret for ever was, of course, impossible, as the practical jokers used certain means of carrying through their jest which caused instant inquiry on the part of the Foreign Office. These inquiries were so pertinent that the majority of the young men sought seclusion, but one of them, bolder than the rest, has remained in London to tell the tale.

Monday's adventure had been brewing for some time, but the exact lines upon which the joke was to be worked were not mapped out till about a fortnight ago. Then the commander-in-chief of the enterprise hied himself to an entirely innocent and unsuspecting costumier of world-wide renown, and requested him to furnish make-up for four Abyssinian princes. Expense appeared to have been of no account and the ringleader actually took to the costumier books showing exactly what the princes should wear. Of course, they could have been fitted out in rough-and-ready fashion at an instant's notice, but this was not in the least the idea of this latest follower of 'Captain Koepepick'. He demanded accuracy of detail, and so some days had to be spent in procuring a rigidly correct make-up.

Indeed, so reckless was he as to what the adventure might cost that he one day rushed out of the shop, declaring that their jewels were of no value – and returned an hour later with £300-worth or so of precious stones purchased from a neighbouring jeweller.

Wonderful Make-up

The make-up when complete was certainly striking. The three young men and the young woman all had their hair cut short and were fitted with black woolly mats which completely covered their skulls. They were all provided with short, crisp, curly black beards and the most complete sets of nigger lips. Their faces, arms and hands were dyed to the proper hue. They wore turbans and flowing robes. Round the neck of each, suspended by a gold chain, was an Early Christian cross. Their persons fairly glittered with costly jewels.

But even in this 'make-up' the humour of the instigator of the plot struck a dominant note. The Abyssinian princes were all furnished with enormously long pointed, elastic-sided patent-leather boots. The princes were indeed a glorious sight.

The man who was to pass as the interpreter – supposedly a German – looked his part. The dress of the Foreign Office attaché was, of course, an easy matter to furnish.

On the day selected for the raid on Portland all the conspirators were so anxious that their appearance should present no blemish that they arrived at the costumier's at six o'clock in the morning, and were not satisfied with their Abyssinian toilets until after noon had struck.

Then, unfortunately, they allowed their determination and the exuberance of their spirits slightly to outrun their judgement, and the following telegram was despatched to the Commander-in-Chief of the Home Fleet at Portland:–

'Prince Makalin and suite will arrive at Weymouth at 4.20. Kindly make all arrangements to receive them.'

Splendid Reception

This telegram, it must regretfully be said, bore the name of a high official whose lightest wishes were likely to be received with respect.

And so it was that the 'princely' visitors were received on board the flagship, and marines presented arms as 'Prince Makalin' and his gorgeous suite stepped over the side.

Here it may be mentioned that all the 'princes' bore names which had been specially invented for the occasion on the journey down from town; the name chosen for the lady was 'Prince Mendax'.

Still, no one suspected even the mendacious Mendax.

With characteristic hospitality, the officers of the battleship strove their utmost to shower honours and attentions on their guests. There was unfortunately no Abyssinian flag on board, so as a makeshift the flag of Zanzibar was hoisted to the main-mast. Unluckily too, the National Anthem of Abyssinia could not be discovered among the music. Again Zanzibar was brought to the rescue, and the National Anthem of that State was rendered quite efficiently, considering the short notice the band had received.

Shown Everything

The attaché from the Foreign Office was charming, and his explanations were complete. He told what pleasure it would give the 'princes' to see over the warship, and informed one of the officers that the 'princes' were on a visit to this country in order to make arrangements for sending their sons and nephews to school at Eton.

So the 'princes' were shown everything – the wireless, the guns, and the torpedoes, and at every fresh sight they murmured in chorus, 'Bunga-bunga,' which, being interpreted, means 'Isn't it lovely.' That is to say, three of the 'princes' did, but the fourth 'prince', being afraid to reveal her naturally treble voice, assumed a cold, and murmured, 'Cuck-a-choi, chuck-a-choi', by which she intended to convey her great appreciation of her surroundings.

After the inspection of the ship a grave peril for a few moments con-fronted the conspirators. They were asked to take tea, but this was not to be thought of, as it would certainly have ended in the 'princes'' false lips becoming detached. 'Prince Makalin', apparently overcome by the hospitality which had been shown him, desired to present an officer with the Grand Cross of Abyssinia. The officer regretfully explained that he could not receive the Order. No one apparently stopped to ask whether there were Grand Crosses in Abyssinia.

Then the 'princes' left. They were delighted, and the officers were delighted, too. It was altogether a most pleasant afternoon.

The Daily Express, 12 February 1910.

A fortnight later, the following exchange took place in the House of Commons:

Colonel Lockwood asked the First Lord of the Admiralty, whether a hoax had been played upon the naval authorities by the pretended visit of some Abyssinian princes; and if so, whether he will take steps to prevent such conduct in the future.

The First Lord of the Admiralty (Mr McKenna): I understand that a number of persons have put themselves to considerable trouble and expense in pretending to be a party of Abyssinians, and in this disguise visited one of His Majesty's ships. The question is being considered whether any breach of the law has been committed which can be brought home to the offenders.

Mr WILLIAM REDMOND: Will the right hon. Gentleman include in his inquiry an inquiry as to whether it is not a fact that these gentlemen conferred the Royal Abyssinian Order on the Admiral, who wrote to the King to know whether he could wear it, and will he wear it?

Mr McKENNA: I shall be relieved from the necessity of inquiring into that matter because I know it not to be true.

Colonel LOCKWOOD: Does the right hon. Gentleman think with me that the joke was a direct insult to His Majesty's flag?

Mr McKENNA: I think I have answered the question on the paper fully. The hon. and gallant Gentleman will not ask me to go further into a matter which is obviously the work of foolish persons.

Hansard, 24 February 1910.

....

Uproar in the Theatre

Première of Stravinsky's Rite of Spring

The Russian-born musician Igor Stravinsky (1882–1971) was the twentieth century's most influential composer. In the early part of his career he was considered an iconoclast, especially with his scoring of the ballet The Rite of Spring, *with Sergei Diaghilev, the founder of the Ballet Russe.*

The première performance of The Rite of Spring *in Paris caused an uproar because of his new approach to rhythm and his asymmetrical musical patterns. The public reaction was mixed, to say the least, as shown in this excerpt from Richard Buckle's book on Vaslav Nijinsky, the greatest male dancer of the twentieth century.*

Not since the reception of Tannhäuser *at the old Opéra in the rue Le Peletier in 1861, or even since the first night of Hugo's* Hernani *at the Comédie Française in 1830, had there been such a battle as took place at the new Théâtre des Champs-Elysées on 29 May 1913. Valentine Gross, a hundred of whose studies of the Russian Ballet (including fifty of Nijinsky) were on exhibition in the foyer, describes it well:*

I look back with delight at the uproar of that evening. At that time in the new theatre there was an ambulatory between the boxes of the *corbeille* and the big boxes – and in those days there were no *strapontins* [folding seats]. It was here that stood all the painters, poets, journalists, and musicians who were friends of Diaghilev, all the representatives of the new ideas and movements of that marvellous period. This band of Apollo was like a delightful river – calm, for the most part – flowing between the ramparts of the boxes, which were ablaze with diamonds and pearls. I knew already that the music of this ballet outstripped in violence and in dangerous experiment anything that had gone before. I also knew that the choreography had necessitated an incredible amount of work and that Nijinsky had shown a terrible determination during the countless and arduous rehearsals – had even, one day at the theatre, lost his temper to such an extent, teaching the ballet to the company, that he had literally nearly hit the ceiling of the rehearsal room – but I was expecting neither so great a work of art, nor such a scandal.

Nothing that has ever been written about the battle of 'Le Sacre du printemps' has given a faint idea of what actually took place. The theatre seemed to be shaken by an earthquake. It seemed to shudder. People shouted insults, howled and whistled, drowning the music. There was slapping and even punching. Words are inadequate to describe such a scene. Calm was briefly restored when the order was suddenly given to put up the house lights. It amused me to see how certain boxes whose occupants had been so noisy and vindictive in the dark quietened down when the lights went on. I must admit that our calm river had become a raging torrent. I saw Maurice Delage, beetroot-red with indignation, little Maurice Ravel truculent as a fighting-cock and Léon-Paul Fargue spitting out crushing remarks at the hissing boxes. I cannot think how it was possible for this ballet, which the public of 1913 found so difficult, to be danced through to the end in such an uproar. The dancers could not hear the music … Diaghilev thundered orders from his box … I missed nothing of the show which was taking place as much offstage as on. Standing between the two middle boxes, I felt quite at ease at the heart of the maelstrom, applauding with my friends. I thought there was something wonderful about the titanic struggle which must have been going on in order to keep these inaudible musicians and these deafened dancers together, in obedience to the laws of their invisible choreographer. The ballet was astoundingly beautiful.

Jean Cocteau thought the public's reaction inevitable:

All the elements of a scandal were present. The smart audience in tails and tulle, diamonds and ospreys was interspersed with the suits and *bandeaux* of the aesthetic crowd. The latter would applaud novelty simply to show their contempt for the people in the boxes ... Innumerable shades of snobbery, super-snobbery and inverted snobbery were represented, which would need a chapter to themselves ... The audience played the role that was written for it ...

Between the two scenes the police were called in to seek out and eject the most violent demonstrators. But it was in vain. No sooner had the curtain risen on the trembling girls of Part II, their tilted heads propped on the back of their hands, than a voice called out *'Un docteur'*, then another: *'Un dentiste!'*, followed by another: *'Deux dentistes!'* There was laughter, shouting and whistling; and the battle was renewed. One smart lady in an orchestra box stood up and slapped the face of a man in the box next-door, who was hissing. Her escort rose and cards were exchanged by the two men, who fought a duel next day. Another society woman spat in the face of one of the demonstrators. Comtesse René de Pourtalès (whose photograph reveals an expression of fatuous pride) rose to her feet in her box, tiara askew, and cried out, brandishing her fan, 'I am sixty years old and this is the first time anyone has dared to make fun of me!' Florent Schmitt shouted at the boxes *'Taisez-vous, les garces du seizième!'* of which the London equivalent might be 'Shut up, you Kensington bitches!' And a woman called Ravel 'a dirty Jew'. Carl van Vechten described how 'The young man seated behind me in the box stood up during the course of the ballet to enable him to see more clearly. The intense excitement under which he was labouring betrayed itself presently when he began to beat rhythmically on the top of my head with his fists. My emotion was so great that I did not feel the blows for some time.' At one point Diaghilev climbed to the gallery, and his voice was heard by the dancers coming from very far away, calling *'Je vous prie. Laissez s'achever le spectacle!'* Leaning from his box, Astruc shouted, *'Ecoutez d'abord. Vous sifflerez après!'*

Stravinsky later wrote:

I was sitting in the fourth or fifth row on the right, and the image of Monteux's back is more vivid in my mind today than the picture of the stage. He stood there apparently impervious and as nerveless as a crocodile. It is still almost incredible to me that he actually brought the orchestra through to the end ...

After the 'performance', we were excited, angry, disgusted, and ... happy.

I went with Diaghilev and Nijinsky to a restaurant. So far from weeping and reciting Puskhin in the Bois de Boulogne as the legend is, Diaghilev's only comment was: 'Exactly what I wanted'. He certainly looked contented. No one could have been quicker to understand the publicity value and he immediately understood the good thing that had happened in that respect. Quite probably he had already thought about the possibility of such a scandal when I first played him the score, months before, in the east ground room of the Grand Hotel in Venice.

Richard Buckle, Nijinsky (Penguin Books, 1971), pp. 356–60.

....

'The Saviour of the Punjab'

Brigadier Dyer orders troops to open fire

The Amritsar Massacre in Punjab in April 1919 was one of the worst crimes ever perpetrated by the British Army. For the Indian Nationalists, it was the turning point for the Raj in the Subcontinent. Brigadier General R. E. H. Dyer, the commanding officer in the holy city of the Sikhs, ordered fifty riflemen to open fire on a defenceless rally of approximately twenty thousand people in an enclosed garden next to the Golden Temple, Sikhdom's most sacred shrine. There had been unrest throughout India after the passing of the Rowlatt Act which endorsed a continuation of Emergency Powers in India after the end of the First World War. In Amritsar, several British residents had been murdered and an Englishwoman assaulted a week before the massacre. Dyer ordered a curfew but the residents persisted in holding a rally. There was no evidence that a single person at the rally was even armed, but Dyer was determined 'to teach them a lesson'. Although many of the more blinkered English residents treated him as a hero, he was censured by the Hunter Commission and resigned. The following is his official account of the massacre.

I entered the Jallianwala Bagh by a very narrow lane which necessitated leaving my armoured cars behind. On entering I saw a dense crowd, estimated at about 5,000 [those present put it at 15,000 to 20,000]; a man on a raised platform addressing the audience and making gesticulations with his hands.

I realised that my force was small and to hesitate might induce attack. I immediately opened fire and dispersed the mob. I estimated that between 200 and 300 of the crowd were killed. My party fired 1650 rounds.

I returned to my headquarters about 1800 hours. At 2200 hours, accompanied by a force, I visited all my pickets and marched through the city in order to make sure that my order as to inhabitants not being out of their homes after 2000 hours had been obeyed. The city was absolutely quiet and not a soul was to be seen. I returned to headquarters at midnight. The inhabitants have asked permission to bury the dead in accordance with my orders. This I am allowing.

R. E. H. Dyer, Brigadier-General, Commanding 45th Brigade.

Alfred Draper, *The Amritsar Massacre* (Cassell, 1981), p. 96.

Dyer's report shows that he did not bother to offer any assistance to the thousand or so wounded for several hours, but this did not prevent the lieutenant-governor, Sir Michael O'Dwyer, sending Dyer a personal message by aeroplane which stated:

Your action correct and Lieutenant-Governor approves.

In 1941, Udham Singh, who had been wounded at the massacre site by Dyer's troops, avenged Sikh pride by shooting Sir Michael O'Dwyer dead at a public meeting in London. Udham Singh was hanged for the assassination.

....

£50,000 for the Honour

Lloyd George's sale of honours

David Lloyd George, the British Prime Minister from 1916 until 1922, treated the Honours system with contempt in the final years of his Prime Ministership. He did however consider the system useful as a form of fund-raising for the

Liberal Party. He needed several million pounds as a campaign fund and confided to a colleague, 'You and I know that the sale of honours is the cleanest way of raising money for a political party.' Just after the First World War, baronetcies were available for as much as £50,000 but any businessman worth his salt could get the price knocked down. There was public unrest at the granting of a peerage to the meat packager Sir William Vestey in 1922 for 'immense service' during the war for providing cold-storage facilities for the war effort in France 'gratuitously'. It transpired that Vestey had been paid generously for these services and then had moved his business to Buenos Aires to avoid being taxed on his excessive profits. However, the case that really caused public outrage was the following one involving Sir Joseph Robinson (who had been fined £50 for fraud), who later was forced to decline his honour. King George V actually wrote to Lloyd George complaining about 'the excessive number of honours conferred; the personality of some of the recipients; and the questionable circumstances under which the honours in certain instances have been granted'. In another comment on the Honours scandal, the king said the Birthday Honours list of 1922 was 'an insult to the Crown and to the House of Lords'. Maundy Gregory, the publisher of The Whitehall Gazette, *was the go-between for the purchase of honours from the Lloyd George Government. A total of 91 peers were created by Lloyd George, more than double the number of his two predecessors. The following editorial appeared in* The Spectator *in July 1922.*

The Government will have to answer satisfactorily, or in the alternative to yield to, the strong public criticisms of the traffic in honours. There is a widespread conviction that the granting of honours in exchange for money, though the transactions are disguised, amounts to corruption which, if it is allowed to continue, will bring democracy into putrefaction ... When Sir Joseph Robinson was recently granted a peerage it was announced in the *Gazette* that he had rendered 'national and Imperial services', and that he was Chairman of the Robinson South Africa Banking Company. That bank, however, ceased to exist in 1905.

In 1908 Mr Robinson was made a baronet. When Lord Harris brought up the question of Sir Joseph Robinson's peerage in the House of Lords on June 22nd, he quoted the remarks of the Chief Justice of South Africa upon the conduct of Sir Joseph Robinson in a certain case. The Chief Justice's remarks were very strong, and the Lords are quite right to resent having Sir Joseph Robinson added to their number unless he disposes satisfactorily of those strictures. Lord Buxton and Lord Selborne declared that during their Governorships of South Africa they had never heard of any national or Imperial service done by Sir Joseph Robinson. General Smuts, the Prime Minister of the Union, had not even been consulted.

Lord Selborne went on to state, without reservation, that immense sums of money continued to flow into the party chests from the sale of honours and that in recent years 'the evil had become much greater'.

In the House of Commons on Tuesday, Mr Lloyd George declared that he had 'never departed from precedent'. All we can say is that precedent in this matter has never been above reproach. We do not defend the old methods as such, but just because they were more scrupulously used than they are to-day by Mr Lloyd George they were the less harmful. We cannot remember that Prime Ministers like Lord Salisbury and Mr Gladstone made recommendations that sent an honest shudder through the nation.

Of course, the Prime Minister may truthfully say that he does not know whether the recipients of honours have paid money or not, or, if they have paid, how much they have paid. But somebody knows. It is a familiar practice for the man at the head, the man ultimately responsible, to leave the 'dirty work' – the phrase is Lord Selborne's – to be done by agents. The Prime Minister said that the Departments, the Party Whips and the Patronage Secretary all made recommendations. Who recommended Sir Joseph Robinson? When the Prime Minister was asked that question he did not answer. We join with the *Morning Post* in expressing our curiosity about the Patronage Secretary. We should like to know more about the nature of his work.

The Morning Post declared on Wednesday that it had evidence that the agents of the Government do in fact approach strangers with offers of honours in return for money. It then goes on: 'There is even a regular tariff. The price of a knighthood ranges from £10,000 to £12,000. A baronetcy is scheduled at from £30,000 to £40,000. Then, of course, there are the higher realms, with prices in proportion. The aspirant is, further, very kindly furnished with a catechism or questionnaire, which we have seen.'

The Spectator, July 1922.

The controversy surrounding the Honours for Sale scandal led to the Conservatives withdrawing support for the coalition government, which fell in October 1922. In 1925, the Honours (Prevention of Abuses) Act was passed and in 1933 Gregory was jailed after a failed attempt to extract £2,000 from a naval lieutenant commander in return for a knighthood. Gregory, who was suspected of murdering a woman friend in 1932 for her inheritance, moved to France after his release from prison and eventually committed suicide in 1941.

Hunnish Scenes of the Future Lord Ampthill

How had Mrs Russell become pregnant?

In 1923, the Honourable John Hugo Russell sought the dissolution of his marriage to his wife, Christabel, because she became pregnant. Russell claimed he could not be the father as the couple had an agreement that he could not sleep with his wife. He accused her of adultery with at least three different men, while she claimed in court that the pregnancy stemmed from what she called her husband's 'hunnish scenes'. The court case exercised the minds of London society as shown in the following extracts published in The Daily Telegraph.

Great public interest followed the proceedings last July [1922], the disputed paternity of Mrs Russell's son involving the question of the succession to the barony of Ampthill. The case also raised questions of much interest to the medical profession.

Sir Edward Marshall-Hall, continuing his outline of the petitioner's case, said that on June 23, 1921, Mr Russell left his wife to go to St Pancras Station, leaving her in London. Mrs Russell had sent for her husband, telling him she wanted to say something to him, which could not be written. She then told him the extraordinary story counsel had related to the jury the previous day. The jury had heard the statements made by Mrs Russell to her husband. What did they, as men and women of the world, think was the intention of Mrs Russell when she made the statements to her husband? Counsel could only suggest that, first of all, Mrs Russell had only just discovered that she was going to have a child, that the fortune-teller had told her the story, that she was seven and a half months pregnant, that the petitioner (according to her) was the father, and that her condition had been brought about in consequence of intercourse between her husband and herself. Proceeding, counsel said he had already read to the jury a letter in which Mrs Russell used the term 'Hunnish' as applying to a person who would not do something she wanted; but the sense in which Mrs Russell had used the expression as applying to the alleged conduct of her husband meant something totally distinct and apart from any form of modified intercourse that had taken place between them at any time.

That being so, the jury had to consider what she meant. In effect this is what she said: 'I am going to have a child. It is your child. I know perfectly well that there has been no intercourse in the proper sense of the word, and I am driven to difficulties. How on earth did I get with child? It was the result of some intercourse while you were making Hunnish scenes at Curzon Street, while you were walking in your sleep.' But Mr Russell could not understand, and did not know what she was driving at. Continuing, counsel said that when Mr Russell, after leaving his wife, went to St Pancras Station he found he had a considerable time to wait for his train. He then wrote his wife a letter – a letter, added counsel, which did him credit:

June 23, 1921

Darling Chris – After what you've just told me my brain is still rather in a whirl, but I would like you to quite definitely understand one or two things which are at any rate absolutely clear in my mind.

Firstly, although I was going to institute nullity proceedings next week, I still put you first in my mind, and it would hurt horribly to have gone through with it. My reasons for starting seriously to consider it were that I was more or less convinced that we should never manage to get on together – after all that has passed – and it would be best for both our future happiness to annul it before it might be too late.

This it appears to me, and, although it does complicate things a little, I can't help feeling glad, although I am most awfully sorry for you because life at No. 1 with 'mad' husband must have simply been awful. I can only say that I did not know anything about it at all – if only you had told me I would have padlocked myself to my bed rather than such things should have happened. I am very sorry: but I shall like being a papa to a boy or a girl. I wonder if you would like being a mamma?

As regards our mutual positions I would merely say this, that my feelings for you are as ever, and if you care to blot out the past I'm your man and I will never refer to it by word or deed. I don't enjoy or from choice prefer being on the somewhat chance acquaintance terms we are now – but it is your move, old thing, and till you say the word a more cold and distant husband you will not meet, externally, anyway – internally, no, never. I should now make an impassioned appeal for us to revert to normal man and wife relations for the sake of the child!!! I won't because although I think it will be damned rough on the poor kiddie if ma and pa don't get on, I do think it is useless trying to pretend to be fond of one another unless both feel there is something in it. If you do feel this tell me, won't you? If you don't feel this, we will discuss plans as regards deeds of separation later on – if this will make things easier and pleasanter for you –

I will be ready to agree; it's useless to pretend I should like it, but after all, happiness is what really everyone wants and must have, and time would heal all sores – but I do feel our baby ought to have a chance in its infancy.

I don't expect you will read as far as this, or if you do will find it rather incoherent, but do remember I am most awfully happy about the baby. I would be perfectly happy if only I could feel you were happy too, and I will try to do all I can to make you so. – Your loving husband, John.

The Daily Telegraph, 2 March 1923.

Despite the husband's insistence that intercourse had never taken place, the jury found in favour of Mrs Russell. She later speculated that her pregnancy might have stemmed from the injudicious use of a sponge after her husband had been in the bath. There was another controversy over who should succeed to the title in the 1980s, with the eventual successor being the child of Mrs Russell.

....

The Teapot Dome Scandal

Sale of US Government leases on oil reserve

Until the Watergate affair, the Teapot Dome scandal was the worst one to involve the American Government this century. The case centred around government leases on a naval oil reserve site in Teapot Dome, Wyoming and another at Elk Hills in California being 'privatised'. The Bush Administration attempted to sell off the Teapot Dome and Elk Hills leases in 1989, but Congress was too superstitious to risk such a move again. Although the scandal is associated with the name of President Warren Harding, who was the most corrupt American president this century, he was, in fact, dead when the story broke in February 1924. The following account was written by Nathan Miller.

Under the pressure of the oil companies, Congress, in 1920, passed the Oil Land Leasing Act which permitted the government to lease drilling rights on public lands to private operators. The three naval petroleum reserves were included, with the intent of allowing the tapping of government reserves to prevent them from being drained off by wells on adjoining private lands. Royalties from the oil taken from the reserves under the terms of the 1920 law went into the general revenues – a fact that created considerable unhappiness in the navy. Faced with the increasing power of Japan in the Pacific, naval strategists believed that the United States must have a two-ocean navy. The admirals wished to build fuel-oil storage facilities at the new base at Pearl Harbor in Hawaii and along both coasts. But an economy-minded Congress, which could see no need to prepare for a war that was not likely to occur, refused to appropriate the money for these installations and barred the navy from using the oil royalties for that purpose.

It was at this point that Albert Fall became Secretary of the Interior. Almost as soon as he was firmly in the saddle, he launched a vigorous campaign to wrest control of the petroleum reserves from the Navy Department preparatory to fulfilling his plan to lease them to private developers. Fall lost no time in convincing [President] Harding that it would be more efficient to have the reserves administered by his department than by the navy. Thus armed, he turned his attention to Edwin Denby, the Navy Secretary. Denby, who seems to have had little interest in his department except to administer it with the least possible annoyance to himself, readily acquiesced in the transfer.

On May 31, 1921, after the Harding administration had been in office less than three months, the President signed an executive order placed before him by Fall which transferred control of the petroleum reserves from the Navy to the Interior Department. No questions were asked and no explanations were given. News of the order was buried in the inside pages of a few newspapers. With final authority over the petroleum reserves safely in his hands, Fall proceeded to enter into a series of deals that were to make Teapot Dome part of the folklore of American politics.

Two months later, Fall awarded the first drilling contract for offset wells in the Elk Hills reserve to the Pan-American Petroleum and Transport Company, headed by Edward Doheny. The contract was publicly advertised, and although there were some misgivings among conservationists and naval officers, there was no great outcry as the wells were supposedly aimed at preventing drainage from the reserve. Fall and Doheny were old friends. In fact, as young men they had been fellow prospectors. While Fall's luck was bad, Doheny had struck it rich, discovering oil fields in California and Mexico. 'There is nothing extraordinary about me,' Doheny once proclaimed. 'I am just an ordinary, old-time, impulsive, irresponsible, improvident sort of a prospector.' Unlike most old prospectors, however, he was worth more than $100 million.

Doheny was soon complaining that the royalties that he had to pay for pumping oil from his wells in Elk Hills were too high. Inasmuch as the payments had been set in public bidding, Fall could not reduce them, but promised his old friend that he would have preferential rights to any additional leases in the California reserves under a scheme soon to be put into effect. To placate the navy for the loss of control of its reserves, Fall produced a plan in which private developers would pay the navy for the crude oil pumped from the reserves with certificates good for fuel oil rather than cash. The companies would also agree to build storage facilities at Pearl Harbor, or on the Atlantic and Pacific coasts, as the navy desired. Thus, the navy would circumvent the annoying legal requirement that all funds received for the sale of government oil be placed in the Treasury.

On November 28, 1921, Doheny made a formal bid to construct storage tanks at Pearl Harbor in exchange for oil from the Elk Hills reserve. The next day, Fall telephoned Doheny in New York and informed him that he 'was prepared now to receive that loan'. Doheny dispatched his son, Edward L. Doheny, Jr., to Fall's suite in the Wardman Park. The younger Doheny carried a little black bag with him that contained $100,000 in cash. Not long afterward, Doheny was given a fifteen year lease on the reserve. 'We will be in bad luck,' said the old prospector, 'if we do not get $100 million profit.'

Albert Fall's customer for the reserve at Teapot Dome was Harry F. Sinclair, of the Sinclair Consolidated Oil Company. Sinclair was a one-time Kansas pharmacist who had become a swashbuckling international wheeler-dealer with interests in all parts of the globe and a fortune in excess of $300 million. In 1924, Albania asked him to become its ruler and settle its problems. By then, however, Sinclair had his own difficulties.

They began at the end of 1921, when he visited Fall at his ranch and the two men reached a mutually satisfactory settlement concerning the future of the Wyoming petroleum reserve. As a token of friendship, Sinclair ordered some expensive stock shipped from his breeding farm to New Mexico. Even before he returned to Washington on the tycoon's private railroad car, Fall instructed his aides to prepare the necessary documents turning Teapot Dome over to the Mammoth Oil Company, a subsidiary formed by Sinclair solely for the operation of the lease.

This was the second lucrative triumph scored by Sinclair in as many months. Just a few weeks before, on November 21, 1921, a small group of oil barons negotiated a deal that cast a brilliant light on the business ethics of the age – and was to play a vital part in eventually unravelling the Teapot Dome scandal. Those present included Colonel E. A. Humphreys, owner of the newly discovered Mexia oil field in east Texas; H. M. Blackmer, of the Midwest Oil Company; James E. O'Neil of the Prairie Oil Company; Colonel Robert W. Stewart, board chairman of Standard Oil of Indiana; and Harry Sinclair. Humphreys agreed to sell 33,333,333 barrels of oil from his field at $1.50 a barrel, $50 million, to the other men – but not directly to their companies. Instead, the sale was made to a newly established Canadian firm, the Continental Trading Company, Ltd. Continental then entered into an agreement to sell the oil to the companies represented at the meeting – not at $1.50 a barrel, but for $1.75. Thus, these executives diverted into their own pockets an $8 million windfall which would be paid by their stockholders. These enormous profits were to be paid in Liberty Bonds instead of cash.

The lease granting Mammoth Oil the exclusive right to extract oil and gas from the Teapot Dome reserve for twenty years was signed on April 7, 1922. Fall locked it in his desk, and his subordinates were told to give out no information about it. In return for the lease, Sinclair promised to build oil storage tanks at points along the Atlantic coast designated by the navy and to fill them with fuel oil. Royalty certificates exchanged for Teapot Dome oil were to be used as payment. Sinclair estimated his potential profits as high as $100 million. A month later, Fall sent M. T. Everhart, his son-in-law, to see Sinclair, whose private car was in the Washington rail yards. Sinclair gave him $198,000 in Liberty Bonds, which were part of the loot realised from the Continental Trading deal. He either overlooked the fact, or possibly he didn't care, that such bonds have serial numbers. Another payment of $35,000 in bonds and about $70,000 in cash followed.

So, in exchange for about $400,000 in cash and bonds, Albert Fall had given away navy petroleum reserves then conservatively valued at $200 million – and worth considerably more.

Shortly after Fall had been appointed to Harding's Cabinet, his neighbours in New Mexico were puzzled to see a rapid change in his fortunes. While they were forced to turn their livestock out on the open range to graze down into Mexico in search of food, Fall was suddenly prosperous. Back taxes on his ranch were paid, and his house was put into repair. New fences were erected and blooded stock began to appear on his range. Fall also added two sizeable parcels of land to his property – one valued at $91,500 and the other at $33,000 – bringing his total holdings to 700,000 acres. Such improvements obviously could not be supported on his $12,000-a-year salary. As he had no other source of income to explain his sudden prosperity, suspicions were aroused.

The realisation that something was amiss with Fall's stewardship of the naval petroleum reserves, dawned upon a number of men in different parts of the country at almost the same time. Harry A. Slattery, a Washington lawyer with a strong interest in conservation, learned from acquaintances in various government agencies that Fall had leased Teapot Dome to Harry Sinclair. Even before the lease had been signed, the rumour mill was at work. 'I understand the Interior Department is just about to close a contract to lease Teapot Dome,' a Standard Oil of New Jersey official told Albert Lasker, head of the Shipping Board. 'You should tell the President that it smells – that he must not permit it to go through.' That evening, Lasker told Harding what he had heard. 'This isn't the first time that this rumour has come to me,' was the President's reply, 'but if Albert Fall isn't an honest man, I'm not fit to be President of the United States.'

A few months later, the gusher of the Teapot Dome spilled over, forever burying Harding's reputation in scandal. The long-awaited hearings by the Senate Committee on Public Lands and Surveys into the letting of the oil leases began on October 22, 1923, with Albert Fall as the first major witness. The hearings were held in the cavernous caucus room of the Senate Office Building – a room all marble and glittering chandeliers. Swaggering up to the witness table, Fall bore himself with 'something more than his usual touch of quiet arrogance', said Mark Sullivan. Senator Reed Smoot, the Utah Republican who was chairman of the committee, and the other majority members had no desire to embarrass their own administration, so the leadership passed by default to a Democrat, Senator Thomas Walsh of Montana. He was a skilled and doggedly persistent interrogator. The mountain of documents that Fall had submitted to the committee had, as designed, intimidated the other members, but Walsh had penetrated into the paper jungle deep enough to become convinced there was something radically wrong with Fall's activities.

Senator Walsh's investigation had uncovered the fact that Doheny had given Fall $100,000, but there was still no proof that Sinclair had paid off the Secretary. To find the missing link between Sinclair and Fall, Roberts put a four-man team of Secret Service men to combing banks all across the West for accounts in Fall's name. The investigators struck pay dirt in a bank in Pueblo, Colorado after a lengthy search. Records on file disclosed that two years before, $233,500 in Liberty Bonds with consecutive serial numbers had passed through an account bearing Fall's name. These numbers were checked against records in the Treasury and ultimately led to a Toronto bank and then by devious paths to the mysterious Continental Trading Company – and Harry Sinclair.

Fall did not go on trial until October 7, 1929. This time he had taken the precaution of having the flamboyant Frank Hogan as his attorney. Hogan made his client's entry into the courtroom a pathetic scene guaranteed to wring a tear from the most hardened juror. Haggard and gasping for breath, Fall arrived in a wheelchair, clutching a cane and wearing a shirt-collar three sizes too big for him. After the first day of the trial, the prosecution said it would move for a mistrial unless the jury was absent until Fall was lifted from his wheelchair, tucked into a large leather chair, and covered by blankets and shawls. Hogan pleaded with the jury to send this dying man 'back to the sunshine of New Mexico', which prompted Judge William Hitz to observe with some asperity: 'Neither you nor I have anything to do with sunshine. We are here to decide this case on the evidence and nothing else.' The jury agreed. Fall was found guilty and sentenced to serve a year in jail and pay a fine of $100,000. Nevertheless, another jury refused to convict Doheny of having given the bribe for which Fall was jailed.

On July 18, 1931, Albert B. Fall achieved the unhappy distinction of being the first Cabinet officer in American history to go to prison.

Nathan Miller, *The Foundling Finaglers* (Mackay, 1976),
pp. 318–23, 334, 343, 348.

....

Making News as Well as Owning It

The spendthrift lifestyle of Mr and Mrs Edward McLean

Earlier this century, Edward McLean (1886–1941) and his wife Evalyn were notorious in the United States for their spendthrift ways and adventurous lifestyle. The children of nouveau-riche parents, they were each given $100,000 for the 'young people to enjoy themselves' on their honeymoon. It was almost but not quite enough and they had to cable their parents to pay their last hotel bill. Evalyn purchased extraordinarily expensive diamonds while her feckless husband carried on the pretence of being the publisher of The Washington Post *and the* Cincinnati Enquirer, *which he had inherited from his father.*

Edward McLean thought that his son Vinson should have a negro boy to play with because he had one when he was young. Mrs McLean admitted that 'We could not buy a colored boy, of course ... although it was our habit to buy anything we wanted.' They settled on an arrangement with the parents of a five-year-old black child who relinquished control of their son for a decade while he worked for the McLeans. It was not a great success, with Mrs McLean complaining that 'I would have done as well to have borrowed a playmate from the zoo.' Her husband, Ned, lived at a high pitch, eventually ending his days in a mental hospital. In summing up Ned's life, the American journalist Alfred Friendly said he 'reached a new high, or low, in ingenious profligacy, inventive wildness, and general hell-raising of a sort that this enfeebled age ... simply cannot conceive of, much less match':

There was the item of the private train, with its whistle tied down, every time he left Washington for New York; the kidnapping of a *Post* reporter, who woke up, after being drugged, on a ship to Europe simply because McLean wanted trans-Atlantic company; the ten tarts standing nude on pedestals at McLean's garden parties; the stripping of his New Year's Eve guests and their running around the block naked to welcome the new year in; the mad affair with Marion Davies' sister that went on for months, if not years, all over Europe; the inevitable two bodyguards who wrote out orders for new hats to those barflys whose fedoras McLean liked to knock off with his cane; the last stages of his drunkenness, when he had to tie a bar towel around his wrist and make it into a pulley around his neck so that he could get his drinking hand up to his mouth; the coolness of Mrs Harding [The President's wife] because he urinated in the fireplace in the East Room (as well as down the leg of the Belgian Ambassador); the bottle of whiskey delivered daily by a *Post* editorial writer from McLean's inexhaustible cellars to his favorite pet seal, Col. George Harvey; the perjury on behalf of his friend, Albert Fall* to whom he said he had lent $100,000 when, of course, Doheny had actually bribed Fall by that amount ... and so on and on.

Cleveland Amory, *Who Killed Society* (Harper & Brothers, 1960), pp. 158–9.

....

* See the previous item on the Teapot Dome Scandal.

The Happy Valley Set

High life in Kenya

The antics of the English aristocracy in Kenya between the wars have been memorably recreated in James Fox's book White Mischief. *Lord Erroll, who was notorious for his affairs within the white settlers' community, was murdered in 1940 by a cuckolded husband, Sir Evelyn Delves Broughton, Bt. But, even before this incident, Josslyn Erroll had made quite a name for himself in the colony, as described in this extract from* White Mischief.

Josslyn returned to London in 1922, passed the Foreign Office exams, and began to exploit his remarkable sexual attraction in London society, while the older generation began to describe him as 'spoilt'. There was no question about that, but he was vulnerable, too.

The following year he fell in love with Lady Idina Gordon, the married woman with whom he eloped to Kenya. She was born Idina Sackville, the daughter of the 8th Earl De La Warr, and she had been married twice, first to Euan Wallace with whom she had two sons, and secondly to Charles Gordon, whom she divorced in 1923. Gordon did not defend the case.

Idina was apparently irresistible. She was already *mal vue* in society for her 'fast' reputation. She had had many boyfriends during her first two marriages, including Oswald Mosley, who had presented her with a pearl-inlaid dressing table. 'She could whistle a chap off a branch,' said an old acquaintance. 'She didn't pinch other people's men, but if they were left lying about, she'd pick them up.' She had a perfect figure, slight and little girlish, for which she was famous, and much admired; always wore the chicest clothes and walked barefoot wherever possible 'to show off her size three feet'. Her face might have been beautiful were it not for the shotaway chin and, it is said, she was intelligent, well-read, enlivening company.

Josslyn's liaison with Idina became high scandal. Not only was she twice divorced, she was soon to marry a mere boy, eight years younger than herself and the heir to an earldom. In addition she was seen, correctly, to have ended his chances of the Foreign Office career that in spite of the stigma of Josslyn's dismissal from Eton, his father had managed to secure for him. Even after their marriage in September 1923, it was hinted that Joss and Idina would have been 'unwelcome at Ascot' had they stayed in

England. Idina had already lived for a year in Kenya with her second husband, Charles Gordon, and now it seemed the obvious, indeed the only, place to go. Their departure in April 1924 launched the Colony's reputation as a place beyond the reach of society's official censure, and so beyond the pale, although this was tame compared to the scandals that followed. The couple set up house at Slains, a fairly modest bungalow on the slopes of the Aberdares, named after the castle sold by Joss's grandfather.

In 1925, they moved from Slains to a house in the valley called Clouds, a large, low thatched mansion with many guest bedrooms along each of its wings, facing on to a courtyard. Guests began to come out from England in large numbers, and it was often so wet on the escarpment, so difficult to negotiate by car, that it was hardly worth leaving for weeks on end. Idina would make it very difficult for her guests to leave at all.

She was not to come to the height of her powers for another ten years, but she quickly dominated what there was of the social life of that remote part of the White Highlands and it was there, under her influence, that the Happy Valley legend began.

Idina was only happy, according to the survivors of her house parties – and it was held as truth at Government House where she was on the blacklist – if *all* her guests had swapped partners, wives or husbands by nightfall, or certainly by the time the weekend or the invitation was over. She would organise, from time to time, after-dinner games of 'blowing the feather' across a sheet held out by the guests around a table. It was a frantic game that was designed to create near hysteria; when the feather landed all eyes would be on Idina, who, like a high priestess presiding over a sacred ritual, would divine and then announce who was to sleep with whom.

The bedrooms were locked, and Idina had numbered keys with duplicates which were laid out on a table so that bedroom partners could be chosen by an alternative game of chance, or what appeared to be so. 'We always called Idina's bed "the battleground",' said a survivor, 'and we all used to end up in it at various times of the day or night.'

Lady Altrincham (then Lady Grigg, wife of the Governor) put Idina on her blacklist. She remembers visiting Clouds and being shocked to find Idina's clothes and pearls scattered across the floor, the dogs unfed and the servants gone. It was considered that Idina carried on shamelessly in front of Africans and this – the setting of a bad example – was inexcusable. Retrospectively, Idina is even thought by some to have made a significant contribution to Mau Mau and the end of British rule, through her scandalous behaviour.

. . .

Idina's closest neighbours were Comte Frédéric de Janzé and his young American bride, Alice. Frédéric, twenty-six, elegant, laconic, aristocratic, had motor raced at Le Mans, fought in the Rif Mountains and moved in the literary circle of Proust, Anna de Noailles and Maurice Barrés.

De Janzé's *Vertical Land* [Duckworth, 1928] includes anonymous pen portraits of some of the Happy Valley residents, their names pencilled in by the author in my own copy.

. . .

De Janzé described the principal cast of characters, among them Fabian Wallis, a homosexual and a close friend of Josslyn's; Michael Lafone, a fierce womaniser with an eye-glass, who was briefly and disastrously married in Kenya to Elizabeth Byng, daughter of the Earl of Strafford, and above all Raymond de Trafford, the epitome of the remittance man.

Raymond came from a grand English family from Lancashire, and had been in the Coldstream Guards before coming to Kenya. He was devilishly attractive, quick-witted, original, cultivated, hopelessly indiscreet, a heavy gambler and drinker. To women, he could be delightfully attentive when he felt like it, and a great relief to talk to. Evelyn Waugh called him a 'fine desperado', took a great liking to him when he met him in Kenya in 1931, and kept up with him afterwards. 'Something of a handful,' he observed, 'v. nice but so BAD and he fights and fucks and gambles and gets D.D. [disgustingly drunk] all the time.' They stayed together with the Delameres at Elmenteita. Waugh wrote of Trafford in his diary: 'He got very drunk and brought a sluttish girl back to the house. He woke me up later to tell me he had just rogered her and her mama, too.'

There was a music-hall jingle that went the rounds in Nairobi:

> There was a young girl of the Mau
> Who said she didn't know how,
> She went for a cycle with Raymond and Michael,
> She knows all there is to know now.

Along with the champagne, the drugs of the new age, cocaine and morphine, had found their way into Happy Valley. The chief dealer was Frank Greswolde Williams, who got his supplies from Port Said and who openly plied his trade in the Muthaiga Club. One of his best customers was the American Kiki Preston, a Whitney by birth, a beauty who often stayed with Idina. She had had many lovers, including the two Valentinos, de Trafford and Lafone – and the late Duke of Kent.

When her supplies ran low, Kiki would send her aeroplane to Nairobi for a fresh consignment. Cockie Hoogterp was a close friend of Kiki and remembers her extraordinary performance with her silver syringe.

'She was great fun and very witty, never made any bones about morphine. She always looked marvellous. She would be quite open about it, digging the needle into herself while we sat drinking whisky. She never went to bed until 4 a.m. Next morning we were always hung over and sleeping: but she was up at 8 a.m. beautifully dressed, and looking lovely, as if nothing had happened.'

'I'm sorry to say', said Sir Derek Erskine, whose wife had helped the Prince of Wales to destroy the Muthaiga Club dance records, 'that drugs played a very large part in that period. Cocaine was taken like snuff in Happy Valley and certainly didn't do anybody any good.' At another dinner party for the Prince of Wales in 1928, at Muthaiga, Erskine saw Greswolde Williams suddenly being manhandled out of the room by a white hunter called Archie Richie. When Erskine asked what had happened, he was told, 'Well, there is a limit, even in Kenya, and when someone offers cocaine to the heir to the Throne, something has to be done about it, particularly when it is between courses at the dinner table.'

James Fox, White Mischief (Jonathan Cape, 1982), pp. 30–4.

....

The Prostitutes' Padre

Revd Harold Davidson, the rector of Stiffkey

The Reverend Harold Davidson was the most controversial vicar in Britain between the wars. His trial in 1932 was so well publicised that it pushed the yo-yo craze sweeping Britain completely off the front page. This was not his first encounter with fallen women. During the First World War, while he was a chaplain in the Royal Navy, he was arrested during a police raid on a Cairo brothel but escaped conviction by explaining that he was in fact trying to track down a whore who was giving venereal disease to his troops. In the 1920s, he was declared a bankrupt after trying to borrow from moneylenders at 250% per annum to pay for bad investments in Australian mining companies. Davidson claimed that he found his inspiration for his concern with the fate of fallen shopgirls in Christ. 'His attitude towards the woman taken in adultery, and still His close personal friendship with the notorious harlot of Magdala ... have always been my inspiration.'

However, the Church was not prepared to countenance such a connection and after his 1932 convictions for immoral conduct, expelled him from the ministry. Later, he became a seaside entertainer until one day in 1937 he was mauled to death in Skegness by a caged lion that he thought he could tame. His last recorded words were 'Telephone the London newspapers – we still have time to make the first editions.' This account of his 1932 trial appeared in The Daily Express.

The Rev. Harold Francis Davidson, rector of Stiffkey, Norfolk, appeared yesterday before the Norwich Consistory Court, at Church House, Westminster, to answer charges against his moral character.

The court was presided over by the Chancellor of the diocese, Mr F. K. North.

The charges, which were brought by the Bishop of Norwich under the Clergy Discipline Act, 1892, were that Mr Davidson:

1. Has been guilty of immoral conduct from September 1921 until November 1931 with a woman named.

2. In or about the month of August 1922 was guilty of immoral conduct in that he annoyed and made improper suggestions to a waitress at a cafe at Walbrook, London.

3. Was on November 12, 1931, guilty of an immoral act in that he embraced a young woman in a public room at a Chinese restaurant at Bloomsbury.

4. Has during the last five years been guilty of an immoral habit in that he has habitually associated himself with women of a loose character for immoral purposes.

A complete denial of the allegations had been entered on behalf of the rector.

Charges spread over ten years

Counsel for the bishop are Mr Roland Oliver, K. C., Mr Walter Monckton, K. C., and Mr Humphrey King. Counsel for Mr Davidson are Mr R. F. Levy, Mr Ryder Richardson, and Mr K. J. P. Barraclough.

Mr Oliver asked leave to amend the charges by adding a fifth.

'In this additional charge', said Mr Oliver, 'Mr Davidson is charged with the immoral habit of accosting, molesting, and importuning young females for immoral purposes. A list of the young females follows in the particulars, but I will not now read them, and there is a list of the places in which it is alleged that the offences were committed.'

Mr Roland Oliver, opening his case, said that the total effect of the charges was that Mr Davidson, who for many years had been rector of Stiffkey, had for years in London been systematically misbehaving himself with young women.

'For many years, certainly ten, according to this evidence that will be put before you, this clergyman has led rather a remarkable existence.

'The only time, or substantially the only time, he spent in his parish has been Sunday, when he used to attend and conduct divine service. All the rest of the week he spent in London.

Search for 'Mr Gordon'

'He used to travel up very early on Monday, arriving in practically the small hours and leaving London on Saturday night.

'This went on for week after week, month after month, and year after year.

'There were two occupations which the rector seemed to have had principally in London.

'One was looking for a Mr Gordon, who was apparently a gentleman from whom the clergyman had financial expectations. The other main occupation seemed to have been associating with quite young women from the age of sixteen upwards. That was the side of his activities which has got to be inquired into in this court. It has nothing to do with Mr Gordon.

'Whatever the nature of his intentions was in all of his associations with young women, it was an association which caused him to take them to theatres or cinema shows, or out to meals, or for taxicab rides or to pay for their lodgings.

'If he had been a man of means that would have been less remarkable, but he has been an undischarged bankrupt since 1925, with a wife and four children dependent upon him.'

Mr Oliver said that after Mr Davidson's bankruptcy his income fell to something like one-half of what it was before, and there he was, a man with £400 a year, spending money on these girls.

Rescue work had been advanced by the defence, but the time and place at which he met these young women was very significant – bed-sitting-rooms at all hours of the day and night. It seemed a curious place to proselytise young women.

The first case that he proposed to deal with, said Mr Oliver, was under charge four. The particulars of that included the case of a Miss Gwendoline Harris (who would be known in the case as Barbara Harris), Betty Peach, and other women whose names were unknown.

Marble Arch Meeting

Gwendoline Harris was not an innocent girl at the time she appeared in the case, but she was very young. When Mr Davidson met her in September 1930 she was only sixteen and a half. She was living at an address in Victoria. She had a back bed-sitting-room for which she paid 10s. a week and she was out of work. She had no parents.

Mr Davidson met her in the neighbourhood of Marble Arch.

That was the beginning of an association between these two which lasted from September 1930 until January 1932.

'He gave her small sums of money and sometimes paid her rent. He started on a course of what was really a course of seduction. She always resisted him.

'He took her to a house of which you will hear a great deal in this case. It is a house in Macfarlane-road, Shepherd's Bush, which was really his home in London. He had a bed-sitting-room there.

Missed the Last Train

'He took her to that room, and on one occasion the girl missed her last Tube train back to Victoria. She stayed the night. That was in September 1930. She slept in his bed and he slept in a chair.

'So far as we know this was the only place he had to sleep in London. She went there, and for two nights she slept alone. Then he began to arrive in the middle of the night. She used to lock the door, and he made noises, such as tapping on the bathroom window, and eventually she would let him in.

'The Rose Ellis mentioned in the first charge also came to the house, and he behaved in the most familiar manner, kissing and hugging the girls in front of each other.'

Mr Oliver said that on October 30 Davidson took Barbara to a flat in Melcombe-place, Marylebone, which was occupied by Betty Peach.

Dancing Lessons

Mr Davidson for some reason or other apparently had a key to her flat, and could go there whenever he liked, so he took Barbara there on this day. He took them both to a dance school, where he paid for dancing lessons for the two of them.

December arrived and with it another job for the girl which, in justice to Mr Davidson, he must say he got for her.

He took her to an address in Providence-place which was the house of a Mr and Mrs Lake, who would be witnesses.

Mrs Lake was, without question, a woman of a most charitable disposition. He brought this girl to Mrs Lake about 9.30 in the evening, told her he was her legal guardian and undertook to pay the rent of 10s a week.

The girl was installed in a bed-sitting-room in the front on the ground floor, the window of which could be reached from the street.

Every day Mr Davidson called, and when she lost her job he called many times a day at all hours, and even at two o'clock in the morning. At all times he was trying to get into the bed-sitting-room where this girl lived.

Mrs Lake would not allow him in the house, guardian or no guardian, and he had to stop outside. She remained with Mrs Lake until quite recently, and Mrs Lake kept her at her own expense because she was so much upset by the persecution of this young girl by Mr Davidson.

His strenuous efforts to see this girl might have had another explanation, because in December it had come to his knowledge that he was being watched and that Rose Ellis had made a statement.

Mr Oliver said that in February last a rule nisi for contempt of court was obtained from the High Court against Mr Davidson, and on February 23, while his conduct was being investigated by the High Court, he was back at Mrs Lake's.

He said, 'Barbara's name has not been mentioned. I do not want Barbara to be brought into this case, as she is now going straight.'

'Mr Davidson said to Barbara on more than one occasion, "I will marry you. I will divorce my wife because I am not the father of her youngest child." That is a terrible thing to have to mention in court, but it is absolutely vital, if he said it to her, that you should know that he said the same thing to the solicitor instructing us.'

'Rescue Work' Defence

Turning to charge two, Mr Oliver said that the defence of Mr Davidson had been that his concern principally with the young women had been rescue work.

With regard to these other cases they concerned perfectly respectable young women, all in employment and needing no rescuing by Mr Davidson or any one else.

The first girl concerned was Miss Dorothy Burn. In August 1929 she was a waitress at Lyons in Walbrook. She was eighteen and very pretty. On Mr Davidson's first visit to the restaurant he took hold of her hand, said she was lovely, and that he must come again.

'Was that rescue work or what?' asked Mr Oliver. 'The next day he came, and the next day, and every day. He pestered this unfortunate girl to death. Sometimes he would come twice a day.

A Complaint

'She did not like it at all. She complained, and as a result there was an interview with an official of Lyons.'

Mr Davidson was asked to transfer his custom elsewhere.

Mr Oliver said that the fifth charge concerned the pestering of perfectly respectable women who needed no rescuing, and certainly not Mr Davidson's society. He referred to three women employed as waitresses in an ABC cafe in Oxford-street. There were complaints, and he was asked to go.

He said to an official of the ABC that he had been an actor who was known as the musical artists' padre, but he was told to keep away from the cafe or the police would be informed.

Coming to the case of Rose Ellis, Mr Oliver said that this woman, who was now about thirty, had been of immoral character for several years. She had known Davidson for ten years.

They did not propose to call her, for the reason that it would be idle to attach the slightest reliance upon her word, but they were going to ask the court to infer, nevertheless, that the charge, without her evidence, was true.

Mr Davidson had described Ellis as 'half-witted and a bit mentally defective.' It was a very valuable description to give to a girl concerning whom there might be complaints that he had been taking liberties with her.

He had described her at various times as his secretary and his ward. The girl had certainly been taken to the rectory once, possibly many times, but they could only prove once. In 1923 Davidson had a room in Euston-street, and he was constantly visited there by Ellis. He used to stay in his room with her for hours at a time, and sometimes at night.

Rumblings of the Storm

Mr Oliver said he came to the last chapter of the long story when, on November 27 last, Ellis was interviewed, and three days later a statement was taken from her. Mr Davidson got to know about it, how they did not know, but very quickly.

The first rumblings of the storm were heard as far as he was concerned. What he did was to take prompt steps to get the girl to retract everything she said in the statement. He wrote a letter to his bishop, which was simply intended to throw dust in his eyes in order to stop proceedings.

Miss Gwendoline Harris was the first witness.

'I first met Mr Davidson in August 1930,' she said, 'when I was living in a bed-sitting-room at Alderney-street, Victoria, for which I paid ten shillings a week. I was out of employment at the time and had no money.

'I was walking near Marble-arch when I saw Mr Davidson for the first time. He kept on following me, and at last said, "Good evening", adding that he thought I was a friend of his and a film star. We went to a shop to have tea, and there I told him I was out of work and mentioned my address.

'He said that he would help me find a job, and after tea I left him. He came to see me in my bed-sitting-room the next day.'

Mr Oliver: 'How did he behave?' – Miss Harris: 'He was quite all right most of the time.'

Mr Oliver: 'When he did not behave quite all right, what did he do?' – Miss Harris: 'He always apologised.'

Mr Oliver: 'What did he do?' – Miss Harris: 'He started kissing me and caressing me.'

Mr Oliver: 'How soon after his first visit?' – Miss Harris: 'After nearly a fortnight.'

Mr Oliver: 'How often did he kiss you?' – Miss Harris: 'He was always kissing me.'

Mr Oliver: 'Did he ask you things?'

'Yes,' replied Miss Harris in almost a whisper. 'He asked me to give myself, body and soul, to him just once.'

Mr Oliver: 'You would not?' Miss Harris: 'No.'

Kept the door locked

Mr Davidson had a room at Shepherd's Bush and twice when she missed her train she slept there. She occupied his bed, and Mr Davidson slept in a chair.

Miss Harris stated that she was never intimate with Mr Davidson.

Miss Harris said that when she went to Macfarlane-road she went on the understanding that she was to live alone in Mr Davidson's lodgings. He said that he would go to his sister's house. For a week she lived alone, and then he started sneaking into the room, saying he had missed his train.

Mr Oliver: 'Did you keep the door locked?' – Miss Harris: 'Yes.'

Mr Oliver: 'Why?' – Miss Harris: 'To keep him out, because he came back one night and came in.'

Mr Oliver: 'How did he afterwards get in?' Miss Harris: 'He knocked on the window till I opened the door.'

Ran away from the Rectory

Miss Harris then described in detail how she and Rose Ellis went to Stiffkey, ostensibly for a holiday, and were put to do the housework and the cooking, and how they ran away from the rectory.

Mr Oliver: 'Where did you sleep that night? – Miss Harris: 'Under a haystack.'

Mr Oliver: 'Did Mr Davidson come the next day?' – Miss Harris: 'No.'

Mr Oliver: 'Did you and Rose stay there again that night?' – Miss Harris: 'Yes, we slept in a field.'

Mr Oliver: 'What did you eat?' – Miss Harris: 'We hardly ate anything.'

Mr Oliver: 'Was it wet or dry?' – Miss Harris: 'It was raining on the last night. We had had no food since the previous night.'

Mr Oliver: 'So you had no food and it was pouring with rain?' – Miss Harris: 'Yes.'

With Rose Ellis she then walked to Fakenham, where they found a garage. Here Rose Ellis knew someone who drove them to London.

Miss Harris then dealt with her employment at a dentist's in Euston-square, and of her visits to sleep at the room in Macfarlane-road during the week-ends.

Mr Oliver: 'I don't want to ask you these unpleasant questions, but did the time ever come when he left you in peace, or was he always trying to get you?' Miss Harris: 'He was always trying to get me.'

Mr Oliver: 'The whole time, right up to the end?' – Miss Harris: 'Yes.'

'The Queen of his heart'

'Once,' said Miss Harris, 'he said that I was the queen of his heart.'

Mr Oliver: 'Hardly an isolated position, I should think.'

'I asked him what he had done about the other girls,' added Miss Harris, 'and he said that he had given them all up.'

Once they visited Betty Peach for luncheon at her flat. Betty was in bed in her night-gown.

'Betty got out of bed,' said Miss Harris. 'Mr Davidson kissed her and put his arms around her. She showed him what she had been doing at dancing lessons, and did some acrobatics, bending backwards and forwards. He said that he was glad she was getting on so well.'

Mr Davidson paid for her (Miss Harris) to have dancing lessons, too, and later bought her some clothes, paying £5 for them.

That night they went to a theatre, and afterwards he wanted her to go to Macfarlane-road with him. When she demurred he said he only bought her the clothes so that she should go home with him, and added that if she did not he would commit suicide. Eventually she went there with him.

'Did you ever quarrel?' – 'We were always quarrelling – about different things and different girls.'

They used to go nearly every night to a Chinese restaurant, and there Mr Davidson, who never had any strong drink, used to kiss her and put his arms around her.

Armistice Day Telegram

Mr Oliver: 'Did he ever tell you about his wife?' – 'Yes. He said that he very seldom saw her, only once a week, that she did not like him, that he did not like her, and that she got jealous because there were so many girls. He said that he would get a decree because the last child was not his.' He would then marry her.

Miss Harris said that on Armistice Day he missed the five o'clock train in the morning to Stiffkey, where he was supposed to be taking the service in the morning at eleven o'clock. He sent a telegram to Stiffkey, and said he would go to the Cenotaph.

Mr Oliver: 'Why did he miss the train?' – 'He was trying to kiss me all the time.'

'Did he go to the Cenotaph?' – 'No.'

Mr Oliver read a number of letters said to have been written by Mr Davidson to Miss Harris, one of which warned her against steeping her mind in sensational literature, and added, 'Think ideals, and you will become ideal yourself. Help to raise those you meet on life's long way. God bless you.'

Story of Insults

Another ran, 'Everything I have done and said for you has been from my heart and meant only for your benefit.'

Miss Harris explained a phrase in one letter: 'Last night at the Tube station when you insulted me was quite enough.'

'He came up to me while I was with somebody else,' she said, 'and handed me 3s. 6d., saying it was a great responsibility being a guardian. I knocked the money out of his hand. He insulted me, so I insulted him.'

'Did he ever say anything about his home having money?' – 'He said they had none at all. He said they were starving down at Stiffkey . . .'

The Daily Express, 30 March 1932.

The trial dragged on for a further nine weeks, after which Davidson was found guilty and stripped of his living.

....

'You Need a New Rolls-Royce'

Edward James, art patron and eccentric

Edward James, the son of the illegitimate daughter of Edward VII, was involved in a celebrated divorce case with the ballet dancer Tilly Losch, in 1933. He was exceedingly rich and took great delight in sponsoring ballets in Paris and collecting surrealistic works of art, which later formed the basis of his extraordinary collection in Sussex. The marriage was one of fiscal convenience and soon began to fall apart with Tilly arriving at Edward's lavish parties often accompanied by her regular lover, Tom Mitford, while Edward was frequently to be found seeking comfort in the arms of Marie-Laure, a French aristocrat. The divorce was very messy and ended in James's favour, although many in café society cut him on subsequent social occasions, which led him to flee to Mexico. Tilly Losch went on to marry 'Porchy', the 6th Earl of Carnarvon.

James wrote the following extract in his memoir, Swans Reflecting Elephants:

I was in Tilly's room talking to her, and she asked me what I was doing the following day. 'I'm lunching with Oliver Messel,' I said. 'He asked me to lunch. Would you like to come?'

'No, you go. You go with him. I hope he sucks you and sucks you dry.'

This shocked me terribly. I was prudish and I had never imagined such a thing. I was so horrified at these filthy ideas being mouthed by a pretty woman that I pushed over a very heavy, fireproof iron safe which was disguised as a piece of Louis XVI furniture. It crashed to the floor, and the impact caused some of the plaster to fall from the drawing-room ceiling below. I left the house immediately without speaking to Tilly, and she woke up Mitzi and made her measure the distance between the bed and where the safe had fallen so that she could make out that I had thrown the safe at her, in order to build up her case for mental and physical cruelty. The next day she called Randolph [Churchill] and said, 'Look, Edward tried to throw the safe at me.

Randolph roared with laughter and said, 'Five men couldn't lift that safe, let alone throw it.' ...

Mrs Povey had come in one day and found Tilly having it off on the sofa with Randolph [Churchill], in the middle of the afternoon. I wasn't even annoyed about that; I knew that she was irresistibly fascinating and that she had seduced the friends I loved most because she thought she would be able to hurt me. What I did mind was that Randolph had started to spread rumours that I had treated Tilly badly. First of all he started being very offensive, saying such things as: 'You've got to get better cigars in your house for me. I don't like your cigars,' or, 'You need a new Rolls-Royce. I'm tired of your old one and so is Tilly.' It was a sort of drunken joking, but it wasn't funny because he was trying to pick a quarrel; he felt he was a shit for having slept with his best friend's wife and because of something else he had done.

There was an occasion when I had come back to London for a week or two to see my lawyer about raising money to finance the ballets. I had to sell a lot of things to raise the £100,000 necessary to rent the theatre and to pay for the scenery as well as Derain, Serge Tchelitchew and Balanchine. Tilly was still in New York, and Randolph suggested that we have dinner together; I was still fond of him so I agreed, and then he did something very *louche*. After dinner he asked me up to his place for a drink. He had a small, rather squalid room not far from Bond Street, which was all he could afford; a single bedroom and a sort of kitchen on the third floor. We drank quite a lot and even I got drunk; and then he said, 'You don't want to go all the way back to Wimpole Street tonight. Why not stay here? Tom slept in this bed only three days ago and we had a very nice peaceful night.' I thought that this was perfectly innocent and that it would be nice to wake up in the morning with a cheerful friend, and make breakfast and talk again, especially since I was lonely and unhappy, for I had not yet started my affair with Marie-Laure. In the morning Randolph got up with an erection and smiled at me from the foot of the bed, stark naked and rather provocative – he was a very handsome boy – and said, 'What would Tilly think if she knew we'd slept together?'

'I don't suppose she'd think anything. It was innocent enough, wasn't it? After all, Tom slept here last week, and do you suppose his girl-friends think anything?'

'Oh, I'm only kidding. But wouldn't she be jealous?'

'I don't think so, she'd have no cause to be, would she?'

Half laughing, he said, 'You are a dirty beggar, aren't you!'

Randolph at least had the decency not to lie about it to Tilly; he must have reported that nothing had happened. I think he was ambivalent too, like an *agent provocateur*, which was pretty low in one's best friend and Winston's son . . .

After the divorce I discovered who my real friends in England were, and they were awfully few. The two who were most loyal to me were Diana, the mother of Desmond Guinness, and Violet Tree, who was a wonderfully staunch and loyal friend . . . John Betjeman was loyal too. At the theatre one night we met my first cousin Anthony Wynn, with whom I had spent all my days playing games at Monckton, and he cut me dead, because it was the thing to do. I could hardly believe it. Betjeman looked at me and said, 'Hm. This is a historic meeting – or non-meeting.' . . . When I defended myself, it was like a deer being attacked by hounds, with its back to the wall: it starts using its horns and tossing the hounds down. It was as if they were saying that the deer was not supposed to defend itself.

Betjeman told me something very funny. He went to a music-hall, the Victoria Palace, I think it was called, to see Nervo standing in a corner twirling his hands about in a green light and somebody says to Knox, 'What's he doing?' and Knox answered: 'He's Tilly Losch asking for alimony!' . . .

Finally, to show her loyalty, having been a long-standing friend of my father and mother, and Arundel being very near West Dean, the Duchess of Norfolk invited me to a dinner given by Lady Rachel Howard for a couple of dozen people at Norfolk House in St James's Square. I arrived in tails and pearl studs, and immediately ran into Chips Channon. I didn't think that he would bother me much, because he was laying on the flattery to Rachel; unfortunately she had put me next to Honor Channon, and he had forbidden her to speak to me. She sat through the entire dinner with her back to me. The woman on my left talked to me as much as possible, but she didn't have much to say, and I was left alone. It was particularly offensive because this was the same Chips who had tried to get into bed with me in Italy. At this point I said to myself, 'Really, as Lady Cunard says, society is based on a lie, and if you tell the truth you won't be received in decent houses. That's a fact.'

Edward James with George Melly, *Swans Reflecting Elephants*
(Weidenfeld & Nicolson, 1982), pp. 142, 154–6, 167–9.

....

Diary in Blue

Mary Astor's off-screen adventures

Mary Astor was as famous for her off-screen adventures as her on-screen talent. She went through four marriages and had several well-publicised affairs – with actors such as John Barrymore – plus an 'alcohol' problem and at least one suicide attempt. However, the biggest scandal of her career, and arguably the most publicized one in Hollywood during the thirties, involved her romance with playwright George S. Kaufman.

Having dispatched the other major stars of the twenties and thirties in his salacious book Hollywood Babylon, *Kenneth Anger describes the unfortunate consequences of the discovery of Mary Astor's private diary.*

It was the biggest Hollywood scandal of the thirties but did little to alter Miss Astor's powers of recuperation.

The thirties was endowed with another lady luminary with a pronounced penchant for men, an auburn-haired beauty, poised sophisticate with a sensuous throaty voice: Mary Astor, one of the screen's great character actresses.

Since girlhood, Mary's best friend and confidante had been her diary. She told it everything, and delighted in setting down a sublime experience while the memory glowed. She could relive the moment and mark the high spots of her passage through life. Her Hollywood Diary was bound in blue, its pages covered with fine, ultrafeminine, flowing script that graphologists have affirmed is remarkably free from inhibitions. Its contents were as free as her penmanship. The volume for 1935 covered her extramarital trysts with witty playwright George S. Kaufman, with whom she found exquisite rapport; it is odd she didn't keep it well hidden.

The blue book had been kept tossed in a bedroom drawer, in with Mary's undies. One day, her physician husband was hunting a pair of misplaced cufflinks. When Dr Frankly Thorpe idly opened the leather volume, his glance fell on a passage of extravagant admiration:

'... remarkable staying power. I don't see how he does it!'

The admiration was not for Dr Thorpe.

As Dr Thorpe turned the pages, he learned that the man with such fantastic staying power was the urbane Kaufman, man-about-New York. He and Mary had met at the Algonquin during a New York shopping spree she had indulged in during the summer of 1933. This meant the good doctor had been a cuckold for a good sixteen months. Mary recorded her first encounter with her paramour-to-be (introduced by friend Miriam Hopkins) in glowing terms:

'His first initial is G. – George Kaufman – and I fell like a ton of bricks. I met him Friday ... Saturday he called for me at the Ambassador and we went to the Casino for lunch and had a very gay time!'

After taking in a performance of Kaufman's *Of Thee I Sing* at the Music Box Theater, Mary and George did the town for the next few nights – clubs, dives, penthouse parties. The disillusioned doctor's eyes popped as he read his wife's own record of her sexual itinerary:

'Monday – we ducked out of the boring party ... it was very hot so we got a cab and drove around the park a few times and the park, was, well, the park, and he held my hand and said he'd like to kiss me but didn't ...

Tuesday night we had dinner at Twenty-One and on the way to see *Run Little Chillun* he did kiss me – and I don't think either of us remember much what the show was about. We played kneesies during the first two acts, my hand wasn't in my own lap during the third ... It's been years since I've felt up a man in public but I just got carried away ...

Afterwards we had a drink someplace and then we went to a little flat in 73rd Street where we could be alone, and it was all very thrilling and beautiful. Once George lays down his glasses, he is *quite* a different man. His powers of recuperation are amazing, and we made love all night long ...

It all worked perfectly, and we shared our fourth climax at dawn ...
I didn't see much of anybody else the rest of the time – we saw every
show in town, had grand fun together and went frequently to 73rd
Street where he fucked the living daylights out of me ...

One morning about 4 we had a sandwich at Reuben's, and it was
just getting daylight, so we drove through the park in an open cab,
and the birds started singing, and it was a cool and dewy day and it
was pretty heavenly to pet and French ... right out in the open ...

Was any woman ever happier? It seems that George is just hard all
the time ... I don't see how he does it, he is perfect.'

Dr Thorpe then discovered that the heady New York affair had continued
right near his own back yard.

Kaufman and Moss Hart passed a few days in Hollywood in February
1934 before setting up their winter writing headquarters in Palm Springs.
One morning, when Mary told Thorpe she was going to Warner's for a
costume fitting, she raced instead to Kaufman's hotel:

'Monday I went to the Beverly Wilshire and was able to see George
alone for the first time. He greeted me in pyjamas, and we flew into
each other's arms. He was rampant in an instant, and in a few moments
it was just like old times ... he tore out of his pyjamas and I was never
undressed by anyone so fast in all my life ... Later we went to Vendome
for lunch, to a stationer's shop ... then back to the hotel. It was raining
and lovely. It was wonderful to fuck the entire sweet afternoon away
... I left about 6 o'clock.'

On subsequent weekends in Palm Springs:

'Sat around in the sun all day – lunch in the pool with Moss and
George and the Rogers – dinner at the Dunes – a drink in the moonlight
WITHOUT Moss and Rogers. Ah, desert night – with George's body
plunging into mine, naked under the stars ...'

When Thorpe confronted his wife with his discovery, one might suppose
the blue-bound book would go blank for a spell. But Mary couldn't wait
to record her husband's reaction:

'He was very badly broken up for several days, used his final weapon
with me, "*I need you*," with tears.

For the sake of peace and respite from all this emotionalism, I told
him I would do nothing at the present. My main reason for saying
this is, quite honestly, I want to be able to see George for the rest of

his stay here without being all upset – looking like hell. I want to have the last few times of completely enjoying him . . .'

Mary's refusal to break off the affair caused Thorpe to retaliate; soon, he was being seen with so many starlets that his digressions became the talk of the town. When Thorpe sued Mary for divorce in April, 1935, and demanded the custody of their daughter Marilyn (adored by Mary), hundreds of eyebrows were raised.

Mary did not contest the divorce. Thorpe had appropriated her tell-all Diary before she moved out of their Beverly Hills mansion. It was devastating evidence. She could not face the prospect of being deprived of her daughter. She filed a counter-suit on July 15, to retain custody of the child.

Thorpe's lawyers revealed the existence of the Diary the first day of the trial. The judge, 'Goody' Knight, took a peek at the book and excluded it as evidence. But Thorpe's lawyers leaked excerpts to the press which left little doubt as to its tenor; among them was the 'Ah, desert night . . .' passage which quickly entered into folklore. The tabloids gave the Diary full coverage, long excerpts sprinkled with asterisks. The public had a ball filling in the dots for itself.

Older fans recalled another of Mary Astor's passionate *affaires de coeur*, a decade earlier before her marriage, when as a budding film star (during the making of *Don Juan*) she had been John Barrymore's young mistress.

The court got an earful when the nurse of Mary's daughter related what had been going on *chez* Thorpe after Madame Thorpe moved out. The nurse described a scene when starlet Norma Taylor got into a jealous brawl with Thorpe in front of the child. At the time Norma had on red toenail polish and nothing else. Nurse reported that not only Norma, but three other blonde Busby Berkeley showgirls had 'slept in the doctor's bed' on succeeding nights. And Thorpe's whereabouts? Her deadpan reply was: 'He was right there in his bed too!'

Mary got back the mansion and Marilyn, in spite of all the diary revealed of her passion for Kaufman. However, the court did not return her Dearest Friend. The diary was adjudged 'pornography' and consigned to the courthouse stove.

It is significant that these revelations did not injure Mary Astor's career – far from it. Ten years earlier, a case like this would have finished off any star, but the Depression had been a factor, albeit painful, in promoting greater public maturity. In a few years, Mary would score one of her greatest successes as the seductive villainess in *The Maltese Falcon*.

Kaufman had taken a powder [disappeared] during the courtroom proceedings; he sat them out in New York with Hart. He dodged queries concerning the case, but once, when cornered by reporters at the stage door of the Music Box, he allowed: 'You may say I did *not* keep a diary.'

Kenneth Anger, *Hollywood Babylon* (Arrow Books, 1975), pp. 192–8.

....

The Maharajah of Alwar

Extravagance and egoism of a maharajah

In the 1930s the Indian princely states in Rajasthan had more than their fair share of bad and eccentric rulers with few able to compete in this category with the Maharajah of Alwar. He was a fanatical Hindu who loathed physical contact with Britishers, whom he considered to be in effect, untouchables. The Maharajah was also renowned for his temper and once poured petrol over a polo pony that had let him down and then incinerated it. The British officials agonized about what to do with this errant prince, with one of their biggest concerns being the political backlash if it were publicly revealed how outrageous and corrupt his rule had become. One official feared that such disclosures 'made public would be such as to provoke the horror of the whole civilised world'. As his state was teetering on bankruptcy, the Maharajah went into exile, turning up in Italy where he failed to get Mussolini to throw a birthday party for him. He then camped on the steps of the Vatican in a vain attempt to receive an audience with the Pope before turning up uninvited at a Buckingham Palace garden party, much to the fury of King George V. Back in India, at the farewell reception for Lord Willingdon, the Viceroy, the Maharajah said, after shaking the Viceroy's hand, 'Your Excellency, I am sorry to say farewell, but you can leave India knowing that everything you have done to me was entirely justified.' Shortly before the Maharajah died in 1937, a single-minded Scotsman, Arthur Lothian, was appointed as his Prime Minister by the Viceroy, but even he found it hard going. He described his exasperation to one of his colleagues.

I close this report with a brief account of His Highness's personal equation, for he is a very extraordinary character. The Maharajah is now about 53 years of age, and has always kept himself very fit physically with the result that he looks younger than his actual age. Perhaps the main defects in his character are his gross extravagance and his overweening arrogance. As regards his extravagance I have made a rough estimate of the expenditure of the ruler which suggests that it amounts to well over half the total income of the state, and would note that nine lakhs of unpaid bills are now pending against the state, mostly for articles ordered by His Highness. If he plays tennis, a table displaying anything from ten to twenty rackets has to be set out in front of him; so with guns when out shooting; his office table is festooned with gold fountain pens in racks like those one sees in a stationer's shop window.

As regards the Maharajah's arrogance, he cannot bear not being in the centre of every picture. In his own state this is natural enough, but he pursues the same policy elsewhere by staging spectacular late arrivals, the wearing of clothes of the most conspicuous possible hue and headgear of extraordinary shape, and by making speeches on any and every occasion. When to his arrogance there is added a vindictive, capricious and cruel temperament, his officials and attendants never dare put up any proposals which are unpalatable to him. He is currently reported to thrash his ADC's. Be that as it may, and it is quite in keeping with the cruelty in his character, there is a cringing, frightened atmosphere among the members of the Maharajah's staff such as I have never seen in any other state.

I was not sent to Alwar as Censor Morum so I have hitherto refrained from any reference to this aspect of his life. But to complete the picture of conditions in the state, it is necessary to bear in mind that the moral atmosphere of the place is mephitic. The people around the Maharajah have an evil, brutalised look such as I have seen nowhere else. One incident which happened a couple of years ago will give some idea of what goes on under the veil. The Alwar Darbar pressed for the extradition of a man from a neighbouring Rajputana state as a deserter from the Alwar Bodyguard; but the other Darbar flatly refused, because the Alwar Bodyguard was not a military unit at all but was well known to have been recruited for another more personal purpose. Against all this, however, there is something to put on the credit side. He has probably the acutest brain of all the Indian princes. When he cares, he can make himself the most charming host and companion. To see him at a shooting party beguiling the company with story after story of interesting experiences he has had, makes one regret all the more that there is another altogether different side to his character, the Dr Jekyll to his Mr Hyde.

Charles Chenevix Trench, *Viceroy's Agent* (Jonathan Cape, 1987), pp. 146–8.

···

Wee Willie Winkie

Graham Greene on Shirley Temple

This film review by Graham Greene caused immense trouble when it appeared in the literary magazine Night and Day *in 1937. Many people claimed that the out of court settlement with Miss Temple's lawyers caused the closure of the magazine, a point that Greene always strongly denied.*

The owners of a child star are like leaseholders – their property diminishes in value every year. Time's chariot is at their back; before them acres of anonymity. What is Jackie Coogan now but a matrimonial squabble? Miss Shirley Temple's case, though, has peculiar interest: infancy with her is a disguise, her appeal is more secret and more adult. Already two years ago she was a fancy little piece (real childhood, I think, went out after *The Littlest Rebel*). In *Captain January* she wore trousers with the mature suggestiveness of a Dietrich: her neat and well-developed rump twisted in the tap-dance: her eyes had a sidelong searching coquetry. Now in *Wee Willie Winkie*, wearing short kilts, she is a complete totsy. Watch her swaggering stride across the Indian barrack-square: hear the gasp of excited expectation from her antique audience when the sergeant's palm is raised: watch the way she measures a man with agile studio eyes, with dimpled depravity. Adult emotions of love and grief glissade across the mask of childhood, a childhood skin-deep.

It is clever, but it cannot last. Her admirers – middle-aged men and clergymen – respond to her dubious coquetry, to the sight of her well-shaped and desirable little body, packed with enormous vitality, only because the safety curtain of story and dialogue drops between their intelligence and their desire. 'Why are you making my Mummy cry?' – what could be purer than that? And the scene when dressed in a white night-dress she begs grandpa to take Mummy to a dance – what could be more virginal? On those lines her new picture, made by John Ford, who directed *The Informer*, is horrifyingly competent. It isn't hard to stay to the last prattle and the last sob. The story – about an Afghan robber converted by Wee Willie Winkie to the British Raj – is a long way after Kipling. But we needn't be sour about that. Both stories are awful, but on the whole Hollywood's is better.

Graham Greene, Night and Day, 28 October 1937.

'Persecuted but Happy'

Sixty-year-old vicar engaged to seventeen-year-old girl

In August 1937, a sixty-year-old vicar in Somerset became engaged to a teenage parishioner.

The Rev. Gerald Salkeld Stubbs, sixty-year-old rector of Chiselborough and West Chinnock, conducted morning service in Chiselborough's stone church today before a congregation which besides the organist, a verger and myself – consisted of three people.

Four days ago Mr Stubbs announced his engagement to a seventeen-year-old parishioner, Miss Betty Fewings. At the early Communion service today a woman churchwarden had taken the collection – and walked out without taking Communion. Morning service followed. Instead of a sermon, the Litany was read. Afterwards, Mr Stubbs, six-foot, blue-eyed, tanned, said to me: 'I shall not refer to my engagement in any sermon. It is an entirely personal matter. My life has been hell since I announced our engagement. You should see the letters I have had – anonymous, horrible. Worse still, it has affected the parish. There is gossip. I can't understand people who think like the authors of those letters. Our engagement is perfectly decent.

'Miss Fewings has been terribly upset. Horrible letters have been sent to her, too. I am taking legal advice over some of the things that have been written.'

Miss Fewings's mother and father – he gave up his job in the Civil Service to market-garden in West Chinnock – told me of their fight to save their daughter's name from 'malicious gossip'.

Mrs Fewings said: 'We should not have agreed to the engagement if we had not thought Mr Stubbs one of the kindest and finest men in the world. He told us once, "The morning and afternoon of my life have been so sad that I was hoping for a little sunshine in the evening of it."

'Now the storm has broken over him again. It is so cruel. Our doctor says Betty has the mind of a woman of thirty. She has just won the gold medal of the Associated Board of the Royal School of Music. I detest people who make insinuations about them. They are both very happy, despite their persecution.'

Mr Stubbs attended a fete yesterday with Miss Fewings. Today, with her beside him, he addressed a meeting of 1,000 members of the Order of Buffaloes.

The Daily Express, 16 August 1937

....

Peking Society taken Aback

Bride upset at the lack of response from her husband

In December 1937, The Daily Express *reported another scandal involving a marriage, only this time it was in Peking with the Japanese army on the outskirts.*

While battle rages along the railway 30 miles away, Peking society circles are scandalised by a divorce suit against the grandson of the late President Yuan Shih-kai.

Mrs Yuan Chi-lang who also charges her husband with bigamy, seeks £6,000 alimony, says that when he did not speak at their first meeting – the engagement dinner – she thought he was observing ancient Chinese etiquette, but after the wedding she found he was deaf and dumb.

The Daily Express, 24 December 1937.

....

'We Say No!'

Unity Mitford's support for Hitler

The Honourable Unity Mitford was perhaps the most prominent female admirer of Hitler in Britain. Her connections were quite wide, with one sister married to Oswald Mosley, a second to the future Duke of Devonshire, while yet another was the writer Nancy Mitford and a further one, Jessica, was considered by her circle to be a Communist. Unity Mitford showed her singular lack of reality with the following statement in the press which appeared in The Daily Mirror *in March 1939. She was still in Germany after the Second World War began and was so upset at this turn of events that she shot herself. Her friend Hitler allowed her to be evacuated to Britain, where she died in 1948.*

What Miss Mitford would like to See

(We don't agree with her. And the Editor asks what you think!)

The *Daily Mirror* opens this page to-day to Unity Mitford. Miss Mitford is a daughter of Lord Redesdale and a personal friend of Hitler. She has been strongly criticised for her pro-German activities and views. Last year she was attacked by a mob in Hyde Park. The *Daily Mirror* has given her a free hand to express her views to-day. Would she get the same freedom for unpopular views in Germany? We say NO!

Unity Mitford writes:

In 1935 the Naval Pact between Germany and England was signed, limiting Germany's naval power to 35 per cent of that of Great Britain. The pact was an outward and visible sign that Germany never wished to go to war with Britain again. And yet, ever since, a ceaseless flood of propaganda has tried to persuade English people that Nazi Germany intends to attack England. What is the truth about Germany's intentions towards England?

Hitler has often been called a dreamer. He was called a dreamer by his enemies in Germany before he came to power, who laughed at him and said his dreams could never come true. What they did not realise was that, as well as being a dreamer, Hitler was a realist, and that he only dreamed dreams whose fulfilment he knew to be possible, taking into account his genius for achieving the apparently impossible. Many of these apparently impossible dreams have already been

realised. One that has not yet materialised is an Anglo-German friendship and co-operation. The time will come when this dream also
becomes reality; it is already shared by many, many Englishmen, in
spite of intensive anti-German propaganda in this country.

At the time, and on looking back since, Hitler realised the folly and
impracticability of the Kaiser's pre-war policy of rivalry with England.
By reason of her geographical and historical position, Germany is not
so well suited as England to the role of colonial power.

Possession of overseas colonies necessitates a powerful navy. And
Germany's strength has always lain in her land army, not in her navy.
That Germany wishes the return of her former colonies is only natural.
They were taken from her unjustly and the claim for their return is a
claim for justice.

But every German knows that the future of the Reich lies, not in a
large overseas colonial empire, but in an entirely different direction,
a direction in which there is no reason at all why she should come
into conflict with British interests.

Apart from these practical considerations, there is another and
equally important side to the question.

Those who believe that National Socialist Germany wishes to
weaken England show a sad ignorance of Nazi ideology.

And when discussing that ideology, one must remember that
National Socialism is more to Germans than a political creed; it is a
faith.

One of the foundations of Nazi ideology is the racial theory.
Germans believe the Nordic race to be the greatest in the world, which
indeed it is. They believe that the future of Europe stands or falls with
the Nordic race. And they believe that enmity between the two great
Nordic countries would mean its virtual suicide. Humanly speaking,
friendship between England and Germany is the most natural thing
in the world. English people visiting Germany generally feel absolutely
at home, and find the Germans are very much like themselves, with
the same interests and the same outlook on life.

The Englishman or woman is always hospitably welcomed in
Germany. And when during the September crisis, when it was touch
and go whether the British Government would take sides with the
Czechs against them, Germans never became unfriendly towards the
English people, though they were naturally puzzled at the attitude of
England's rulers.

Only recently the former Governor of Gibraltar said in a speech that
he had seen English sailors fraternising with German sailors in a

manner which would be impossible with sailors of any other nationality. If such friendly feelings can exist in the face of such intensive, anti-German propaganda, how much more would they exist if that propaganda were to cease!

The real interests of Britain and Germany do not clash. They are, as the British Ambassador in Berlin said in a speech a few weeks ago, complementary to one another. For that reason a close alliance between the two countries would be perfectly possible. And such an alliance would be a blessing for the whole world. With Germany the greatest Continental power, allied to Britain, the greatest Colonial power, another world war would become an impossibility. The advantages to be gained by such a partnership are incalculable. The German Army, the British Navy and the two Air Forces combined would police the world and keep 'peace in our time'.

I can hardly do better than to end by quoting a passage from the Fuehrer's speech to the Reichstag on January 30 of this year:

'I have stated over and over again that there is no German, and above all, no National Socialist, who even in his secret thoughts has the intention of causing the British Empire any kind of difficulties.

From England, too, the voices of men who think reasonably and calmly express a similar attitude with regard to Germany.

It would be a blessing for the whole world if mutual confidence and co-operation could be established between the two peoples.'

Unity Mitford

Well, Miss Unity Mitford has had her say … And now we'd like to know what YOU think about it all. Can we trust in a real friendship with Germany? Remember Hitler has once again broken his word of honour!

The Daily Mirror, 18 March 1939.

A total of 1,093 readers wrote in, with ninety-two per cent attacking her. One correspondent, a Mr F. J. Clark, pointed out that 'Lions do not mate with jackals.'

....

William Hickey's Closest Shave

Tom Driberg's misadventures

Tom Driberg, the House of Commons' most renowned 'cottager', had several brushes with the law because of his homosexual enthusiasms. In the thirties, while he was writing the 'William Hickey' column for Lord Beaverbrook's Daily Express, *he was acquitted at the Old Bailey of indecent behaviour. Two homeless miners sharing his bed had complained about improper advances. Beaverbrook managed to keep the story out of Fleet Street and the arresting policeman later confessed that had he known that Driberg was 'William Hickey', he would not have allowed the miners to bring charges. The following incident occurred in 1942.*

The narrowest shave of my life – apart from the Old Bailey affair – occurred in Edinburgh, where I had gone, as a newly elected MP, to speak at a by-election for the Northern Midlothian constituency in support of another Independent, Tom Wintringham. The meeting was a crowded one, in the Usher Hall; no doubt we had the customary few drinks afterwards. Later I was walking along Princes Street towards my hotel. The war was still on, and the whole city was blacked out. In such dim lighting as there was, one could just make out the forms of passers-by – and I bumped into a tall figure in a foreign naval uniform. One of us struck a match to light cigarettes. He was a Norwegian sailor, typically Scandinavian in appearance, flaxen-haired and smilingly attractive. He may have had a few drinks, too: he was eager for anything, and perhaps lonely. (Loneliness is as strong an incentive, often, as lust.) I recalled that there was an air-raid shelter under the gardens a few yards from where we were standing. Neither of us could speak the other's language, but he readily came down to the shelter with me. Down there it was completely dark, but another match showed a bench running along one side of the shelter. There was no air-raid, nor alarm, on at the time, so we were alone. In a matter of seconds he had slipped his trousers half-way down, and was sitting on the bench, leaning well back. We embraced and kissed, warmly enough, but my interest was concentrated lower down, on a long, uncircumcised, and tapering, but rock-hard erection; and I was soon on my knees. Too concentrated, and too soon perhaps; for in a few moments the stillness of the shelter was broken by a terrifying sound – the crunching, very near at hand, of boots on the gravelled floor. Instantly the blinding light of a torch shone full on us, and a deep Scottish voice was baying, in a tone of angry disgust: 'Och, ye bastards – ye dirty pair o' whoors ...' No concealment was possible: we were caught almost wet-handed; the sailor pulled his trousers up over a prick that was rapidly losing its pride, and sat forward, his face buried in his hands; and I stood up, to confront a young Scottish policeman, of about the same height as myself, with an older special constable lurking behind him.

He wanted to take us straight to his station ('Ye can do your explaining there'); but I (with, I am sure, a subconscious recollection of the detective-sergeant's remark at the *Express* office) said, with such firmness as I could muster, 'First, you'd better just see who I am.' I was still on the *Express*, and had been equipped with visiting-cards bearing my name, with the words 'Member of Parliament' – and, in the lower left-hand corner, the columnist's pseudonym. The policeman scrutinised the card gravely. Then he exploded. '*William Hickey!*' he said. 'Good God, man, *I've read ye all of my life!* Every morning...'

After a few more exchanges, he turned to his colleague, the special, and told him to go, saying that he would handle the matter himself. My hopes rose a little, but it was not until he shooed away the Norwegian sailor ('Get awa' oot of it, ye bugger' – and get awa' the poor lad did, scampering out of the shelter like a rabbit: I still regret having had to leave that bit of business unfinished; but I don't suppose he picked up anyone else that night) – and it was not until this moment that I began to feel fairly safe, and suggested that we should continue our talk upstairs in the gardens.

So we did. He was seven years my junior, but talked to me 'like a father'. I lied to him as convincingly as I could, swearing that if he would let me off I would never do such a thing again; it worked. In twenty minutes or so, we were good friends, on a writer-and-reader basis. ('Ye must meet a lot o' interesting people ...') His name was George Crowford. He had a ruddy face, and a markedly cleft, strong chin. I liked him and thought him attractive (but judged that it would be going too far, in the circumstances, to make a pass). When we said goodnight, we shook hands, and he gave a – not too formal – salute. I was sure that it would be unwise, as well as wrong, to give him any money; but, having ascertained his address, I sent him from London, a few days later, book-tokens to the value of six guineas. I thought it thoroughly decent – and Scottish – of him not to pretend that this was a surreptitious gift, or bribe, in any way connected with the shelter incident, and to write me a literate, though prim, letter of thanks, telling me that he was spending the tokens on books that he had 'long coveted', I think some special edition, or a life, of Robert Burns.

Tom Driberg, *Ruling Passions* (Jonathan Cape, 1977), pp. 143–5.

....

Confession of a Cuckold

Sir Jock Delves Broughton

The Who's Who *entry for Sir Jock Delves Broughton, 11th baronet (1888–1942) mentions that he was educated at Eton, had one marriage and 'owns about 15,200 acres'. What it fails to mention is that he was also a blackmailing murderer. He had been charged in Kenya in 1941 with the murder of the Earl of Erroll, one of his second wife's numerous lovers, but was acquitted. The following letter only came to light half a century after the murder and paints a revealing picture of his wife's numerous liaisons.*

Diana,

I am determined to punish you for ruining my life in the way you have done. Up to the time we left England, universally popular, respected, millions of friends, and welcome everywhere. I worshipped the ground you stood on, and got divorced in order to marry you. On board the boat you became a stranger to me and a completely different human being. You started a fuck with Tony Mordant under my eyes and I discovered the copy of the letter you wrote to your Italian; the most violent love letter written when living with me on Doddington writing paper. This was the first time I knew you had double crossed me. On the boat you were regretting the whole time that you had not stayed in England and married Rory Moore O'Farrel.

We got to South Africa where at Cape Town you were bloody to me most of the time. When being thoroughly fed up I said I should like to return to England in front of the Bailes family you said 'I shall stay in South Africa, why don't you return to England?' Charming for me. You made such a farce of our marriage that the Registrar almost refused to marry you. If I had not adored you I should not have been fool enough to marry you, but I worshipped you. We came up to Kenya where, for about six weeks, I was happy. You then started double crossing me with Erroll. Do you think any woman has ever treated any man as badly as you did me? Letting him be divorced from a wife he has lived with not unhappily for 25 years, and then telling him she was leaving him two months after she had married him because she herself had fallen in love. Millions of people fall in love, but they have feelings of decency and do not behave like you did. If you had returned to England you would have of course got over it. Erroll was murdered. You say yourself it never even occurred to you to connect me with it till the Police put it into your head. You then in your evidence did all in your power to get me hung. Later you say yourself you were convinced that I had nothing to do with it. After the verdict you were charming to me and were perfectly happy in Ceylon and India. We came back and were quite happy till we went on safari with Gilbert Colville. Since that moment everything has gone wrong. You knew he was the richest settler in Kenya, could be useful to you, was easy money and laid yourself out to ensnare him, quite regardless of how you knew how unhappy and miserable it made me.

Like a fool I bought Oserian [Lord Erroll's farm] because you said you were unhappy at Karen. We have never been anything else but unhappy since we went there on March 1st. I never objected to you having people to stay, but when we had rows you always dinned into me how you were still in love with Erroll. This, your very fervent friendship with Colville and your obvious dislike of being ever alone with me made me depressed, unhappy and hating the place, people, country – everything connected with it. In addition, I was ill with malaria for four months.

I thought things were going better when you had Hugh Strickland to stay, liked him and enjoyed having him, and you were apparently quite happy. Like the poor fool I was I had no idea of what was happening or why you put him in a room with no lock on the door opening straight out into your rooms till Chappy Bailes told me that he was seen kissing you in your bedroom at the Stanley by a highly amused crowd from Torr's Hotel. Even then, thinking that you had always told me the truth about your 'cold temperament' I didn't suspect what was going on till you were so very anxious to get me off to bed one night with a sleeping draught. I watched through the window of your bathroom, and saw you actually go and fetch him and return to your bedroom with him, and then listened to him fucking you through the gauze in your bedroom window not more than three yards away. By the way the whole bed rocked you evidently enjoyed it, like you used to with me. I waited and watched the next two nights, but you both had chills and I saw nothing. The next night I asked for a sleeping draught and went to bed early, and watched, and saw him walk into your bedroom and get into bed, and you followed and got into bed with him. I then took action. After this you had the cheek to suggest that he stayed another four days till you could take him to Nairobi. Like the fool I was, still loving you, I forgave it, but since that moment, you have been more vile to me than anyone would think possible.

... After this catalogue of betrayal and self-hatred, Delves Broughton goes on to both threaten his wife with blackmail while offering yet another opportunity to return to him as if nothing untoward had ever occurred between them. The deed box mentioned below contained a string of pearls belonging to Diana that they conspired to lose just before the war in order to claim £12,000 insurance on them.

I have always been suspicious as to what you had inside the deed box you gave me to give George Green to keep for you. I have cabled him to take it to my solicitors; I have given my agents here a sealed letter with instructions inside it to cable my solicitors at home to open the box, and if my suspicions are correct, to send the contents to the place where they were purchased for verification, and if so verified to send the box and contents to Scotland Yard, on my instructions, and to ask them to await an air mail letter I am sending in duplicate. You will then be sent home for trial. If you were only an accessory it would be exactly the same thing and make no difference. The penalty for this 'offence' is 14 years hard labour. You are now nearly 29 and by the time you were taken home for trial and tried and sentenced it might take nine months and this would keep you from double crossing me and popping into bed with any strange man until you are 44, and prison is very ageing, and I don't think you would find men so easy then. I could, moreover, divorce you for having committed a criminal offence. Moreover any accomplices you may have had would be equally involved (if my suspicions are verified). Do not think this is an empty threat because nothing in this world will stop me doing it. I want you to be punished for ruining my life by ruining yours and punished you shall be, regardless of what happens to me. I should change my name after the trial and go and live where no one knows me. I have no doubt that I can get someone I am fond of to live with me. You have changed me into a fiend thirsting for vengeance. I think of nothing else day and night. I never sleep for thinking of it.

As I said hate and love are very akin, and I still love you. I hate you sometimes like you do me, but I miss you every hour of the day and night, and want you back, and am determined that swine Gilbert Colville, who is the cause of all this shall not have you. When you told me that he and you were going to share Oserian, which of course means that he would have to keep you, and thought how I could punish you both and this is how I am going to do it.

I will give you one last chance and one only. If within ten days of receiving this letter you have packed up all your belongings, and put them on the train for Mombasa and have gone down there yourself to catch the first boat to England, and come back and live with me wherever I elect to live, I will do nothing. You say that you and Colville have fixed up Oserian so that you have the house and he the land. Right, leave it at that. The place will be yours, or I will get Spring Valley to advance the money for taking over the house if he lends the money on mortgage and takes it over, I will settle it on you in strict settlement, but will take no more chances of being a cipher in your house to be treated like dirt and turned out when you wish.

Private Papers

Diana showed the letter to the Kenya Attorney-General, who wired the British authorities to meet Delves Broughton when he arrived at Liverpool. Two CID officers met and questioned him but he committed suicide before any action could be taken.

....

In Brains We Trust

Professor C. E. M. Joad's railway ticket fraud

Professor C. E. M. Joad was a high-profile Oxford don who was well-known throughout Britain for his radio appearances on the Brains Trust. After the following incident in 1948, his reputation was never quite the same.

Dr Cyril Edwin Mitchinson Joad, of East Heath Rd Hampstead, was fined

40s and ordered to pay 25gns costs by Mr H. H. Maddocks at Tower Bridge police court yesterday for travelling on the railway without previously having paid his fare between Waterloo and Salisbury, and with intent to avoid payment.

When the case was before Miss Sybil Campbell on March 25 Mr Ralph Freeman pleaded guilty on behalf of Dr Joad, and explained that Dr Joad was under the impression that he had the return half of a ticket from Waterloo to Salisbury.

Miss Campbell said that Mr Freeman's statement was entirely contrary to the plea, which should have been one of not guilty. The case was then adjourned so that Dr Joad could give him explanation.

Mr J. Platts Mills yesterday represented Dr Joad, who did not attend court. Mr R. E. Seaton, prosecuting, said the offence was 'a common ticket fraud'. Dr Joad and his secretary joined the Exeter train at Waterloo on Jan. 5 and booked two places for dinner. After the train had passed Salisbury he was asked for his ticket. He said he boarded the train at Salisbury and he paid 24s for the fare from there to Exeter.

Booked Two Dinners

When challenged later by the collector, who pointed out that he had booked two dinners on boarding the train at Waterloo, Dr Joad repeated that he had got on at Salisbury. In all, he denied four times that he had travelled from Waterloo, but at Exeter admitted he had made a mistake and tendered the full fare from London. This was not accepted, and next day he forwarded the money.

Sixteen days later his solicitors wrote about the 'extremely unfortunate incident' and referred to the repercussions which any prosecution 'would have on a person of the standing of our client who is, of course, the internationally known lecturer and author'. The solicitor explained that it was the custom for his secretary to obtain the tickets, but on this occasion Dr Joad told her no ticket would be necessary for him to Salisbury as he had a return half to that point. After paying the excess to Exeter he discovered to his dismay that he could not find the return half which he had believed was in his possession.

Mr Platts Mills said the prosecution did not involve Dr Joad in a charge of dishonesty or fraud. The obligation on him was to produce a ticket when it was demanded and he could not do so. His conduct at Waterloo when he ordered dinner that was to be served at Salisbury showed he had no intention to avoid paying his fare.

Mr Maddocks said there was no question that Dr Joad was guilty; in fact, he had pleaded guilty, and there could be only one fine, the maximum of 40s.

The Daily Telegraph, 13 April 1948, p. 5.

....

The Groundnut Fiasco

Plan to harvest groundnuts in East Africa

This scandal did more to damage socialism than anything else done by the post-war British Labour Government. The dream was to harvest vast acres of groundnuts in state-run plantations in East Africa. More than three million acres of scrub and jungle were going to be cleared and, by 1953, a crop of more than half a million tons was forecast. The entire project was a fiasco, as shown in the following report of the Public Accounts Committee in 1950.

The basic fault in the East African groundnuts scheme was the failure to realise the impracticality of the original plans in the conditions which existed immediately after the war. This was the impression of the Committee of Public Accounts. The Committee's report on the accounts of the Overseas Food Corporation, the organisation responsible for the groundnuts scheme, was published yesterday. It deals with the accounts for the period March 1, 1948, to March 31, 1949. It points out, however, that during the first year of the scheme the United Africa Company (Managing Agency Ltd) were in charge in East Africa. 'They must, in the opinion of your committee, take some share of the responsibility for the lack of efficient organisation.' In running the scheme normal commercial methods were a secondary consideration compared with the fastest possible rate of proceeding with the scheme, because of the world shortage of fats.

An immense development and production drive was set on foot at a time when nothing but a second-hand plant and machinery were available and before a balanced administrative, financial and accounting system had been created which could bear the weight of the initial surge of expenditure. 'But the sense of urgency was such that priority was given to clearing and production requirements: administration and accounting, though important, were regarded as secondary to those main purposes.' This sense of urgency was so great that the whole project was pushed forward with a degree of deliberate 'risk taking' in the hope that the 1948 harvest would produce some improvement in a dangerous situation. The desire to economise in time was obvious from the inception of the scheme, for the Wakefield Mission completed their inquiries in nine weeks. They obtained their data from the best sources available to them and formed their conclusions and estimates accordingly. 'In stating that these estimates have proved in the event to have been extremely inaccurate, the scope and originality of the conception and the total lack of any experience of mechanised agriculture on this scale in Africa should be borne in mind.'

Instructions from the Ministry of Food precluded changing over to an experimental policy and pilot schemes. Discontinuance of operations and the establishment of experimental units were considered during 1949, but it was decided to continue the existing scheme on a reduced scale. Sir Leslie Plummer (who is relinquishing his chairmanship of the Corporation) contended in evidence that small scale experiments would not have been of real value in this mechanised project.

'Work, therefore, began under the handicap of a long-term plan which in the event proved to be impracticable. The scheme of work for the first year, the clearing of 150,000 acres, was in itself impossible of fulfilment, owing to the bad state or unsuitability of the only plant and machinery available, the impossibility of obtaining spare parts and repair shops, the inadequacy of the port, storage accommodation and railway facilities and the lack of staff and the means of housing them.

The latest figure of moneys advanced to the Overseas Food Corporation was £34,650,000, up to April 21, 1950. Of this sum £991,320 was for the Queensland scheme for growing sorghum, and £1,908,328 was in respect of railway and port work in East Africa, which will be recovered from the East African Railways and Harbours Administration.

There has so far been no appreciable revenue from the groundnuts scheme. It is hoped that there will be a small amount this year but it is realised that there will be none of any consequence until after the harvest of 1951. In his evidence Sir Leslie Plummer said he hoped that by the harvest of 1954 the Corporation would cease to require any more capital and that they would be making a trading profit – that is a profit on their operations without any provision for amortisation, depreciation, interest, &c.

Sir Frank Lee, Permanent Secretary to the Ministry of Food, said that some of the assumptions which the Corporation made in framing these hypothetical estimates appeared to be over sanguine, but he added that the Ministry put forward no alternative date for the viability of the scheme.

Sir Leslie Plummer gave the following reasons for the failure to produce groundnuts within the time and in the quantities forecast in the original plan:

Extreme Difficulty of Communications

There was no adequate port and Kongwa could be reached only by 200 miles of single track railway, which was barely adequate to their needs.

Intractability of the Soil

The soil at Kongwa presented far more difficulties than expected by the Wakefield Mission. The Mission, the Managing Agency and the Corporation all, in fact, made deductions from comparatively small acreages which proved to be misleading when applied to larger areas.

Lack of Suitable Machinery

There was no machinery in the world which was really suitable for the task which had to be performed.

The Severe Drought of 1949

This ruined the crop that year. At Kongwa rainfall proved to be quite different from that of the two stations a dozen miles away which had provided the Wakefield Mission with the information on which was based the recommendation of Kongwa as a suitable area for growing groundnuts.

Sir Leslie Plummer said that strenuous efforts were made during the last year to correct the situation as revealed by the auditors. The staff of accountants had been increased to 128, compared with 51 in August 1948. The quality of those engaged also improved.

Answering Mr Thurtle, a member of the Committee, Sir Leslie said: 'I think it far too early to say of a scheme of this kind, which has been in operation less than three years and which is planned as a vast piece of agricultural colonial development in an undeveloped area, that it is a failure.'

Mr John Rosa, a former member of the board of the corporation who resigned last year, in general observations on the finance and accounts of the scheme, said in evidence:

One had no plan at all to work to. There was the original White Paper, which was accepted as the original plan. I think fairly soon it became obvious that was not a plan to which one could work; it was unrealistic – it was unattainable anyway. There was no substitute for that plan.

Mr W. A. Faure, formerly in executive overall charge of the United Africa's Managing Agency, told the committee that experts sent to inspect British army lorries in Belgium on behalf of the groundnuts scheme found that 'something like 150' out of 800 or 900 vehicles 'were quite good'.

'They noted the numbers painted on the doors and made a private little scratch on every door so that we would be able to identify the vehicles.

'When these lorries arrived in Kongwa (and I am telling you the complete truth) the numbers and the code scratches were verified, and we were very glad that they were there. But what had happened? They had taken those doors out of the vehicles we had selected and put them on to complete write-offs.'

In the conclusions to the report the committee says that when the corporation took control in March, 1948, the accounts and storekeeping records were in an unsatisfactory state.

'The corporation cannot have been unaware of what had been happening. During the previous five months members-designate had been appointed and had been in very close touch with the managing agents: some of them, including the chairman-designate, had visited East Africa and seen for themselves how badly operations were proceeding.'

The Daily Telegraph, 13 June 1950, p. 51

Piltdown Man Loses his Bite

Celebrated fossil hoax

The Piltdown Man was one of the most notorious scientific hoaxes of the century. In 1912, Charles Dawson, a Sussex solicitor, claimed to have discovered the pieces of what became for forty years the most celebrated humanlike fossils in the world. However, in 1953, The Times *revealed conclusively that Dawson, along with a local jewellery-forger, had perpetrated a fraud.*

The startling discovery that one of the most famous of anthropological specimens, the Piltdown skull, is in important parts – and therefore in general effect – a forgery has been made as a result of investigations just completed in the Department of Geology at the British Museum (National History) and in the Department of Anatomy of the University of Oxford.

The full details of these investigations are being published by Dr J. S. Winer, Dr K. P. Oakley and Professor W. E. Le Gros Clark in the new number of the geological series of the museum's *Bulletin*, to be issued to-day.

Not Genuine Fossils

Briefly, the conclusion of these scientists is that, though the fragments of the cranium are genuine remains of a primitive man, the large piece of mandible and the separate canine tooth 'are actually those of a modern ape (chimpanzee or orang) deliberately faked to simulate fossil specimens'.

That the jaw and tooth were those of an ape has been maintained before now by several distinguished anthropologists, but they have always assumed them to be genuine fossils, and have merely thought that, though found in association with the cranium fragments, they had wrongly been presumed to belong to the same creature. Never until now has it been suspected that they represent a deliberate attempt to mislead.

The various pieces of the Piltdown skull were submitted in 1949 to the test for fluorine content to ascertain their age. It was then clear that neither the cranium nor the mandible was of the Lower Pleistocene period, as they had been widely held to be. The test was not, however, at that time developed to the point of accuracy necessary to distinguish, with the limited material available in this case, Upper Pleistocene from later bones, and there was therefore nothing to show that all the remains were not of that period.

New Tests

Now the fluorine test is more advanced, and the Piltdown remains have been retested, with the result that it is clear that whereas the cranium is Upper Pleistocene (say, about 50,000 years old) the mandible and canine tooth are modern. Another test, that of nitrogen content (which recent American experiments have shown to decrease with time at a more or less uniform rate), has produced the same result.

It therefore became evident that the jawbone and canine tooth, since they were not those of any recent type of man, must be those of an immature ape (whether chimpanzee or orang is not determinable in immaturity) and could not therefore represent any animal native in contemporary England. The jaw and tooth must, in other words, have been brought to Piltdown through some recent agency.

This is not all: it has also been established that the jawbone had been stained with bichromate of potash and iron. This, the writers of the article say, 'seems to be explicable only as a necessary part of the deliberate matching of the jaw of a modern ape with the mineralised cranial fragments'. They also find that the molar teeth of the mandible, and also the isolated canine tooth, have been artificially pared down.

'No Parallel'

The writers add: 'From the evidence which we have obtained, it is clear that the distinguished palaeontologists and archaeologists who took part in the excavations at Piltdown were victims of a most elaborate and carefully prepared hoax. Let it be said, however, in exoneration of those who have assumed the Piltdown fragments to belong to a single individual, or who, having examined the original specimens, either regarded the mandible and canine as those of a fossil ape or else assumed (tacitly or explicitly) that the problem was not capable of solution on the available evidence, that the faking of the mandible and canine is so extraordinarily skilful, and the perpetration of the hoax appears to have been so entirely unscrupulous and inexplicable, as to find no parallel in the history of paleontological discovery.'

The further point is made that the exposure of this fraud 'clarifies very considerably the problem of human evolution'. For Piltdown Man (*Eoanthropus*) as he has hitherto appeared to be, was a curiously aberrant form, entirely out of conformity both in character and time with the evidence of human evolution from other parts of the world.

The authors of the article do not identify the perpetrator of this fraud –

but 'Who did it?' is a question many will ask. The discovery of the 'Piltdown skull' was due to Charles Dawson, a solicitor who lived at Hastings and who was an amateur collector of fossils. He died, highly regarded by scientists, in 1916, aged 52. At some, now uncertain, date workmen, whom Dawson had asked to keep a look out for fossils while working in a gravel pit at Piltdown, in Sussex, found what they called a 'coco-nut', broke it with their pick, and subsequently gave him a piece, the rest having been thrown away. This he recognised as part of a very thick human skull, and by careful search he eventually found four more pieces. These finds he took in 1912 to Sir Arthur Smith Woodward, of the British Museum (National History), an authority of international reputation and unassailable integrity.

Tribute to Research

Woodward was greatly interested and joined Dawson in the further examination of the Piltdown site, which he visited many times. Some more fragments of the cranium were found; then, in Woodward's words, 'on a warm evening after an afternoon's vain search, Mr Dawson was exploring some untouched gravel at the bottom of the pit when we both saw half of the human lower jaw fly out in front of the pick-shaped end of the hammer which he was using.' This was the jawbone, now shown to be that of a modern ape.

In the same way in the next year, an eminent French scholar, Father P. Teilhard de Chardin, then a young priest studying at Hastings, was induced to examine some rain-washed gravel where he found the canine tooth – now also shown to be that of a modern ape. Thus two witnesses of the highest character either found, or helped to find, the bones now known to be spurious, and it is hard to resist the conclusion that the jaw and tooth had been put there, by some third person, in order that they might be so unimpeachably discovered. If that third person were to prove to be Charles Dawson, it would be but one more instance of desire for fame (since money was certainly not here the object) leading a scholar into dishonesty. That the deception – whoever carried it out – has, though cunning and long successful, at least been revealed is a tribute to the persistence and skill of modern palaeontological research.

The Times, 21 November 1953.

Jimmy Goldsmith's Elopement

Goldsmith elopes with 18-year-old Bolivian heiress

There was considerable family opposition to the elopement, in January 1954, of Jimmy Goldsmith with Isabel Patiño, heiress of the Bolivian tin-mining family. Señor Patiño is reported to have objected to a member of his Latin American family marrying a Jewish boy, to which Jimmy is reported to have replied that he imagined his family likewise disapproved of him marrying the granddaughter of a Red Indian.

Señor Antenor Patiño, who succeeded yesterday in getting a Scottish court to stop the runaway wedding of his 18-year-old daughter, Isabel, did so because he had six bachelors of royal descent lined up for her choice.

As the Court of Session in Edinburgh granted the plea of Bolivia's multi-millionaire tin tycoon, the reasons for his angry chase after his daughter were made plain by an officer cadet at Eaton Hall Q.C.T.U., near Chester.

The cadet was Edward Goldsmith, brother of 20-year-old James – with whom Isabel has eloped – and a son of Major Frank Goldsmith, a director of the Savoy and of French hotels.

The wealthy hotelier's son sat in the NAAFI canteen and said: 'I should know about this business. I started it all.

'I knew Isabel, and I introduced my brother to her at her 18th birthday party at Claridge's.

'That was two nights before the Coronation.

'Everyone could see they were immediately attracted to each other, but there was a lot of opposition from her parents.

'They wanted her to marry into royalty. There were half a dozen royal marriages lined up for her.

'Her parents said she was too young, anyway. There were religious difficulties too. My father is Jewish, my mother is Roman Catholic. Isabel's parents are both Roman Catholics.

'But the royalty issue is the main one. You see, Isabel's mother is a Bourbon, a descendant of Louis XIV, and she is the daughter of the Duc de Durcal, whose cousin was King Alfonso of Spain.

'The royal descendants who were considered for Isabel are all good friends of mine. They are all French.

'They are all in the circle of Prince de Beauvau-Craon, who is married to Isabel's sister, and they all have castles.

'They Roared with Laughter'

'But Isabel seems to have preferred Jimmy. The trouble was that though they met at parties in London and Paris, Isabel was always chaperoned.

'So they met in secret whenever Isabel could escape.

'It became more and more obvious that they were very much in love – and her parents became more and more furious.

'But I knew my brother was planning to marry.

'Two weeks ago Jimmy and Isabel drove up in a chauffeur-driven Rolls-Royce to the Grosvenor Arms Hotel at Aldford, where my wife, Jill, is staying – near here.

'They were roaring with laughter and Jimmy told me they were off to Scotland to get married.'

Cadet Goldsmith grinned and said: 'I am sure Jimmy will bring it off, and I wish him all the best.

'We have no idea where they are. But we hope to be at their wedding.'

Wedding Stopped – on the Eve

In Edinburgh Papa Patiño stopped the wedding – for the time being – with less than 24 hours to spare.

For the couple had given the required eight days' notice – ending at 10 a.m. today.

In his three-roomed suite at the Caledonian Hotel Papa organised the court action with his lawyer, Mr George Gordon.

A petition for 'interim interdict' – to prevent two Edinburgh registrars from issuing the marriage licences today – was lodged before 10 a.m. yesterday.

By 11.30 a.m. Lord Birnam, the vacation judge, had granted the postponement.

The plea had been: 'It is easier for a marriage to be stopped than to undo it. Can a marriage under Scots law be regarded as valid in Continental countries?'

Any answer will have to be lodged within seven days and if it is, the matter will be settled by the court. If no answer is lodged, the ban will go on indefinitely.

Mr Charles C. Sinclair, one of Isabel's solicitors in Edinburgh, said: 'We are not letting things stand as they are. We are doing something. We won't let our client down.'

How They Spent Hogmanay

But the 6,400-boliviano (64-dollar) question last night was: Where are they – the lovely hour-glass-figure brunette and the handsome Old Etonian?

Papa Patiño has engaged private detectives to trace them. Newspaper pictures of the couple led to many reports.

They spent Hogmanay in the Golden Lion Hotel at Stirling. They booked in just before lunch on December 31 and left after breakfast next day.

They registered in their own names – Jimmy in a scrawl and Isabel in bold backhand script.

Jimmy asked for two single rooms with baths. They were offered two double rooms with baths – at £3 each a night.

Said Jimmy: 'That's too dear. We'll take ordinary single rooms' – at 21s. 6d. each.

The hotel boots, Tommy Robertson, said last night: 'The man wore a camelhair coat. The girl was wearing a leopard-skin coat.'

During their stay at the Golden Lion Jimmy told the staff: 'If anyone telephones or calls for me, say I am at Dundee.'

They left in a car – a Standard Vanguard No. KVX 688.

Traced – to Grim Mining Town

Before midday yesterday the couple were reported seen in the Rogano, a smart Glasgow restaurant.

Cloakroom attendant Alex McGaw said they made a phone call to Edinburgh.

He said: 'I am quite sure. The man was tall, fair, and wore a camelhair coat. The girl was small and dark and was in a leopard-skin coat with a grey pleated skirt.

'She had brown shoes and was hatless. I got a good look at her because she waited while the man went into the cocktail bar for change.

'When he came out he asked how much a call to Edinburgh would cost. Then he phoned.'

And then the couple were reported in the grim mining town of Cordenbeath, Fife. They arrived in a train from Glasgow at 3.48 p.m. And they were carrying light suitcases.

Footnote: Bridal Orchids Arrive

A lush bridal bouquet – consisting mainly of orchids – was flown into Edinburgh last night and was early today in the office of the couple's solicitors.

The flowers, from an undisclosed donor, had been packed by florists at a stand in London's Ritz Hotel.

They were in a wooden crate addressed to 'James Goldsmith, Esq. c/o Iain Smith . . .' – a partner in the firm of solicitors.

They were delivered to the B.W.A. terminal in George-street. And at 10 p.m., when the terminal offices closed, the flowers had not been collected.

But 40 minutes later, while an official was still working, a courier arrived for them.

The solicitors' caretaker said last night: 'I don't suppose the flowers will keep long enough now. The bride will have to get fresh ones . . .'

The Daily Express, 6 January 1954.

The day after Señor Patiño prevented the couple marrying, he relented. Isabel Goldsmith died shortly after giving birth to a daughter, also called Isabel, who now runs a luxury hotel in Mexico.

....

Vile Bodies

Extract from Evelyn Waugh's diary

Evelyn Waugh's diaries caused quite a stir when they were published because of the often shocking comments he made about his friends and acquaintances. A number of extracts had to be published with the names of the perpetrators missing because of fears of libel. Here is one of the more interesting ones with some of the real names added.

London, Thursday, 23 June 1955

Tried on clothes in Albemarle Street, then, weary, took refuge in White's where I sat until 7 drinking and talking to a succession of friends – mostly to Randolph [Churchill] who, fiery with whisky, poured out the story hitherto unknown to me of— **Sir Anthony Eden's** adultery with— **Lady X**, how the butler photographed them in the act, how— **Lady X** attempted suicide and was evacuated by— **Biddy Monckton** with a stomach pump. All this during the time that— **Y** was supposedly pregnant by him.

Michael Davie (ed.), The Diary of Evelyn Waugh
(Weidenfeld & Nicolson, 1976), p. 725.

....

Spies, Spies and More Spies

Philby, Burgess and Maclean

Kim Philby (1911–88), the most audacious spy of the twentieth century, managed to escape detection and prosecution for much of his career as a double agent. After the sensational defection of his two Cambridge contemporaries, Guy Burgess and Donald Maclean in 1951, the finger of suspicion once again pointed at Philby, who was rightly suspected of having tipped off Maclean that he was under scrutiny from MI6 and the CIA. The subsequent British White Paper on the Burgess–Maclean affair failed to mention that Kim Philby was the prime suspect. J. Edgar Hoover, the head of the FBI, was furious at this omission and so arranged for Philby's name to be leaked in the New York Sunday News *on 23 October 1955. Two days later, Marcus Lipton, a Labour MP, asked the following question in the House of Commons:*

Has the Prime Minister made up his mind to cover up at all costs the dubious third man activities of Mr Harold Philby who was First Secretary at the Washington Embassy a little time ago, and is he determined to stifle all discussion on the very great matters which were evaded in the wretched White Paper, which is an insult to the intelligence of the country?

Hansard, 25 October 1955.

Although many in the intelligence services rightly suspected Philby, it was not possible to prove his guilt in a court of law. There was also an underlying distaste in the Macmillan government for the entire secret service. Macmillan's private secretary, Lord Egremont, who thought the intelligence agencies were a complete waste of time, echoed this when he said 'Much better if the Russians saw the Cabinet minutes twice a week. Prevent all that fucking dangerous guesswork.'

A fortnight after his name was aired in the Commons, Philby was virtually given a clean bill of health there by Macmillan who declared:

No evidence has been found that Philby was responsible for warning Burgess or Maclean. While in government he carried out his duties ably and conscientiously. I have no reason to conclude that Mr Philby has at any time betrayed the interests of this country, or to identify him with the so-called 'third man', if, indeed, there was one.

Hansard, 13 November 1955.

Although Philby had been sacked by MI6, he continued as a freelance contributor to The Observer *and* The Economist *before finally defecting from Beirut to the Soviet Union in 1963.*

During the brief contact Burgess and MacLean had with British journalists in Moscow while delivering their statement, Burgess wore his Old Etonian tie, although the Reuters correspondent failed to notice this beyond mentioning that he wore 'a dark blue tie with light blue stripes'.

Guy Burgess and Donald Maclean, former members of the British Foreign Office, wish to make the following statement:

It seems to us that the doubts as to our whereabouts and speculations about our past actions may be a small but contributing factor that has been and may again be exploited by the opponents of Anglo–Soviet understanding. Accordingly, we have thought it best to issue the following statement: We both of us came to the Soviet Union to work for the aim of better understanding between the Soviet Union and the West, having both of us become convinced from official knowledge in our possession that neither the British, nor, still more, the American Government was at that time seriously working for this aim.

We had in the positions we occupied every reason to believe that such an understanding was essential if peace was to be safe. We had every reason to conclude that such an understanding was the aim of Soviet policy. We had had every opportunity to know and grounds for fearing the plans and outlook of the few but powerful people who opposed this understanding.

At Cambridge we had both been Communists. We abandoned our

political activities not because we in any way disagreed with the Marxist analysis of the situation in which we still both find ourselves, but because we thought, wrongly, it is now clear to us, that in the public service we could do more to put these ideas into practical effect than elsewhere. It was probably our action in necessarily giving up political activities by entering the public service that, falsely analysed, led the Foreign Office to say through its spokesman it 'believed' we had been Soviet agents at Cambridge. The Foreign Office can, of course, 'believe' anything it wishes. The important point, however, is that on this question we know, and it does not. We neither of us have ever been Communist agents.

So far the ground was common for us both. Details of our subsequent careers were completely different and had, therefore, better be dealt with separately. As regards Maclean, he worked in London and in Paris, Washington and Cairo as a regular member of the Foreign Service from 1935 until 1951 and as such, was part of the machine which, with the exception of the war period, carried out a policy unacceptable not only to him but to many others. He was by no means alone inside the Foreign Service in objecting to British foreign policy before the war, particularly as regards Abyssinia, the Spanish Civil War and Munich. But he was increasingly isolated in doing so after the war. It became more and more difficult to find anyone willing to think or speak of anything but the 'menace of Communism' or to understand the folly and danger of American policy in the Far East and in Europe. Further work in the Foreign Office was becoming impossible. In May, 1951, there were clear signs that whatever future course he might work out for himself, the Foreign Office and Security authorities had plans of their own.

His telephones in his office and private house were used as microphones. Plain clothes policemen followed him wherever he went, and one of his colleagues was put up to act as provocateur. Maclean therefore decided to come to the Soviet Union and do whatever he could to further understanding between East and West from there. The difficulty of leaving the country while being tailed by the police was solved by a meeting with Burgess shortly after the latter's return from the Washington Embassy to London. The latter not only agreed to make arrangements for the journey but to come too. The risks of such a journey would have been too great for Mrs Maclean, who was shortly expecting a child. She and the children came to the Soviet Union in 1953.

As regards Burgess, when he decided to leave Cambridge, he joined the BBC. Subsequently positions were offered to him which he accepted first in a department of the Secret Service and secondly in the Foreign Office. Throughout he sympathised with Soviet policy and became increasingly alarmed by the post-war trend of Anglo–American policy. Most alarming of all was its failure first to reach, and later even to seek to reach, a modus vivendi between East and West.

Neither in the BBC nor in the Foreign Office nor during the period that he was associated with the Secret Service and also MI5 itself did he make any secret from his friends or his colleagues either of his views or the fact that he had been a Communist.

His attitude in these positions was completely incompatible with the allegation that he was a Soviet agent. This statement of Burgess's position is necessary to understand the situation which arose a week or so after his return to London from Washington in 1951. He went to see Maclean as head of the American Department of the Foreign Office. They found that their information and opinions about the political situation and the danger of war were in agreement. What now happened was determined by the following acts. Burgess, who some months previously had himself initiated arrangements to obtain a new job with a view to leaving the Foreign Office, was faced with the fact that the Foreign Office had independently and subsequently decided that they would no longer employ him. It is, of course, obvious that no agent would take the initiative in arranging to leave the Foreign Office. However, when the break came, Burgess was doubtful whether he wanted or could conscientiously do the new job he had been arranging. Therefore when Maclean told Burgess that he himself had decided he could no longer work for the Foreign Office and its policies and suggested that they should both go to the USSR, Burgess had no difficulty in agreeing. There alone there appeared to both to be some chance of putting into practice in some form the conviction they had always held. As the result of living in the USSR we both of us are convinced that we were right in doing what we did. We are handing this statement to the press.

Donald Maclean, Guy Burgess.

'Snake Bite, Sir!'

Unfortunate photograph of Prime Minister of Ceylon

Sir John Kotelawala, who was Prime Minister of Ceylon (Sri Lanka) in the 1950s, blamed his election defeat on the grandness of his house and his parties, pictures of which occasionally appeared in the newspapers. Sir John also told Michael Ondaatje of another incident at his residence in Colombo.

He tells us of one of the most scandalous photographs organised by the Opposition. A demure young couple visited him along with a third friend who had a camera. They asked if he minded their taking some photographs and he gave them permission. The photographer took several pictures of the couple. Suddenly the man dropped to his knees, lifted up the woman's sari and started chewing away at her upper thigh. Sir John who was watching casually a few yards away rushed forward and asked what was happening. The man on his knees unburied his head and grinned at him saying, 'snake bite, sir,' and returned to the thigh of the woman.

A week later three photographs appeared in the newspapers of this blatantly sexual act with Sir John also in the picture chatting casually to the woman whose face was in the throes of sexual ecstasy.

Michael Ondaatje, *Running in the Family*
(Victor Gollancz, 1983), pp. 159–60.

The Orr Case

Sidney Sparkes Orr and the teenage student

In the mid-fifties in Tasmania, the case of Sidney Sparkes Orr, Professor of Philosophy at the University of Tasmania, became Australia's equivalent to the Dreyfus case. Professor Orr was sacked for having an affair with a teenaged student but his supporters insisted it was because of his leftist politics. After his dismissal, the Philosophy chair remained blacked by the international academic community for a decade.

HOBART, October 1956—A reference to an 'association with royalty' in his parentage arose during cross-examination of a professor about his conversation with a girl student in a Supreme Court action today.

Sydney Sparkes Orr, 41, Professor of Philosophy, is claiming £10,000 damages from the University of Tasmania for breach of contract.

Orr seeks an injunction against the university to restrain it from excluding him from the discharge of his duties and the privileges of his office.

The defence admits termination of the appointment, but claims it was for misconduct, inconsistent with the due and faithful discharge of his duty as a professor.

Among the allegations submitted by the defence is one of an improper association with an 18-year-old student, Suzanne Kemp.

Orr spent the day in the witness box today, under cross examination by Mr R. O. Wright (for the university).

He was cross-examined at length on an alleged conversation with Miss Kemp on his parentage, and denied he had said to her he was upset about the publicity given to Princess Margaret, and then remarked: 'It is another instance of the failure of Royal romances.'

Professor Orr replied to the question, 'What an astonishing thing to say.'

Mr Wright: 'Did she ask you "What are you talking about"? And did you reply: "I am Royalty"?'

Orr: 'That is ridiculous.'

'Did you make any comment on the likeness of yourself to a Royal person?'

'Not to Miss Kemp.'

'Even to the stoop and the eyes?' – 'No.'

'I put it to you that you then referred to your parentage and broke down and wept?' – 'No.'

'Did you say anything as to your father?' – 'I did not.'

'Did you say you did not know who he was?' – 'I did not.'

'Did you say your mother was coming out from Ireland, but passed away on the voyage?' – 'I did not.'

'Was that the fact?' – 'It was the fact.'

'Did you say it was fitting that you should not see her (your mother) again?' – 'No.'

'Did you say that ever since your childhood you knew there was something wrong, and you had been hunting to find out who your father was?' – 'I did not say that to Miss Kemp.'

'My Birth is a Mystery'

At this stage, Professor Orr dramatically appealed to the judge to allow him to make a statement.

'My birth is a mystery,' he said.

'It has been a source of great distress to me all my life. I do not know whether my purported parents are my real parents, whether I am adopted or illegitimate.

'This fact was told to Dr Milanov [a university lecturer in philosophy] in the confidence of psychoanalysis – a sacred confidence.

'It was told to nobody else except the Bishop of Tasmania.

'I told Dr Milanov I had searched for my father all my life, without discovering any trace whatever except the suggestion.'

Mr Wright: 'I put it to you that you said that to Miss Kemp.'

Orr: 'It is the most sacred secret of my life, and I should not tell it to an irresponsible teenager.'

Asked if he then broke down and wept, he said he did not.

'It is not a matter about which one weeps,' he added.

Orr said the story was among many stories circulated for months, and he heard it being circulated first through one of his colleagues, and he was shocked.

It went the rounds. Everyone had it, and no doubt Miss Kemp had it in a distorted form.

Orr also was cross-examined about a Greek inscription in a book he said he had given Miss Kemp.

He translated it: 'An unexamined life is not worth living.'

Throughout his cross-examination Orr repeatedly denied suggestions of improper relations with the student at a number of places in and around Hobart.

He was asked whether he considered a sexual relationship between a student and a professor was in any way proper.

He said in no circumstances would he consider it proper unless the parties intended to marry.

On the part of a married professor he would find no excuse whatever for it.

Free Love

Orr denied he had mentioned to Miss Kemp any association among undergraduates for the practice of free love or such things.

Mr Wright: 'Did you enter into denunciation of the church in not facing up to the real problems of society?'

Orr: 'That could be so. I hold very strong views on that.'

He said he had discussed with Miss Kemp her belief that genuine true feeling was the only basis of true living, got largely from a book by Krishnamurti, an Indian philosopher, and also Professor John McMurray's views on freedom in the modern world.

He admitted that discussion of philosophical problems with Miss Kemp became more personal, but denied he told her he was becoming emotionally involved.

In Group

Orr denied he told Miss Kemp of a friend who practised the ideas of McMurray, who was professor of Moral Philosophy in Edinburgh.

He said he possibly referred to McMurray's views, but it was more likely to have been in a group of people.

He said he objected to saddling Professor McMurray with the term 'free love'.

Questioned on a university sub-committee's investigation, he said he felt he was being subjected to 'something in the nature of a star chamber'.

He said he refused to go further than to give a categorical denial to the allegations.

The Age, 17 October 1956.

Dr Cassandra Pybus, a Tasmanian academic, wrote a book on the subject. As she points out:

'His dismissal was seen as a blatant act of intellectual suppression akin to the McCarthyite reprisals in the USA.

  'Re-reading documents of the controversy in 1991 reveals a very different story, however, and raises concerns about the motives of those who sought to make an academic martyr of Orr. I don't want it to flash upon the public gaze as a sordid tale of sex in a small town, which is what it lends itself to.

  'I think it is a universally true fact, whether it be in the 50s, 60s, 70s, 80s or 90s, that a young woman confronting an older, powerful man is to be given some credibility ... As a person who has spent much time on university campuses, I have been disturbed by exploitative relationships between staff and students.

  'Some of my peers have been deeply hurt and distressed by the relationships they had, when they were young students, with powerful males who were academics. Any woman responds to the Orr case completely differently. There are no women academics who support Orr.'

....

The Rogue's Guide to Tangier

Scandal in Tangier

Since the Second World War, Tangier has been a recipient of a considerable amount of the West's flotsam and jetsam, where 'bed and boy' was extremely cheap, not to mention the availability of a kaleidoscope of exotic drugs. A number of these Remittance Men and ne'er-do-wells are charmingly described in a booklet published locally by Bert and Mabel Winter in the seventies, called The Rogue's Guide to Tangier.

Characters of Yesteryear

In its heyday, Tangier really was an incredible Sinville on Sea, full of villains, smugglers, exiled writers, tax-avoiding American millionaires, on-the-run SS officers, Vichy French, drug addicts, disgraced blue-bloods given a monthly allowance for keeping out of England, paedophiles with long police files and a wide variety of spies and counter spies. Some of the old characters are still talked about in pavement cafes and bars.

PAUL AXEL LUND was the son of a respectable Birmingham family who had a good start in life but went wrong and ended up serving eight years in jail, two of them on Dartmoor. In January 1954 he came to Tangier as a wanted man on the run from police in the North of England and opened a small, six-stooled drinking spot in the centre of town named the Bar Navarra which became quite notorious as a meeting place for shady characters and oddballs, your authors included, as well as tourists.

Paul's stories, told as he drank neat brandy and spat theatrically into a spittoon, kept him busy and surrounded by a wide variety of gullibles from all walks of life. As the bar prospered, Paul's stories grew taller. The tallest being that he had been involved in the mystery double explosion in the Tangier harbour in 1957 when the British-owned motor-vessel the 'Barra' and a similar vessel the 'Red Witch' were blown out of the water.

Both had been fitted with special engines to give them extra speed and Paul claimed they were owned by Britishers smuggling American cigarettes from Italy to Spain via Tangier. Paul said the boats had been blown up by locally based and rival smugglers but political sources tell a different story. This is that both boats had allegedly been used to smuggle arms and ammunition to rebels fighting the French in Algeria and after a Tangier-based French Intelligence operative named 'FRENCH CHARLES' had tipped off Paris, two French cruisers had anchored outside the port so that frogmen could swim underwater and secretly attach limpet mines to both the 'Barra' and the 'Red Witch'. Six hours later, when the French cruisers had long sailed away, both boats were blown to pieces, killing a night-watchman and making world headlines with cleverly planted stories that misled most people to believe it was just a 'smugglers' vendetta'.

Paul Lund's greatest admirers were the idle rich remittance matrons who lived in Tangier and sat enthralled as he recounted his tall tales judiciously laced with underworld jargon and Cockney rhyming slang. Only one lady customer had any impact on Paul. This was Carol, an attractive and intelligent girl from the most respectable of families. She realised Paul was not the hard nut he claimed to be. In turn, Paul was captivated by this cultured and elegant girl from good stock. They were married and Carol was clearly a good influence because Paul toned down his language and cut down on his drinking...

In 1966 Paul Lund died choking in blood when one of his lungs collapsed. Typically, most people were sad that another odd character had passed on...

One famous eccentric who lived in Tangier was RUPERT CROFT-COOKE, who ably documented Paul Lund's life story in a book entitled *Smiling Damned Villain*, which is a must for those wishing to understand the criminal mentality. During World War II, Rupert was in the Intelligence Corps, for which he was awarded the British Empire Medal. After the war he was caught in bed with a young male friend, and London Society dropped him like a hot brick when he was jailed in Wormwood Scrubs.

On being freed, Rupert retaliated by writing a book about his homosexuality and the criminal conviction this had brought him. Sarcastically entitled *The Verdict of You ALL*, the book was quite sensational for the early fifties as it pointed out that the antiquated laws on the subject of homosexuality were hypocritical. This made Rupert a total outcast from straight society so he settled in Tangier with Joseph Susei Mari, a highly intelligent young Hindu who acted as his secretary and companion but was a talented author in his own right...

In 1970, when his love for Tangier turned sour, Rupert wrote *The Exiles*, which, although it claimed to be fiction, was the most vitriolic attack ever made on local British and American residents. His pen portraits were mostly accurate but incredibly bitchy and although he used false names, every character was instantly recognisable and Rupert became the most hated writer in this city.

In 1974 he delivered another devastating attack on local Britishers when he wrote *The Caves of Hercules* which was rightly denounced by the *Journal de Tangier* as 'an evil and cowardly book' because Rupert had quit Tangier. After various trips he settled in the south of England where he died a few months later.

Rupert Croft-Cooke had one main weakness. He was an intellectual snob who sneered at the 'ignorant masses and tradespeople'. This flaw was used to devastating effect by a Tangier-based journalist when Rupert died. The journalist discovered and exposed the strange fact that Rupert, using a pen name, had secretly written many trashy cowboy and thriller paperbacks for schoolboys over a period of 15 years as a way of making the extra money he needed to keep up his image as a gentlemanly man of letters.

... the wealthiest Westerner to have lived in Tangier was BARBARA HUTTON ... She settled in Tangier in 1946 and bought a house in the Kasbah which she filled with a bonanza of antique furniture worth millions ... In an attempt to enhance her social status in the eyes of Tangier's snobby set, Miss Hutton had a book published, at her own cost, of poems she claimed to have written. Babs always had a hang-up about being a shopkeeper's grand-daughter and did everything to gain Grace Kelly-style princess status. She never found herself a king or a world-recognised prince, but at her fabulous parties in Tangier she sat on a gold throne wearing an emerald and diamond tiara once owned by Empress Catherine of Russia and at her feet were priceless antique silk rugs she had bought from that zillionaire, the Shah of Persia.

Barbara Hutton spent thousands of dollars on silk underwear every year but she never had to worry about rinsing out her smalls. After wearing them once, she threw them out. When she felt like a change of scenery, Babs flew to Paris and occupied a luxury suite at the Ritz Hotel. Today, you can rent the same suite for a mere £3,500 a night. While in Morocco she fed her camels on rose petals and when a group of socialites lingered on until dawn at one of her private house parties she walked round dishing out wads of dollars to make them go.

The only thing Babs could not buy was love. She spent her life buying seven husbands and hundreds of young, one-night beach boy lovers.

Bert and Mabel Winter, *The Rogue's Guide to Tangier* (undated booklet).

....

London Has Never Known a More Evil Racketeer

Rachman and his racketeering

Rachmanism has become a byword for evil exploitative landlords who are solely concerned with how much profit they can wring out of slum tenements. With increased immigration from the Caribbean from 1950 onwards, West Indians arrived in London to find many landlords had posted 'No blacks' in the windows of much of the available accommodation. One landlord who positively encouraged the immigrants was Peter Rachman, who owned a slum empire of hundreds of properties in Notting Hill. Rachman found he could charge tenants exorbitant rents and that they did not dare to ask for any repairs to their dilapidated flats. But the main charge against Rachman was that he terrorised his tenants for rent. It has subsequently been revealed that while Rachman was obviously a crook, there were those who were perhaps even more sinister – especially the notorious Michael de Freitas, alias Michael X – and Rachman himself was a somewhat more complicated character, as this account from The People *describes.*

Perec Rachman, a Polish ex-soldier, came to Britain after the war with £65 in his pocket. He died last November – few people accept the startling suggestion made in the Commons that he may still be alive.

Between the years 1952 and 1961 he built up an empire based on vice and drugs, violence and blackmail, extortion and slum landlordism, the like of which this country has never seen. And, let us hope, will never see again.

He turned that £65 into a fortune estimated at more than a million pounds.

He lived life at a fantastic pace which eventually killed him by its excesses.

And in his wake he left a heartbreaking trail of human misery which worried him not one jot.

How could he do it? How could he get away with it? How was it that so evil a man could operate against society for so long without collecting even a parking summons from the police?

The answer is that Perec Rachman, the man named in the Stephen Ward case as the 'protector' of Mandy Rice-Davies, was as astute as he was evil.

His Power

His empire of seedy tenement houses was split into no less than 40 separate companies.

Part of each company was interlocked with parts of other companies.

He cocooned his sordid empire inside a bewildering web of false trails and numerous 'front men'. Perec Rachman was always the man in the shadows.

His power grew slowly – he started by buying one tenement house in St Stephen's Gardens, Paddington. By 1959 he owned more than 100 houses.

The flood of West Indian immigrants to Britain was at its height. Rachman soon found that he could make fantastic money if he could force out white families and pack each room with seven or eight immigrants.

And even greater profits could be made by putting prostitutes into the rooms.

This newspaper began to investigate his activities. Night after night observations were kept on Rachman houses.

There was obvious evidence of the purpose for which many of his houses were being used.

But, because Mr Rachman had covered his trail so well, there was not sufficient positive proof linking Rachman with the activities in these houses.

Our dossier had to remain unpublished. For the libel laws protect even men as evil as Rachman.

But at least this newspaper can take pride in the fact that Rachman got out of his evil properties in 1961 because he feared we would be in a position to expose him.

Now Rachman's death has opened lips sealed by fear during his lifetime.

Our dossier on this evil man, fortified by the confessions of people who worked for him, can now be published.

It reads like mob-ruled Chicago at its worst. And it all happened here ... in England ... in the heart of London.

Rachman began his career by buying up a few dilapidated houses on 100 per cent mortgages arranged through a 'benefactor'.

He set out on a cold, calculated plan to force out the white tenants in these houses whose rents were controlled, and pack each room with coloured immigrants.

To force out the white families he used methods brutally obvious (like hints of 'an accident' to their children). If that failed, he switched to more subtle tactics.

One method was to introduce at least one set of West Indians into an all-white house.

They were encouraged to have rowdy parties, to play musical instruments into the early hours, to use the doorways of white families' rooms as lavatories. This would go on for weeks, if necessary. Until, finally, the white people could stand it no longer and left.

Then Rachman would pack every room in the house with coloured people – often two, three or four to one room, and each individual paying rent.

Rachman's income from these houses was prodigious. He used it all to buy more and more houses in the Kensington, Paddington, Notting Hill and Bayswater areas.

His Thugs

The houses were controlled for him by a gang of strong-arm thugs and a team of rent collectors who turned Alsatian dogs on anyone who refused to pay the rents demanded.

Some of these rents were as high as £20 for one room. Only prostitutes pay that kind of money.

Most of these vice houses were in the Notting Hill and Bayswater areas.

They included houses in St Stephen's Gardens, Lancaster Gardens, Monmouth Road, Chepstow Road, Powis Terrace, Powis Gardens, Leinster Terrace, Westbourne Park Road, Great Western Road, Sussex Gardens, St George's Drive, Battersea, Wymering Road, Maida Vale, and several houses in Earls Court.

White tenants who threatened to complain to the rent tribunals about their treatment were 'persuaded' against such unwise action.

Our investigators learned that at one rent tribunal five applications for a reduction in rent had been withdrawn by the tenants.

Each notice of withdrawal was typed on the same machine – a machine traced to one of Rachman's companies.

As Rachman's empire grew, so did his fear of violence against him. He surrounded himself with a bodyguard of tough men.

One of these men, 'The People' can now disclose, was Peter Rann, ex-world welter-weight wrestler. He was Rachman's personal bodyguard. Last week 'People' investigators secured a full confession from him to add to our Rachman dossier.

The Evidence of the Bodyguard

'I was introduced to Rachman about six years ago through one of his rent collectors.

The original deal he had in mind fell through, but Rachman asked if I would be his bodyguard.

Then he asked me to recruit a squad of men who would throw out any of his tenants whom he wanted to get rid of – perhaps they were not paying their rents promptly.

I got together this squad and the first job we did was to throw out all the occupants of a house in Westbourne Park Road.

There were about 15 people in this house – all coloured. Six of us got there about 10 a.m. and stormed the house. We rushed in like a band of thugs.

We went through every room, removing all the tenants and every bit of their furniture. We had to jostle them along a bit. All their cases and furniture we piled up on the pavement and we left them there.

My squad were used to throw people out of five or six houses.

Something like 50 per cent of Rachman's houses had prostitutes using rooms in them. In some houses there were seven or eight girls paying £20 each for a room.

In the basements of many of the houses in Notting Hill and Bayswater Rachman set up sordid little drinking clubs.

In these clubs you could get anything – girls, marijuana. Rachman knew what was going on, but he didn't ask any questions.'

Peter Rann gave evidence of other ways in which 'awkward' tenants were forced out.

'One old couple who had lived for years in a house suddenly bought up by Rachman, refused to move out.

The next they knew was that the new landlord sent a painter to decorate the flat for them. They decided the new landlord really had a heart after all.

But the painter insisted on working throughout the night, trampling on their bed, keeping the light on and sloshing paint all over the place. This went on until the old couple, in desperation, moved out.

Another couple complained that their windows did not fit properly. Rachman sent round someone to take out the windows, but they didn't fit new windows in their place.

This was in the middle of winter and, not surprisingly, the old couple couldn't stand the cold and they were moved out by relatives.'

Peter Rann's association with Rachman lasted until his death. He was one of the few people who knew Rachman intimately.

'His philosophy in life amounted to this: Everybody can be bought for a price.

He boasted that he could always buy off anyone who might create difficulties – police, council officials, property surveyors.

He claimed he had all the protection he needed in high places.

But he had a great fear of being exposed by a newspaper or in Parliament.'

Another man who worked for Rachman was Frank Rudolph Davis. From 1957 to 1961 he collected rents at Rachman houses in the Bayswater area.

Davis collected rents of about £360 a week from a handful of houses. Another Rachman collector traced by 'The People' collected £1,000 a week.

Davis saw at first hand what happened when anyone refused to pay the extortionate rents demanded.

The Evidence of the Rent Collector

'In 1957 I was in a bad financial position when I was offered this job.

On my second day on the job I saw four Alsatian dogs in the basement of Rachman's office in Westbourne Grove. They were so fierce they had to be muzzled.

In my four years working for Rachman I saw these dogs used many times on tenants who were "causing trouble". It was never a pretty sight.

All Rachman's rent collectors had instructions to telephone his Polish aide if they had any trouble with tenants. Then the strong-arm boys moved in.

On my second day there I was in the office when a collector phoned in. Two strong-arm boys took the Alsatians round to the house and I went with them.

The tenant "causing trouble" was a big coloured man.

On this occasion the sight of the four snarling dogs on their leashes was enough. He was thrown out of his room with his baggage and threatened with iron bars.

If tenants were really awkward the dogs were let off the leashes and set at them.

Rachman always kept himself well clear of things. It amazed me how he could stay behind the scenes out of trouble.

He just threw his side-kicks to the wolves when it was necessary.

Rachman liked to give the impression of being tough. But he always got someone else to do his dirty work for him.

I remember the day two men tried to take one of his girl friends away from him. Rachman's thugs beat them up with bottles and pieces of lead piping.

He even had his own prostitutes beaten up. One girl was refusing to pay the rent for her room – £18 a week.

She was beaten up and her face was slashed. She vanished.

His Clubs

Another girl, a hostess at one of his clubs, was caught helping herself out of the till. She was beaten up ... we never saw her again.

Rachman used to go to one of his own clubs near his office where they put on exhibitions of nude women wrestling. He liked that.

By 1961 I began to realise that I was running the risk of becoming involved in something really serious. So I got out.

But I was too much in debt and so I went back to Rachman doing small jobs in the office. I was connected with him until he died.'

Rachman learned to live with danger. His bodyguards and strong-arm thugs were always around to protect him. But he never took risks.

He wrote a lot of his business letters in a post office in South Kensington.

His very sound theory was: You're less likely to get 'cut up' in a crowded street.

One man who supplies fascinating evidence to this chapter of the Rachman dossier is Karol Zbyszewski, a journalist on the staff of the 'Polish Daily', a newspaper for Poles in Britain.

The Evidence of the Polish Journalist

'I met Rachman a few years ago at the Daquise Cafe near South Kensington tube station.

For months we played a weekly game of chess and talked our native Polish.

I never realised what kind of a man he was.

I often saw him standing outside the cafe, often in the pouring rain, conducting his business. He was usually there for two hours, between 3 p.m. and 6 p.m.

His agents and contacts knew he would be there. They arrived in cars and taxis. Rachman would have a few moments of conversation with them on the pavement. I saw money and documents change hands.

I learned things about Rachman which made me ashamed to be Polish.

I know he sent strong-arm men to meet the immigrant trains arriving at Victoria.

As the bewildered West Indian families came through the ticket barriers they were approached by Rachman's agents with tempting offers of accommodation.'

Throughout these years Rachman lived life at a pace which even the strongest body could not withstand.

By 1961 his doctor was warning him that his sexual excesses would kill him unless they were curbed.

He ignored the warning. He gambled in the clubs throughout the night. He would wager £5,000 on a hand of chemmy. And he had dozens of different girl friends.

One of his former girl friends added the following to our dossier:

The Evidence of an Ex-Girl Friend

'Rachman sometimes made love to five different women in a day.

He had his regular girl friend of the moment – and various temporary associations.

He preferred tall, slender blondes. He was crazy about Mandy Rice-Davies. She hated him, but she knew when she was "on to a good thing". After all, he gave her £80 a week spending money.

She used to throw fits about his sleeping with other women and wreck his flat.

Rachman hated Christine Keeler because he thought she had a hold over Mandy.

His one desire was to have a child of his own. But he couldn't.

People say he always came off best in the strong-arm stuff. But I remember one occasion when he didn't.

Some notorious London gangsters moved into his territory and demanded £5,000 protection money – or else.

There was a big rumble in the underworld and it seemed a gang fight would break out.

But Rachman got scared – and paid up the £5,000.'

It will be a long time yet before London is finally cleansed of all Mr Rachman's vile operations.

Even today, eight months after his death, rent tribunals are still dealing with cases in the file marked 'P. Rachman.'

Peter Forbes, *The People*, 14 July 1963.

....

'Something's Blown Up'

The Profumo affair

One of the great scandals of the century, the Profumo affair played a significant role in the downfall of the Macmillan Government in Britain. It is a popularly held view that John Profumo, the Minister for War, had to resign primarily because he had lied to Parliament by denying there was any truth in the stories that he had an affair with call girl Christine Keeler.

The publication of this letter did not help his case either.

Profumo's Letter to Christine Keeler

9/8/61

Darling

In great haste & because I can get no reply from your phone –

Alas something's blown up tomorrow night & I can't therefore make it. I'm terribly sorry especially as I leave the next day for various trips & then a holiday so won't be able to see you again until some time in September. Blast it.

Please take great care of yourself & don't run away.

Love J

I'm writing this cos I know you're off for the day tomorrow & I want you to know before you go if I still can't reach you by phone.

The Sunday Mirror, 9 June 1963, p. 1.

The following cryptic dispatch in Private Eye *was the first public reference to the involvement of Profumo in the growing scandal.*

Idle Talk Reveals Lunchtime O' Booze

Mr Silas Jones, a West Indian immigrant of no fixed abode, was today sentenced at the Old Bailey to 24 years' Preventive Detention for being in possession of an offensive water pistol.

The chief 'witness' in the case, gay fun-loving Miss Gaye Funloving, a 21-year-old 'model', was not actually present in court. She has, in fact, disappeared. It is believed that normally, in cases of this type, a Warrant is issued for the arrest of the missing witness.

'Parties'

One of Miss Funloving's close 'friends', Dr Spook of Harley Street, revealed last night that he could add nothing to what had already been insinuated.

Dr Spook is believed to have 'more than half the Cabinet on his list of patients'. He also has a 'weekend' cottage on the Berkshire estate of Lord*, and is believed to have attended many 'parties' in the neighbourhood.

Among those it is believed have also attended 'parties' of this type are Mr Vladimir Bolokhov, the well-known Soviet Spy attached to the Russian Embassy, and a well-known Cabinet Minister.

Resignation?

Mr James Montesi, a well-known Cabinet Minister, was last night reported to have proffered his 'resignation' to the Prime Minister, on 'personal grounds'.

It is alleged that the Prime Minister refused to accept his alleged 'resignation'. Mr Montesi today denied the allegations that he had ever allegedly offered his alleged 'resignation' to the alleged 'Prime Minister'.

Mr Silas Jones is serving his 24-year sentence in a prison of the type it is believed is a long way from Fleet Street. Miss Funloving is still 'in hiding'.

In the Dark

The public is still in the dark. And so am I, which is why I have had to compile this whole ridiculous story from other newspaper cuttings.

So what?

Private Eye, No. 33, 22 May 1963.

Christine Keeler's 'confessions' in The News of the World *ensured that the story had a considerable amount of life in it, especially as they were stretched over three issues. Miss Keeler wished to emphasise that while she is portrayed as the author of the following article, she was not responsible for its literary style.*

The first time I met Jack Profumo he was in a dinner jacket and I was clutching a towel around me. My hair was hanging in strings, water was pouring off me – and I was acutely embarrassed.

It happened like this. That particular night in July, 1961, was a rare one for an English Summer. Hot and sultry. I'd been in a club in London and met a young man whose name I don't even remember now. I'd called in there before going on to see my friend Dr Stephen Ward who that weekend was staying in his country cottage on Lord Astor's estate at Cliveden in Buckinghamshire. But the way it worked out I took along this nice young chap I met in the club – and on the way, at a bus stop near London Airport, I spotted a girl. We pulled up and asked her if she'd like a lift. She said she would and as we drove along, I asked her if she'd like to go to a party. She said 'Yes'.

Just Him

Of course, when we got to Stephen's place, there was no party. Just him. But it didn't matter. We had the usual talk, a few drinks after introductions.

But it was such a beautiful Summer evening. Lord Astor's swimming pool not far away shimmered in the moonlight. It was irresistible. That was how we came to wander up there for a midnight swim.

It didn't matter about having our own costumes, because Bill Astor, which is what we called him, always had costumes hanging up in the changing cubicles – ready for emergency swims such as this.

There was nobody about and I plunged in. I love swimming. Even as a child they used to say I was very good at it. But Stephen is such a joker. He must do something to liven things up.

I'd known him for about two years. We were very close friends – and at the time I was living in his London flat.

Dared Me

When he dared me to swim in the nude, just for the sheer hell of it, I said I would.

In I went again, with Stephen standing on the side of the walled pool. Then it happened.

There had been a dinner party in Lord Astor's house, which is right next door to the pool. The wall around the pool makes it impossible to hear or see who is coming.

Suddenly in came two figures in dinner jackets. One was Bill (Lord) Astor, and the other Jack Profumo. I'd met Bill before of course. I didn't even know who the other fellow was at that moment.

All I knew was that I was as naked as the day I was born – and I swam like mad into the far end of the pool from where they had entered.

It was then that Stephen played another one of his little jokes. Laughing his head off, he tossed my costume clean into the bushes or somewhere.

Dripping

I hardly saw it go. I just knew I was in the water naked.

I had one chance. At the far end of the pool I jumped out and grabbed a towel, wrapping it round me quickly. Then the two visitors were up to me.

I remember Bill Astor making the introduction. I felt such a fool, standing there dripping, trying to wrap this rather inadequate towel round my figure.

But worse was to come. There were more voices – and in came the remainder of Bill's dinner guests. Including his wife, the former top model Bronwen Pugh – and of course Valerie Hobson, Jack's wife.

I can hear her saying it now – words which, because of all the dreadful things that have happened to Jack and me since that balmy Summer night, have such a tremendous significance.

Valerie said, 'Haven't you got a costume?' I couldn't very well say Stephen had thrown mine away, let alone try to explain why I decided to swim nude.

I just made a vague nod of the head and stepped back into the costume she offered.

So for the first time I met her husband I also took her bathing costume.

Fate

But I didn't plan it that way at all. It was just fate, like so much of all the trouble has been fate.

Well, obviously, we didn't feel much like swimming after this. We got dressed and Bill invited us back into his famous country home.

Looking back, there is no doubt about it. Jack was attracted to me from that moment. And I must admit I was attracted to him.

It was Jack who somehow showed me round that lovely house by himself.

But before that, the men dressed me up in some of the armour. I remember the women looked rather furious, but the men laughed like hell.

It was in one of the rooms which Jack was showing me over that he grabbed me. It was just a bit of fun, I thought.

I liked it – I don't mind admitting. Anyway, it was late at night and we'd all had a good time.

Round about 1:30 in the morning, Stephen and I left the house and drove back to London. But obviously, since there was a fine spell of weather, we readily accepted Bill's invitation to go back the next day with a party.

Eugene

It was some party that drove down that day. Stephen took some friends – but I was driven down by the Russian whose name you have heard so much recently, Captain Eugene Ivanov.

I had known him for some time because he was a friend of Stephen's and often used to visit our flat in Wimpole-mews.

It was in the afternoon and the first thing we did was to go to the pool. This was the memorable afternoon when Ivanov met the British War Minister, Mr John Profumo, for the first time.

Now I liked Ivanov. He was a MAN. He was rugged with a hairy chest, strong and agile. But somehow when we decided to have a water piggy-back fight, it was Jack Profumo's shoulders I climbed on.

We had a great time pulling one another into the water, then Eugene, Jack and Bill had a swimming race.

The idea was that they were not supposed to use their legs. But old Jack he cheated somehow and came first by using his legs in such a way that at first we couldn't spot it.

It was all good clean fun. Jack was like that, always gay, lively and out for a laugh. It was this personality of his which I found strangely fascinating and relaxing.

But it was not with Jack that I decided to leave the party early. It was Eugene, the hairy-chested Russian.

As we were saying our good-byes, Jack asked me for my telephone number. He said, 'When can I see you again?'

I replied, in a hurry, 'Talk with Stephen. He has my number' – which was our number, since I was living in Stephen's flat at the time.

I thought no more about it as we drove to Wimpole-mews in Eugene's Austin Westminster. I noticed he had a bottle of vodka stowed away, and he took it with him into the flat when we arrived.

As we drank the vodka we had quite a discussion about common English terms. He had no idea of our colloquial expressions.

Explained

He didn't know what a 'queer' was, and when I explained, he said stoutly, 'We have none of this in Russia.' I laughed and said they must have as it goes on all over the world. But he wouldn't have it.

Eugene seemed to have one thing in his life, and that was his country. But then we left serious discussion and I yielded to this wonderful huggy bear of a man...

But I did tell Stephen in later months that I didn't trust Eugene, because he seemed too nice and too simple.

A few days later I got a phone call from Jack. He said, 'What about a drive?' I replied, 'Hi – nice to hear from you again.'

The upshot was that he came round to the flat while Stephen was out. We drank, chatted and mucked about in general. I didn't think he was handsome, but his ways appealed to me.

He was so gentlemanly and he seemed so honest. I could have really liked him. I was very fond of him. I could feel myself warming to him. Mentally speaking, we got very close to each other.

The Start

But then as was often to happen in our future meetings at the flat, I had to say, 'Stephen will be back very soon' and as always when Stephen's name was mentioned, Jack got up and said that he had better be going. I didn't know when I would see Jack again. As I was to learn later, his duties kept him for anything up to a week before he could even phone me.

But we managed to meet once more at Stephen's flat before the fatal time when Jack Profumo and I became lovers.

It was the third time that he came round. I didn't anticipate what was going to happen. We started talking and laughing as usual, and then suddenly we both stopped.

There was one of those electric, potent silences – and then without a word we were embracing, and he was kissing me and I was returning his kisses with everything that I suddenly felt for him.

That was how it all started. He continued to meet me at the flat, always after phoning first. But always while Stephen was out.

I don't believe Stephen really liked Jack. Sometimes Stephen and Eugene would have left the flat only by a minute before Jack would arrive.

Our meetings were very discreet. Jack drove a little red mini car. We never once dined out, or had a drink in a pub or went anywhere. If we were not in the flat, then we would just drive and drive for hours. I felt safe being locked up in that little car.

Of course, it was impossible that our discretion would be absolutely complete. There was that amazing evening when Jack was round, and an army colonel showed up suddenly looking for Stephen.

I had to let him in, and introduce him to the War Minister. The colonel couldn't believe it. Jack nearly died. The funny thing was I never used to think of Jack as a Minister. I cannot bow down to a man who has got just money or position. I've got to like them. And I liked Jack as a MAN.

Looking back on it now, I realise what a strange contrast there was between the three men in my life at that time. There was Stephen Ward, an extrovert, excitable, always eager to attract attention to me and to him.

He had an extraordinary sense of humour and loved creating a sensation. For instance, one of his little jokes was to put a dog collar round my neck and take me along the street on a lead. Ivanov was often with us, and we would go into a pub and talk as if there was nothing unusual.

I would be sitting beside Stephen with the collar round my neck, and we would pretend not to notice the reactions of the other customers.

Afterwards Ivanov would roar with laughter about it all. Then there was the fact that unlike Jack, Ivanov was a party boy and loved to take me out to the bright spots, wining and dining me.

Jack never took me anywhere, except for drives all over London and even then he was so anxious to be discreet that he used to borrow a big black car from Mr John Hare, the Minister of Labour.

It had a silver hare on the bonnet as a mascot.

But despite our discretion in what speedily became an idyllic relationship the cloud which was inevitable because of Jack's position soon descended upon us.

Stephen had a visit from MI5 ... I remember the man coming. I opened the door to him. I half expected a man with a cloak held over his face. Instead, there was a little man with a bowler hat and an umbrella.

I don't know what he said to Stephen as I didn't stick around. They didn't seem to want me to.

Checking

But afterwards Stephen told me that it was perfectly all right. It was just that they were checking up on who I was, because Ivanov was also a frequent visitor to our flat. After that, Stephen and I used to get up to jokes on the telephone. We suspected our line was being tapped. So we would ring one another up and say curt things like, 'Is it all right? Have you got the plans? Right!'

But though we made make believe in a kid fashion, the fact remained that Jack never really trusted Stephen. He was also worried about the Press finding out about us – and above all he was worried about Valerie.

The end of our affair came as suddenly as it had begun. It seemed a normal evening. Jack picked me up in his car and we went for a little drive around London.

Then he said his wife was away in Ireland, and would I like to see his London home.

We drove to near Regent's Park where he had this beautiful Nash house – the house which the great architect built for himself.

It was late. The butler and the rest of the staff were in bed, and Jack let us in with his own key. We crept round the lovely rooms. And then we got to THEIR bedroom.

I knew he loved Valerie. I didn't want to take him away from her. Yet I loved him terribly. His devotion to Valerie used to play on his conscience when we were in the flat. He was always worried about it, and quite suddenly would get up and say he had to go.

But now I was in their bedroom. I was terribly jealous – God how terribly jealous I was! I wanted Jack so much at that moment. Perhaps you can't understand this – but this was when I loved him more than ever.

Afterwards we drove round and saw a former Secretary of State, Mr George Ward (now Viscount Ward). George was very friendly and I flirted with him just to tease Jack.

This time it was Jack's turn to get jealous.

Now we were getting towards the end of the affair. He drove me back to Wimpole-mews. We sat in the car talking.

He wanted me to leave the flat, saying it was too risky for him to keep coming there. But I wouldn't go.

Stephen was so close to me, though we had never been lovers.

Jack said he wouldn't come to see me if I didn't leave. I told him he must make his choice – got out and slammed the door. I never met him again.

But I received three letters from him. One said, 'Darling, I can't get you on the phone. I can't wait to get hold of you. Please don't run away . . .'

When the news of Jack's resignation came through I wasn't surprised. But I was hurt.

It's never nice to know that somebody you have loved very dearly is in deep trouble because of it all.

Christine Keeler, 'Confessions of Christine', *News of the World*, June 1963.

Profumo, a wealthy man, left politics for good and has since devoted himself to charity work in the East End of London.

....

Would You Like to See My Etchings?

Douglas Fairbanks and Mandy Rice-Davies

Mandy Rice-Davies, the other girl in the Profumo scandal, was slightly put out when it came to the intentions of Mr Douglas Fairbanks, Jnr.

I was seriously thinking of becoming an actress, it was one step on, I thought, from modelling, and making commercials had given me an idea of how to work with cameras and lights. I met Douglas Fairbanks, Jnr. with his wife and daughter Melissa at Cliveden and was able to talk to him about the film business. I was flattered by his interest when he telephoned me a few days later and invited me to lunch at the Dorchester.

Even then, in his fifties, he was a remarkably good-looking man as well as being an amusing companion and I felt strongly attracted to him. After lunch he suggested we go upstairs to his suite there, and I did. We went to bed. There were several of these little afternoon interludes. A pleasant lunch, an hour in bed. I was genuinely fond of him. And I imagined he felt something similar for me.

He suggested I went along to see a producer friend of his at Shepperton Studios where they were casting a new TV series called *One Step Beyond*. He went even further, he phoned and booked the appointment for me and paved the way.

However, arriving for the meeting I had a rude awakening. Certainly the producer was interested, but it seemed to me that he first needed an indication of what he could expect in return. That was it. I felt I had been sent as a piece of meat. I pretended to be totally thick and not understand the proposition and left. I felt deeply hurt, I could not disguise the implication. Over our next lunch, I told Douglas what had happened and my embarrassment. We never made love again.

Mandy Rice-Davies with Shirley Flack, *Mandy*
(Michael Joseph, 1980), pp. 64–5.

....

'Her Attitude ... was Wholly Immoral...'

The divorce case of the Duchess of Argyll

The Profumo affair overshadowed another scandalous highpoint of the year, the divorce case of the then Duchess of Argyll. The Duchess had been in the news for more than three decades; her name usually coupled with that of a wealthy man by whom she was seen being escorted or from whom she was about to be divorced. The Daily Express *ran the following account of the divorce case.*

The Duke of Argyll yesterday won his marathon £50,000-divorce action. And in the Edinburgh Court of Session the judge, 55-year-old Lord Wheatley, said of the 49-year-old duchess, a famed beauty and mother of the Duchess of Rutland:

'There is enough in her own admissions to establish that by 1969 she was a completely promiscuous woman whose sexual appetite could only be satisfied by a number of men, and whose attitude to the sanctity of marriage could only be described as wholly immoral.'

The 59-year-old 11th duke, hereditary master of the Royal Household, Scotland (motto: Forget not), was awarded a decree on the grounds of his duchess's misconduct with Mr Harvey Christian Rupert Peter Combe, of Muir of Ord, Ross and Cromarty. He is aged 37 and a former press officer at the Savoy Hotel, London.

The judge said the duchess also committed misconduct with Baron Sigismund Von Braun and Mr Jack Cohane, and also with a man with whom she was photographed in the nude 'engaging in a sexual association'. Only this man's body was showing and the judge said he accepted that it was not the duke.

Lord Wheatley ruled that the duchess's misconduct with Von Braun and the man in the photographs had been condoned. But, he rejected a plea of condonation in respect of Cohane. The duchess had denied the duke's allegations and pleaded condonation in respect of the allegations relating to Von Braun and Cohane. Combe had denied the allegations concerning him. It was in March that the evidence was heard, but the judge had put off his 'verdict' until yesterday. It was 10.30 a.m. when Lord Wheatley began his 64,000-word reserved judgement. First he spoke of:

The Early Days

The duke and the duchess were married in 1951 and lived together until 1959 – the exact date being in dispute. There are no children of the marriage. The duke had been married twice before. By his first wife he had a daughter and by his second wife two sons, both now over 16. The second wife divorced him in 1951 for adultery with the present duchess.

The duchess was married once before, and that marriage was dissolved in 1947. She had a son and a daughter by that marriage and both were over 16. The relationship of the duke and duchess was said to be unhappy, the judge went on. The duke attributed this to the duchess's insatiable desire to participate in social life, while he preferred a quiet existence. The duchess said his drinking habits and dislike of social engagements left her dependent on the company of others. The judge said what seemed reasonably clear was that by the beginning of 1959 relations were certainly strained. About that time the duke and duchess went on a world cruise during the course of which the duke taxed the duchess with misconduct with a man not named in the present action.

The duke said she admitted that. But the duchess denied it. The duke, however, returned from this trip certain that his wife had been unfaithful. The judge spoke of the duke's search for evidence and of a locksmith he employed to open a cupboard in their Upper Grosvenor Street house where the duchess was living. In the cupboard were:

The Photographs

Also in the cupboard were letters from Von Braun and Cohane which formed the basis of the duke's case for misconduct with these two men. The photographs formed the case for misconduct with the unnamed man or men. The duke said he found in the cupboard what he considered the most important document of all – a mock-up of fragmented documents pasted onto a piece of note-paper from an hotel. This appeared to be a letter written and signed by the duke's second wife, and the contents of this were highly derogatory to the duke and the children of the second wife. The duke was suspicious that the duchess was the author of a campaign and stated that the finding of this document confirmed his suspicions.

Lord Wheatley said that in April 1959 the couple had a violent quarrel and had had no marital relations since, except one night in June of that year. He went on: 'The duke says that on May 12, 1959, he had a bolt put on his bedroom door to prevent the defender (the duchess) getting into his room and into bed with him.'

Then the judge turned to: ·

The Three Diaries

One was grabbed from the duchess's bedroom in September 1959, when the duke, accompanied by his daughter, let himself into the Upper Grosvenor Street house.

The other two diaries – one dated 1948–51 and the other relating to the years 1952–5 were taken from a desk earlier when the duke and duchess were living together. The duke's purpose in obtaining the third diary was the hope that it would provide evidence of his wife's infidelity.

Lord Wheatley, dealing at length with this diary and with two other diaries, said it had been the duchess's practice to write up the diaries late at night.

He went on: 'These diaries did not record her innermost thoughts. The general pattern was a record of places she had stayed at, the weather, her engagements and an occasional reference to her health.

'In the last diary there was an occasional cryptic symbol "B" which the duke held meant she had had intercourse with Von Braun on that date.

'In support of this, he points out that his own initial appears in her diary for April 4, 1950, when he first had intercourse with the duchess, at that time being married to his second wife.

'In any event this seems to be somewhat double-edged as there is no "J" on the date on which the duke alleges that the duchess misconducted herself with John Cohane.

'This leads to the conclusion that on the standard of proof required it would be wrong to attach much evidential significance to a symbol that it was an admission that intercourse took place.' [The duchess claimed that the initials merely marked the times she was given flowers by her various admirers.]

'The diaries' only evidential value is to establish where the duchess was in 1949 and 1950.'

Dealing with allegations of misconduct in 1956 the judge told about:

The Nude Duchess

Lord Wheatley said some of the allegations were based on letters to the duchess from Von Braun and Cohane, and the third was based on the photographs.

'The photographs,' he went on, 'are said to be indicating an association between the duchess and an unknown man or men.

'Two of the photographs not only establish that she was carrying on an adulterous association with those other men or man but revealed that she was a highly sexed woman who had ceased to be satisfied with normal relations and had started to indulge in what I can only describe as disgusting sexual activities to gratify a basic sexual appetite.'

Two of the pictures showed the duchess in the nude with a naked man. But only the man's body was shown, not his head.

'I have no doubts that the woman in the photographs was the duchess,' said the judge.

Lord Wheatley said he would spare the duchess the indignity of describing the photographs. The only inference that could be drawn from them was that the persons in the photographs were indulging themselves in a gross form of sexual relationship.

An expert had made an examination of the duke and a comparison of the photographs, and had come to the conclusion that the man in the photographs was the same in each case and that it was not the duke. He accepted the opinion of that matter.

The judge said the camera used to take the photographs was of a Polaroid type, which also printed the films, which was an advantage to people who wished to take that type of pornographic photograph.

The judgement then brought Lord Wheatley to:

The Duke's Joke

The duchess, he said, denied keeping the photographs and suggested they were part of a catalogue of pornographic photographs kept by the duke.

Lord Wheatley said the duke had admitted showing photographs to a mixed party in New York and seemed to think it was a joke.

'I do not commend his standard of tastes and habits,' commented the judge.

The judge said the photographs seemed from the contents and positions, to be more the type of photograph carried by a woman with a sex perversion than by a man with a sex perversion.

Dealing with the accusation involving Cohane, Lord Wheatley spoke of:

The Invitation

He said that during a visit to New York the duchess went to a party on January 10, 1956 and Cohane tried to date her. But he only succeeded in getting an invitation to cocktails on January 12 in her hotel suite.

He took her to the airport on her return to England on January 13 and later wrote letters to her.

Misconduct was alleged to have taken place on January 13 in the duchess's suite and the allegations were based on an entry in her diary, 'Jackie 9–10'.

Lord Wheatley said he had had the advantage of seeing the duchess in the witness box but not of seeing Cohane, whose evidence was taken on commission.

Cohane's evidence was more unreliable. He was a voluble witness and some of his explanations became more incredible as a result of his verbosity.

'Even she, with all her quickness of mind, could not find ways of squaring some parts of his evidence with her own,' said the judge.

He said that Cohane claimed the duchess was not introduced to him as the duchess but by her former name.

'This I doubt,' said the judge. 'I doubt if a New York hostess would miss the opportunity of introducing a duchess to her guests.'

He added: 'Cohane was a self-confessed wolf who admitted he was immediately attracted physically to the duchess and wanted to set in train the machinery culminating in sexual relations.'

The duchess was only concerned at getting back to her husband. But despite the lack of response to his advances, Cohane stated he was anxious to pursue his assault on the chastity of the woman and tried to date her for lunch or dinner engagements, and admitted he was not in the duchess's suite on the day she went to the airport, therefore contradicting the duchess.

Lord Wheatley said he could place no reliance on Cohane's evidence once he departed from the facts, and went on to describe:

The Letters

They were exchanged between Cohane and the duchess. They were written on scraps of paper in Cohane's office. In the first of these he had asked the duchess to write to him. The judge said that it 'could be assumed from various expressions in these letters, such as "dearest Margaret" and "darling Margaret", that a close personal relationship existed between the two'.

The judge said he did not regard the letters as consistent with a situation in which Cohane's advances had been repulsed by a married woman who wanted nothing to do with him.

Cohane's phrase: 'You are an incredibly exciting woman' was further proof of the nonsense of the explanation that there was nothing in their relationship.

Another letter from Cohane said: 'I am completely frustrated as to how we can get together. I would like to be with you in Paris – but I just can't get away.

'I really would love to be with you, even for a few days, and my not having written does not mean that you are not inflaming my imagination.'

This passage, said the judge, was the basis of the duke's contention that the duchess and Cohane had committed misconduct.

The letter went on: 'I have thought of a number of new, highly intriguing things that we might do or I might do to you.'

The clear implication, said the judge, was that they had already engaged in a number of 'highly intriguing things'. He thought it was conclusive of a previous adulterous association. When he turned to the allegations about Von Braun, the judge referred to:

The Torn Pages

Lord Wheatley said he would spare the duchess further embarrassment of quoting in detail from letters written during a time when she was having a sexual relationship with Von Braun.

She claimed that this was between 1946 and 1947 and in 1950, before her marriage to the duke.

In some letters the top of the full page had been torn off. And the duchess suggested that this had been done by the duke after he had recovered the letters.

But Lord Wheatley said he did not accept this suggestion, which was typical of many suggestions advanced by the duchess in the course of her evidence.

The judge referred to an arrangement between the duchess and Von Braun that they exchanged self-addressed envelopes. She had advanced what could be described as 'a fantastic story' to explain the arrangement.

He also referred to a cablegram in which there was a reference to 'ghosts all around me'. The duchess said that was from the duke.

'I don't believe her,' said Lord Wheatley. 'There is a reference to ghosts in the correspondence and I find that this would seem to be an expression used between Von Braun and the duchess.'

She admitted this but she asserted that this was an expression also used between herself and the duke. 'I don't believe her,' said the judge.

Lord Wheatley said he found that the letters between Von Braun and the duchess in relation to 1956 spelled out in large capitals that they were engaging in an adulterous association. In speaking of the duchess's evidence about condonation the judge said it was unconvincing, and he went on to refer to her attitude to:

The Moral Code

Lord Wheatley said: 'Her explanations of many of these incriminating documents were unconvincing and I formed the view that she was lying on various points.

'She did not shrink from casting aspersions on anyone who seemed to be giving evidence contrary to her interests. She seemed to be a malicious woman.

'When a woman's chastity and character are being impugned it is not surprising that she is hostile to those whose evidence seems to support the attack, but the general effect of her evidence, particularly on the questions touching her adultery, was most unfavourable.'

Lord Wheatley said in considering the allegation of misconduct with Combe, it was desirable to refer to the principle of law that a condoned act of misconduct could be taken into account in assessing whether the duchess's conduct on a subsequent occasion could be given an innocent or guilty interpretation.

'In the present case there was sufficient evidence to establish that the duchess was a sexually promiscuous woman. On her own admission she committed adultery with the duke prior to her marriage and with Von Braun in the years 1947 to 1950.

'And she was proved to have committed adultery with Cohane and Von Braun.

'She seemed to think association with a married man, or indeed adultery with a married man, was not a serious breach of the moral code if the man was not happy with his wife.

'There is enough in her own admissions to establish that by 1960 she was a completely promiscuous woman whose sexual appetite could only be satisfied by a number of men, and whose attitude to the sanctity of marriage was what moderns would call enlightened, but in plain language could only be described as wholly immoral.'

Lord Wheatley said these might seem harsh words to use about a woman, but the duchess had qualified for them by her own actions, and reference to them was necessary for the proper examination of the law and the administration of justice.

'It is the actions of a woman of such character and mentality that I have to consider in relation to the events of 1960,' he said.

It was clear that the duke claimed the duchess was associating with Combe, and the judge talking of them told of:

The Watchers

They were two private detectives who kept watch after Combe had been acting as the duchess's escort in London. On the night of July 13, at about 9.10 Combe arrived at the duchess's house in 'a very old Ford car'. He went into the house and then came out and took three dogs back in with him.

'The duchess and Combe came out and went to a night club and drove back to the duchess's house at 1.25 a.m. Combe left with the dogs at 3 a.m.'

The duchess's explanation for Combe's long stay was that he had to clean up a terrible mess made by the dogs and that he also had a good-night drink.

Lord Wheatley said that if the time spent in the house was one and a half hours some explanation was called for, if the old-fashioned if realistic inference was not to be drawn. Their evidence, he said, was far from convincing. He found it difficult to believe the dogs were given free run of the house. Witnesses differed over the damage to the furniture and the mess the dogs made...

Speaking of the relationship of the duchess and Combe, who denied misconduct, the judge referred to:

The Trip Abroad

Lord Wheatley said that despite the duchess's assertion that it was impossible for her to commit misconduct with Combe, it was admitted that he
was in her bedroom shortly after arrival, drinking champagne.

The reason for their trip abroad had been given as an interest in the
acquisition of land. Her real interest was another matter.

Combe was uncertain about a number of important details such as
where the land was to be acquired, what was to be done with it and how
much money would be needed.

'The fact that no land has been acquired is not a surprising sequel to
the whole affair,' said the judge. The duchess appeared vague about where
the land was to be acquired, and Lord Wheatley said he reached the
conclusion that the so-called business trip was an excuse to enable her to
spend a few days with Combe with whom she had a close association ...

'When the escort chosen is a close friend, it may be that there would be
an opportunity to be something more than just friends. Such a woman
might be prepared to satisfy her sexual urges and take risks that a normal
woman would not have taken.'

The judge took four and a half hours to deliver his judgement. Then
came submissions from counsel about payment of the expenses of the
action – one of the longest and costliest in Scottish legal history.

'The Divorce of Margaret, Duchess of Argyll', *The Daily Express*, 9 May 1963.

....

Incident at 'Pinkville'
– the My Lai Massacre

American massacre of South Vietnamese villagers

*America's worst war crime remained undetected for twenty months, despite the
attempts of various people to force the Army to investigate it. On 16 March
1968, an American Army company under the command of Lieutenant William
Calley murdered between 450 and 500 South Vietnamese civilians in cold blood*

in a tiny hamlet called My Lai 4. Although the residents were sympathetic to the National Liberation Front – the Communist guerrillas – there were none in the village when the Americans attacked and there were no shots fired at the Americans. In fact, the sole American casualty was a soldier who shot himself in the foot to avoid participating in the slaughter. A day after the massacre, an American Army colonel conducted an investigation, but concluded that nothing untoward occurred at My Lai 4. The South Vietnamese Government had numerous reports of the atrocity but did not wish to embarrass their American allies, so did not pursue the matter. Nine months after the massacre, gruesome photographs of the hundreds of dead taken by an American Army photographer were actually shown by him at Rotary Club dinners in Ohio, but again, nobody thought it worth investigating further.

Captain Ron Ridenhour, who had served in South Vietnam as a door gunner on a helicopter gunship, was disturbed by the various first-hand accounts he had heard about the massacre. He wrote the following letter and sent it off to the Pentagon, the White House and twenty-four Congressmen.

Phoenix, Arizona
29 March 1969

Gentlemen:

It was late in April, 1968 that I first heard of 'Pinkville' and what allegedly happened there. I received that first report with some scepticism, but in the following months I was to hear similar stories from such a wide variety of people that it became impossible for me to disbelieve that something rather dark and bloody did indeed occur sometime in March, 1968 in a village called 'Pinkville' in the Republic of Viet Nam...

In late April, 1968 I was awaiting orders for a transfer from HHC, 11th Brigade to Company 'E', 51st Inf. (LRP), when I happened to run into Pfc 'Butch' Gruver, whom I had known in Hawaii. Gruver told me he had been assigned to 'C' Company 1st of the 20th until April 1st when he transferred to the unit that I was headed for. During the course of our conversation he told me the first of many reports I was to hear of 'Pinkville'.

'Charlie' Company 1/20 had been assigned to Task Force Barker in late February, 1968 to help conduct 'search and destroy' operations in the Batangan Peninsula, Barker's area of operation. The task force was operating out of L. F. Dottie, located five or six miles north of Quang Nhai city on Viet Namese National Highway 1. Gruver said that Charlie Company had sustained casualties, primarily from mines and booby traps, almost every day from the first day they arrived on the peninsula. One village area was particularly troublesome and seemed to be infested with booby traps and enemy soldiers. It was located about six miles Northeast of Quang

Nhai city at approximate co-ordinates B.S. 728795. It was a notorious area and the men of Task Force Barker had a special name for it: they called it 'Pinkville'. One morning in the later part of March, Task Force Barker moved out from its firebase headed for 'Pinkville'. Its mission: destroy the trouble spot and all of its inhabitants.

When 'Butch' told me this I didn't quite believe that what he was telling me was true, but he assured me that it was and went on to describe what had happened. The other two companies that made up the task force cordoned off the village so that 'Charlie' Company could move through to destroy the structures and kill the inhabitants. Any villagers who ran from Charlie Company were stopped by the encircling companies. I asked 'Butch' several times if all the people were killed. He said he thought they were, men, women and children. He recalled seeing a small boy, about three or four years old, standing by the trail with a gunshot wound in one arm. The boy was clutching his wounded arm with his other hand, while blood trickled between his fingers. He was staring around himself in shock and disbelief at what he saw. 'He just stood there with big eyes staring around like he didn't understand; he didn't believe what was happening. The captain's RTO (radio operator) put a burst of 16 (M-16 rifle) fire into him.' It was so bad, Gruver said, that one of the men in his squad shot himself in the foot in order to be medivac-ed out of the area so that he would not have to participate in the slaughter. Although he had not seen it, Gruver had been told by people he considered trustworthy that one of the company's officers, 2nd Lieutenant Kally (this spelling may be incorrect), had rounded up several groups of villagers (each group consisting of a minimum of 20 persons of both sexes and all ages). According to the story, Kally then machine-gunned each group. Gruver estimated that the population of the village had been 300 to 400 people and that very few, if any, escaped.

After hearing this account I couldn't quite accept it. Somehow I just couldn't believe that not only had so many young American men participated in such an act of barbarism, but that their officers had ordered it. There were other men in the unit I was soon to be assigned to, 'E' Company, 51st Infantry (LRP), who had been in Charlie Company at the time that Gruver alleged the incident at 'Pinkville' had occurred. I became determined to ask them about 'Pinkville' so that I might compare their accounts with Pfc Gruver's.

When I arrived at 'Echo' Company, 51st Infantry (LRP) the first men I looked for were Pfcs Michael Terry and William Doherty. Both were veterans of 'Charlie' Company, 1/20 and 'Pinkville'. Instead of contradicting 'Butch' Gruver's story they corroborated it, adding some tasty tidbits of information of their own. Terry and Doherty had been in the same squad and their platoon was the third platoon of 'C' Company to pass through the village. Most of the people they came to were already dead. Those that weren't were sought out and shot. The platoon left nothing alive, neither livestock nor people. Around noon the two soldiers' squad stopped to eat. 'Billy and I started to get out our chow,' Terry said, 'but close to us was a bunch of Vietnamese in a heap, and some of them were moaning. Kally (2nd Lt. Kally) had been through before us and all of them had been shot, but many weren't dead. It was obvious that they weren't going to get any medical attention so Billy and I got up and went over to where they were. I guess we sort of finished them off.' Terry went on to say that he and Doherty then returned to where their packs were and ate lunch. He estimated the size of the village to be 200 to 300 people. Doherty thought that the population of 'Pinkville' had been 400 people.

If Terry, Doherty and Gruver could be believed, then not only had 'Charlie' Company received orders to slaughter all the inhabitants of the village, but those orders had come from the commanding officer of Task Force Barker, or possibly even higher in the chain of command. Pfc Terry stated that when Captain Medina (Charlie Company's commanding officer Captain Ernest Medina) issued the order for the destruction of 'Pinkville' he had been hesitant, as if it were something he didn't want to do but had to. Others I spoke to concurred with Terry on this.

It was June before I spoke to anyone who had something of significance to add to what I had already been told of the 'Pinkville' incident. It was the end of June, 1968 when I ran into Sergeant Larry La Croix at the USO in Chu Lai. La Croix had been in 2nd Lt. Kally's platoon on the day Task Force Barker swept through 'Pinkville'. What he told me verified the stories of the others, but he also had something new to add. He had been witness to Kally's gunning down of at least three separate groups of villagers. 'It was terrible. They were slaughtering the villagers like so many sheep.' Kally's men were dragging people out of bunkers and hootches and putting them together in a group. The people in the group were men, women and children of all ages. As soon as he felt that the group was big enough, Kally ordered an M-60 (machine-gun) set up and the people killed. La Croix said that he bore witness to this procedure at least three times. The three groups were of different sizes, one of about twenty people, one of about thirty people, and one of about forty people. When the first group was put together Kally ordered Pfc Torres to man the machine-gun and open fire on the villagers that had been grouped together. This Torres did, but before everyone in the group was down he ceased fire and refused to fire again. After ordering Torres to recommence firing several times,

Lieutenant Kally took over the M-60 and finished shooting the remaining villagers in that first group himself. Sergeant La Croix told me that Kally didn't bother to order anyone to take the machine-gun when the other two groups of villagers were formed. He simply manned it himself and shot down all villagers in both groups.

This account of Sergeant La Croix's confirmed the rumours that Gruver, Terry and Doherty had previously told me about Lieutenant Kally. It also convinced me that there was a very substantial amount of truth to the stories that all of these men had told. If I needed more convincing, I was to receive it.

It was in the middle of November, 1968, just a few weeks before I was to return to the United States for separation from the army that I talked to Pfc Michael Bernhardt. Bernhardt had served his entire year in Viet Nam in 'Charlie' Company 1/20 and he too was about to go home. 'Bernie' substantiated the tales told by the other men I had talked to in vivid, bloody detail and added this: 'Bernie' had absolutely refused to take part in the massacres of the villagers of 'Pinkville' that morning and he thought that it was rather strange that the officers of the company had not made an issue of it. But that evening 'Medina' (Captain Ernest Medina) came up to me ('Bernie') and told me not to do anything stupid like write my congressman' about what had happened that day. Bernhardt assured Captain Medina that he had no such thing in mind. He had nine months left in Viet Nam and felt that it was dangerous enough just fighting the acknowledged enemy.

Exactly what did, in fact, occur in the village of 'Pinkville' in March, 1968, I do not know for *certain*, but I am convinced that it was something very black indeed. I remain irrevocably persuaded that if you and I do truly believe in the principles of justice and the equality of every man, however humble, before the laws that form the very backbone that this country is founded on, then we must press forward a widespread and public investigation of this matter with all our combined efforts. I think that it was Winston Churchill who once said 'A country without a conscience is a country without a soul, and a country without a soul is a country that cannot survive.' I feel that I must take some positive action on this matter. I hope that you will launch an investigation immediately and keep me informed of your progress. If you cannot, then I don't know what other course of action to take.

I have considered sending this to newspapers, magazines and broadcasting companies, but I somehow feel that investigation and action by the Congress of the United States is the appropriate procedure, and as a conscientious citizen I have no desire to further besmirch the image of the American serviceman in the eyes of the world. I feel that this action, while probably it would promote attention, would not bring about the constructive actions that the direct actions of the Congress of the United States would.

Sincerely,
Ron Ridenhour

The majority of the recipients of this letter, including the White House, ignored it. Two Arizona Senators decided to pursue it, as did President Nixon's Secretary of Defence, Melvin Laird, who began the Army investigation. Ridenhour was not aware that the Army were now seriously following up the story so he wrote to various news magazines but it was not until Seymour Hersh, a young Washington reporter, pursued the story and actually interviewed Calley that the facts were aired in public.

Six months after a thorough Army investigation, Lieutenant 'Rusty' Calley was charged with premeditated murder of 109 civilians. Anxious to assist their American allies, the South Vietnamese Government immediately denounced the stories as being completely untrue and nearly half of Americans polled even believed that the photographs of the massacre were staged. Eventually, twelve officers were charged with murder, including Calley's superior, Captain Ernest 'Mad Dog' Medina, but Calley was the only one convicted and in 1971 was sentenced to life imprisonment. In 1974, his sentence was reduced to 10 years with President Nixon considering further action was inappropriate. In 1975 Calley was released on parole.

Some supporters of the American war treated him as a hero. Nobody knows how many people were massacred by Calley and his troops in March 1968, but it is likely to have been between 450 and 500, with the vast majority of the victims women and children, some as young as a few months.

'It Wiggles, It's Shapely and Its Name is Ainsley Gotto'

Australian Prime Minister and his secretary Ainsley Gotto

The furore caused in 1969 by this description of Australian Prime Minister John Gorton's personal secretary heralded the beginning of a more personal approach to Australian affairs both by politicians and the media.

Canberra—Miss Ainsley Gotto has conferred with the Prime Minister, Mr John Gorton, on allegations levelled against her by former Minister for Air, Mr Dudley Erwin.

The bitterness of the personal allegations made by Mr Erwin against the Prime Minister's private secretary has shocked the Liberal Party. In a statement last night, Mr Erwin said:

- The political manoeuvre used to get him out of office 'wiggles, it's shapely and its name is Ainsley Gotto'.
- Several times Miss Gotto had prevented him speaking to the Prime Minister.
- Miss Gotto 'ruled with a ruthless authority'.
- Young girls of Miss Gotto's age – she is 23 – should not be placed in such a responsible position when so young.

Miss Gotto would not comment today on any of Mr Erwin's allegations.

The Age, 13 November 1969.

Chappaquiddick – Crossing the Bridge When He Comes to It

Edward Kennedy and Mary Jo Kopechne's death

Senator Edward Kennedy, the sole surviving brother of President John F. Kennedy, never recovered politically from the damage caused by the Chappaquiddick scandal. It involved the drowning of his passenger, Mary Jo Kopechne, in a mishap off the resort island of Martha's Vineyard in Massachusetts, after a party in July 1969 for his office staff. The drowning itself was not the cause of the scandal – it was the fact that Kennedy never bothered to notify anybody about the incident until the following morning. This 1970 report in The New York Times *spelled out the reasons why Teddy would never try to follow in his assassinated brother's political footsteps. Even apart from this scandal, it is doubtful whether Kennedy would have had the wherewithal to be a serious presidential candidate. He has done outstanding work in the Senate but until his recent remarriage, never quite lost his image as a ladies' man. Joseph Lelyveld, the author of the report, later distinguished himself as a foreign correspondent before being appointed Editor of* The New York Times.

The judge at the inquest into the death of Mary Jo Kopechne reported that he could not accept as the truth key elements of Senator Edward M. Kennedy's sworn testimony at the hearing.

Judge James A. Boyle of the Dukes County District Court found neither 'responsible' nor 'probable' these assertions by the Senator about the drowning of Miss Kopechne last July:

• The Senator's testimony that he and Miss Kopechne had left a party at a cottage on Chappaquiddick Island with the intention of catching a ferry back to Martha's Vineyard.

• His testimony that it was a wrong turn that took him onto a dirt road that led to a narrow, unmarked bridge on Chappaquiddick.

Judge Boyle, who conducted the inquest six months after the Senator's car plunged off the wooden bridge, also took note of the testimony showing that both Mr Kennedy and Miss Kopechne had been driven over the same bridge earlier on the day of the accident.

From this he concluded that there was 'probable cause' to believe that the Senator had been driving negligently and that such driving might have contributed to Miss Kopechne's death.

It was a decision by the local authorities not to proceed with prosecution that cleared the way for the release here this afternoon, by the Massachusetts Superior Court, of Judge Boyle's findings and the 763-page transcript of the inquest. No explanations for that decision were available here today.

A spokesman for Robert H. Quinn, the Attorney General of Massachusetts, said that prosecution could have been initiated by Judge Boyle himself, by District Attorney Edmund Dinis of New Bedford, or by Police Chief Dominick Arena of Edgartown on Martha's Vineyard. Since none of these officials acted, the spokesman said, 'the matter is at the end as far as the Attorney General is concerned.'

Mr Dinis, at his office in New Bedford, declined to comment.

The release of the transcript appeared to constitute the final act of a legal drama that has lasted more than nine months since Miss Kopechne was trapped and drowned in the Senator's overturned Oldsmobile the night of last July 18–19.

When Mr Kennedy testified at the inquest last Jan. 5, it was the first time that he had submitted to questioning about the accident. His testimony did not appear to contradict his earlier statements.

The judge's 'presumptions of fact' as to what really happened on the night of the accident were based on testimony that Miss Kopechne left her purse in the cottage when she left with the Senator and that she told none of her friends where she was going. According to the testimony, Mr Kennedy spoke only to his driver, John B. Crimmins, when he asked for the keys to the car.

Judge Boyle apparently found it strange that Mr Kennedy did not ask Mr Crimmins to drive him and Miss Kopechne back to their hotels at Martha's Vineyard. This would have enabled the driver to bring the car back to Chappaquiddick and pick up the other girls who had not been planning to spend the night in the small cottage where the party was held.

Cross-Examination Barred

However, Senator Kennedy was not subjected to aggressive cross-examination during nearly two hours on the stand. The judge held that cross-examination was not appropriate in an inquest.

At no point were Senator Kennedy or any of his companions at the party asked directly whether they had ever considered concealing his involvement in the accident.

Mr Kennedy testified that he had never been on Chappaquiddick before the day of the accident and that he himself had not been at the wheel of his car when he visited the island earlier in the day.

Asked whether he realised that he was not heading to the ferry after turning onto the dirt road, he replied: 'At the moment I went off the bridge, I certainly did.'

The next thing he was conscious of, the Senator said, was Miss Kopechne struggling next to him on the front seat of the car as it overturned in the water, then 'the rushing of the water, the blackness, the fact that it was impossible even to hold it back.'

Mr Kennedy, who testified that he was 'absolutely sober' when the car went off the bridge, told of diving to the point of exhaustion to save Miss Kopechne, after struggling out of the car, then of being swept out into the pond by a strong current.

Denies Seeing Lights

He said he never saw the lights of the houses near the bridge, and returned to the cottage where the party was being held to get help.

Asked why he did not then try to phone the police, Mr Kennedy said he had intended to do so.

But first, he said, he returned with Joseph Gargan, his cousin; and Paul Markham, a former United States Attorney for Massachusetts, who dived for 45 minutes in an attempt to reach Miss Kopechne.

According to the Senator's testimony, it was past 1 a.m. when Mr Gargan and Mr Markham drove him to the ferry clip. On the way, he said, they repeatedly stressed the importance of his phoning the police when he reached Edgartown on Martha's Vineyard.

Mr Kennedy said he agreed but was more preoccupied by worries about how he would meet his duty to notify Miss Kopechne's parents or his own family. This concern led him to the desperate hope, he said, that what he knew to be fact was only nightmare.

'To See Her Walking'

'I was almost looking out the front window and windows trying to see her walking down that road,' he said. 'I related this to Gargan and Markham and they said they understood this feeling, but it was necessary to report it.'

Before diving impulsively into the channel to swim to Edgartown, he said, he told his companions, 'You take care of the girls, I will take care of the accident.'

Mr Gargan said he was not worried by the Senator's sudden dive because he knew his cousin to be a strong swimmer. But Mr Kennedy testified that the swim nearly cost him his life and left him in an even deeper state of confusion and exhaustion.

Back in his hotel room, the Senator testified, he continued to wrestle with his hope that Mary Jo Kopechne was still alive. 'I somehow believed that when the sun came up and it was a new morning that what had happened the night before would not have happened and did not happen,' he said.

He could not find, he said, 'the strength within me, the moral strength to call Mrs Kopechne at 2 o'clock in the morning and tell her that her daughter was dead.'

Tells of Phone Call

The only reason he returned to Chappaquiddick Island the next morning, he testified, was to make a call in private to Burke Marshall, a family friend and former high Justice Department official under Robert Kennedy. That done, he said, he went directly to the police.

Edmund Dinis, the District Attorney questioning the Senator, noted the discrepancy between this testimony and his original statement that he went 'immediately' to the police in the morning. But Judge Boyle would not let him ask Mr Kennedy to explain it.

When Mr Markham took the stand at the inquest, he testified that Mr Kennedy had tried to keep him and Mr Gargan from becoming implicated in the case. 'Look,' he quoted the Senator as saying, 'I don't want you people in the middle of this thing ... As far as you know, you didn't know anything about the accident last night.'

Esther Newburgh, one of the five young women who remained behind in the cottage, said that Mr Gargan collapsed on a couch after returning there. According to the testimony, Mr Markham, also exhausted from the diving, dropped on a couch too and slumped across a girl's legs.

He testified that the young woman was annoyed – that all the young women were in an irritated mood over having been stranded at the cottage, but apparently unaware still that anything serious had happened.

All the witnesses agreed there had been no heavy drinking at the party. Mr Crimmins told of taking the leftover vodka and rum back to his cottage in the Kennedy compound in Hyannis Port.

The only corroboration for Senator Kennedy's testimony that Miss Kopechne wanted to leave the party because she was tired came from Mr Crimmins. 'She was bothered by the sun on the beach that day,' the driver said.

A series of five affidavits and medical reports were introduced in evidence by Senator Kennedy's lawyers to demonstrate that he suffered a concussion in the accident and that his disoriented frame of mind was not unusual, in the opinion of specialists, for persons in that condition.

Mr Kennedy did not attempt to resolve a discrepancy over the time of the accident between his testimony and that of Christopher Lock, Jr., who testified that he was almost certain he had seen the Senator's car some 90 minutes after the accident occurred if the times given by Mr Kennedy were accepted as correct.

Judge Boyle did not attempt to resolve this discrepancy either. His report put the time of the accident between 11.15 p.m. and 1 a.m.

The only charge ever brought against Senator Kennedy in the case was for leaving the scene of an accident. He pleaded guilty before Judge Boyle on July 25, and thereby was spared cross-examination. The judge gave him a two-month suspended sentence.

The following week the case was reopened by Mr Dinis, who chose to call for an inquest into Miss Kopechne's death rather than to take the more usual route of bringing it before a grand jury himself.

The closed inquest lasted from Jan. 5 to Jan. 8. A grand jury eventually did study the case but took no action.

Joseph Lelyveld, *The New York Times*, 30 April 1970.

Kennedy never managed to shake off the effect of the Chappaquiddick affair on his political career. In 1980, he pulled out of his race to gain the Democratic Party presidential nomination after it was felt that he failed to give plausible answers to questions on the affair in a television interview.

'A Cause for National Shame'

Sunday Times *campaign for victims of thalidomide drug*

The campaign in the early seventies by the Insight team of The Sunday Times *on behalf of the victims of the drug thalidomide was a brilliant success. Several hundred children were born without limbs after their mothers had taken the drug during pregnancy. Distillers, the company who made the drug, which was taken as a tranquillizer during the early stages of pregnancy, initially offered a compensation package of less than £3 million but following the publication of the article below, the offer was raised to more than £20 million. Distillers fought a lengthy battle to prevent further articles on the background of how the worst drug tragedy in recent history had occurred. Eventually the case was thrown out and other pieces appeared.*

TOMORROW week, the civil law courts will reopen for the Michaelmas Term. It will be, near enough, the tenth anniversary of the first legal action taken to obtain compensation for children who were deformed by the drug thalidomide.

This may seem an apt – if none too expeditious – moment to settle the bulk of outstanding claims, and provide some disposable cash for 370 children whose afflictions date back to the early sixties. And it seems clear that in the new term, lawyers acting for Distillers Biochemicals, who made thalidomide, will appear with lawyers acting for the children, to seek court approval for a settlement which has been worked out in private over the past few months.

Unhappily, the settlement is one which is grotesquely out of proportion to the appalling injuries the thalidomide children suffered. Essentially, the offer is that Distillers set up a trust for the children and their families, worth some £3.25m.

This is not a large sum in the context of Distillers' commercial operations (a little less than 10 per cent of last year's after-tax profits, a little more than 1 per cent of the money made in the ten years since thalidomide). It may seem larger in the context of a claim for damages – until one reckons up the price of providing for a legless, armless infant who still has, in inflationary times, some fifty years of life to be endured.

No firm predictions can be made about individuals, for one feature of the trust is that no family can know what its own case will be worth. They have all been told that they must sign up 'blind' or not at all. But there is a rough estimate that a family whose child is in the 'top bracket' of deformity (that is, an entirely limbless trunk) might receive about £15,000.

To put that sum in perspective, there is an actuarial estimate that such a case would need not less than £100,000 to support a reasonable existence over the likely span of life. And that estimate deals in the necessities of subsistence and special care: to provide the traditional compensation for 'pain and suffering' would require a good deal more.

Fairly plainly, the proposed trust will be too small to make proper amends for suffering. Worse still, in the 'top bracket' cases it will probably be insufficient to ward off simple destitution. Yet this proposed settlement is the result of much devoted legal craftsmanship, and its acceptance is being strongly – even passionately – urged, not only by Distillers' lawyers, but also by the lawyers acting for the afflicted families.

What has gone wrong?

In the decade since thalidomide was invented, marketed and withdrawn, it has become a symbol of the havoc that a technically complex society can wreak upon its own members. In almost every country where the miraculous new 'tranquillizer' was sold, it caused a national disaster. In British terms, it was one of the worst of all peacetime accidents – worse than Aberfan, or the typhoid outbreaks, or any of our rare aircraft accidents.

Classic disasters tend to produce social reform, and thalidomide was no exception. A decade ago, it was possible for Distillers to promote thalidomide as being unusually suitable for pregnant women. Today, under the new rules which govern the pharmaceutical industry, such a campaign would be virtually impossible. Drug manufacturers must be much more circumspect in their claims.

Our new safety, of course, has been bought at the cost of several hundred distorted lives: essentially, the reason that the thalidomide victims are being offered such slender recompense for their exemplary and involuntary sufferings is that, although their disaster effected a revolution in pharmacology, it has not yet caused any change in the system of law.

Yet the legal conventions under which this settlement was devised are already, by one good test, obsolete. The Law Commission, which is the body officially charged with proposing law reforms, has already decided that the present methods of fixing damages for personal injuries lacks 'any mathematical, actuarial, statistical or other scientific basis' – and should undergo major reconstruction.

The Commission's proposals may never become law, and certainly will not do so in the coming Michaelmas Terms. Equally certainly, Distillers are quite within their rights to fight their case hard, and defend their position, on the basis of present law, however absurd that may be.

Even so, our laws on personal injury and damages are notoriously ramshackle: almost certainly, they *are* going to be reformed. If, in the meantime, the most important of recent claims for personal injury should have been disposed of on an old and unfair basis, it would rank as one of the worst single failures of the English legal system.

'Our thalidomide children: a cause for national shame', *The Sunday Times*, 24 September 1972.

....

Lord Lambton's Political Waterloo

Lord Lambton found in bed with two prostitutes

Lord Lambton, disclaimed heir to the Earldom of Durham, promptly resigned from his post as Air Minister in 1973 when it was revealed to him that he had been photographed in bed smoking marijuana with two prostitutes. When asked by the police about one of the women, Lord Lambton replied, 'She's a kind of prostitute . . . I liked her, but she played no important part in my life whatsoever.' However, he later told the press his behaviour was 'credulous stupidity'. The following day, Earl Jellicoe, Lord Privy Seal and leader of the House of Lords, also resigned following his admission that he too had been involved with call girls, albeit different ones to Lord Lambton. The concern about possible security repercussions led Prime Minister Edward Heath to set up a security commission, which quickly reported back that there were no security breaches in either case. Nor were Lord Lambton or Lord Jellicoe found to be part of 'a top people's vice ring', as the article below alleged.

Colin Levy, the husband of one of the call girls who was photographed in bed with Lord Lambton, has told the *News of the World* his amazing story.

We have also talked exclusively to his wife, Norma, the attractive 26-

year-old girl in the middle of the biggest sex scandal to hit Britain for a decade.

Their amazing revelations are the climax to nine months of painstaking investigation by *News of the World* reporters.

This investigation revealed the names of London's landlords who have become rich by letting flats to prostitutes. More important, reporter Peter Earle also obtained information about the existence of a top people's vice ring.

Before Levy or his wife talked to the *News of the World*, our investigators possessed accurate information that the two Government Ministers who resigned last week – Lord Lambton, the Under-Secretary of State at the Ministry of Defence, and Lord Jellicoe, the Lord Privy Seal and Leader of the House of Lords – were among those involved.

Levy claims he decided to tell all after a lover's tiff with his call girl wife put MI5 and the police on his trail. After hours of talks with him and his wife I can today reveal the full facts.

Blackmail

Because of the grave risk of blackmail and Lord Lambton's position at the Ministry of Defence which gave him access to military secrets the *News of the World*, using normal journalistic enterprise, decided to check the story further.

Levy came to the *News of the World* because, he said, he was in fear for his life.

In Levy's own words when he first walked into my office: 'I'm terrified. I've got a terrible feeling that someone is going to get me.

'As long as I know that someone else knows what's been going on I'll feel safe.'

Levy came along with his close friend 32-year-old Peter Goodsell. They had left Mrs Norma Levy at home in her luxury £40,000 flat at Marlborough, Edgware Road, Maida Vale, London.

- They told me they had conclusive proof of a high-class international call-girl ring operating in London, Paris, Detroit and Stuttgart.
- They had two undeveloped colour cine films taken on May 3 and May 5 which they alleged showed Lord Lambton entering the flat, leaving it and participating in sex acts with Mrs Levy and another person. They allege that the second person in this instance was not the girl Kim Pinder, who was later pictured in bed with Mrs Levy and Lord Lambton.
- They had Photostat copies of seven pages containing addresses, phone

numbers, nationalities, and personal physical descriptions of girls in the London ring which they claimed was organised by Miss Jean Horn, who lived in a luxury flat at St John's Wood.

• They had what they claimed was an original cheque made out in Lord Lambton's own handwriting drawn in favour of N. Russell (Mrs Norma Levy's maiden name) in the sum of £50 and dated April 24, 1973.

• They had five £20 notes allegedly paid to Mrs Levy by Lord Lambton – all in numerical sequence.

• They claimed these had been paid by him on May 3, May 5 and May 8.

Scared

• They had the names and addresses of eight high-class 'Madams' dotted throughout the world, two in Paris, two in Detroit, and others in New York, Stuttgart, Zurich and London.

• They also had tape recordings.

I immediately asked Levy and Goodsell the reason why they had gone to such lengths to obtain all this information.

Goodsell replied: 'Because we're scared that someone is going to get us. Don't think we're being melodramatic. MI5 have been brought into this. The flat has been searched. We're certain it's bugged.'

At this point, Levy, who was white-faced and shaking, said: 'One officer told me: "If you don't cooperate with us we'll get you."

'As soon as that threat was made, we started collecting evidence so that we could protect ourselves and raise enough money to get Norma, Peter and myself out of the country.

'We reckon we need a minimum of £30,000 from a newspaper for our story to get us to a country from which we can't be extradited.'

Levy then explained how a 'lovers' tiff' alerted the security forces and the police to the existence of an international vice ring which catered for the titled, political and famous people who could afford to pay for high-class and high-priced call girls.

'I love my wife, Norma, very much,' he told me. 'But as anyone who knows her understands, she's highly-strung and extremely jealous of me.

'Early in April I told her I was leaving the country on a business trip. For certain reasons I couldn't tell her where I was going.

'After I'd left she became very worried, believing that I'd gone off with some other woman.

'In her panic, she thought up the idea of getting me arrested and brought back to England. She rushed down to Scotland Yard, saw an officer of the

Drugs Squad and blurted out the story that I was involved with a high-class call-girl ring and had taken secret photographs of a Government Minister.

'At that time it was totally untrue! The drugs man told Special Branch and I think they told the Prime Minister.'

Levy told me how when he returned to London Airport 'several Special Branch officers' and policemen from Det. Chief Supt Albert Wickstead's Serious Crimes Squad moved across to the plane as it taxied to a halt on the tarmac.

'I told them Norma was lying,' said Mr Levy. 'But they didn't believe me. Then one of the men made that remark which I took to be a serious threat.

'Peter and I discussed the matter and decided to get together as much evidence as we could.'

On one occasion Levy noticed that Lord Lambton, who used the code name 'Lucas' when visiting call girls, arrived outside Norma's flat in a chauffeur-driven Daimler limousine.

A pennant was flying on the bonnet and the registration plate indicated it was a military car.

A quick piece of detective work and he knew the man was Lord Lambton.

And in preparation for the Minister's next visit to the flat he and Goodsell scraped the silver from the back of a bronze-coloured mirror which was fitted into the back of a wardrobe in the main bedroom.

Tape

Behind this mirror was the wall of a spare bedroom. They knocked a hole through the wall large enough to enable them to operate a cine camera.

In the spare bedroom they rigged up a tape recorder with a wire leading into the main bedroom, along the carpet edge and up into the body of a large teddy-bear which was seated in a chair.

After removing the bear's nose, they connected a microphone to the wire and blacked over the silver end.

On one occasion compromising pictures, which I have seen, were taken of Lord Lambton.

In two other instances every single incident which occurred on the bed between Lord Lambton and the other people present was filmed, according to Goodsell and Levy.

In addition, they even filmed him leaving the flat, walking round the corner to his house in Hamilton Terrace, St John's Wood, climbing the steps to his front door, opening it with a latch-key and disappearing inside.

Levy told me how, during the course of filming one sequence a pet Burmese cat owned by Norma climbed into the wardrobe and obscured the camera's view.

Adamant

On several occasions during my meetings with Levy and Goodsell, I questioned them closely as to whether they had ever considered black-mailing anyone involved in the vice ring. Both were adamant.

'We aren't exactly good guys, but we'd never stoop to that,' they said.

Indeed, they pointed out that it would be impossible to contemplate such a venture as both Scotland Yard and MI5 already knew of the connection between themselves, Norma Levy and Lord Lambton.

Within three hours of my first meeting with Levy and Goodsell, I persuaded them to hand into my custody both undeveloped colour films which are said to show acts being committed by Lord Lambton.

Those films were hidden in a place known only to two people. Later I handed them to the police.

Colin and Norma Levy had a stormy relationship. Norma was living on her nerves during the time I knew them.

I found her elegant rather than beautiful. Her speaking voice is refined, but when she gets angry she lapses into an Irish accent.

She came over to England from County Cork, Eire, with her family eight years ago.

She soon became bored with her family life in a council house in Stockton on Tees, Co. Durham, and went to Manchester and began working in a club.

After one row with her husband two weeks ago she went to visit her parents for three days.

Even after I told Levy and Goodsell that the *News of the World* was not willing to pay them anything for their story under any circumstances, I stayed in touch with them.

Sadism

Levy told me: 'Some of the girls specialise in way-out forms of sadism. When they lay it on a client, they really enjoy it.

'On some occasions with a very rich client a girl has been in the room while the man concerned has indulged in forms of homosexuality with a fairly young man. I don't know his exact age, but think he is about 17 or 18.'

This particular incident was also confirmed to me by Mrs Levy.

In a somewhat pathetic and, in the event, fruitless, effort to retain anonymity for themselves, most of the clients were awarded and accepted pseudonyms.

With Lord Lambton it was 'Lucas'. That is the name he used with Mrs Norma Levy.

And that is the name he used with another call girl who said she worked for the London ring and whom I interviewed three days ago.

Nervous

She is beautiful, well-spoken and so nervous about the present situation that she begged me not to reveal her name. I later went with her to Scotland Yard, where she made a lengthy statement to Deputy Assistant Commissioner Ernest Bond.

She told me: 'I know this man Lucas who paid to indulge in sex with me on two occasions. He was extremely polite but I am afraid I don't think I satisfied him. I must have been a disappointment.

'He came late at night on two dates in April and paid rather more than I got from most clients. I never knew his name until I saw his photograph in the paper. It was definitely Lord Lambton.'

From inquiries made by a team of *News of the World* reporters we have gained evidence which shows that most clients of the London 'Madam' visited many of the girls on her list until such time as they found special rapport with one who gave them complete satisfaction.

Again and again the same client's name would occur.

A well-known television broadcaster, an elderly and highly respected member of the judiciary and a foreign prince are included.

Throughout the whole of the time in which I was in daily contact with Levy and Goodsell I knew that at least one of them kept in close contact with a senior officer at Scotland Yard.

Levy expressed to me the desire to get his wife out of the country as quickly as possible because she was fast becoming neurotic about the situation.

Indeed, on Friday, May 18, Levy was asked to visit a senior officer at Scotland Yard's Serious Crime squad's headquarters, Tintagel House, Victoria.

Later that afternoon I met Levy outside the *News of the World* offices. He was sitting in his car, pale-faced and shaking with nerves.

Duty

He told me he was too frightened to go to meet the officer concerned. I advised him that it was his duty to keep the appointment. After persuasion he agreed to go and drove off.

I subsequently discovered that he had kept the appointment and had later gone to Scotland Yard and been interviewed by Mr Bond.

I also found that by that time the police had in their possession a photograph of Lord Lambton together with the coloured girl Kim Pinder and Mrs Norma Levy – plus a photostat copy of the original Lord Lambton cheque.

News of the World, 27 May 1973.

Lord Lambton has since decamped to Tuscany, where he lives in considerable style in Cetinale, a Renaissance villa once owned by the powerful Chigi family. Lord Jellicoe returned to public life with various business interests and was recently appointed President of the Royal Geographical Society.

....

Spiro's Demise

Vice-President Spiro Agnew accepts bribes

Spiro Agnew, President Richard Nixon's disgraced Vice President, resigned in 1973 after pleading nolo contendere *(not exactly a guilty plea but a statement of unwillingness to contest charges, which technically has the same effect) to an income tax evasion charge on payments made to him by contractors when he was governor of Maryland in 1967. He was fined $10,000 and placed on probation for three years. The prosecution then submitted forty pages of evidence of further charges they would have brought against him. Spiro Agnew, who made a political career out of his hostility to intellectuals and radical students, was later disbarred from practising law.*

The following is Attorney-General Elliott Richardson's statement read to the U.S. District Court dealing with Agnew's case. A few months after Agnew's departure, Nixon sacked Richardson, after he declined to get rid of Professor

Archibald Cox, the independent Watergate prosecutor who was seeking answers to questions that eventually led to Nixon's resignation less than a year later.

May it please the court, I am, like every other participant in these pro-ceedings, deeply conscious of the critical national interests which surround them. The agreement between the parties now before the court is one which must be just and honourable, and which must be perceived to be just and honourable, not simply to the parties but above all to the Amer-ican people.

From the outset of these negotiations which have culminated in these proceedings, the Department of Justice has regarded as an integral require-ment of any agreement a full disclosure of the surrounding circumstances, for only with knowledge of these circumstances can the American people fairly judge the justice of the outcome. One critical component of these circumstances is the Government's evidence. In accordance, therefore, with the agreement of counsel, I offer for the permanent record of these proceedings an exposition of the evidence accumulated by the inves-tigation against the defendant conducted by the office of the United States Attorney for the District of Maryland as of Oct. 10, 1973. Because this exposition is complete and detailed, it is sufficient for present purposes simply to state that this evidence establishes a pattern of substantial cash payments to the defendant during the period when he served as Governor of Maryland in return for engineering contracts with the State of Maryland. Payments by the principal in one large engineering firm began while the defendant was County Executive of Baltimore County in the early nineteen-sixties and continued into 1971. The evidence also discloses payments by another engineer up to and including December, 1972. None of the Government's major witnesses has been promised immunity from prosecution, and each of the witnesses who would testify to having made direct payments to the Vice President has signed a sworn statement subject to the penalties of perjury.

In the light of the serious wrongdoing shown by its evidence, the Government might have insisted, if permitted by the court to do so, on pressing forward with the return of an indictment charging bribery and extortion. To have done this, however, would have been likely to inflict upon the nation serious and permanent scars. It would have been the defendant's right to put the prosecution to its proof. The Department of Justice has conceded the power of Congress, once an indictment had been returned, to proceed by impeachment. The Congress could well have elected to exercise this constitutional power. If the Congress chose not to act, the defendant could, while retaining office, either have insisted upon his right to a trial by jury or have continued to contest the right of the Government to try an incumbent Vice President. Whichever of these courses were followed would have consumed not simply months but years – with potentially disastrous consequences to vital interests of the United States. Confidence in the adequacy of our fundamental institutions would itself have been put to severe trial. It is unthinkable that this nation should have been required to endure the anguish and uncertainty of a prolonged period in which the man next in line of succession to the Presidency was fighting the charges brought against him by his own Government.

On the basis of these considerations, I am satisfied that the public interest is better served by this Court's acceptance of the defendant's plea of *nolo contendere* to a single count information charging income tax evasion.

There remains the question of the Government's position toward the sentence to be imposed. One possible course would have been to avoid this difficult and painful issue by declining to make an affirmative recommendation. It became apparent, however, in the course of the negotiations that without such a recommendation no agreement could be achieved. No agreement could have been achieved, moreover, if that recommendation did not include an appeal for leniency.

I am firmly convinced that in all the circumstances leniency is justified. I am keenly aware, first, of the historic magnitude of the penalties inherent in the Vice President's resignation from his high office and his acceptance of a judgement of conviction for a felony. To propose that a man who has suffered these penalties should, in addition, be incarcerated in a penal institution, however briefly, is more than I, as head of the Government's prosecuting arm, can recommend or wish.

Also deserving of consideration is the public service rendered by the defendant during more than four and one-half years as the nation's second highest elected official. He has been an effective spokesman for the executive branch in the councils of state and local government. He has knowledgeably and articulately represented the United States in meetings with the heads of other governments. He has participated actively and constructively in the deliberations of the Government in a diverse range of fields.

Out of compassion for the man, out of respect for the office he has held, and out of appreciation for the fact that by his resignation he has spared the nation the prolonged agony that would have attended upon his trial, I urge that the sentence imposed on the defendant by this court not include confinement.

US District Court, Baltimore, 10 October 1973.

In his 1980 memoir, Go quietly ... Or Else, *Agnew claimed he was framed by overzealous Baltimore prosecutors. While admitting to receiving the payments, he said they were in fact campaign contributions and that he would have favoured the contractors regardless. His fines and legal costs of approximately $160,000 were paid for him by his friend the entertainer Frank Sinatra. A year later, in 1981, a Maryland court ordered him to repay the state of Maryland a quarter of a million dollars in alleged kickbacks plus interest, that he had actually taken while Governor of Maryland and later as Vice President.*

The real impact of Agnew's resignation was that replacing him with the dull but honest congressman Gerald Ford enabled Congress to contemplate impeaching President Richard Nixon because of his role in the Watergate affair. As long as Agnew stood to inherit the presidency, there were virtually no politicians of either party willing to contemplate Nixon's removal.

....

Cardinal Danielou

Danielou's death in cabaret blonde's flat

Cardinal Jean Danielou's death in the early seventies was as memorable as that of President Faure. Governor Nelson Rockefeller and the Australian Billy Snedden continued the ignoble tradition less than a decade later. The Cardinal's brother was a distinguished mystic who spent a long time studying in Benares on the Ganges in India.

Police Probe Cardinal's Death

French police are investigating the circumstances in which Cardinal Jean Danielou, a senior figure in the French Catholic Church, collapsed and died in the flat of an attractive young blonde who works in an all-night cabaret in Paris.

The police report on the 59-year-old cardinal's death says it assumed that he called on 24-year-old Mrs J. Santoni in the 17th district of Paris to act as her father confessor.

The *Canard Enchaine*, the French satirical weekly, reports in its current issue that requests were made to several French newspapers by Father Coste, head of the Jesuit Order in Paris, asking them to maintain 'extreme discretion' in reporting Cardinal Danielou's death, which was on 20 May. Fr. Coste asked Paris newspapers, according to the *Canard*, to suggest that the Cardinal died in the street.

Mrs Santoni, in an interview published in the Paris newspaper *Meilleur* yesterday, says: 'Too much fuss is being made about this quite unimportant affair. I can confirm that the Cardinal died in my apartment and not in the street. He was fully dressed and collapsed after climbing the four storeys to my flat.'

Last week church officials said that Cardinal Danielou had been calling at Mrs Santoni's flat for about three months to discuss the settlement of an incident involving blackmail of a 'highly placed personage among the cardinal's close circle of friends'. Mrs Santoni told police after the cardinal's death that she did not know he was a cardinal until she saw his photograph on television and that he rarely wore clerical garb when he called.

Cardinal Danielou was a member of the Académie Française, the author of 14 books on theology and head of the theological faculty at Paris University.

Antony Terry, *The Sunday Times*, 9 June 1974.

....

Watergate: The 'Smoking Gun' Tape

Extracts from Watergate tapes

The Watergate affair was the most influential scandal in American history. It forced the resignation of President Richard Nixon, who was about to be impeached over accusations that he attempted to cover up evidence of wrongdoing. It began as a burglary of the Democratic National Headquarters in the Watergate Complex in Washington, D.C., on 17 June 1972. The burglars were, in fact, hired by the Republican Committee to Re-elect the President – or CREEP *as it was more familiarly known – which was answerable to senior White House staff.*

Although Nixon never actually ordered the break-in and may not have even known about it in advance, he obstructed the FBI *investigation and then lied about it. Most of the key work on the press investigation was done by two relatively junior reporters for* The Washington Post *– Carl Bernstein and Robert Woodward. Apart from forcing the removal of a disgraced President, 'Woodstein' created a fashion in Washington for investigative journalism that continues to this day. The other extraordinary thing about the Watergate affair is that it revealed that Nixon actually taped all of his conversations in the Oval Office of the White House. It was the following transcript – the so-called 'smoking gun' tape, recorded less than a week after the break-in – which eventually caused his downfall.*

Nixon further weakened his position by not even bothering to tell his own defence counsel about how damaging the tape was until he was forced by a Congressional Committee to reveal it. After being ordered to release it, Nixon conceded that 'portions ... are at variance with certain of my previous statements', adding feebly that 'the record, in its entirety, does not justify the extreme step of impeachment and removal of a president.'

Congress thought otherwise and he resigned three days after the transcript was released. The following excerpts relate to conversations on 23 June 1972, between Nixon and Robert Haldeman, his Chief of Staff. Interestingly, the amount of time on the transcripts devoted to the cover-up is quite small. The remainder is devoted to minor campaign details and comments on press coverage regarding other political topics. It also includes gems such as Nixon saying 'The arts you know, they're Jews, they're left-wing – in other words, stay away.'

Meeting between Nixon and Haldeman in the Oval Office:

HALDEMAN: Now, on the investigation, you know the Democrat break-in thing, we're back in the problem area because the FBI is not under control, because Gray [Patrick Gray, the FBI Director] doesn't know exactly how to control it and they have – their investigation is now leading into some productive areas – because they've been able to trace the money – not through the money itself – but through the bank sources – the banker. And, and it goes in some directions we don't want it to go. Ah, also there have been some things – like an informant came in off the street to the FBI in Miami who was a photographer or has a friend who is a photographer who developed some films through this guy Barker [Bernard L. Barker, one of the Watergate burglars] and the films had pictures of Democratic National Committee letterhead documents and things. So it's things like that that are filtering in. Mitchell [John Mitchell, former Attorney-General and then head of CREEP] came up with yesterday, and John Dean [John W. Dean III, White House counsel and later Nixon's chief accuser] analysed very carefully last night and concludes, concurs now with Mitchell's recommendation that the only way to solve this, and we're set up beautifully to do it, ah, in that and that – the only network that paid any attention to it last night was NBC – they did a massive story on the Cuban thing.

PRESIDENT: That's right.

H: That the way to handle this now is for us to have Walters [Vernon Walters, deputy director of the CIA] call Pat Gray and just say, 'stay to hell out of this – this is ah, business here we don't want you to go any further on it.' That's not an unusual development, and ah, that would take care of it.

P: What about Pat Gray – you mean Pat Gray doesn't want to?

H: Pat does want to. He doesn't know how to, and he doesn't have, he doesn't have any basis for doing it. Given this, he will then have the basis. He'll call Mark Felt in, and the two of them – and Mark Felt wants to cooperate because he's ambitious—

P: Yeah.

H: He'll call him in and say, 'We've got the signal from across the river to put the hold on this.' And that will fit rather well because the FBI agents who are working on the case, at this point, feel that's what it is.

P: This is CIA? They've traced the money? Who'd they trace it to?

H: Well, they've traced it to a name, but they haven't gotten to the guy yet.

P: Would it be somebody here?

H: Ken Dahlberg.

P: Who the hell is Ken Dahlberg?

H: He gave $25,000 in Minnesota and ah, the check went directly to this guy Barker.

P: It isn't from the Committee though, from Stans [Maurice Stans, finance chairman of CREEP]?

H: Yeah. It is. It's directly traceable and there's some more through some Texas people that went to the Mexican bank which can also be traced to the Mexican bank – They'll get their names today.

H: – and (pause).

P: Well, I mean, there's no way – I'm just thinking if they don't co- operate, what do they say? That they were approached by the Cubans. That's what Dahlberg has to say, the Texans too, that they—

H: Well, if they will. But then we're relying on more and more people all the time. That's the problem and they'll stop if we could take this other route.

P: All right.

H: They say the only way to do that is from White House instructions. And it's got to be Helms [Richard Helms, director of the CIA] and to – ah, what's his name – ? Walters.

P: Walters.

H: And the proposal would be that Ehrlichman and I call them in, and say, ah –

P: All right, fine. How do you call him in – I mean you just – well, we protected Helms from one hell of a lot of things.

H: That's what Ehrlichman says.

P: Of course, this Hunt [E. Howard Hunt, White House 'plumber' and burglar], that will uncover a lot of things. You open that scab there's a hell of a lot of things and we just feel that it would be very detrimental to have this thing go any further. This involves these Cubans, Hunt and a lot of hanky-panky that we have nothing to do with ourselves. Well, what the hell, did Mitchell know about this?

H: I think so. I don't think he knew the details, but I think he knew.

P: He didn't know how it was going to be handled though – with Dahlberg and the Texans and so forth? Well, who was the asshole that did? Is it Liddy [G. Gordon Liddy, another 'plumber', burglar and official at CREEP]? Is that the fellow? He must be a little nuts.

H: He is.

P: I mean he just isn't well screwed on is he? Is that the problem?

H: No, but he was under pressure, apparently, to get more information and as he got more pressure, he pushed the people harder to move harder—

P: Pressure from Mitchell?

H: Apparently.

P: Oh, Mitchell. Mitchell was at the point (unintelligible).

H: Yea.

P: All right, fine, I understand it all. We won't second-guess Mitchell and the rest. Thank God it wasn't Colson [Charles Colson, Nixon's special counsel].

H: The FBI interviewed Colson yesterday. They determined that would be a good thing to do. To have him take an interrogation, which he did, and that – the FBI guys working on the case concluded that there were

one or two possibilities – one, that this is a White House – they don't
think that there is anything at the election committee – they think that
it was either a White House operation and they had some obscure
reasons for it – non-political, or it was a Cuban and the CIA. And after
their interrogation of Colson yesterday, they concluded it was not the
White House, but are now convinced it is a CIA thing, so the CIA turnoff
would—

P: Well, not sure of their analysis, I'm not going to get that involved. I'm
(unintelligible).

H: No, sir, we don't want you to.

P: You call them in.

H: Good deal.

P: Play it tough. That's the way they play it and that's the way we are
going to play it.

H: OK.

P: When I saw the news summary, I questioned whether it's a bunch of
crap, I thought, er, well, it's good to have them off us awhile, because
when they start bugging us, which they have, our little boys will not
know how to handle it. I hope they will though.

H: You never know.

P: Good.

US Senate Watergate Committee Hearings, Washington, DC.

....

Northern Corruption

Poulson's corrupt architectural practice

*Throughout the 1960s, John Poulson ran the largest architectural practice in
Europe, taking annual fees in excess of £1 million. His success stemmed from
his use of political figures such as Reginald Maudling, as well as a local Northern
political figure from the Labour Party, T. Dan Smith. Smith set up a string of
public relations companies which employed key local politicians who then fed
work from their councils to Poulson. He overextended himself and while he was*

assiduous in paying off his political contacts, he neglected to do the same to the taxman, so he filed for bankruptcy in 1972. A subsequent investigation revealed the corruption of the entire enterprise, ending with Poulson being imprisoned.

The following exchange occurred in court between a QC and Poulson concerning a senior civil servant at the Scottish Office, George Pottinger.

QC: If we look at this list, we start with 'H. Huntsman, tailor, £95 13s. 6d.', and surely by no stretch of the imagination, Mr Poulson, could anybody writing up any book of yours have put down a tailor's bill with 'Pottinger' beside it if he had not been told?

ARCHITECT: I'm jolly sure that could have happened many times, and did do, because I found they put all sorts of things against me and...

QC: Yes, but look; I mean, by the greatest stretch of the imagination, could any audit clerk writing down your tailor's bill write down the name of a prominent civil servant alongside it?

ARCHITECT: I don't know.

QC: Is the world full of Pottingers?

ARCHITECT: I've never heard of one before...

QC: Well, look, this is a chap you know, and I suppose you saw him from time to time, did you not?

ARCHITECT: Yes, but I didn't see him much during the course of the house-building, because I hadn't anything to go to Scotland for.

QC: Yes, but, I mean, he said, 'I want a house' – is that right? – and you said 'I'll build it for you', and then you said, I suppose, 'How much do you want it to cost you?', and he said, 'Do I have to worry about that? – is that right?

ARCHITECT: No, he didn't.

QC: Well, you tell me what he did say.

ARCHITECT: I can't remember how it happened, but I am quite sure...

QC: Oh, come. How many houses in the country have you built for senior civil servants? Is it too difficult to remember this one?

ARCHITECT: No, but we don't do many houses...

QC: You will not, of course, have it, will you Mr Poulson, that this was a payment for any sort of services rendered?

ARCHITECT: Of course not. I should be...

QC: Of course not. It would be dreadful, scandalous, would it not?

ARCHITECT: Well, it wouldn't be honest.

Alan Doig, *Corruption and Misconduct in Contemporary British Politics*
(Penguin Books, 1984), pp. 19–20.

'He was a Warrior, a Roman'

Lord Lucan

The disappearance of Lord Lucan in 1973 after the murder of his nanny remains one of the great unsolved mysteries of post-war Britain. There are still occasional stories or television documentaries claiming that he is alive although the most likely explanation is that his corpse ended up somewhere in the English Channel after the bungled murder of his wife. James Fox, a journalist on The Sunday Times, *wrote the most detailed and accurate accounts of the whole affair.*

Just after 10.45pm on Thursday, 7 November last year, four dinner guests invited by Lord Lucan sat down in the Clermont Club, a gambling club in Berkeley Square. The party had been to the Mermaid Theatre to see a musical and Lord Lucan had said that he would meet them later at the club. He was not, however, there when they arrived. Lord Lucan had booked a table for only four people – one place too few. His guests started without him.

Looking back at that evening and at the 48 hours which preceded it, Lord Lucan's small oversight is not, for a gambler, of more than marginal significance. His schedule had involved his meeting a fair number of his regular acquaintances – people who were to become very familiar to the police over the next few weeks.

The previous day he had visited his old friend – and his piano teacher – Caroline Hill at Old Church Street, at about noon. In the afternoon he had gone to Heywood Hill's Bookshop in Curzon Street, where he bought a book about the Greek shipping millionaires. That evening he attended a buffet supper given by Selim Zikha, chairman of the Mothercare chain of shops, for some 40 guests. He played bridge with his friend John Aspinall, founder of the Clermont Club, Aspinall's wife Sarah and Charles Benson – 'Scout' racing correspondent of *The Daily Express*. He went on to the Clermont to play backgammon, and met Andrina Colquhoun, a friend who had got to know him in recent months. He left late. He was drinking heavily, but he had been doing so for several weeks, a fact noted by another friend, Dominick Elwes, the painter.

On Thursday, the day of his disappearance, Lucan rose early – unusual perhaps, since he was an insomniac who tended to stay up late at the gaming tables until he felt he could sleep. He would then stay in bed until late into the morning.

And he telephoned his lawyers. At 10.30am he was telephoned by Andy Colquhoun, who asked him about his dinner plans. She found them 'rather a muddle'. She looked for him at lunchtime and when she couldn't find him decided to drive down to the country instead.

Then there is a gap until 1pm when Lucan called in at his chemist, asking them to identify a pill belonging to his wife which he had brought with him. The chemist told him it was a tranquilliser.

Later that afternoon he visited Michael Hicks Beach, old Etonian and literary agent, for a drink in the flat in Elizabeth Street, Belgravia, where Lucan had lived since the separation almost two years previously from his wife Veronica. He and Hicks Beach discussed an article Lucan was writing on gambling for an Oxford magazine. At about 4pm he drove Hicks Beach home to his flat in Fulham in a Corsair GT he had borrowed two weeks before from another friend, Michael Stoop, old Rugbeian and a top-class backgammon player. He had a few more drinks, returned to his flat in Elizabeth Street, where he changed into a roll-neck sweater and a sleeveless brown pullover. He switched to his Mercedes and drove past the Clermont Club, and talked through the window to Billy, the doorman. He asked whether any of his friends had yet arrived. The answer was 'No'.

In the meantime the Clermont had been getting into full swing. The backgammon had given way to dinner, and the bigger games, chemmy and blackjack, were starting upstairs. There could hardly be a more elegant setting in Europe in which to win or lose the fortunes which the high stakes provided for: the last William Kent house in London, designed in 1742, an architectural masterpiece in marble and gold.

The regulars, the people who took refuge there every night 'because the other places are too vulgar', were settling in. By the time Lucan's guests had arrived the place was full. They included Greville Howard, Old Etonian, one-time assistant to Enoch Powell, now an executive at Slater Walker, who lived in Lucan's mews house, and a friend, Sarah Smith-Ryland. It needed only their host to make up the party.

A mile-and-a-half away, in Belgravia, the house in Lower Belgrave Street where Lady Lucan lived with their three children and a nanny was already teeming with policemen and forensic experts. They had been summoned after a distraught figure had burst into the nearby Plumbers Arms, blood pouring from large gashes in her head. It was Veronica, Countess of Lucan, screaming about an intruder. 'He's in the house ... The children are in the house ... He's murdered the nanny.' Then she collapsed.

At about the same time Lucan was on his way to Uckfield in Sussex, 44 miles away, driving Michael Stoop's Corsair, arriving at 11.30pm at the house of a friend, Susan Maxwell-Scott. (It was not until 48 hours after the murder that Mrs Maxwell-Scott let it be known that Lucan had visited her. 'I had no reason to go to the police,' she said.) On the way to Uckfield, Lucan made a telephone call to his mother in St John's Wood. The call came neither from a call box nor through an operator.

At Mrs Maxwell-Scott's he wrote three letters, whose contents give a confusing picture of his state of mind. Two were written to Bill Shand-Kydd, his brother-in-law, and one to Michael Stoop. He wrote that he had surprised an intruder in the house struggling with his wife. He had rushed inside but the man managed to escape, then ran off. 'I have had a traumatic night of unbelievable coincidence,' he wrote. Lucan thought the evidence looked bad against him for something he had not done, and decided to 'lie doggo for a while'.

His handwriting appears shaky. Mrs Maxwell-Scott told the Press that Lucan had left the house at 1.30am, intending to return to London and to contact the police in the morning. But the car was found at Newhaven, 16 miles away. It was parked in Norman Road, near the harbour, some time between 5am and 8am on Friday morning. How it got there is not known, and here the trail goes cold.

The detectives assigned to the case, Roy Ranson and David Gerring, are both policemen with long experience. Ranson, a former Flying Squad officer in charge of the area that covers Whitehall, Buckingham Palace and Westminster, had recently been working on the Princess Anne shooting case.

He was, and still is, investigating Harold Wilson's missing tax papers. Gerring, 40, had been a divisional officer for 20 years and had worked among other things on the misdeeds of the Richardson gang.

Squad cars from Gerald Road police station arrived at the house in Lower Belgrave Street within a few minutes of the commotion at the Plumbers Arms. Graham Forsythe, a detective sergeant who was to become Veronica Lucan's permanent bodyguard – and almost her only companion for several months, until it was felt that the danger had passed – had the initial task of keeping the children out of sight in the general confusion. Lucan's mother the Dowager Countess Lucan, socialist peeress, arrived soon afterwards. They found, at the bottom of the stairs leading to the basement, the teacups that Sandra Rivett had dropped when her attacker struck. They found the light bulb, removed, lying on a chair. And they found the body of Sandra Rivett in a US mail bag, hideously beaten. They also found the murder weapon – a piece of lead piping carefully wrapped in Elastoplast. A welded iron banister had been prised away by Lady Lucan as she had struggled, successfully, with the attacker. There was blood everywhere.

Three days later Ranson and Gerring were granted a warrant for the arrest of Lucan on a charge of murder and attempted murder. They pressed ahead with their investigations, building up a dossier which includes the names of no fewer than 93 witnesses useful to the prosecution. They launched a massive search for the person, or the body, of Lord Lucan who had vanished into the night.

Ranson and Gerring pieced together the events of the night. Lucan had visited the house in Lower Belgrave Street, but, as his letter confirms, had left in a hurry. He had telephoned a friend in Chester Square, whose children went to school with his own. She remembers very little of the call except that she was certain that it was Lucan. A few minutes before the telephone call she heard a prolonged ringing on her doorbell but was too terrified to go down. (She did not tell the police about this until the Monday. 'It's the police's problem actually,' she explained. 'They're obviously trained to discern these things.') Later she was to find blood on her doorstep.

After the police had made their forensic tests, it proved remarkably difficult to obliterate; the painter Dominick Elwes found himself trying to scrub the stains from the Portland stone.

Lucan's address books provided Ranson and Gerring with an enormous task of investigation. As they dug into the upper crust in alphabetical order, jokes about the antics of 'the nob squad' became social currency, and in return the class feeling in Gerald Road police station built up as they came up against what they saw as a condescending, almost patronising attitude. One witness described how she had been telephoned early next morning and instructed by a friend to say nothing, not to answer the telephone, to get a briefing before talking to the police.

On that same day, Friday, John Aspinall held a lunch for the Lucan inner circle to discuss what might have happened to him. It included Stephen Raphael, 62-year-old stockbroker, who managed whatever stocks Lucan had; William Shand-Kydd, millionaire and amateur jockey, married to Christina, the sister of Veronica Lucan; Daniel Meinhertzhagen, son of a merchant banker, a gambler since leaving Eton; Charles Benson, who had been in Lucan's house at Eton; Jimmy Goldsmith*, Old Etonian, chairman of Cavenham Foods, 7 per cent holder in the Rothschild bank in France; and Dominick Elwes, portrait painter, Old Etonian.

'People were worried,' says John Aspinall, 'about what to do if he (Lucan) turned up. He might have turned up at Howletts (Aspinall's country house and zoo), he might have telephoned from Brazil, so every contingency

* Jimmy Goldsmith was not present at this lunch. (Ed.)

was looked at.' 'Some of the ideas at the meeting,' said Charles Benson, 'were more melodramatic and ludicrous than others.'

At the same time Lady Lucan was lying in hospital with wounds which looked almost as bad as those which had killed Sandra Rivett. She was clearly in need of sympathy. Yet her only visitors were her sister, Christina, her brother-in-law, Hugh Bingham, and Dominick Elwes. They had got to her bedside with some difficulty, to hear her first-hand account of events. Lucan's marriage had become something of a war of attrition between man and wife.

'I went to their marriage with a certain foreboding,' said Aspinall. 'To be blunt, she had no money, she wasn't particularly pretty, and she had a shrewish temperament.'

As the murder story broke, rumours about Lady Lucan began to spring up in quarters where the truth could not conceivably have been known. None had any basis in fact, but their style suggested a morbid imagination. There was a common assumption that she was, to put it mildly, a 'difficult woman' and that therefore Lucan was a man to be sympathised with. 'Lucky' Lucan, as he was sometimes known, became indeed a popular hero – even to those who had only read about him. His wife, according to one married woman who frequents the Clermont, 'was the most disliked woman in London'. The married woman in question had, in fact, never met her. She added: 'You know how it is – when you hear that someone is so disliked, you think she must be awful.'

By the time of the murder, the couple had been separated for almost two years. Lady Lucan had been awarded custody of the children, Lady Frances, Lady Camilla and Lord Bingham. She had been ostracised from the social world of her husband. She was alone. 'The board went down on her, with everyone, stage by stage,' says Aspinall. 'And Lucan's long attachment to her began to curdle.'

Lucan was widely seen, on the other hand, as the model husband, the perfect gentleman, whose patience in a war waged by his wife had bled him dry. There is, however, a different version which may give a wider perspective to the affair. Lucan was an earl in decline, buoyed up by an introverted, almost exclusively male world of smart professional gamblers. His fortunes, and his marriage, were crumbling. Many of his Eton friends had sought refuge in what one of them referred to as 'the boys' clubs', to lead what Dominick Elwes calls, 'a hypercivilised patrician kind of life'. But it was out of tune with the times. Lucan himself seemed almost a throwback, with his strange Crimean face, and views which appeared to be degenerating, under pressure, from paternalistic feudalism to the extreme Right wing – views echoed by many of his friends.

'Lucan,' says Aspinall, 'was my fifth, sixth or seventh best friend. I had known him for 20 years. I saw him as a figure like myself – born out of his own time. His qualities were the old-fashioned ones – loyalty, honesty, reliability. He had the *dignitas* of an aristocrat without the impertinence that goes with a great name or possessions. Lucan was really a leader of men. In fact he wasn't but in more rigorous times he would have found a better role in life. In other words, in a state of war Lucan would have been a valuable acquisition to a country. He wouldn't have had any difficulty in getting loyalty from his men. He was a warrior, a Roman. He was quite capable of falling on his sword, as it were.'

Under the heavy, emotionless face, which one person who played backgammon with him described as 'not so much control as blankness', Lucan's warrior blood would occasionally burst forth. A close friend says: 'Very occasionally one did see a flash of temper, and then it was quite unpleasant. He would get very tensed up and shake – the classic bellicose effect. He would get angry with golf caddies who wouldn't listen, and so on.' Lucan was also proud of the great strength of his Doberman pinscher which would sleep on his bed and chew enormous bones on the Wilton carpet in the drawing room at Lower Belgrave Street. Otto, as it was called, would, however, brutalise Alsatians in the park, and had to be sent away. In his flat in Elizabeth St, Lucan had a collection of Hitler's recorded speeches, many books on psychiatric illness and countless detective novels. His wardrobe contained rows of identical pin-striped suits. He also had a grand piano, had taught himself to play Bach and latterly Scott Joplin rags. 'This was one of the things that he disguised from the world,' says Dominick Elwes, 'because people would have thought it soppy.' Elwes describes his almost fastidious politeness, his *'gentilhommerie'*.

James Fox, *The Sunday Times*, 1974.

CIA's Domestic Agenda

The illegal domestic spying of the CIA

This story led to a number of other equally extraordinary revelations, including those of the Church Committee in the U.S. Senate, which investigated various CIA schemes to assassinate foreign leaders. Seymour Hersh, the Pulitzer-Prize-winning journalist and author, who wrote this article in The New York Times, *also wrote the best follow-up accounts of the My Lai massacre.*

WASHINGTON, Dec. 21 [1974]—The Central Intelligence Agency, directly violating its charter, conducted a massive, illegal domestic intelligence operation during the Nixon Administration against the antiwar movement and other dissident groups in the United States, according to well-placed Government sources.

An extensive investigation by *The New York Times* has established that intelligence files on at least 10,000 American citizens were maintained by a special unit of the CIA that was reporting directly to Richard Helms, then the Director of Central Intelligence and now the Ambassador to Iran.

In addition, the sources said, a check of the CIA's domestic files ordered last year by Mr Helms's successor, James R. Schlesinger, produced evidence of dozens of other illegal activities by members of the CIA inside the United States, beginning in the nineteen-fifties, including break-ins, wire-tapping and the surreptitious inspection of mail.

A Different Category

Mr Schlesinger was succeeded at the CIA by William E. Colby in September, 1973.

Those other alleged operations, in the fifties, while also prohibited by law, were not targeted at dissident American citizens, the sources said, but were a different category of domestic activities that were secretly carried out as part of operations aimed at suspected foreign intelligence agents operating in the United States.

Under the 1947 act setting up the CIA, the agency was forbidden to have 'police, subpoena, law enforcement powers or internal security functions' inside the United States. Those responsibilities fall to the FBI, which maintains a special internal security unit to deal with foreign intelligence threats.

Helms Unavailable

Mr Helms, who became head of the CIA in 1966 and left the agency in February, 1973, for his new post in Teheran, could not be reached despite telephone calls there yesterday and today.

Charles Cline, a duty officer at the American Embassy in Teheran, said today that a note informing Mr Helms of the request by *The Times* for comment had been delivered to Mr Helms's quarters this morning. By late evening Mr Helms had not returned the call.

The information about the CIA came as the Senate Armed Services Committee issued a report today condemning the Pentagon for spying on the White House National Security Council. But the report said the Pentagon spying incidents in 1970 and 1971 were isolated and presented no threat to civilian control of the military.

The disclosure of alleged illegal CIA activities is the first possible connection to rumors that have been circulating in Washington for some time. A number of mysterious burglaries and incidents have come to light since the break-in at Democratic party headquarters in the Watergate complex on June 17, 1972.

Duping Charged

Throughout the public hearings and courtroom testimony on Watergate, Mr Helms and other high-level officials said that the CIA had been 'duped' into its Watergate involvement by the White House.

As part of its alleged effort against dissident Americans in the late nineteen-sixties and early nineteen-seventies, *The Times*'s sources said, the CIA authorized agents to follow and photograph participants in antiwar and other demonstrations. The CIA also set up a network of informants who were ordered to penetrate antiwar groups, the sources said.

At least one avowedly antiwar member of Congress was among those placed under surveillance by the CIA, the sources said. Other members of Congress were said to be included in the CIA's dossier on dissident Americans.

The names of the various Congressmen could not be learned, nor could any specific information about domestic CIA break-ins and wiretappings be obtained.

It also could not be determined whether Mr Helms had had specific authority from the President or any of his top officials to initiate the alleged domestic surveillance, or whether Mr Helms had informed the President of the fruits, if any, of the alleged operations.

Distress Reported

These alleged activities are known to have distressed both Mr Schlesinger, now the Secretary of Defense, and Mr Colby. Mr Colby has reportedly told associates that he is considering the possibility of asking the Attorney General to institute legal action against some of those who had been involved in the alleged domestic activities . . .

When confronted with *The Times*'s information about the CIA's domestic operations earlier this week, high-ranking American intelligence officials confirmed its basic accuracy, but cautioned against drawing 'unwarranted conclusions' . . .

Two months ago, *Rolling Stone* magazine published a lengthy list of more than a dozen unsolved break-ins and burglaries and suggested that they might be linked to as yet undisclosed CIA or FBI activities.

Senator Howard H. Baker Jr., Republican of Tennessee, who was vice chairman of the Senate Watergate committee, has publicly spoken of mysterious CIA links to Watergate. The White House transcripts of June 23, 1972, show President Nixon saying to H. R. Haldeman, his chief of staff, 'Well, we protected Helms from one hell of a lot of things.'

The remark, commented upon by many officials during recent interviews, could indicate Presidential knowledge about the CIA's alleged domestic activities.

The possible Watergate link is but one of the many questions posed by the disclosures about the CIA that *The Times*' sources say they believe can be unravelled only by extensive Congressional hearings.

The CIA domestic activities during the Nixon Administration were directed, the source said, by James Angleton, who is still in charge of the Counterintelligence Department, the agency's most powerful and mysterious unit.

As head of counterintelligence, Mr Angleton is in charge of maintaining the CIA's 'sources and methods of intelligence,' which means that he and his men must ensure that foreign intelligence agents do not penetrate the CIA.

The Times's sources, who included me with access to firsthand knowledge of the CIA's alleged domestic activities, took sharp exception to the official suggestion that such activities were the result of legitimate counter-intelligence needs.

'Look, that's how it started,' one man said. 'They were looking for evidence of foreign involvement in the antiwar movement. But that's not how it ended up. This just grew and mushroomed internally.'

One former CIA official who participated in the 1969 and 1970 White House-directed studies of alleged foreign involvement in the antiwar movement said that Mr Angleton 'undoubtedly believes that foreign agents were behind the student movement, but he doesn't know what he's talking about.'

The official also raised a question about the bureaucratic procedures of the CIA under Mr Helms and suggested that his penchant for secrecy apparently kept the most complete intelligence information from being forwarded to the White House.

'We dealt with Ober and we dealt with Angleton on these studies, went over them point by point,' the official said, 'and Angleton, while not exactly enthusiastic, signed off' – that is, he initiated the study indicating that it represented the views of the Counterintelligence Department.

The former CIA official said that he could not reconcile Mr Angleton's decision to permit the studies, which reported no evidence of foreign involvement, while being involved in an elaborate and secret domestic security operation to root out alleged foreign activities in the antiwar movement. The results of the studies were forwarded to Henry A. Kissinger, then President Nixon's national security adviser.

A number of former FBI officials said in interviews that the CIA's alleged decision to mount domestic break-ins, wiretaps and similarly illegal counterintelligence operations undoubtedly reflected, in part, the long-standing mistrust between the two agencies.

In 1970, Mr Hoover reportedly ordered his bureau to break off all but formal liaison contact with the CIA, forcing lower level CIA and FBI officials to make clandestine arrangements to exchange information.

By the late sixties, one former FBI official said, all but token co-operation between the two agencies on counterintelligence and counterespionage had ended.

'The CIA was never satisfied with the FBI and I can't blame them,' the former official said. 'We did hit-or-miss jobs.'

'Cutting Throats'

'We were constantly cutting the throats of the CIA in our dealings with them. If the White House knew about it, they were too afraid of Hoover to do anything about it.' . . .

Before Mr Hoover's decision to cut off the working relationship, the former official added, the FBI – as the agency responsible for domestic counterintelligence – would, as a matter of policy, conduct a major clandestine inquiry into the past and present CIA men.

Despite Mr Hoover's provocative actions, the former FBI man said, the CIA still was not justified in taking domestic action.

'If they did any surreptitious bag jobs [break-ins],' he said, 'they'd better not have told me about it.'

Seymour M. Hersh, The New York Times, 22 December 1974.

....

The Commissioned Prince

Prince Bernhard of the Netherlands and the Lockheed scandal

Prince Bernhard was the most publicised victim of the fallout from the Lockheed bribery scandal in the 1970s. It affected politicians around the globe, including the Japanese Prime Minister Tanaka.

After the allegations against Prince Bernhard were investigated by a Dutch government enquiry, he stepped down from his position as Inspector General of the Dutch armed forces. While the enquiry failed to find conclusive evidence of the payment to the prince, payments had been made by the company from a Swiss bank account to an associate of the prince's mother. Two other letters came to light in which the prince asked Lockheed for a commission of $US1 million to be paid to him but these particular orders never actually went through. The report's conclusions were hardly a clean bill of health, saying that the German-born prince had 'entered much too lightly into transactions which were bound to create the impression that he was susceptible to favours' and that he had 'showed himself open to dishonourable requests and offers'. The Dutch Prime Minister accepted the commission's conclusions and that they had damaged the national interest. The prince also accepted the report and withdrew from all his military and business connections.

He had told the commission that the million dollars was actually destined for the World Wildlife Fund, of which he was president, but the Fund later denied receiving any money from this source and Prince Bernhard wrote to the Fund to announce that he would step down as president when his term expired in December 1976.

BRUSSELS – Feb. 7—Revelations to a United States Senate subcommittee that the Lockheed Aircraft Corporation had paid $1.1 million to a high Dutch official to aid the 1959 sale of Starfighter jet aircraft to the Dutch forces has raised a storm around Prince Bernhard of the Netherlands, who has been identified by a source close to the investigation in Washington as the official.

The Prince's name was first linked with Lockheed two months ago by a former Lockheed employee, Ernst F. Hauser, who said he had learned from a third source that the Prince had accepted money from the company.

Last night the Dutch Prime Minister, Joop M. den Uyl, said at a news conference that the Dutch Government had no reason at present to accuse the 65-year-old Prince of wrongdoing, but he said that he had instructed the Dutch Ambassador in Washington to obtain all evidence from the subcommittee that could implicate a Dutch official. Foreign Minister Max van der Stoel was in frequent contact with Washington today concerning the affair.

Prime Minister den Uyl stressed the need for good faith and fair play, but added that if evidence arose that proved any Dutchman had been bribed, 'we will not hesitate for a minute to take the necessary steps.'

He also said that if Prince Bernhard was involved, a special act of Parliament that would have to be signed by the Queen would be required for him to be brought to trial.

Today the Dutch press voiced strong suspicions that the Prince, who is the husband of Queen Juliana and serves as inspector general of the Dutch armed forces, was the official who was said by the Lockheed president and vice chairman, A. C. Kotchian, to have received the money.

While the Senate subcommittee on multinational corporations has refused to reveal the name of the Dutch official, a source close to the committee confirmed yesterday in Washington that the official was Prince Bernhard. Today the Amsterdam daily *De Volkskrant* said that its Washington correspondent had also been told by a committee source that the official was the Prince.

Mr Kotchian, in testimony yesterday before the Senate subcommittee headed by Senator Frank Church, Democrat of Idaho, gave details of how Lockheed had paid large bribes overseas to help promote its sales. The company had previously acknowledged that such payments totalled at least $22 million.

Today in The Hague, the Dutch capital, a spokesman for Prince Bernhard said that the Prince had in the past strongly denied accusations similar to those that arose yesterday and that he had no new statement to make.

Meeting with Prince Cited

Prime Minister den Uyl said at his news conference that he had discussed the matter with Prince Bernhard a few months ago when the first accusations arose and that after those talks he had seen no ground for suspicion or for Government action.

However, Piet Dankert, a Labor Party member of the Dutch lower house, declared: 'I think Prince Bernhard's name has popped up too often in press reports here for us not to be suspicious, but we want to know more.'

Mr Dankert and other members of the Dutch Parliament plan to travel to Washington within two weeks to talk to members of the Senate subcommittee about the accusations and try to get more evidence. 'The Dutch Government now has to find out who took the money,' Mr Dankert said. 'The Senate has solved a U.S. problem with Lockheed but has created a Dutch problem.'

Prince Bernhard's name was also linked with the Northrop Corporation earlier this year as a result of United States Senate hearings. During testimony that a Dutch businessman, Teengs Gerritsen, had been paid to represent Northrop interests in the Netherlands, it was revealed that the Northop president, Thomas V. Jones, had once made contact with the Prince, an old acquaintance, for advice on choosing a Northrop representative in the Netherlands.

Calls for Inquiry Rejected

At that time a spokesman for the Prince said there had been nothing improper about the contacts. Calls in Parliament for an investigation of the Prince's activities as inspector general of the forces were turned aside.

Today, Dutch press reports pointed out that as a member of the board of the Fokker–V.F.W. Aircraft Company, which co-operated on the contract for the Lockheed F–104 Starfighters, Prince Bernhard was in a good position to influence the Dutch choice of airplanes.

Prince Bernhard, who is well known to the public as the head of the World Wildlife Foundation and an organizer of discussion groups on international affairs, has also acted for a long time as a good-will ambassador for Dutch business interests.

The House of Orange, of which his wife, Queen Juliana, is the head, is known to be very wealthy, owning, among other things, a sizeable share of the Royal Dutch Shell oil company.

The Lockheed and Northrop affairs are only two of a series of influence-peddling cases that have caused major political interest in the Netherlands in the last year.

The New York Times, 8 February 1976.

....

Some Very Curious Material

Jeremy Thorpe and Norman Scott

This mention was the first inkling that the scandal surrounding Jeremy Thorpe, the leader of the Liberal Party, was about to break, which it did with a vengeance shortly afterwards.

JEREMY THORPE
'A Mr Norman Scott has sent me some very curious material concerning his close friend, the Liberal leader Jeremy Thorpe.

If Mr Thorpe would send me my usual fee of £5, I will send him the dossier and say no more.'

Private Eye, 14 November 1975.

By February 1976, the situation had unravelled enough for the following article to appear, also in Private Eye.

Old but true

'There are things that one passionately wants to keep private, things that are no-one's business. What isn't realised is how professionally I don't expose what I don't want to.'

—*Jeremy Thorpe: 'Behind the Image'*, by Susan Barnes (Cape, 1974).

If Jeremy Thorpe hopes that he has heard the last of the Scott affair he is making a mistake – likewise those Liberals who may be thinking that after a suitable interval when people have forgotten all about the scandal, their leader will step quietly down for reasons other than Scott.

The trouble with such thinking is a) that there may well be more shocks to come and b) that too many loose ends have been left untied after the first batch of revelations.

The first hurdle for the Liberals comes this week when airline pilot Andrew Gino Newton appears before Minehead Magistrates on February 20 charged with possessing a Mauser pistol and ammunition with intent to endanger life.

The charge follows an incident last October when a Great Dane belonging to Norman Scott was found shot dead on Exmoor with Scott weeping over it.

Scott will be the chief prosecution witness and may well take the opportunity to make further remarks about the wretched Thorpe.

This may have been in the Liberal leader's mind when he addressed a gathering of hacks last week and warned them of a 'confrontation' between press and Parliament if the freedom of the witness box was abused and if the papers continued to publish the wild allegations of deranged homosexuals.

Meanwhile it has been reported (*Daily Mail*, Feb. 6) that the police have re-opened an enquiry that began last year as a result of statements made by Scott.

Among matters that they can be expected to investigate are: 1) The role of Peter Bessell, former Liberal MP for Bodmin and business partner of Thorpe. Bessell first said (*Daily Mail*, Feb. 3) that he made a number of payments to Scott as an act of 'charity' – 'I was genuinely sorry for the man and I wanted to help him – as I would any other constituent'.

There was no evidence that Mr Bessell's 'charity' extended to anyone else apart from Scott. Furthermore Bessell reversed himself and told the *Mail* (Feb. 4) it was because 'he began to know too much about my personal life', in particular about his affair with a secretary. . . .

3) There is also the matter of whether any other offences may have been committed. At the time, between 1960 and 1966, that Scott alleged that he had 'a sexual relationship' with Thorpe, such a relationship, should it have existed which the Liberal leader denies, would have been illegal.

But there are many other loose ends which, if they do not interest the police, certainly intrigue the Liberal party and Fleet Street. Among these are: 1) The circumstances in which the Liberal leader met Scott, and also the date of their meeting. Thorpe has merely stated that: 'It is well over 12 years since I last saw or spoke to Mr Scott'.

2) Why Thorpe, who took Scott to his mother's home and arranged for him to stay in Devon with another Liberal candidate, and Bessell, who made such efforts to get Scott his National Insurance cards without ever telling him to adopt the usual procedure for replacing lost cards, went to such lengths to help 'an unfortunate person'.

3) Why there are so many contradictions between Bessell's version of his own meeting and dealings with Scott and the version of Scott himself which on certain points is corroborated.

4) Who was the emissary – 'not someone in the Liberal party' – who came to see the supposedly uncontactable Bessell in New York before Christmas to obtain a statement 'for possible use in a court case for supporting evidence' regarding his payments to Scott – a statement then made public out of court despite a gentleman's agreement not to do so?

5) How and why it was that the Liberal party knew where Bessell was when his creditors were told that the MP had disappeared in 1974.

Even if these matters can be satisfactorily explained there remains the danger, for Thorpe, of further publicity.

By issuing blanket denials of Scott's allegations first to the Liberal party 'kangaroo court' in 1971 as well as earlier this month, Thorpe would run the risk of ending up in a 'Profumo situation' if there was any evidence to contradict him.

Regardless of his personal habits which of course are his own affair, the fact that he told a lie would be eagerly seized on by his enemies as a good reason to give up the leadership of the Liberals. The issue would then change, as it did in the Profumo case, from private morality to 'public interest'.

Private Eye, No. 370, 20 February 1976, p. 16.

Thorpe, who was leader of the Liberal Party from 1967 until 1976, resigned after his sensational acquittal of conspiracy to murder Norman Scott, his alleged former lover.

....

Removing the Executors

The estate of Mark Rothko and Marlborough Galleries

The affair of artist Mark Rothko's estate was perhaps the biggest post-war art scandal. Frank Lloyd, who revolutionised the art market from his Marlborough Fine Art Galleries in London and New York, fled to his home on Paradise Island in the Bahamas to avoid accusations of criminal malfeasance. He was found guilty of tampering with evidence in connection with the lawsuit against him after he surrendered to the New York attorney-general in 1982. Although he faced a prison sentence of up to 12 years, after the fines were paid he was merely forced to set up scholarships to improve art appreciation amongst New York's youth.

Russian-born Rothko came to the United States in 1913, when he was 10 years old. After studying at Yale, he settled in New York, where he went through various artistic phases before arriving at his distinctive style of creating large, looming shapes suspended in space on big rectangular canvases.

Surrogate [an American Judge of Probate] Millard L. Midonick of Manhattan removed yesterday the three executors of the estate of Mark Rothko, the abstract expressionist painter, and assessed damages and fines totalling $9,252,000 against the executors, Frank Lloyd and Mr Lloyd's Marlborough Galleries.

The judge found that the executors had acted in a conflict of interest or negligently in selling and consigning 798 of the artist's paintings to Mr Lloyd for much less than their true value and under terms that were highly disadvantageous to the estate.

The surrogate cancelled the contracts for the transfer of the 798 paintings and directed the return to the estate of any unsold paintings and any others that Mr Lloyd can retrieve.

The case, involving the work of one of the major painters of the abstract expressionist school and one of the most powerful art dealers in the world, was both extremely complex and closely watched. Reacting to the decision yesterday, art dealers and collectors here said that one result could be a reform in the marketing of high-priced art.

The 87-page decision granted most of the requests of Rothko's two children, Kate and Christopher, and of the state's Attorney General, Louis J. Lefkowitz, who joined their suit because Mr Rothko left half of his estate to a charitable foundation.

The damages of $9,252,000 include a fine of $3.3 million against Mr Lloyd and his galleries, which the judge said could be mitigated by return of paintings Mr Lloyd sold in violation of a court order issued after the suit began. Mr Lloyd was held in contempt of court for these sales, which he swore at the trial were made before the injunction.

Rothko committed suicide at 67 on Feb. 25, 1970, in his studio on East 69th Street, leaving an estate consisting principally of the 798 paintings. Art experts testified at the lengthy trial that he was one of the great painters of the 20th century, one of fewer than a dozen leaders in the abstract expressionist movement. One expert, put on the stand by Assistant Attorney General Gustav Harrow, who handled the case for Mr Lefkowitz, testified that the paintings Rothko left were worth $32 million.

The disputed contracts, which Judge Midonick cancelled yesterday, provided for the sale of 100 of the paintings to Marlborough at an average price of $18,000 each and consigned the 698 others to the gallery to be sold at a commission of 50 per cent.

Owner of Global Chain

The contracts were made by Mr Lloyd, owner of a world-wide chain of galleries, and the three executors, within three months of the artist's death. The executors were Bernard J. Reis, an 81-year-old accountant and art collector; Theodoros Stamos, a painter, and Morton Levine, a professor of anthropology.

All three men had been close friends of Rothko's, and Marlborough Gallery had been handling the artist's paintings at his death.

Judge Midonick held yesterday that Mr Reis, who was secretary-treasurer of Marlborough Gallery in New York at the time the contract was signed, and Mr Stamos, who became its client later, acted in conflict of interest. He held them liable, with Mr Lloyd and the Marlborough Galleries, for the total amount of damages and fines – $9,252,000 – individually and severally.

Mr Levine broke from the other two executors, engaged his own lawyer, and testified at the trial that the two other executors had 'pressured' him into signing the contracts. Judge Midonick ruled yesterday that Mr Levine was negligent, and liable for $6 million of the damages. The damages are to be paid to the Rothko estate, in which the Rothko children and a charitable foundation share equally.

Commissions Are Denied

The case began when a suit was filed on behalf of Kate Rothko, then a minor, on Nov. 23, 1971. The guardian of her younger brother, Christopher, joined the suit and the Attorney General also entered it. They all alleged that the executors had wasted the assets of the estate and demanded their dismissal and cancellation of the contracts.

Surrogate Midonick, in his decision yesterday, said that evidence adduced at the trial showed a 'curious atmosphere involving absence of hard bargaining, arm's-length negotiations, deliberate consideration and the presence of improvidence and waste verging upon gross negligence on the part of all the executors as well as breach of duty of disinterested loyalty on the part of the executor Reis and the executor Stamos'.

'The acts and failures-to-act of the three executors were clearly improper,' the contracts they made had 'unconscionably low provision as to price and ... unreasonably long payout-term ... indefiniteness of minimum price provision,' Judge Midonick held.

He added that 'the fact that Levine did not receive any personal gain will not free him from responsibility to the beneficiaries since his improvident actions assisted in causing loss to the estate. The court is therefore constrained to hold Levine liable for his participation in the wrongful acts of his two co-fiduciaries.'

Mr Lloyd was not named in the original suit. During the trial, Mr Harrow, who went to Europe during a short recess to do some detective work in art galleries, asked the judge to hold Mr Lloyd in contempt for selling Rothko estate paintings in violation of the court's injunction.

Mr Lloyd, a dapper, Viennese-born third-generation art dealer, denied the charge, and produced documents to rebut it. He also testified that he had not been served with a copy of the injunction.

In his decision yesterday, Judge Midonick said, 'It is clear that this litigation was the occasion for a sale of consigned paintings at inadequate prices.' The Marlborough Galleries, the judge continued, 'at the discretion of Lloyd, wilfully disposed of estate paintings in bulk resulting in falsely low prices at the time of such sales.'

The judge also found that the 100 canvases sold by the executors to Marlborough were re-sold by the gallery and its affiliates 'at retail from 6 to 10 times' the purchase price.

The gallery and its affiliates 'were certainly aware of the conflict of interest and as such are chargeable with notice that the executors were committing a breach of their duty,' the judge said. And at another point he said 'the conclusion must be that Lloyd is Marlborough.'

Edith Evans Asbury, *The New York Times*, 19 December 1975.

....

'The Sky Is The Limit with Beauty, Ability'

Junie Morosi and Jim Cairns

Miss Junie Morosi was a key assistant for Dr Jim Cairns, the former deputy Prime Minister of Australia under Gough Whitlam. Dr Cairns, a former policeman who studied part time before going to University to earn a doctorate, was a well-known radical who was at the forefront of the Australian protest movement against the war in Vietnam. Dr Cairns has retired from politics and now devotes himself to green politics. This account of Miss Morosi appeared in 1975.

Miss Junie Morosi's seven-month leap to stardom as Australia's most talked about Girl Friday coincided with the equally meteoric decline of her boss, Dr Jim Cairns.

Few outside her own circle of friends and business acquaintances had heard of the good-looking, 41-year-old mother-of-three until she joined Dr Cairns's staff last December.

Three years ago an article appeared on her as a busy sales manager of an airline. 'The sky is the limit with beauty, ability' was the headline. She was a newsmaker again last August as one of Australia's first civil marriage celebrants.

But it was on December 1 of last year that the nation began to hear of Miss Morosi with an intensity that at times rivalled coverage of a major war.

With the first reports of her pending appointment as the office co-ordinator of the Deputy Prime Minister and new Treasurer, Dr Cairns, Miss Morosi was a star, the details of her public and private life part of the common knowledge.

Photographs showing her Eurasian good looks helped to spice the drama of the many controversies that have engulfed Miss Morosi and Dr Cairns since December.

On December 4, amid questions about her qualifications for the job in Dr Cairns's office, a letter from the then Attorney-General, Senator Lionel Murphy, to the Minister for the Capital Territory, Mr Gordon Bryant, was leaked. The letter asked that Miss Morosi be given a priority allocation of a cheap government flat in Canberra, enabling her to jump a three-year waiting list.

The Morosi Affair, as it quickly and popularly became known, almost ended with that letter and the series of revelations and accusations that followed in rapid succession.

Her husband, Mr David Ditchburn, an airline executive, was reported to have been appointed to the Government's Film Review Board. Questions were raised in Parliament about the couple's business transactions. By 5 December, just four days after the furore began, Miss Morosi announced she would quit her job.

The decision brought relief to Labor MPs who feared the controversy over Miss Morosi would prove costly to Dr Cairns, Senator Murphy (now a High Court judge) and the Labor Government as a whole. But their relief proved to be short-lived. On December 11, Dr Cairns announced she would work for him after all. A NSW Corporate Affairs Commission investigation found no grounds for legal action.

Her job status resembled a Ping-Pong match for weeks. She was staying, she was quitting. Finally she stayed and the controversy simmered.

On January 17, her home in Sydney was broken into and a government document taken. Dr Cairns told Parliament that several Liberal Party MPs were part of the burglary conspiracy and he once again emotionally defended his secretary.

But the burglary was soon in the background, overwhelmed by a fresh series of allegations over Miss Morosi's business dealings.

The allegations made on February 20 renewed pressure on Dr Cairns to sack his secretary. He refused, saying he would rather quit first. As before, the controversy faded away, and as before Miss Morosi stayed on the job.

Miss Morosi was never far from the limelight; she accompanied her boss in mid-March on an official trip to the Middle East, attracting the fancy of photographers at every stop.

She was by then a full-fledged media superstar. It was news when she was ill in early April; it was news when she went on another business trip with Dr Cairns in mid-April; it was news when Dr Cairns hired other women for his staff; and what Junie Morosi thought about love and sex and career women was news.

Her birth in Shanghai, her first marriage in Manila at 15, her three sons by the time she was 18, her jobs as a reporter, saleswoman, airline hostess had all become important.

When Dr Cairns was forced to step down in early June from the Treasurer's post to the junior portfolio of Minister for the Environment, it was Miss Morosi who was photographed at his side as he went to get the bad news in Parliament House.

She remained with him as his private secretary when he switched portfolios. She was remaining loyal to Dr Cairns, the man whose political career was on the line, the man who had defended her against all critics, the man who had called her a victim of sexism, racism and sensationalism.

The Australian, 2 July 1975.

Two years later, this story appeared in The Herald:

Morosi Job an Affront – Jury

SYDNEY—A Supreme Court jury found yesterday that Junie Morosi was a 'disreputable and incompetent person'.

It also found that her civil service appointment was an affront to the nation and the feelings of the community.

The 12-man jury's findings were made in reply to a series of questions about the imputations and truth of stories published about Morosi between December 5, 1974, and November 25, 1975.

Morosi, 43, a personal assistant to the former Deputy Prime Minister and Treasurer, Dr Cairns, claims she was defamed by Mirror Newspapers Ltd. in eight articles and one cartoon published in *The Daily Telegraph*, *The Sunday Telegraph* and *The Australian*.

The jury returned with its decision at 2 p.m. yesterday, after being sent out at 11 a.m. Monday by the Chief Judge at Common Law, Mr Justice Taylor.

Discreditably

Other imputations contained in the stories which the jury found to be substantially true were:

She was an undesirable person lacking in the qualities and capacities demanded of a public servant.

She was involved in shady business and company transactions and suspicious commercial transactions which required close investigation.

She became an embarrassment and liability to the Labor Government in general and Mr Whitlam, Senator Murphy and Dr Cairns in particular.

She was discreditably connected with the alleged misdeeds, scandals and improprieties of the Whitlam Government. She was discreditably connected with the alleged incompetence of the Whitlam Government. She and her appointment to the civil service were contributing factors to the unpopularity of the Whitlam Government. She and her appointment to the civil service was one of the scandals and improprieties attributed to the Whitlam Government.

Imputations contained in the stories which the jury found were not substantially true were:

That the then Prime Minister, Mr Whitlam, disapproved of her, considered her unfit for her job and ordered her to be dismissed.

That she had attempted to get preferential treatment by means of improper pressure and influence.

That she was a promiscuous person.

That she was a disreputable individual whose employment with the Labor Government endangered that Government and the reputations of those in it.

The jury also found that one of the stories imputed she had a romantic attachment with Dr Cairns. They were not asked to find whether this was substantially true or not.

They were also not asked to decide the truth of another imputation that she unlawfully obtained and gained access to certain persons and places for improper purposes and for her own advancement and profit.

The imputation that Morosi's dismissal was canvassed by parliamentarians was true.

Mr Justice Taylor dismissed the jury for the afternoon after receiving its answer and heard legal argument from Mr A. B. Shand, QC, for Mirror Newspapers, and Mr C. R. Evatt, QC, for Morosi.

The argument centred around the imputations which the jury failed to find were substantially true.

The Herald (Melbourne), 20 April 1977.

The Case of the Exploding Cigar

The CIA plot to assassinate Fidel Castro

US Senator Frank Church's 1975 Commission into the CIA was the most candid account ever released about a government's intelligence service attempts to assassinate foreign leaders. Although there were several foreign leaders on the CIA's hit list, none of the plans managed to achieve their objective. The plots against Cuba's Communist dictator Fidel Castro were the most bizarre. Richard Helms was the former head of the CIA and Richard Bissell the CIA official in charge of Operation Mongoose, the code name describing the various assassination plots.

(iv) Castro

The efforts to assassinate Fidel Castro took place in an atmosphere of extreme pressure by Eisenhower and Kennedy Administration officials to discredit and overthrow the Castro regime. Shortly after Castro's ascendancy to power, Allen Dulles directed that 'thorough consideration' be given to the 'elimination' of Castro. Richard Helms recalled that:

> I remember vividly [that the pressure] was very intense. And therefore, when you go into the record, you find a lot of nutty schemes there and those nutty schemes were borne of the intensity of the pressure. And we were quite frustrated.

Bissell recalled that:

> During that entire period, the Administration was extremely sensitive about the defeat that had been inflicted, as they felt, on the U.S. at the Bay of Pigs, and were pursuing every possible means of getting rid of Castro.

Another CIA official stated that sometime in the Fall of 1961 Bissell was:

> *** chewed out in the Cabinet Room in the White House by both the President and the Attorney General for, as he put it, sitting on his ass and not doing anything about getting rid of Castro and the Castro Regime.

General Lansdale informed the agencies co-operating in Operation MON-GOOSE that 'you're in a combat situation where we have been given full command.' Secretary of Defense McNamara confirmed that 'we were hysterical about Castro at the time of the Bay of Pigs and thereafter.'

Many of the plans that were discussed and often approved contemplated violent action against Cuba. The operation which resulted in the Bay of Pigs was a major paramilitary onslaught that had the approval of the highest government officials, including the two Presidents. Thereafter, Attorney General Kennedy vehemently exhorted the Special Group (Augmented) that 'a solution to the Cuban problem today carried top priority *** no time, money, effort – or manpower is to be spared.' Subsequently, Operation MONGOOSE involved propaganda and sabotage operations aimed toward spurring a revolt of the Cuban people against Castro. Measures which were considered by the top policymakers included incapacitating sugar workers during harvest season by the use of chemicals; blowing up bridges and production plants; sabotaging merchandise in third countries – even those allied with the United States – prior to its delivery to Cuba; and arming insurgents on the island. Programs undertaken at the urging of the Administration included intensive efforts to recruit and arm dissidents within Cuba, and raids on plants, mines, and harbors. Consideration and approval of these measures may understandably have led the CIA to conclude that violent actions were an acceptable means of accomplishing important objectives.

Discussions at the Special Group and NSC meetings might well have contributed to the perception of some CIA officials that assassination was a permissible tool in the effort to overthrow the Castro Regime. At a Special Group meeting in November 1960, Under-secretary Merchant inquired whether any planning had been undertaken for 'direct, positive action' against Che Guevara, Raul Castro, and Fidel Castro. Cabell replied that such a capability did not exist, but he might well have left the meeting with the impression that assassination was not out of bounds. Lansdale's plan, which was submitted to the Special Group in January 1962, aimed at inducing 'open revolt and overthrow of the Communist regime.' Included in its final phase was an 'attack on the cadre of this regime, including key leaders'. The proposal stated that 'this should be a "Special Target" operation ***. Gangster elements might have proved the best recruitment potential against police ***.' Although Lansdale's proposal was shelved, the type of aggressive action contemplated was not formally ruled out. Minutes from several Special group meetings contain language such as 'possible removal of Castro from the Cuban scene'.

On several occasions, the subject of assassination was discussed in the presence of senior Administration officials. Those officials never consented to actual assassination efforts, but they failed to indicate that assassination was impermissible as a matter of principle.

In early 1961, McGeorge Bundy was informed of a CIA project described as the development of a capability to assassinate. Bundy raised no objection and, according to Bissell, may have been more affirmative. Bissell stated that he did not construe Bundy's remarks as authorization for the underworld plot against Castro that was then underway. But the fact that he believed that the development of an assassination capability had, as he subsequently told Harvey, been approved by the White House, may well have contributed to the general perception that assassination was not prohibited.

Documents received by the Committee indicate that in May 1961, Attorney General Kennedy and the Director of the FBI received information that the CIA was engaged in clandestine efforts against Castro which included the use of Sam Giancana and other underworld figures. The various documents referred to 'dirty business', 'clandestine efforts', and 'plans' which were still 'working' and might eventually 'pay off'. The Committee is unable to determine whether Hoover and the Attorney General ever inquired into the nature of the CIA operation, although there is no evidence that they did so inquire. The Committee believes that they should have inquired, and that their failure to do so was a dereliction of their duties.

Documents indicate that in May 1962, Attorney General Kennedy was told that the CIA had sought to assassinate Castro prior to the Bay of Pigs. According to the CIA officials who were present at the briefing, the Attorney General indicated his displeasure about the lack of consultation rather than about the impropriety of the attempt itself. There is no evidence that the Attorney General told the CIA that it must not engage in assassination plots in the future.

At a meeting of the Special Group (Augmented) in August 1962, well after the assassination efforts were underway, Robert McNamara is said to have raised the question of whether the assassination of Cuban leaders should be explored, and General Lansdale issued an action memorandum assigning the CIA the task of preparing contingency plans for the assassination of Cuban leaders. While McCone testified that he had immediately made it clear that assassination was not to be discussed or condoned, Harvey's testimony and documents which he wrote after the event indicate that Harvey may have been confused over whether McCone had objected to the use of assassination, or whether he was only concerned that the subject not be put in writing. In any event, McCone went no further. He issued no general order banning consideration of assassination within the Agency.

One of the programs forwarded to General Lansdale by the Defense Department in the MONGOOSE program was entitled 'Operation Bounty' and envisioned dropping leaflets in Cuba offering rewards for the assassination of Government leaders. Although the plan was vetoed by Lansdale, it indicates that persons in agencies other than the CIA perceived that assassination might be permissible.

While the ambivalence of Administration officials does not excuse the misleading conduct by Agency officials or justify their failure to seek explicit permission, this attitude displayed an insufficient concern about assassination which may have contributed to the perception that assassination was an acceptable tactic in accomplishing the Government's general objectives.

Moreover, with the exception of the tight guidelines issued by the Special Group (Augmented) concerning Operation MONGOOSE, precise limitations were never imposed on the CIA requiring prior permission for the details of other proposed covert operations against Cuba.

No general policy banning assassination was promulgated until Helms' intra-agency order in 1972. Considering the number of times the subject of assassination had arisen, Administration officials were remiss in not explicitly forbidding such activity.

The committee notes that many of the occasions on which CIA officials should have informed their superiors of the assassination efforts but failed to do so, or did so in a misleading manner, were also occasions on which Administration officials paradoxically may have reinforced the perception that assassination was permissible.

For example, when Bissell spoke with Bundy about an Executive Action capability, Bissell failed to indicate that an actual assassination operation was underway, but Bundy failed to rule out assassination as a tactic.

In May 1962, the Attorney General was misleadingly told about the effort to assassinate Castro prior to the Bay of Pigs, but not about the operation that was then going on. The Attorney General, however, did not state that assassination was improper.

When a senior Administration official raised the question of whether assassination should be explored at a Special Group meeting, the assassination operation should have been revealed. A firm written order against engaging in assassination should also have been issued by McCone if, as he testified, he had exhibited strong aversion to assassination.

5. PRACTICES CURRENT AT THE TIME IN WHICH THE ASSASSIN-

ATION PLOTS OCCURRED WERE REVEALED BY THE RECORD TO
CREATE THE RISK OF CONFUSION, RASHNESS AND IRRES-
PONSIBILITY IN THE VERY AREAS WHERE CLARITY AND SOBER
JUDGEMENT WERE MOST NECESSARY

Various witnesses described elements of the system within which the
assassination plots were conceived. The Committee is disturbed by the
custom that permitted the most sensitive matters to be presented to the
highest levels of Government with the least clarity. We view the following
points as particularly dangerous:

(1) The expansion of the doctrine of 'plausible denial' beyond its
intended purpose of hiding the involvement of the United States from
other countries into an effort to shield higher officials from knowledge,
and hence responsibility, for certain operations.

(2) The use of circumlocution or euphemism to describe serious matters –
such as assassination – when precise meanings ought to be made
clear.

(3) The theory that general approval of broad covert action programs is
sufficient to justify specific actions such as assassination or the passage of
weapons.

(4) The theory that authority granted, or assumed to be granted, by one
DCI or one Administration could be presumed to continue without the
necessity for reaffirming the authority with successor officials.

(5) The creation of covert capabilities without careful review and authorization by policymakers, and the further risk that such capabilities, once
created, might be used without specific authorization.

(a) The danger inherent in overextending the doctrine of 'plausible denial'

The original concept of 'plausible denial' envisioned implementing covert
actions in a manner calculated to conceal American involvement if the
actions were exposed. The doctrine was at times a delusion and at times a
snare. It was naive for policymakers to assume that sponsorship of actions
as big as the Bay of Pigs invasion could be concealed. The Committee's
investigation of assassination and the public disclosures which preceded
the inquiry demonstrate that when the United States resorted to cloak-
and-dagger tactics, its hand was ultimately exposed. We were particularly
disturbed to find little evidence that the risks and consequences of disclosure were considered.

We find that the likelihood of reckless action is substantially increased when policymakers believe that their decisions will never be revealed. Whatever can be said in defense of the original purpose of plausible denial – a purpose which intends to conceal United States involvement from the outside world – the extension of the doctrine to the internal decision-making process of the Government is absurd. Any theory which, as a matter of doctrine, places elected officials on the periphery of the decision-making process is an invitation to error, an abdication of responsibility, and a perversion of democratic government. The doctrine is the antithesis of accountability.

(b) The danger of using 'Circumlocution' and 'Euphemism'

According to Richard Bissell, the extension of 'plausible denial' to internal decision-making required the use of circumlocution and euphemism in speaking with Presidents and other senior officials.

Explaining this concept only heightens its absurdity. On the one hand, it assumes that senior officials should be shielded from the truth to enable them to deny knowledge if the truth comes out. On the other hand, the concept assumes that senior officials must be told enough, by way of double talk, to grasp the subject. As a consequence, the theory fails to accomplish its objective and only increases the risk of misunderstanding, Subordinate officials should describe their proposals in clear, precise, and brutally frank language; superiors are entitled to, and should demand, no less.

Euphemism may actually have been preferred – not because of 'plausible denial' – but because the persons involved could not bring themselves to state in plain language what they intended to do. In some instances, moreover, subordinates may have assumed, rightly or wrongly, that the listening superiors did not want the issue squarely placed before them. 'Assassinate,' 'murder' and 'kill' are words many people do not want to speak or hear. They describe acts which should not even be proposed, let alone plotted. Failing to call dirty business by its rightful names may have increased the risk of dirty business being done.

(c) The danger of generalized instructions

Permitting specific acts to be taken on the basis of general approvals of broad strategies (e.g., keep Allende from assuming office, get rid of the Castro regime) blurs responsibility and accountability. Worse still, it increases the danger that subordinates may take steps which would have been disapproved if the policymakers had been informed. A further danger is that policymakers might intentionally use loose general instructions to evade responsibility for embarrassing activities.

In either event, we find that the gap between the general policy objectives and the specific actions undertaken to achieve them was far too wide.

It is important that policymakers review the manner in which their directives are implemented, particularly when the activities are sensitive, secret, and immune from public scrutiny.

(d) The danger of 'Floating Authorization'

One justification advanced by Richard Helms and William Harvey for not informing John McCone about the use of underworld figures to attempt to assassinate Fidel Castro was their assertion that the project had already been approved by McCone's predecessor, Allen Dulles, and that further authorization was unnecessary, at least until the operation had reached a more advanced state.

We find that the idea that authority might continue or 'float' from one administration or director to the next and that there is no duty to reaffirm authority inhibits responsible decision-making. Circumstances may change or judgements differ. New officials should be given the opportunity to review significant programs.

(e) The problems connected with creating new covert capabilities

The development of a new capability raises numerous problems. Having a capability to engage in certain covert activity increases the probability that the activity will occur, since the capability represents a tool available for use. There is the further danger that authorization for the mere creation of a capability may be misunderstood as permitting its use without requiring further authorization.

Finally, an assassination capability should never have been created.

Church Commission Report, 1975

....

I Danced with a Man, Who Slept with a Girl . . .

President Kennedy and Mrs Exner

President John F. Kennedy was probably the most libidinous American President in history, once famously confiding to a startled British Prime Minister (Harold Macmillan) that he always suffered from a headache if he did not manage coitus at least once a day. It later transpired that he and his brother Robert had both enjoyed the favours of Marilyn Monroe while Kennedy was President. JFK managed to keep his affairs completely secret during his Presidency. This was partly because of his numerous friendships with Washington journalists who knew exactly what he was getting up to but would never dream of writing about it. A decade later, in the wake of the Watergate scandal, there was no such restraint exercised by the media, as shown by this 1975 account, the first of many to appear in The New York Times. *In this instance, it was his girlfriend's indirect connections with organised crime that caused the problem. After the revelations of Mrs Exner's relationship with the President were published, her former husbands expressed surprise, describing her as a 'quiet, family kind of girl'.*

SAN DIEGO. Dec. 17—Judith Campbell Exner maintained today that, although she had had a close personal relationship with President Kennedy while she was dating two leaders of a Chicago crime syndicate, she had never acted as an intermediary between the mafia and the White House.

At a news conference here called to dispel what she termed 'wild-eyed speculation', Mrs Exner, who is about 41 years old, said she had never discussed with Mr Kennedy her relationships with the late Sam Giancana, then head of the Chicago syndicate, or John Rosselli, an associate of Mr Giancana.

Nor, she said, had she ever been aware during the time she was seeing President Kennedy and the two crime figures that Mr Giancana and Mr Rosselli were helping the Central Intelligence Agency to recruit agents in an unsuccessful plot to assassinate Prime Minister Fidel Castro of Cuba.

Mr Castro's name, the woman said, was never mentioned in the numerous telephone conversations she had with Mr Kennedy, beginning in March 1961, or during what she said were a number of private White House lunches in the President's office.

Mrs Exner, whose tanned face was partly hidden behind saucer-shaped sunglasses, said that all of her discussions with the President, whom she said she had also seen on some occasions while he was travelling outside of Washington, were entirely 'of a personal nature'.

Mrs Exner declined to comment on a report that she had spent some time with Mr Kennedy in Palm Beach, Florida, but she said that she had paid for whatever trips she had taken to meet Mr Kennedy when he was travelling around the country.

She added that, although she had not worked during the two years that she was close to Mr Kennedy, she 'was always financially able to take care of myself'. She said she got her money from her family.

She repeatedly declined to elaborate on her relationship with any of the three men and replied with a 'no comment' when asked whether she had also known the late Robert F. Kennedy, the President's brother, who served as Attorney General in the Kennedy Administration.

A Government source said, however, that Mrs Exner was known to have attended 'a party or two' with Robert Kennedy when he was the Attorney General.

In a prepared statement read before reporters and cameramen crowded into a suite at the downtown Westgate Hotel, Mrs Exner, who was accompanied by her attorney, Brian Monaghan, and her husband of eight months, Daniel Exner, said that she hoped to 'set the record straight' about her relationships with the Mafia, which have been the subject of leaks to newsmen from the Senate Select Committee on Intelligence, and about what she called 'distortions' concerning her friendship with 'Jack Kennedy' by former White House aides . . .

Mrs Exner declined today to name the friend who introduced her to Mr Kennedy and then to Mr Giancana, but Senate sources identified him as Frank Sinatra, the singer.

Lawyers for Mr Sinatra, whom Mrs Exner described as a 'friend', had no immediate comment on his alleged involvement.

Asked whether she had been aware at the time that Mr Giancana and Mr Rosselli were important figures in the Mafia, Mrs Exner said at first that she 'didn't really know', but conceded later that she 'probably knew they were members of the underworld'.

Although she said that, to her knowledge, Mr Kennedy had not known that she was also seeing the two Mafia figures, Mrs Exner added that she thought Mr Giancana was aware of her relationship with the President, although she said she never told him of it or discussed it with the Chicago crime leader. Mr Giancana was slain last June 20 at his home in Oak Park, Illinois.

Mrs Exner emphatically denied reports that she had called Mr Kennedy at the White House from a telephone in Mr Giancana's home. One source familiar with the records obtained by the Senate committee said they showed at least one such call from Oak Park, although not necessarily from the Giancana residence.

Asked whether she had ever called Mr Kennedy from her own home in Los Angeles or anywhere else, Mrs Exner, who seemed nervous during most of her 45-minute appearance, quickly answered, 'Oh, yes.'...

Jack Warner, a spokesman for the Secret Service in Washington, declined today to say whether his organization had any record that Mrs Exner had ever been cleared for admission to the White House or to the President's office.

Mr O'Donnell was travelling and could not be reached for comment. Mrs Lincoln, [President Kennedy's private secretary] according to the Senate report, told the committee that she had received a copy of Mr Hoover's Feb. 27 memorandum describing Mrs Exner's Mafia associations and 'believed she would have shown it to the President'.

Angie Novello, who was Robert Kennedy's secretary when he was Attorney General, said in a telephone interview today that, while she did not recall seeing the memorandum, it might have been delivered directly to the Attorney General by the F.B.I. agent who then acted as the bureau's liaison with the Justice Department.

Worked in Primary

Mrs Lincoln reportedly told the Senate panel that she recalled Mrs Exner only as a worker in the President's California primary campaign in 1960, and did not believe the woman had ever seen Mr Kennedy at the White House or anywhere else after his election in November 1960. Mr O'Donnell reportedly endorsed this recollection.

Mrs Exner expressed irritation today at what she characterized as efforts by Mrs Lincoln and Mr O'Donnell 'to sully or distort my personal relationship with Jack Kennedy'.

'To me he was Jack Kennedy and not the President,' Mrs Exner said.

Mrs Lincoln's friends said she was travelling in Europe and could not be reached for comment. Mrs Exner said that, whenever she called the White House, she would 'always talk to Evelyn Lincoln first', and would then be put through to the President immediately, 'if that was my purpose for calling'.

Pressed by reporters to say what other reason she might have had for calling the White House, Mrs Exner said she could think of none...

One source familiar with the evidence said there was 'some indication' that Miss Campbell attempted to call the President after March 22, 1962, but that she was rebuffed.

Mrs Exner said today, however, that 'Jack Kennedy and I last talked in late 1962,' about a year before the President was assassinated in Dallas on Nov. 22, 1963.

She said she last spoke to Mr Giancana toward the end of 1964, and had not talked to Mr Rosselli for 'five or six years'.

Mrs Exner said that the Senate committee staff had read portions of the file compiled on her by the FBI in the course of her testimony, and that what she heard seemed 'prying, insidious and sounded more like a scandal sheet than a governmental investigation'.

John M. Crewsden, *The New York Times*, 18 December 1975

···

The Resignation Honours 'Farce'

Harold Wilson's resignation Honours List

The list of recipients of peerages and knighthoods from Sir Harold Wilson's last Government in 1976 raised almost as much of a storm as the Lloyd George list half a century earlier. Known also as 'The Lavender List', because it was allegedly based on a list prepared on the lavender-coloured notepaper of Lady Falkender, Wilson's private secretary, it included some individuals whose companies contributed to the Conservative Party. A columnist in The Times *claimed that 'No honours list, resignation or otherwise, has ever been attended by such farce' while the normally sympathetic* Guardian *called it 'frankly distressing'.*

Some of Wilson's inner circle accused Lady Falkender of being responsible for the inclusion of such unlikely friends of the Labour Party – a charge she heatedly denied. Instead, she thought the comments were a 'sanctimonious protest by the unimaginative half of the Establishment on their own behalf'. However, Joe Haines, Wilson's press secretary, claimed that 'the substantial majority of the knights and peers who were in the published list were those originally proposed by Lady Falkender.' The Times published the following editorial on the whole affair the day after the story broke.

Sir Harold Wilson's resignation Honours List had been widely leaked beforehand and the leaks have proved largely correct. There seems to have been one or two revisions but the list remains a bizarre one for a socialist ex-Prime Minister. If one takes the baronies and knighthoods, a majority go to people who are very clearly capitalists, and capitalists of tough, risk-taking types. These are not, by and large, the men who run the great industrial companies, but men who have carved out their own fortunes with their own sharp swords.

Some of them are men that one would genuinely admire and like. Sir Max Rayne is one of the kindest and most philanthropic men in London, but when one reads the roll of honour: Delfont, Grade, Kagan, Rayne, Weidenfeld, Goldsmith, Hanson, Miller, Sternberg, the impression it creates with cumulative and striking force is one of unrepentant Darwinism, of the business survival of the fittest and of nature red in tooth and claw.

There is a view, with which we have some sympathy, that the dismal lack of enterprise that has overcome Britain in the years since 1964 can only be overcome by an injection of a more ruthless, capitalist, spirit. Certainly, if the more than Egyptian lassitude of the socialist years is to be shaken into life, it will be done by men of this kind, rather than by the more bureaucratic and under-ambitious leaders of British industry. These men represent the surviving wild strains of capitalists in their threatened habitat, and it is very appropriate that Mr Goldsmith's knighthood should refer to his service to ecology.

Whether these untamed capitalists hold theoretically socialist views or not, it is they – the tigers and the wild dogs free ranging on the veldt – rather than the captive pseudo-capitalists on display in the safari park of the CBI, who are capable of destroying socialism. They mostly have to a high degree the real capitalist motive as the great principle of their lives. They are men who want to make money, and most of them know how to do it. One would not choose to thrust oneself between them and their objective, but they probably serve a better social purpose than more gentle and acceptable men.

That is sufficient for those of us who believe that Sir Harold Wilson's various governments left the state of Britain worse than he found it, but how can it be good enough for Sir Harold? These are the very people whose lives are the contradiction of everything for which the Labour Party stands. Is it really true that they are the people he most admires? Is it really true that they are the people he wants to thank for having helped him with his administration? Are they his friends for whom he feels the warmth of personal gratitude? If they are, what secret hunger for the company of capitalists led him to form so many ultra-capitalist friendships? It is rather pleasant to see the wilder shores of capitalism once again hung with coronets, but it remains very odd that such a scene should be set by the ex-Prime Minister of a socialist party.

The Times, 27 May 1976.

....

The Tate Drops a Costly Brick

Tate Gallery buys Carl Andre's pile of bricks

This 1976 article in The Sunday Times *by Colin Simpson led to a widespread series of attacks on the absurdity of modern art and questioning of the acquisitions policy of the Tate Gallery. Ironically, Carl Andre's bricks turned out to be one of the shrewdest commercial purchases by the gallery.*

The Tate Gallery receives an annual grant of £500,000 from public funds. This is five times as much as the Victoria and Albert Museum, and £100,000 more than all provincial museums and galleries put together. The money is spent by the trustees, who account for their stewardship every two years.

Their latest report is raising eyebrows at the Treasury and in academic – as opposed to artistic – circles. The underlying message of the sumptuously illustrated 275-page catalogue is that modern art is alive and well, and some of its practitioners are laughing their way to the bank. Some forms of public expenditure, it seems, are still sacred.

'The function of the Tate,' write the Trustees, 'is to reflect the art of our time.' The Tate, they claim, 'is *the* national collection and has a responsibility to show the greatest achievements ... such collections set standards and are the focal points in the cultural life of the nation. They provide an incentive and a yardstick for those who are responsible ... for promoting the idea that art is worthwhile.'

Carl Andre, a sculptor, and the John Weber Gallery of New York would agree with this dignified and admirable sentiment. In the summer of 1965, while on a canoeing holiday, Andre suddenly decided it was time to create low sculptures. He bought 120 bricks from a brickyard, arranged them in a low pile on the floor of an art gallery, put a price tag of $12,000 on them and waited for customers. None came. Being short of money, he took the bricks back to the brickyard and got his money back. The tale thereafter has an inevitability worthy of the late Gerald Hoffnung. In 1972 the Tate saw a photograph of Andre's bricks and offered to buy them. Andre went back to the brickyard only to find it had closed. However, nothing daunted, he found some other bricks, which in due course were crated and sent to London together with careful instructions on their assembly.

The Tate is understandably coy about how much it paid for this insouciant masterpiece. One trustee explained: 'If we published one price, every artist in the country would come and ask for more. It would ruin the market.'

Andre's bricks can be assembled fairly quickly, but Victor Burgin's work of art took twelve months to create. It consists of 18 sheets of foolscap, each with a few words typed on it. It is called 'Room 1970' and the idea is that the sheets are to be pinned up around any room. 'Mr Burgin,' writes the Trustees, 'values economy of expression and will avoid 12-page solutions when he can get away with half a page.' Nevertheless, the catalogue entry explaining Burgin's economy of expression runs to more than a thousand words.

Once again the Tate declines to reveal how much it paid Burgin for his year's work, but Sir Norman Reid, director of the gallery, does concede that possibly in one or two purchases, the Tate is 'skating on rather thin ice'.

The 'clou' of the conceptual collection is undoubtedly Claes Oldenburg's 'Lipsticks in Piccadilly Circus, London 1966'. Oldenburg has been even more economical than Burgin, as his offering consists of a magazine cutting stuck on a postcard measuring four and a half inches by five and a half inches. He explains his creative process in the catalogue:

'My first grasp of London was the tide of the Thames, and the constant rising and falling ... So I devised a giant copper ball which could be placed in the river, and which would rise and fall with the tide like the plumbing in a toilet.'

The idea did not meet with the wholehearted co-operation of either the GLC or the Department of the Environment, and the project foundered when the file was sent to the Port of London Authority. However, Oldenburg kindly offered to design a new monument to replace Eros in Piccadilly Circus. His first project was a giant retractable lipstick made to rise and fall according to the state of the tide, but the Tate settled for an alternative design using a cluster of lipsticks instead – possibly in an effort to be different from Yale University, which commissioned from Oldenburg a retractable lipstick monument mounted on caterpillar tracks.

The City of London is well represented by no fewer than four works by a gently ribald artistic partnership called Gilbert and George who operate a modest company called Art for All of Fournier Street, E1. The catalogue tells that Gilbert and George 'were almost teetotal until they tried to communicate their art to the public. They started to drink because they found that drink was a catalyst of communication, a way of presenting their work to the public. They consider drinking to be a duty rather than a pleasure and told the trustees that for some time, drinking has been part of their work.'

Their favourite medium is the videotape, and the Tate has a splendid one called 'Gordons makes us drunk,' which lasts for 12 minutes. It shows the two artists sitting in the front room of 12 Fournier Street drinking gin, while George murmurs several times 'Gordons makes us drunk ... very drunk.'

Gilbert and George are sculptors, but the Tate has no examples of their work in that field. They have managed, however, to acquire a collection of photographs taken by the two sculptors in their local pub. These are all framed together in *passe-partout* and the assemblage is titled 'Balls'.

Colin Simpson, *The Sunday Times*, 1976.

John Stonehouse and a Case of Mistaken Identity

In November 1974, John Stonehouse, Labour MP and former Government min-
ister, disappeared on a Miami beach. He had left the hotel in a pair of shorts
and it was assumed that he had drowned. However, a month later he was
arrested in Melbourne, Australia, where he was living under an assumed name.
He had disappeared rather than pay back money he had lost various investors
in some disastrous business deals.

In January 1975, the House of Commons set up a select committee and politely
requested him to appear before it. He replied that 'it would be extremely dangerous
to his psychiatric health' if he did so. The following year, he was sentenced to
seven years' imprisonment on various charges of credit card misuse, forgery, false
pretences, theft and fraud. After losing his appeal to the House of Lords, he
resigned from the Privy Council and went to prison. He refused to accept his
guilt. Just before he died in 1989, he said, 'I just wanted to get away and become
a plain human being again. All right, so it wasn't a normal thing to do. I wasn't
in a normal state of mind.'

Disaster, or near disaster, attended the whole of John Stonehouse's career.
He has been described as a potential Prime Minister, only prevented by
recently-developed fatal flaws from progressing smoothly to the top. The
facts are different.

Of all the young Labour MPs of his generation (he was elected to
Wednesbury, Staffordshire, in 1957 at the age of 31) he was the one
predicted as most likely to succeed. He seemed to have everything on his
side – qualities which indeed he still retains – charm, looks, a kind of
cleverness, and an enormous capacity for hard graft. But despite it all, the
seeds of failure were planted early on. There are those who – perhaps with
the benefit of hindsight – say they mistrusted him from an early age. The
'brilliance' which the media perceived in him is questioned by his tutors
at the London School of Economics, to which he went in 1947. One,
William Pickles, the political scientist, says: 'He was certainly not as clever
as he thought he was. He was over-bearing with his fellow-students,
thought he knew everything, and was very sure of himself. His worst

weakness was the way he overrated his own ability, and he was totally unable to see anyone else's point of view but his own. He was a sort of conspiracy by himself against himself. I find it easy, *post hoc*, to think he is a crook. He looked shifty; he always looked over your left shoulder when he talked to you.'

Another, Professor Richard Pear, says: 'He was extremely self-centred, always out for himself – a whingeing complaining type.' Of Stonehouse's fellow LSE students, Bernard Levin has remained publicly loyal to him; Stonehouse's talent for alienation (he was, said a contemporary, an 'overweening' Chairman of the Labour Club) had already shown itself. It was to be reinforced by his succeeding experience, culminating in the devastating loneliness of the last two years.

His mother, Rose, says 'John always knew what he wanted.' One trouble was that he made it all too clear, right from the beginning. The British like their Labour politicians to make at least a pretence of humility, of being just an ordinary chap. Stonehouse never bothered.

Even in his first job – working for the co-op in East Africa between 1952 and 1954 – his idealism was to a large extent nullified by his egoism. The job consisted of setting up co-operative farms. Some succeeded, many attempts had disastrous results ... Stonehouse's interest in Africa continued and it was genuinely idealistic as well as intensely curious. In 1960, he went to the Congo to investigate the war. Although he was, by now, a fairly well-known MP, he masqueraded as a reporter, 'Mr Smith', the first recorded instance of him adopting a phoney personality, if in this case for reasons which might be thought admirable ... But he was not widely liked among politicians. After he won Wednesbury, he made an arrogant acceptance speech and refused to shake hands with his opponent, Peter Tapsell – though, typically, he later wrote him a graceful letter. His maiden speech in the House of Commons was described as 'ranting' and 'uncontrolled'. In the House of Commons, one colleague says, 'he never fitted into the club. He was never around in the tea-room.'

He offended the sensibilities of other MPs in paradoxical ways – for instance, by working too hard when they were drinking or gossiping. He broke unwritten rules right to the end – astonishingly, a couple of weeks after being released on bail last autumn, he took his mistress, Sheila Buckley, to lunch in the members' cafeteria and was genuinely surprised when no one talked to him. Despite his unpopularity, however, and the feeling that he was a bit too obviously on the make, Harold Wilson recognised ability in him – perhaps, precisely his ability make money. In 1964 he was appointed Parliamentary Secretary to the Ministry of Aviation and proved something of a super-salesman. But he took his chief failure –

to sell the Super VC10 to BOAC – personally, and expressed it vehemently to the Cabinet. He felt that it was wrong that an American plane (the Boeing 707) should be preferred to a British one, and if the reason was that more money was needed, then more money should have been forthcoming. A portent? One of his commercial colleagues of the Seventies says: 'John was a great believer in spending for ultimate profit – constant injections of credit, fluid money. The trouble is that he would do this when everyone else in sight was drawing in their horns.'

His successes were often marred by sheer insensitivity. On an all-party visit to Mauritius to discuss their new constitution, he took the opportunity of making a party political speech, roundly abusing his Conservative Party colleagues. When he was Under Secretary of State for the Colonies, he earned great admiration in Zambia for the constitution he was instrumental in producing – and then misbehaved at the independence celebrations. His colleague Humphrey Berkeley recalls that the car in which Stonehouse was travelling in the state procession got held up when a white man accidentally drove through the parade. Stonehouse leapt out, seized hold of the nearest (black) policeman and shouted at him, 'Arrest that man! Arrest that man!' It is said, though, that it was his ability constantly to 'get away' in these jobs that kept him going at all. Certainly he has always been some sort of escapist, even if it only involved travelling round Britain rather than staying at the House or in his constituency, on the end of a phone.

He always enjoyed boyish competition, like the time when, holidaying in Yugoslavia, he challenged his friend and fellow-MP Andrew Faulds to swim round a distant island with him. Faulds refused: Stonehouse plunged in and was not seen for four hours. When he 'disappeared off Miami', Faulds was convinced that he had been playing the same sort of solitary game – and drowned. Escapism may even be a family trait – his elder brother Bill, a BOAC pilot, took a job in Singapore a few years ago and then left home overnight, without a word to his wife or children. Bill is now said to be 'making a new life in New Zealand'.

John Stonehouse's Government-sponsored globetrotting came to an end in 1967, when he was made Minister of State for Technology. It was the mixture as before: the unfortunate impression Stonehouse made on some of his political associates, their reaction, his counter-reaction. If he had been thought 'arrogant' in the House previously, as a Minister he was often thought intolerable. He made the headlines, as he had done a decade before, but now they ran: 'Stonehouse speech height of irresponsibility'; 'Stonehouse in Row after Row'.

He began to be paranoid about the Press – a paranoia, which, incidentally, culminated in 1975, when he accused *The Sunday Times* of 'starting his whole problem by its malicious article in November 1972 on the British Bangladesh Trust ...' The message began, apparently, to seep through to Harold Wilson.

There are several MPs who will say, off the record, that when Wilson gave Stonehouse the job of Postmaster-General, 'he hoped he'd mess it up so that he'd have an excuse to get rid of him.' By now Stonehouse's certainty that he was destined for greatness was more obsessive than ever, and he began to acquire what he regarded as the trappings of power. He took a flat in Westminster, and asked a pretty young woman close to the Labour Party to look it over. When she arrived, he said abruptly 'I think it's time I had a mistress' – he had, of course, had several girl friends, but this was to be different. The girl inspected the flat, which was fine – but was somewhat dismayed to discover that the only telephone was a payphone. She turned the offer down. The flat's new incumbent was to be Mrs Sheila Buckley, for whom (understandably) several young MPs were competing. Stonehouse is not the first or the last MP to keep a mistress, but Sheila Buckley's competence and loyalty encouraged him to take on more and more business commitments. It is said that because these were known, even then, to be questionable, Wilson refused to give Stonehouse a portfolio in the 1970 Shadow Cabinet ... By now, Stonehouse was convinced that Wilson was after him. His colleague Bruce Douglas-Mann says: 'If he wasn't going to be PM then he'd show that he could succeed in any field – he would come back into politics as a Maxwell figure, the tycoon, the independent MP not dependent on the party machine.' Stonehouse has never lived ostentatiously; it was greed for power which accounted for his increased determination to succeed in business, to move from thousands to millions. His main directorships, notably of Global Imex and the Bangladesh Trust, date from the early Seventies. One of his colleagues in Global-Imex describes the way he behaved: 'He saw himself as being the overriding genius. He had a dictatorial nature. If Stonehouse said this was going to be the case, then it was the case. He told me he wanted to be PM but to be independent of any financial burden. Everything was pre-arranged before the board meetings.' And, tellingly, 'He had an inability to pick the right people. He was a bad picker, and there were some real bums on the boards of his companies ... he was clutching at straws and hoping for a miracle.'

If Stonehouse had one fatal flaw, it was of always knowing best. Before his Old Bailey trial, he said to me, 'Nobody in authority thinks things through rationally, everyone is working in compartments with no connection with each other. There's so much malaise, we're due for fire and brimstone.' It was pretty clear who he thought was the country's only possible saviour. Perhaps he even believes it still.

Corinna Adam, The Sunday Times, 8 August 1977.

....

Bogeyman

Donald Beves accused of being 'Fourth Man'

Donald Beves, a blameless Cambridge don, was wrongfully accused of being the 'Fourth Man' in a series of articles in The Times *published in 1977, before it was officially acknowledged that in fact it was Anthony Blunt, the former Keeper of the Queen's Pictures. There was an immediate and furious response to these allegations against Beves by his former colleagues and pupils and eventually* The Times *admitted that it had got it completely wrong due to misinformation from the discredited British Intelligence Service, MI5.*

The 25-year-old mystery of how H. A. R. (Kim) Philby, Donald Maclean and Guy Burgess were changed from undergraduate communists at Cambridge in the early 1930s into agents of the Soviet secret service has never been resolved. Inquiries by *The Times* have now established that Mr Donald Beves, a wealthy Cambridge don, was suspected by security circles of having played a critical role in that transformation.

A scholar of sixteenth-century French literature, a former Clerk of the House of Commons, and a fellow of King's College from 1924, Mr Beves died in 1961. His name figured strongly in the intensive investigation of the Cambridge connection by MI5 in the early 1950s after Burgess and Maclean had defected to Moscow and Philby had undergone interrogation in London.

Speculation about the individual who recruited the three traitors into Soviet service has been rife for several years. The names canvassed have included the late Mr Maurice Dobb, the economic historian who was for many years a fellow of Trinity College, Cambridge, as well as other open communists.

But the MI5 inquiry found it misleading to ascribe the recruiting role to an individual. Cambridge was awash with young communists in 1932–3, providing a large, self-selected and obvious pool of Soviet sympathisers for the Comintern to recruit from.

The crucial factor was the subsequent move underground by a handful of those people, and the covers they assumed to mask their new role as agents and to explain away their earlier public convictions. Many, including Burgess, were extremely reluctant to abandon the public practice of extreme left-wing politics.

It was in assisting those who were chosen to take up a covert role that Mr Beves emerged as the main suspect.

MI5 adopted what is known as the 'nodal' approach to trace association between Philby, Burgess, Maclean and other individuals under varying degrees of suspicion. The inquiry pointed to Beves as one of the points of frequent contact; his name cropped up at several points in connection with the three traitors.

He would have been admirably placed to assist the three in disguising their treachery and planning their future careers. A large, jolly man, he was the best amateur actor of his generation, the life and soul of the Marlowe Society and the social circles that revolved round the theatrical side of Cambridge life.

A famous giver of parties, ubiquitous and much loved, he was known as the old-fashioned type of unmarried don who devoted all his energies to his pupils, his friends and his exquisite collection of eighteenth-century glassware.

His efforts at shaping the future roles of Philby, Burgess and Maclean may have begun in 1932 and 1933 when he was in his late thirties and a well-established figure of Cambridge society.

Burgess left Trinity College in 1935, jettisoned his overt communist beliefs and publicly assumed a neo-fascist, pro-imperialist line. He began to assert that the Indian masses must be saved from communism, that only the right wing of the British Conservative Party could do it in allegiance with the extreme right-wing in Europe as typified by the Nazis.

Three years later, Burgess confessed to his friend, Mr Goronwy Rees, former Principal of University College, Aberystwyth, that he had been a Comintern agent since leaving Cambridge. Mr Rees refused to believe him. According to Mr Rees's book, *A Chapter of Accidents*, Burgess replied:

'Why not? Why else do you think I've behaved as I have since I left Cambridge? Why should I have left Cambridge at all? Why should I have left the party and pretended to become a fascist? I hope you didn't believe all that ridiculous rigmarole about India and the Conservatives and the

Nazis; but I had to invent something to say. They told me that before going underground I must break off all connection with the party as publicly and dramatically as possible, and with anyone connected with it, and try to start a new career of some kind. So I did it. And all that nonsense worked.'

In 1933 Maclean wrote to his mother, Lady Maclean, widow of Sir Donald, the former Liberal Cabinet minister, that he had dropped his beliefs about the Russian Revolution. Instead of going to Russia as a teacher when he left Trinity Hall, he had decided to seek a career as a diplomat in the Foreign Office.

Philby made his transition to a new image more slowly. On leaving Trinity College in 1933 he travelled to Vienna and was involved in the battles between Austrian communists and fascists the following year.

By 1936, he had begun to assume the guise of a right-wing Conservative of Nazi sympathies, as his public association with the Anglo-German Fellowship indicated. In 1937 he covered the Spanish Civil War as a freelance journalist attached to the fascist forces, reporting for *The Times* among other journals.

Eventually the three men did irreparable harm to the West. Attached to the Washington Embassy from 1944 to 1948, Maclean passed to Russia invaluable information about Anglo–American–Canadian co-operation on the control of atomic energy and the manufacture of atomic weapons.

In 1947–8 he had access to the files of the Combined Policy Committee, which co-ordinated the activities of the three partners. His efforts are said to have been crucial in enabling the Soviet Union to manufacture and test its own atomic bomb several years sooner than its own technology would have allowed.

Philby rose to become head of section V of MI6, which handled counter-espionage for the British Secret Service, directed, in particular, against the Soviet Union from the last years of the Second World War.

The post he held in 1951, when Burgess and Maclean fled, tipped off by his activities as the 'third man', was that of MI6 station chief in Washington and liaison officer between the British Secret Service and the American CIA.

Philby's treachery nullified much of the work of the British and American intelligence communities during the early years of the cold war. It led to the death of many men and the failure of several operations against the communist bloc.

The most influential post held by Burgess was probably that of personal secretary to the late Mr Hector McNeil between 1947 and 1949 during the latter's period as Minister of State at the Foreign Office.

He was the messenger who carried the news from Philby in Washington to Maclean in London which confirmed to Maclean that he had been 'blown', thereby precipitating their flight and the celebrated scandal of the 'missing diplomats'.

The nature of the evidence against Philby after 1951 is thought to have been similar to that concerning Beves. The security service knew of the interconnections between the four men but, as often happens in such cases, the evidence was not of the type that could be used against them in a court of law.

The evidence against Beves amounted to strong suspicion, but fell short, and still falls short, of conclusive proof.

Philby fled to Moscow from Beirut in 1963. Almost two years before, Beves died from a heart attack in his rooms at King's, a beloved Cambridge figure to the end.

MI5 recently decided that information concerning Beves and the Cambridge connection should not be made public as the time for its disclosure was not yet ripe.

Peter Hennessy, *The Times*, 15 June 1977.

....

Sir Anthony Blunt – The Fourth Man

Blunt revealed as former Soviet spy

Sir Anthony Blunt, former Surveyor of the Queen's Pictures and one of Britain's most distinguished art historians, was named in 1979 as the 'Fourth Man' in Britain's biggest post-war espionage fiasco. Although there had been innuendoes published in Private Eye *following the completion of a book on the subject by Anthony Boyle, the truth finally came out in Parliament when Prime Minister Thatcher told the House the full details of Sir Anthony's links with the Russians before and during World War II. Shortly afterwards, his knighthood was withdrawn. However, less than a week later, The Times managed to get an exclusive interview with the former traitor, which took place after Blunt was a luncheon guest in the newspaper's boardroom.*

What was the most extraordinary aspect of the entire affair was the way that Blunt, a self-confessed traitor, had been able to strike a deal for immunity and secrecy and even work with a monarch. The other aspect that was commented on at the time was that Blunt appeared to offer no apologies or regrets for his behaviour, which one author found obnoxious because of the way he attempted to justify his misdeeds on the grounds of his conscience.

Professor Blunt describes double life as MI5 man and Soviet agent

Professor Anthony Blunt, in an interview in the offices of *The Times* in London yesterday, explained how he provided information to the Russians when he worked for MI5 during the war. But he denied giving the Russians information after the war or that he tipped off Guy Burgess and Donald Maclean in 1951 that they were in danger of arrest. He said Mr Burgess recruited him at Cambridge in the 1930s when fascism was the greatest threat.

Like any spy who had come in from the cold, Professor Anthony Blunt yesterday disclosed a great deal about his activities as a spy for the Soviet Union, but not all. He claimed he was inhibited by the Official Secrets Act, but it also seemed he remained loyal to his friends, alive and dead.

Throughout the interview, held in the offices of *The Times*, he was remarkably composed and clearly believed that his confession to MI5 in 1964 and the immunity granted to him was an absolution. In Roman Catholic terms, he was in a state of grace.

He admitted that he was a talent spotter for Soviet Intelligence at Cambridge in the 1930s, and that he provided information to the Russians when he worked for MI5 during the Second World War. He denied that he had given a warning to Guy Burgess and Donald Maclean that they were about to be arrested in 1951. He did not, and could not, have told them. Kim Philby did.

Professor Blunt added: 'I didn't and couldn't have … It was simply Philby … When Guy came back from America, which was a week – it might have been 10 days – before they left, (Philby) told him that they were closing in.'

'Did you not feel obliged to warn the security services?'

'No, because they were my friends.'

Mr Burgess had a contact and put Professor Blunt in touch with him because he rightly supposed that he was in danger and would be a prime suspect 'if things got critical'.

He met the contact and was ordered to go to Russia, probably because they thought he was still one of them. He went home and decided not to go. Professor Blunt said that he became a Communist, or more particularly a Marxist, in 1935 or 1936. He had been on a sabbatical, and on his return to Cambridge found that his friends and almost all the bright undergraduates had become Marxists under the impact of Hitler.

The most intelligent was Mr Burgess, who had become a totally convinced Marxist and a member of the Communist Party. Mr Burgess convinced him that the Marxist interpretation of history was correct.

When Mr Burgess put it to him, he decided that the best way of opposing fascism was to become a talent spotter – that is, he gave Mr Burgess the names of likely recruits.

Professor Blunt said that he spotted very few before he left Cambridge in 1937 to work at the Warburg Institute. He insisted that he did not report to Samuel Cahan, the Chief Soviet intelligence agent in Britain, or to any other Russian at that time. He admitted that he was rejected by Military Intelligence when he applied for a posting at the beginning of the war.

He then joined the Intelligence Corps and served in France until the evacuation.

On his return to Britain he joined MI5, the security service, largely because of the old-boy network. He received only a routine vetting because everybody was too busy.

The Ribbentrop–Molotov Pact, which led many British Communists to recant, did not diminish Professor Blunt's loyalty. He argued that it was a tactical necessity to help the Soviet Union gain time and prepare for war, and while working at MI5 he passed on information to the Russians. His brief was to report anything interesting, but at first his junior rank limited his activities. He mainly reported the names of MI5 officers. He had access to more information by the time of the invasion of Russia, and with the Russians as allies he continued his espionage activities with a clearer conscience. The information was more interesting, but he claimed that it was almost entirely about German intelligence in Europe.

Professor Blunt said that he passed the information to English friends and a Soviet agent, whom he met in London. He did not know his name, but assumed he was attached to the Soviet Embassy.

Professor Blunt claimed that he ceased to report to the Russians after the war. He could have contacted them through Mr Burgess, but he had nothing to report – certainly nothing from the Palace, where he was employed as Surveyor of the King's Pictures.

Professor Blunt said: 'There has been some reference to confidential papers which I might have seen at Buckingham Palace. This is, of course, nonsense.' Nevertheless, he kept in touch with Mr Burgess but not Mr Maclean, who was frequently posted abroad. Mr Burgess could be tiresome and difficult, but was highly intelligent. They discussed everything but politics.

Professor Blunt claimed that he became disenchanted with Communism and the Soviet Union after the war. It was a gradual process, but after the events in Russia and the occupation of Eastern Europe he was finally convinced that the British way of life and constitution were the best.

After the defection of Mr Burgess and Mr Maclean, in 1951, he was frequently interrogated by MI5. They were comfortable conversations, often with people he had known. He had the impression that some believed that he was guilty of espionage, but others did not. He was approached by MI5 again in 1964, and it was obvious that they knew a lot about his past activities. Their offer was a plain statement: he could have immunity in exchange for information. He had the impression that the offer had been decided by high authority, from the Prime Minister.

Professor Blunt said that he did not know if they thought that he was still in touch with Soviet intelligence and could be used as a double agent. He refused to discuss the information he gave in return for immunity, except that it was regarded as important. Although out of date, it could start a line of research which might be useful.

Professor Blunt said that afterwards he was told specifically that the Palace had not been informed. Later, in about 1972, he was given to understand that the Private Secretary had been told, but he did not know if the Queen was informed. He said that he rarely met the Queen when he worked at the Palace. His job was concerned with pictures, and they met only when a decision had to be made about rehanging or restoring a picture.

He had not considered the possibility that the Queen would be deeply embarrassed if his past was disclosed. He had assumed that it would never come out, and thought that his job was important. Professor Blunt did not believe that homosexuals were more liable than others to become spies and traitors. Mr Philby was not a homosexual, and Mr Maclean was essentially normal with perhaps a slight homosexual tendency.

Louis Heren and Stewart Tendler, The Times, 21 November 1979.

Paedophiles Anonymous

Sir Peter Hayman and the Paedophile Information Exchange

The British satirical magazine Private Eye *likes nothing more than an Establishment scandal, especially if it involves homosexuality and a cover-up. In October 1980, they revealed that Sir Peter Hayman, former British High Commissioner to Canada, had escaped prosecution for receiving paedophile literature through the post. The following issue revealed tensions within the legal departments of the government.*

A flaming row has broken out between the Attorney General and the Director of Public Prosecutions following the revelation (*Eye*, 492) of the reckless sexual exploits and fantasies of retired ambassador Sir Peter Hayman KCMG, CVO, MBE.

Hayman joined the Paedophile Information Exchange under the name of Henderson and conducted obscene correspondence with other PIE members through a flat he rented at 95 Linden Gardens, W2.

In October 1978, Hayman was questioned by Obscene Publications Squad officers after pornographic literature addressed to 'Henderson' was left on a bus. Whereas several of his PIE correspondents now face trial at the Old Bailey this month, Hayman was merely cautioned not to send obscene material through the post again. This appears to have been the result of an Establishment 'fix'.

The most worrying aspect of the Hayman affair lies in what was discovered at his Linden Gardens love-nest: pornographic photos, articles of female clothing indicating the regular entertainment of prostitutes, and 46 quarto diaries, each of some 80 pages, cataloguing six years of deviant sexual activity.

The earlier diaries cover part of Sir Peter's term as British High Commissioner in Canada from 1970 to 1974 and would have made him a certain victim of blackmail had they fallen into the wrong hands. Hayman had previously held top posts in the Ministry of Defence and the UK delegation to NATO.

The *Eye* exposé of Hayman's activities horrified the Attorney General, Sir Michael Havers ... Havers demanded that the Beast of Berlin's writings be sent to his office so he could read them himself...

When the diaries were eventually forwarded to Havers it became clear that he wasn't the only person who'd been kept in the dark. The security services had not been informed of their blackmail potential either. Nor had Willie Whitelaw, as Home Secretary, the Cabinet Minister responsible for security matters. Nor, indeed, had the Prime Minister.

Meanwhile, back at the Dipper's Office in Queen Anne's Gate, there was an ... attempt to lower the charges facing Hayman's paedophiliac cronies so that they would willingly plead guilty in return for a token fine. This would keep the public revelation of the evidence to a minimum ...

To the Attorney General's credit, he refused to contemplate any such deal and demanded that the charges stand. It now seems likely, therefore, that the dangerous weaknesses of one of Britain's most trusted post-war security and diplomatic figures may yet be formally revealed. But the lewd contents of Hayman's diaries will not be read out because they form no part of the case against his fellow paedophiles.

Doubtless the diaries will not be mislaid or shredded while in the Attorney General's care but will be returned in due course to their owner and creator.

Sir Peter Hayman has not seen fit to resign his directorships with either Delta Metal (Overseas) or Matthew Hall (International Development). He has retained his job as Governor of the International Students House, a hostel in Great Portland Street, W1 for young university students from all over the world.

Private Eye, 7 November 1980.

Sir Peter fled to France to avoid the growing publicity over the affair but soon returned. A year later, he was cautioned for his behaviour with a lorry driver in a public lavatory.

'He's very European'

Claus Von Bulow's trial for his wife's murder

After gaining a law degree at Cambridge in the fifties, Danish-born Claus Von Bulow worked for John Paul Getty before ending up in New York, where he married 'Sunny', who was formerly the wife of an Austrian prince (see pp. 372–4). For a while the marriage seemed like a fairy tale with considerable entertaining done in the couple's Manhattan apartment or at their summer house in Newport, Rhode Island. The scandal erupted when Sunny slipped into a coma and Von Bulow was charged and convicted of poisoning his wife with insulin injections. After a sensational re-trial in 1981, which included evidence from a mistress, with whom he was having an affair during his marriage, that he intended to divorce his wife, the conviction was overturned and Von Bulow was able to keep the fortune he inherited from Sunny, who remained comatose in a New York hospital. A decade after the case, he returned to live in London.

NEWPORT, R. I., July 11—It is considered one of the more restrained nesting places of the social birds, but Newport was just about as agog as it could get this week. From Bailey's Beach Club to the Reading Room and Tennis Hall of Fame to private lunch and dinner parties in the mansions that pass for cottages here, the name on everyone's lips was Von Bulow.

'There's little talk about anything else,' said Helen Windslow, whose husband, John, is president of the Newport Preservation Society.

'The place is buzzing, it's just wild, unreal,' said Mary McLain Mead, a Texan who has been the center of a round of parties given to celebrate her marriage here today to Rudolph (Foxy) Carter, a former Foreign Service officer whose family has long been associated with this enclave of status and wealth.

But the most commonly used word for the developments that began on Tuesday and were still rocking the summer colony was tragedy. It was on Tuesday that a Rhode Island indictment charged Claus Von Bulow, a New York financial consultant, with twice attempting to kill his wife with insulin injections – in December 1979 and December 1980. Mrs Von Bulow, the former Martha Sharp Crawford, suffers from low blood sugar and went into a coma from hypoglycemic shock last December. She has never regained consciousness and is now a patient at Columbia Presbyterian Medical Center in Manhattan.

The investigation that resulted in the indictment was begun early this year after Maria Schrallhammer, Mrs Von Bulow's maid, became suspicious about the illness that caused the repeated hospitalizations. The maid apparently reported her fears to Prince Alexander Auersperg and Princess Annie-Laurie Auersperg, Mrs Von Bulow's children from her first marriage, to Prince Alfred Auersperg of Austria. The children then engaged Richard H. Kuh, a lawyer and former Manhattan District Attorney, to look into the matter. The 54-year-old Mr Von Bulow is to be arraigned in Providence on Tuesday.

John F. Sheehan of Providence, who is sharing Mr Von Bulow's defence with Herald Price Fahringer, a Manhattan lawyer, denied reports that Mrs Von Bulow, shortly before her hospitalization, was considering divorce. The Von Bulows – he is a Danish-born British citizen and a former official of the Getty Oil Company – were married in 1966.

He maintained, too, that hospital records showed that Mrs Von Bulow's hospitalization in 1979 was traceable to 'barbiturates and alcohol and hypoglycemia', not an insulin injection.

'Mr Von Bulow is so devastated by this that he can't comprehend it,' Mr Sheehan said.

Although few people were willing to talk for attribution, several described Mr Von Bulow, who was a barrister of the Middle Temple, one of the Inns of Court in London and who also holds a master's degree from Trinity College of Cambridge University, as brilliant, knowledgeable, a fascinating conversationalist and a man no one really knew well.

'He's a tall, handsome, austere kind of man,' said a woman who has known the couple for more than a decade. 'He doesn't cosy up to anybody.'

'He's one of the most controversial people here,' said another. 'He always has been, and I don't know why. He's very European.'

'He's not the most favored person in Newport,' said a member of one of the summer colony's oldest and most prestigious families.

Although there is little doubt that many of the couple's social contacts were based on a fondness for Mrs Von Bulow and her mother, Annie-Laurie Aitken, who also has a home here, Mr Von Bulow is highly regarded by others.

'He's a very good friend of ours,' said one woman. 'I don't think we should talk about him.'

'There's Been No Defense Yet'

'All the evidence has been presented by the prosecution, and there's been no defense yet,' said Mr Winslow of the Newport Preservation Society.

'He's a nice sort of man, and he's always been a great help to me in every way.' Mr Von Bulow is a vice president of the society.

Mrs Von Bulow, whose father was George W. Crawford, former chairman of the board of the Columbia Gas and Electric Corporation of Pittsburgh, has holdings estimated at between $30 million and $35 million. She and Mr Von Bulow have a daughter, Cosima, who is now 14.

The Von Bulow residence here, Clarendon Court, is a stone mansion styled after an 18th-century English manor house and protected by a vine-covered wall and wrought-iron gates. The mansion, on Bellevue Avenue, or 'Millionaires' Row', was the setting for the film 'High Society'.

Mr Von Bulow visited the house Wednesday with his lawyers. According to Mr Sheehan, the Von Auersperg children, who are living there, were 'cordial'. Cosima, who has also been staying at Clarendon Court, will spend the rest of the summer at tennis camp.

Despite the lavish house with its museum-quality French furniture and spectacular arrangements of fresh flowers, the Von Bulows were never among the colony's most active residents socially, and in the last few years their entertaining became even less frequent. Mrs Von Bulow, who is 49, was described as shy with people she did not know well, but with a disposition that earned her the nickname Sunny, a good sense of humour and a small circle of close friends with whom she felt at ease.

'We all knew of this investigation back in February,' said one of them, 'but we never talked about it. It was the most amazing silence I've ever heard of in any community. It was a show of loyalty to her. We closed ranks.'

The New York Times, 12 July 1981.

Bokassa Ministers 'Dined on Body of Colleague'

Cannibalism and corruption in the Central African Republic

'Emperor' Bokassa was one of the more grotesque rulers of the seventies. Feted by the West, he held an obscenely expensive coronation service when he declared himself Emperor of his bankrupt country which he renamed the Central African Empire.

There was an earlier incident of high farce when Bokassa declared his wish to meet up again with a daughter that he had fathered while serving as a non-commissioned officer with the French forces in Indochina. Not surprisingly, a number of young ladies of Afro–Vietnamese origins declared that they were the rightful heirs of the dictator. In the end, two of the contestants were flown to the Central African Republic, where eventually one was chosen as the legitimate illegitimate daughter.

Ministers who were invited to dinner by the now deposed Emperor Jean Bedel Bokassa were told after the meal that they had just eaten a former colleague, according to Mr Fred Copperman, British Honorary Consul in Bangui.

Mr Copperman, a businessman in the Central African Republic, said the incident took place some weeks before the coup when Bokassa's fortunes were in sharp decline, plagued by student unrest and international opinion.

Claims about cannibalism were too well documented to be ignored, although no-one appeared willing to admit to having eaten human flesh with Bokassa.

Mr Copperman says he believes that 'human flesh prepared as joints' was found in the deep freeze of one of Bokassa's residences following the coup which brought Mr David Dacko to power in Bangui while Bokassa was in Libya.

Bokassa came from the small M'Baka tribe, renowned for its addiction to cannibalism. A French Guyana governess confirmed a report that Bokassa would sometimes order all servants out of the house to do the cooking himself.

Tattoo on Torso

One body in the deep freeze was identified as Gaston Wengue by the tattoo on the chest. The arms, one leg and head were missing – parts traditionally favoured by cannibals.

His niece, Albertine Kettego, 16, said Wengue was picked up on Aug. 11 near the Bokassa residence on a minor traffic offence.

Another body was that of Mr Jean-Robert Massanquet, 25, who was arrested on Aug. 26 after Bokassa had harangued him over the student unrest. It also showed signs of having been eaten in the traditional manner.

Photos in France

French newspapers have published pictures of the bodies of the three victims in the Bokassa deep freeze. All these charges are now being investigated by a national commission of inquiry into the Bokassa regime which began work yesterday to investigate reports of cannibalism, killing and embezzlement of public funds.

The commission is headed by Mr Etienne Yanibada, chief prosecutor of the Supreme Court, and it will formulate charges that could be used to have the deposed emperor and members of his family extradited from the Ivory Coast to stand trial.

The most grisly of the claims made yesterday concerned cannibalism, but others involved his alleged embezzlement of public funds.

One senior diplomat in Bangui reported that on the day before Bokassa left the capital on his recent trip to Libya, he summarily withdrew $1,500,000 (£685,000) in cash from a leading local bank.

Drew £9m a Year

Estimates in diplomatic circles claim that in the 13 years he held power, Bokassa may have withdrawn about $20,000,000 (£9,132,000) a year, investing it mainly in France.

Bokassa had various sources of income, not least the lucrative ivory trade in which he was involved with a vivacious Belgian woman, the sister of one of his wives.

The woman left Bangui on the eve of the coup d'etat nearly a fortnight ago. She was the only foreigner on the list of people to be arrested by forces loyal to Mr Dacko's new regime.

Bruce Loudon, *The Daily Telegraph*, 3 October 1979.

Later, Valéry Giscard d'Estaing was named as the beneficiary of free diamonds from the 'Emperor'.

A claim that the deposed Emperor Bokassa gave President Giscard d'Estaing diamonds worth more than £100,000 in 1973 grew into a French scandal yesterday.

A curt statement by the Elysée Palace did nothing to halt misgivings about the allegation, in the satirical weekly *Le Canard Enchainé*.

It said the exchange of 'presents of a traditional character, particularly on the occasion of visits by members of the government to foreign states, have in no case either the character or value mentioned by certain publications concerning Central Africa.'

'Truth and Honour'

'To dispute the "character" and the "value" of presents is not the same as to deny their nature and certainly not their existence,' *Le Monde* said yesterday.

The influential Paris newspaper, which reproduced the list for the *Canard* allegations, also commented on the wider implications of the affair as a matter of 'truth and honour'.

'Since the document (a paper by Bokassa ordering the delivery of 30 carats of diamonds to Giscard), appears to be authentic, the only possible clarification would be to announce that this royal present was returned to its sender,' wrote M. Jacques Fauvet, editor.

He suggested it was essential to accept a request for a Parliamentary commission of inquiry into French relations with Bokassa's regime.

The request, made on Oct. 4 by M. Mitterrand, the Socialist leader, was renewed after the 'diamonds' affair came to light.

'Orchestrated Campaign'

M. Pierre Hunt, Elysée spokesman, said at yesterday's daily briefing that he did not think it 'very dignified for the office of President to have to justify or reply to information savouring more of defamation or an orchestrated campaign, rather than real news.'

A battle is raging between pro and anti-government newspapers on the subject. *Le Figaro* yesterday reproached *Le Monde* for making so much of the affair.

Michael Field, *The Daily Telegraph*, 5 November 1989.

In his autobiography published in 1991, Giscard said the diamond affair was like 'a painful bite in the heart'. He claimed that the diamonds had remained in a drawer for eight years when he decided to have them valued. They were subsequently auctioned off for £10,000 and the proceeds were given to the Central African Red Cross.

....

I Would Do Anything to Win a Pulitzer Prize

Hoax story wins Janet Cooke a Pulitzer

The following dramatic story about Jimmy, an eight-year-old heroin addict, appeared in The Washington Post *in 1980 and won its author, Janet Cooke, a Pulitzer Prize. For the newspaper that had almost single-handedly brought down President Nixon because of his cover-up of the Watergate scandal, it was one more feather in its cap and confirmed its pre-eminence in the journalism world. It was also personally gratifying for Bob Woodward, one of the famous Watergate duo, as he was the newspaper executive on the* Post *who had supervised the Jimmy story. The story also led to angry demands for something to be done and accusations that the Washington Police had failed in their duty by not finding Jimmy before he ended up overdosing. To their credit, the city authorities immediately questioned the veracity of the story and demanded access to the reporter's evidence, which was denied on the basis of the Second Amendment, which protects press freedom in the USA.*

A few months later Bob Woodward discovered that the entire story was a hoax and that Jimmy did not exist. The Washington Post *published a deeply embarrassing editorial apologizing for its mistake. It came to light when various colleges telephoned the* Post *in puzzlement after the prize-winner announced she had been one of their alumni. What made the extraordinary fiasco more poignant was that Janet Cooke, like her fictional victim, is black.*

Jimmy is 8 years old and a third-generation heroin addict, a precocious little boy with sandy hair, velvety brown eyes and needle marks freckling the baby-smooth skin of his thin brown arms.

 He nestles in a large, beige reclining chair in the living room of his comfortably furnished home in Southeast Washington. There is an almost cherubic expression on his small, round face as he talks about life – clothes, money, the Baltimore Orioles and heroin. He has been an addict since the age of 5.

 His hands are clasped behind his head, fancy running shoes adorn his feet and a striped Izod T-shirt hangs over his thin frame. 'Bad, ain't it,' he boasts to a reporter visiting recently. 'I got me six of these.'

 Jimmy's is a world of hard drugs, fast money and the good life he believes both can bring. Every day, junkies casually buy heroin from Ron, his mother's live-in lover, in the dining room of Jimmy's home. They 'cook' it in the kitchen and 'fire up' in the bedrooms. And every day, Ron or someone else fires up Jimmy, plunging a needle into his bony arm, sending the fourth grader into a hypnotic nod.

 Jimmy prefers this atmosphere to school, where only one subject seems relevant to fulfilling his dreams. 'I want to have me a bad car and dress good and also have me a good place to live,' he says. 'So, I pretty much pay attention in math because I know I got to keep up when I finally get me something to sell.'

 Jimmy wants to sell drugs, maybe even on the District's meanest street, Condon Terrace SE, and some day real heroin, he says, 'just like my man Ron.'

 Ron, 27, and recently up from the South, was the one who first turned Jimmy on. 'He'd be buggin' me all the time about what the shots were and what people was doin' and one day he said, "When can I get off?"' Ron says, leaning against a wall in a narcotic haze, his eyes half closed, yet piercing. 'I said, "Well, s—, you can have some now." I let him snort a little and, damn, the little dude really did get off.'

 Six months later, Jimmy was hooked. 'I felt like I was part of what was goin' down,' he says. 'I can't really tell you how it feel. You never done any? Sort of like them rides at King's Dominion ... like if you was to go on all of them in one day.

 'It be real different from herb (marijuana). That's baby s—. Don't nobody here hardly ever smoke no herb. You can't hardly get none right now, anyway.'

 Jimmy's mother Andrea accepts her son's habit as a fact of life, although she will not inject the child herself and does not like to see others do it.

 'I don't really like to see him fire up,' she says. 'But, you know, I think he would have got into it one day, anyway. Everybody does. When you live in the ghetto, it's all a matter of survival. If he wants to get away from it when he's older, then that's his thing. But right now, things are better for us than they've ever been ... Drugs and black folk been together for a very long time.'

Heroin has become a part of life in many of Washington's neighborhoods, affecting thousands of teen-agers and adults who feel cut off from the world around them, and filtering down to untold numbers of children like Jimmy who are bored with school and battered by life.

On street corners and playgrounds across the city, youngsters often no older than 10 relate with uncanny accuracy the names of important dealers in their neighborhoods, and the going rate for their wares. For the uninitiated they can recite the colour, taste, and smell of things such as heroin, cocaine, and marijuana, and rattle off all the colours in a rainbow made of pills.

The heroin problem in the District has grown to what some call epidemic proportions, with the daily influx of so-called 'Golden Crescent' heroin from Iran, Pakistan and Afghanistan, making the city fourth among six listed by the U.S. Drug Enforcement Agency as major points of entry for heroin in the United States. The 'Golden Crescent' heroin is stronger and cheaper than the Southeast Asian and Mexican varieties previously available on the street, and its easy accessibility has added to what has long been a serious problem in the nation's capital.

David G. Canaday, special agent in charge of the DEA's office here, says the agency 'can't do anything about it [Golden Crescent heroin] because we have virtually no diplomatic ties in that part of the world.' While judiciously avoiding the use of the term epidemic, Canaday does say that the city's heroin problem is 'sizeable'.

Medical experts, such as Dr Alyce Gullatte, director of the Howard University Drug Abuse Institute, say that heroin is destroying the city. And D.C.'s medical examiner, James Luke, has recorded a substantial increase in the number of deaths from heroin overdose, from seven in 1978 to 43 so far this year.

Death has not yet been visitor to the house where Jimmy lives.

The kitchen and upstairs bedrooms are a human collage. People of all shapes and sizes drift into the dwelling and its various rooms, some jittery, uptight and anxious for a fix, others calm and serene after they finally 'get off'.

A fat woman wearing a white uniform and blond wig with a needle jabbed in it like a hatpin, totters down the staircase announcing that she is 'feeling fine'. A teen-age couple drift through the front door, the girl proudly pulling a syringe of the type used by diabetics from the hip pocket of her Gloria Vanderbilt jeans. 'Got me a new one,' she says to no one in particular as she and her boyfriend wander off into the kitchen to cook their smack and shoot each other up.

These are normal occurrences in Jimmy's world. Unlike most children his age, he doesn't usually go to school, preferring instead to hang with older boys between the ages of 11 and 16 who spend their day getting high on herb or PCP and doing a little dealing to collect spare change.

When Jimmy does find his way to the classroom, it is to learn more about his favourite subject – math.

'You got to know how to do some figuring if you want to go into business,' he says pragmatically. Using his mathematical skills in any other line of work is a completely foreign notion.

'They don't BE no jobs,' Jimmy says. 'You got to have some money to do anything, got to make some cash. Got to be selling something people always want to buy. Ron say people always want to buy some horse. My mama say it, too. She be using it and her mama be using it. It's always gonna be somebody who can use it . . .

'The rest of them dudes on the street is sharp. You got to know how many of them are out there, how much they charge for all the different s—, who gonna buy from them and where their spots be . . . they bad, you know, 'cause they in business for themselves. Ain't nobody really telling them how they got to act.'

In a city overflowing with what many consider positive role models for a black child with almost any ambition – doctors, lawyers, politicians, bank presidents – Jimmy wants most to be a good dope dealer. He says that when he is older, 'maybe about 11', he would like to 'go over to Condon Terrace (notorious for its open selling of drugs and violent way of life) or somewhere else and sell.' With the money he says he would buy a German Shepherd dog and a bicycle, maybe a basket ball, and save the rest 'so I could buy some real s— and sell it.'

His mother doesn't view Jimmy's ambitions with alarm, perhaps because drugs are as much a part of Andrea's world as they are of her son's.

She never knew her father. Like her son, Andrea spent her childhood with her mother and the man with whom she lived for 15 years. She recalls that her mother's boyfriend routinely forced her and her younger sister to have sex with him, and Jimmy is the product of one of those rapes.

Depressed and discouraged after his birth ('I didn't even name him, you know? My sister liked the name Jimmy and I said "OK, call him that, who gives a fu—? I guess we got to call him something, don't we?" ') she quickly accepted the offer of heroin from a woman who used to shoot up with her mother.

'It was like nothing I ever knew about before; you be in another world, you know? No more baby, no more mama ... I could quit thinking about it. After I got off, I didn't have to be thinking about nothing.'

Three years later, the family moved after police discovered the shooting gallery in their home, and many of Andrea's sources of heroin dried up. She turned to prostitution and shoplifting to support a $60-a-day habit. Soon after, she met Ron, who had just arrived in Washington and was selling a variety of pills, angel dust and some heroin. She saw him as a way to get off the street and readily agreed when he asked her to move in with him.

'I was tired of sleeping with all those different dudes and boosting (shoplifting) at Woodies. And I didn't think it would be bad for Jimmy to have some kind of man around,' she says.

Indeed, social workers in the Southeast Washington community say that so many black children become involved with drugs because there is no male authority figure present in the home.

'A lot of these parents (of children involved with drugs) are the unwed mothers of the 60s, and they are bringing up their children by trial and error,' says Linda Gilbert, a social worker at Southeast Neighborhood House.

'The family structure is not there so they [the children] establish relationships with their peers. If the peers are into drugs, it won't be very long before the kids are, too ... They don't view drugs as illegal, and if they are making money, too, then it's going to be OK in the eyes of an economically deprived community.'

Addicts who have been feeding their habits for 35 years or more are not uncommon in Jimmy's world, and although medical experts say that there is an extremely high risk of his death from an overdose, it is not inconceivable that he will live to reach adulthood.

'He might already be close to getting a lethal dose,' Dr Dorynne Czechowicz of the National Institute of Drug Abuse says. 'Much of this depends on the amount he's getting and the frequency with which he's getting it. But I would hate to say that his early death is inevitable. If he were to get treatment, it probably isn't too late to help him. And assuming he doesn't OD before then, he could certainly grow into an addicted adult.'

At the end of an evening of strange questions about his life, Jimmy slowly changes into a different child. The calm and self-assured little man recedes. The jittery and ill-behaved boy takes over as he begins going into withdrawal. He is twisting uncomfortably in his chair one minute, irritatingly raising and lowering a vinyl window blind the next.

'Be cool,' Ron admonishes him, walking out of the room.

Jimmy picks up a green 'Star Wars' force beam toy and begins flicking the light on and off.

Ron comes back into the living room, syringe in hand, and calls the little boy over to his chair: 'Let me see your arm.'

He grabs Jimmy's left arm just above the elbow, his massive hand tightly encircling the child's small limb. The needle slides into the boy's soft skin like a straw pushed into the centre of a freshly baked cake. Liquid ebbs out of the syringe, replaced by bright red blood. The blood is then reinjected into the child.

Jimmy has closed his eyes during the whole procedure, but now he opens them, looking quickly around the room. He climbs into a rocking-chair and sits, his head dipping and snapping upright again, in what addicts call 'the nod'.

'Pretty soon, man,' Ron says, 'you got to learn how to do this for yourself.'

Janet Cooke, *The Washington Post*, 1980.

Cecil Parkinson's 'Love Child'

Parkinson and the Sarah Keays scandal

Cecil Parkinson was one of Prime Minister Margaret Thatcher's most loyal lieutenants. Secretary of State for Trade and Industry and Chairman of the Conservative Party from 1981 until 1983, he was credited with having been instrumental in helping the Conservatives win the 1983 election and was tipped by some commentators as Mrs Thatcher's likely successor.

In October 1983, a small item appeared in Private Eye *saying 'Why was Cecil Parkinson asked to step down as Tory Party Chairman?' I can assure readers that it had nothing to do with his marital difficulties which have recently caused raised eyebrows in Tory circles. Now comes the news that Parkinson's fun-loving secretary Ms Sarah Keays is expecting a baby in three months' time.'*

Later the magazine had to pay damages for some of the libellous comments about those mentioned but it did bring the story into the open and prompted Mrs Thatcher to state that she wished Mr Parkinson to remain in office. It looked as if Parkinson would remain, despite the revelation that he had allegedly promised to marry Ms Keays but had changed his mind. Parkinson was riding high, especially after his performance at the Conservative Party Conference a week after the Private Eye *article appeared and his interview on the then BBC TV flagship current affairs programme* Panorama. *On the same evening, Ms Keays revealed her side of the story in the following interview which appeared in* The Times.

Miss Sara Keays, former secretary to Mr Cecil Parkinson, Secretary of State for Trade and Industry, who is expecting his child in January, told *The Times* last night that he had first proposed to her four years ago and had repeated the proposal again on election day.

But seven weeks later, after a holiday abroad with his family, Mr Parkinson had told her that he no longer intended to marry her.

Speaking at her father's home near Bath, Miss Keays said that she had 'implored' Mr Parkinson to tell the Prime Minister during May and June of this year, but he had refused.

He had finally told Mrs Margaret Thatcher on June 9, polling day, that he intended to marry Miss Keays and she agreed to leave her job at the House of Commons at the end of June.

She said she had met Mr Parkinson in secret on September 1 at an office in London where he told her that he no longer intended to marry her. 'Later that day I telephoned him to say that I thought it essential that he should inform the Prime Minister,' she said.

When it became apparent during the following weeks that the affair was being discussed in political circles and pursued by newspapers she told Mr Parkinson that if he did not issue a statement through his solicitors she would be obliged to defend herself.

Miss Keays said she had decided to speak only because of her 'duty to do so'.

Telephone calls from Miss Keays's family to *The Times* yesterday afternoon were followed by an invitation from her for members of the staff of *The Times* to go to Bath, where she gave them the following statement:

'I agreed for the sake of my family that we would not discuss with the press the statement made by Mr Parkinson last week. I hoped that it would not become necessary for me to say anything. However, I now feel that I have a duty to do so.

On Friday, October 7, *The Times* said that 'Mr Parkinson has made a sad and silly blunder'. Like the Government, the editor believes this should have remained a 'private matter'.

For the *Daily Telegraph* (Monday, October 10) 'the moral logic is that a quiet abortion is greatly to be preferred to a scandal'. I was not aware that political expediency was sufficient grounds for an abortion under the 1967 Act, quite apart from the fact that I could not have contemplated it.

On Monday night, in spite of the understanding expressed in his statement, Mr Parkinson saw fit to answer questions about the matter in a much publicised *Panorama* programme. It appeared from that programme that the Prime Minister had been kept fully informed and that the statement issued by Mr Parkinson contained the full facts.

The full facts have *not* been made public. Press judgements and public opinion have been influenced by inadequate information, speculation, and the Government's desire to restore Mr Parkinson's position – as someone else put it, to 'rehabilitate' him.

    1. It has been implied that I tried to trap Mr Parkinson into marriage;

    2. that I sought to destroy his reputation; and

    3. that the matter should have remained private.

This last presumes that I should hide from public view and declare on the baby's birth certificate 'father unknown', so casting further doubt on my reputation and denying the child his fundamental right to know the identity of his father.

According to the view expressed in the *Telegraph*, I should have sacrificed my baby's life for Mr Parkinson's career and the Government's reputation.

I wish therefore to make known the following chronology of events:

    1. My baby was conceived in a long-standing, loving relationship which I had allowed to continue because I believed in our eventual marriage. It has been suggested that Mr Parkinson only asked me to marry him after I became pregnant, when in fact he first did so in 1979.

    2. In May, when I knew of my pregnancy, Mr Parkinson decided he no longer wished to marry me.

I told him that, while I had to accept the fact that he was not going to marry me, I could not deny my baby his right to know the identity of his father.

    3. I did, however, implore Mr Parkinson, during May and early June, to inform the Prime Minister because his name and mine were sufficiently linked in political circles for speculation to be inevitable and it was essential that the Prime Minister was made aware of the situation before forming her new Government. He would not agree to this.

4. On polling day, Mr Parkinson sought a reconciliation and asked me to marry him. I gladly accepted. He said that he was about to see the Prime Minister to inform her of our relationship and to tell her that he would be obtaining a divorce in order to marry me. That evening he told me he had so informed her.

He also told other members of my family of his intention. He asked me to give him time to arrange matters and to leave my job at the House of Commons, which I did at the end of June. I and my family assured him of our full co-operation and that we would give him such time as he needed.

5. On August 5, Mr Parkinson went on holiday abroad with his wife and family, having reassured me of his intention to marry me.

6. On August 23, I was visited at my London home by reporters from the *Daily Mirror* who demanded to know if it was true that I was pregnant by Mr Parkinson. At that very same moment others from the same newspaper called on my father and younger sister.

Later that night, as I was driving a girl friend to her home, I was pursued by two cars which I believed to be driven by reporters from the *Daily Mirror*, who tried to force me to stop and on[c]e their cars collided with mine. I had to take refuge in Rochester Row Police Station.

7. On August 24, I informed Mr Parkinson, who was still abroad, of the incident with the *Daily Mirror*. I assured him that neither I nor any member of my family had told them anything, but I was concerned that the press would shortly confront him.

He advised me to leave London, which I did, and he said he would speak to me again on his return to England the following week. He gave me no indication that matters between us had in any way changed.

8. On September 1, Mr Parkinson asked me to meet him secretly at an office in London, where he informed me that he was not going to marry me after all. Later that day I telephoned him to say that I thought it essential that he should inform the Prime Minister.

9. I subsequently instructed solicitors with a view to Mr Parkinson and myself issuing a joint statement. In the ensuing weeks it became clear that other newspapers were pursuing the story and that it was being talked about in political circles.

10. On Wednesday, October 5, when I was informed of what had been published in *Private Eye*, I telephoned Mr Parkinson and told him that if he did not issue the statement which solicitors had been discussing for some weeks, then I would be obliged to defend myself.

Press comment, government pronouncements, and the continued speculation about this matter have put me in an impossible position. I feel that I have both a public duty and a duty to my family to put the record straight.

Richard Dowden, The Times, 14 October 1983.

Cecil Parkinson announced his resignation from the party post while the Conference was still in progress. It effectively dashed his hopes of higher office although he did return as Secretary of State for Energy in 1987 and later as Secretary of State for Transport. In 1992, he left the Commons and took a peerage. Ms Keays gave birth to a daughter. She has remained unmarried.

....

'Follow Me Around ... I'm Serious'

Downfall of American presidential hopeful Gary Hart

In 1987, Gary Hart, an American Democratic presidential contender, brought about his own downfall from the race by inviting suspicious journalists to follow him around just to prove that stories of his womanising were untrue. It followed reports in The Miami Herald *that he had accompanied a 29-year-old actress and model Donna Rice on a yacht called* Monkey Business.

The Miami Herald decided to take Mr Hart at his word, which prompted the following story in The Washington Post *on 7 May 1987.*

The *Miami Herald* reported yesterday that a news team that staked out Democratic presidential front-runner Gary Hart's Capitol Hill town house determined that a young woman from Miami spent Friday night and Saturday with him while his wife was in Denver.

Hart, whose campaign has been debating for three weeks how to deal with questions of alleged 'womanising', denounced the story as 'preposterous' and 'inaccurate'. He said he is the victim of 'character assassination' by unethical and 'outrageous' journalism that is 'reduced to hiding in bushes, peeking in windows and personal harassment'.

The paper, which spread the story across the top of its front page, said that a team of five *Herald* and Knight-Ridder reporters kept the front and rear entrances of Hart's town house under surveillance from Friday evening until Saturday night, except for a period between 3 a.m. and 5 a.m. They said they saw Hart and the woman enter the house about 11.15 p.m. Friday and saw no one leave or enter until Hart and the woman came out at about 8.40 p.m. Saturday.

Members of the *Herald* team said they would have seen anyone entering or leaving the house during those hours, except for the predawn period. According to one of them, they 'napped' during that time.

Approached by the reporters later Saturday night, Hart denied having any 'personal relationship' with the woman, denied that she had spent the night at his house and said that she had come to Washington to visit friends. He said that the woman, identified by the Hart campaign as Donna Rice, was in his town house for only a few minutes and that she and a female friend from Miami had stayed at the home of William Broadhurst, a Washington attorney and friend of Hart. Telephones at Broadhurst's office and home were not answered yesterday.

Hart told the reporters, however, that he had called Rice in Miami several times in the past two months from campaign stops around the country. He described the calls as 'casual, political'. Hart said he did not know what Rice's occupation is.

'The story in its facts and in its inferences is totally inaccurate,' Hart's campaign manager, William Dixon, said in a statement. 'Gary Hart will not dignify it with a comment because it's character assassination. It's harassment. He's offended and he's outraged. He's furious. He's a victim. Someone has got to say at some point that enough is enough ...'

'As you know, Mr Hart has suggested the press follow him to disprove the allegations on womanising,' *Herald* Executive Editor, Heath Meriwether, replied in a statement. 'We observed Hart's town house for more than 24 hours from a respectable distance and we conducted ourselves in a professional manner throughout. We never engaged in the practices suggested by Mr Dixon. The womanising issue has become a major one in Hart's campaign because it raises questions concerning the candidate's judgement and integrity. That's why we reported on this story.'

The story appeared just three weeks after Hart formally announced his candidacy. During that time, he was faced with questions about womanising and his unpaid $1.3 million debt from his 1984 presidential race. His advisers had hoped that the focus would be more on substantive issues.

The story's publication also coincided with an Iowa poll showing that Hart has increased his enormous lead over rivals in that state, which will hold the first 1988 presidential caucus. His share of the vote increased to 65 percent from 59 percent, followed by Jesse L. Jackson with 9 percent, Rep. Richard A. Gephardt (D-Mo.) with 7 percent and Gov. Michael S. Dukakis of Massachusetts with 3 percent.

Yesterday's *New York Times* magazine also featured a cover story about Hart that quotes him on the womanising issue:

'Follow me around ... I'm serious. If anybody wants to put a tail on me, go ahead. They'd be very bored.'

Hart supporters speculated that a great deal now depends on the reaction of Hart's wife, Lee.

'If it's true, it's incredibly self-destructive because it means he's been womanising all the time he was denying it,' said one supporter and contributor.

Dixon, Hart's campaign manager, expressed confidence that the voters would see the story as false and react accordingly.

'If fair people are given the opportunity to reach a fair conclusion, then we're not afraid of it,' he said. 'This raises the whole question of journalistic ethics. It raises a question of at what point the question becomes character assassination.'

Dixon said yesterday that Hart apparently met Rice last New Year's Eve in Aspen, Colo., at a party hosted by Don Henley, a member of the Eagles rock group. He said that Lee Hart was with Hart at the party.

Hart and Rice met again in March – March 1, according to the *Miami Herald* – when Hart and Broadhurst were in Miami, where Hart had a fund-raising event. They were on a chartered boat, and Rice and a friend, Lynn Armandt, came on board for about an hour, Dixon said. He said Hart did not remember Rice from the first meeting, so she said to him, 'Hey, I know you, you're Senator Hart.'

At the time, Armandt told Broadhurst that she was looking for a job in Washington and he offered to interview her as a caretaker for the town houses he owns on Capitol Hill, Dixon said. Armandt came up last Friday for the interview and asked Rice to accompany her because she wasn't comfortable staying alone in the home of a stranger.

According to Dixon, Armandt's job interview took place mid-afternoon Friday, then Broadhurst drove her to the airport to meet Rice. Coincidentally, Hart flew in to National Airport about the same time and the four of them drove back to Broadhurst's house where they had dinner together.

At about 11.15 p.m. the four walked to Hart's Capitol Hill town house, which is about three blocks away on 6th Street SE, according to Dixon. He said they wanted to see a deck being built on the top of Hart's town house; then Broadhurst, Armandt and Rice returned to Broadhurst's apartment while Hart stayed at his house alone.

This statement contradicts the *Herald* report.

The *Herald* said it was told by a 'confidential source' that Hart was interested in a Miami woman and that she planned to go to Washington for the weekend. The *Herald* did not know Rice's name and had no information beyond a general description of her as an attractive blond actress in her late 20s, according to Jim Savage, a Knight-Ridder editor who was on the surveillance team.

Investigative reporter Jim McGee boarded Eastern flight 996 last Friday afternoon and saw two women on the plane who met the general description. One was 'lovingly' met in Washington by a boyfriend, and McGee lost track of the second. After checking in with the Knight-Ridder bureau, he went to Hart's house and saw the second woman emerge with Hart at about 9.15 p.m., according to Savage.

'We almost didn't send anyone up to Washington because our information was so minimal,' Savage said. 'It was just an informed coincidence that Jim was on the same plane, and that's what got us charged up.'

Herald reporter Tom Fiedler said the *Herald* team had the front and rear entrance to Hart's Capitol Hill town house under surveillance from about 9 p.m. Friday to about 10 p.m. Saturday.

The *Herald* surveillance team included reporters Fiedler and McGee, editors Savage and Doug Clifton and photographer Brian Smith.

'We had three cars that we parked legally on the street, where we had a view of the front and rear entrance of the town house,' Fiedler said. 'There were a minimum of two people who watched through Friday night and five of us at various times on Saturday.' Fiedler said he joined the group about 10 a.m. Saturday.

The *Herald* reporters parked one of their cars across the street from Hart's town house. 'We had a clear vantage point of his front door,' Fiedler said. The second car was parked in the alley driveway that runs by the rear door to the town house, he said. A third car was parked near the corner of 6th and E streets, he said.

At 9.30 p.m., according to Fiedler, McGee saw Hart and the Miami woman leave Hart's town house. McGee saw them return to the town house at about 11.17 p.m. Friday.

The team of McGee and Clifton remained on surveillance until about 10.30 a.m. Saturday, when they were relieved by Fiedler, Savage and Smith.

McGee and Clifton, after napping and eating, returned to the Hart town house at about 4 p.m. Saturday, Fiedler said.

'All five of us were there when Hart and the girl emerged at about 8.50 p.m. Saturday,' Fiedler said. The pair left by the rear entrance and walked around the block towards Hart's car. But instead of getting into the car, the two returned to the town house by the front door.

Hart came out alone about 30 minutes later, drove around the block, parked and walked several nearby streets.

Fiedler said that Hart apparently became aware that he was being watched Saturday evening when he came out of the town house with the woman. 'That is when he seemed to get very spooked and dashed back into the house, instead of getting into the car,' Fiedler said.

At about 10 p.m. Saturday, as Hart was about to reenter his town house, he was met by Fiedler, McGee and Savage. 'We didn't go inside,' Fiedler said. 'We stood outside and interviewed him.'

It was during this interview that Hart denied having a personal relationship with Rice but acknowledged telephoning her from around the country.

James R. Dickenson and Paul Taylor, *The Washington Post*, 4 May 1987.

Hart's denials continued but he withdrew from the race, allegedly just before The Washington Post *was about to provide details of other relationships he had had. In December 1987, Hart decided to run for the presidential nomination after all but in March 1988, after a series of humiliating defeats, he withdrew from active political life.*

Iran–Contra Story

Colonel Oliver North helps fund arms to Nicaraguan Contras

This was the biggest scandal of the Reagan years. It came out because several senior members of the White House covertly used profits from a secret arms deal with the Iranian regime to fund the Nicaraguan 'Contras' in their war against the leftist Sandinista government. The reason this became such big news is that Congress had specifically forbidden the Reagan Administration from funding the Contras. The person responsible for arranging both the arms deals and the Contra funding was Colonel Oliver North, who worked in the White House.

North became a hero of sorts to right-wing Americans because of his dedication to keeping the Contras alive 'body and soul'. During the televised Congressional hearings into the scandal, North admitted to error, falsehood, obstruction and destruction of evidence, but, in the manner of fanatics throughout history, justified it as being all for a higher cause. 'Lying does not come easy to me,' he said. 'But we all have to weigh in the balance the difference between lies and lives.'

In May 1989, North was convicted of aiding and abetting the obstruction of Congress, falsifying and destroying documents and accepting an illegal gratuity. He was given a three-year suspended sentence and two years' probation. Eventually, because of complications arising out of the limited Congressional immunity granted to him and several other defendants, all the remaining charges against North were dropped in 1991. President Bush said he was 'very pleased' with the result. Bush always contended that he was 'out of the loop' when it came to involvement in the Iran–Contra scandal, a position which has been challenged but never actually disproved.

It may remain this way indefinitely as just before he left office, Bush unilaterally pardoned six key people involved in the scandal, including his former Defense Secretary, Caspar Weinberger. Lawrence E. Walsh, the special prosecutor during the hearings, said there had been 'a disturbing pattern of deception and obstruction that permeated the highest levels of the Reagan and Bush Administrations.' The 82-year-old former federal judge and life-long Republican concluded: 'The Iran–Contra cover-up, which has been continued for more than six years, has now been completed with the pardon of Caspar Weinberger.'

Many commentators contended that, in effect, Bush was pardoning himself. North concluded that President Reagan was fully aware of the scandal from the beginning but here, too, there was no conclusive evidence. North went on to narrowly miss winning the Virginia Senate seat in the 1994 mid-term elections.

Retired Air Force Major General Richard V. Secord, ending months of silence, revealed at the opening of congressional hearings into the Iran–Contra affair yesterday that about $3.5 million of the $18 million profit from the 1985–86 sale of US arms to Iran was used to finance the airlift of military supplies and equipment to the rebels fighting in Nicaragua. Secord, the pivotal private operator in the affair that has haunted the Reagan administration since it was exposed last November, also told the opening joint session of the Senate and House select committees that some of the money went to three other operations at the direction of the then-White House aide Lt Col. Oliver L. North. These, he said, included purchase of $100,000 in radio and telephone equipment for an unnamed Caribbean country, procurement of a small ship in April, 1986, and payment of Drug Enforcement Administration agents working on a separate project to locate and rescue some American hostages in Lebanon.

The Caribbean expenditures were used to support a covert project directed against Castro's Cuba and the ship purchase last year was intended for clandestine transmission of signals into Libya, according to a source familiar with earlier investigations into the Iran–Contra affair. The Iran arms sale profits became a 'slush fund' for covert projects world-wide run by North from the White House, the source said. He added that the $8 million that Secord testified was in Swiss accounts still controlled by his partner, Albert A. Hakim, originally was to be available for the North operation. Secord appeared as the leadoff witness at the unusual joint hearings and immediately levelled a bitter attack on Attorney General Edwin Meese III for 'prematurely [going] public with grossly inaccurate disclosures about our operations' last November.

'The decision of Mr Meese, and possibly others, to succumb to anxiety and ignorance is particularly unforgivable in light of the fact that had he been receptive he could have been advised of the facts surrounding these events before his announcement' that funds from arms sales to Iran had been diverted to aid the Contras fighting the government of Nicaragua. 'This reasonable option was rejected, and we were, instead, betrayed, abandoned and left to defend ourselves.'

Patrick Korten, a Justice Department spokesman, said yesterday that the department had no comment on Secord's testimony. Korten called attention to Meese's statement at the November news conference that 'the president directed that we make this information immediately available to the Congress and to the public.'

Secord also testified yesterday that then-CIA director William J. Casey and a handful of other high government officials in both the Central Intelligence Agency and the State Department did give support to his activities on behalf of the Contras. For the first time, Secord disclosed that he had met privately with Casey to plead for assistance to his operation during a time when Congress had barred the CIA from providing such assistance. On one occasion, Secord testified, Casey said he would look into the matter. Secord said he had no evidence that Casey had done anything, but in a final meeting Casey mused that Secord could get $10 million from a foreign country, and believed 'George could make such an approach.' It was a reference to Secretary of State George P. Shultz, who has acknowledged that he authorised the solicitation of a $10 million donation from an unidentified government that has since been identified as Brunei.

Dan Morgan and Walter Pincus, *The Washington Post*, 6 May 1989.

Ronald Ferguson's Predilections

Major Ferguson's visits to Soho massage parlour

Major Ronald Ferguson, the father of the Duchess of York, failed to be re-elected as director of the Guards Polo Club four months after this article appeared in the News of the World.

Exclusive: How Royal in-law liked massage beauty to wear lace knickers
FERGIE'S DAD REFUSED TO TAKE PRECAUTIONS!

Major Ronnie Ferguson never took precautions when he had sex with blonde massage girl Barbara Ashley, it was revealed last night.

The fear of catching AIDS terrified shapely 25-year-old Barbara, who says she made love to Fergie's dad TEN TIMES in two years.

But she was too frightened to order him to use a contraceptive – in case he stopped visiting the VIP vice den in Marylebone Lane, West London.

Barbara, known to her wealthy clients as Lorraine, says the major paid her £50 a time for sexual intercourse at the plush Wigmore Club.

She said yesterday: 'He never used condoms before or after the AIDS scare, and I was very concerned.

'I knew the dangers but I didn't want to upset him.

'In the back of your mind you're always afraid that you'll lose the client if you don't do what he wants.

'But I once stopped working at the club for three weeks and it was a relief because I didn't have to have sex with Major Ferguson.'

Married

Barbara, who had up to four clients a day, said fear of AIDS meant that most of her married clients insisted on taking precautions.

She said: 'They were as paranoid as I was about catching it.'

Barbara revealed that she had regular AIDS tests at St Mary's Clinic in Paddington, West London.

She explained that the exclusive clients of the Wigmore Club always expected clean girls, and said she had dozens of blood tests for other sexually-transmitted diseases.

Barbara added: 'I've had two tests for AIDS recently. Thank God, they were negative.'

She said that Major Ferguson was a generous man and a favourite among the other vice girls.

And she revealed that the twice-married major liked to be smothered in baby oil.

'It happened every time I saw him,' she said.

'He liked straight sex and nothing kinky. He was a very caring lover.

'He had a really good body and I thought he was in great shape for a man of his age.

'He treated me like a real woman. He was a very caring person.'

Barbara, who earns £800 a week, said she first saw the major about the time of Sarah Ferguson's wedding.

'I couldn't help but recognise him because I'd seen his face all over the TV and newspapers.

'I never asked him once about his daughter.

'As far as I was concerned it was none of my business.'

She revealed they kissed passionately on the mouth with no holds barred.

And he liked her to wear sexy, lacy knickers and ordered her to give him a special 'tickly massage' on his back.

'I kissed him passionately as though we were real lovers. It was a full kiss on the mouth,' she said.

'It never occurred to me that he might be kissing me that afternoon and then kissing the Queen when he'd left. As far as I was concerned, I was just doing a job.'

Major Ferguson's sordid sessions with her took place on a couch in a dimly-lit cubicle.

Barbara said Prince Charles's polo manager was whisked in secret to the club, where she would be waiting in a white clinical overall.

But underneath she would have on only the special knickers he liked.

She said the major would have a shower and lie naked on the couch while she massaged him with BABY OIL.

She then stripped off and they had intercourse.

Barbara said she was his favourite and he lavished presents on her – but he did go with other girls as well.

Royal massage girl Barbara's lifelong dream was to become a qualified beautician.

She headed for London from her Middlesbrough home seven years ago – penniless but full of ambition.

By day she was a student at the Shaw College of Beauty in London's West End.

But by night she worked as a vice girl – to pay her living expenses.

One of her clients recommended her to the Wigmore.

The skills she learned on the beauty course – including massage, manicure and makeup – were used to satisfy the sex fantasies of her clients.

Soon she was earning big money and driving a flash car. She bought a flat in Middlesex.

Barbara said: 'I was just a working girl like anybody else, trying to earn a living.'

The Wigmore girls have made a fortune out of their vice activities.

One girl from Penang, in Malaysia, lives in a £250,000 luxury flat just off the Finchley Road, North London.

Cheated

Another, also a petite Malaysian, bought a £150,000 house in Bounds Green, North London – and paid in CASH!

But Barbara revealed how one famous client in the TV world left without paying the right money.

'He came in for his usual hand relief but he got carried away and we made love,' she said.

'Of course I faked my orgasm, but then he had the cheek to walk out without coughing up the full amount. I felt really cheated.'

Barbara says she now wants to return to Middlesbrough and start afresh.

She explained: 'After all this fuss I've retired. I'd like to set up a little shop in the North East.

'I want to move out of the fast lane and live a quiet life.

'I'm tired of being a rich man's plaything.'

Greg Miskiw, James Weatherup and John Chapman,
News of the World, 15 May 1985.

....

Fiona's Pink Padlocked Diary

Ralph Halpern's mistress tells her story

This account of a London businessman's private affairs published in the News of the World *in 1988, raised considerable interest amongst middle-aged men of flagging potency.*

Randy Burton boss Sir Ralph Halpern boasted of GOOSING Mrs Thatcher at 10 Downing Street, his ex-mistress claimed last night.

Blonde Fiona Wright – whose secret diaries we publish today – revealed: 'Ralph told me he found Mrs T very sexy.

'He thought she had an attractive bottom.

'A picture of the Prime Minister had pride of place in his bedroom, and he kept on bragging about how he was always going to No 10.'

She added that Sir Ralph told her: 'I've nipped Maggie's backside several times when I've been with her at Downing Street. She's just laughed.

'I just went and stood next to her and did it.

'She didn't seem to mind at all. In fact she had a good giggle about it.'

Fiona said: 'He had a strange obsession with Mrs Thatcher.

'And he was convinced she fancied him too.

'He once told me that Margaret had described him as one of her favourite men.

'He used to videotape her TV appearances and play them over and over again, saying, "Isn't she marvellous?"

'He said he found her very stimulating. He thought about what she would be like if she was 30 years younger.'

Sir Ralph made frequent visits to Downing Street to discuss the economy.

The REAL truth about 5 times a night tycoon

POOR OLD HALPERN NEEDED PORN VIDEOS TO WAKE HIM UP

I give him 5 out of 10 for sex

Battle of the Bimbos blonde Fiona Wright always boasted she had sex with randy Burton boss Sir Ralph Halpern five times a night.

But the ageing tycoon – he was 48, she was 18 – needed PORN videos to turn him on.

And in her sensational diaries Fiona gave him a score of just FIVE out of TEN!

Their steamy bedroom romps – and her affairs with OTHER big names – are recounted in her neat, schoolgirlish handwriting in three saucy volumes she titled Fiona's Pink Padlocked Diary.

They mysteriously vanished and this week a court cleared her former flatmate, model Jacqui Bell, of stealing them.

Now the *News of the World* has obtained a copy of the diaries all Britain is dying to read:

JANUARY 1986: I saw Ralph at the studio. We went out for dinner at an Italian restaurant in West Hampstead. He played a porn video about two lesbians having oral sex.

I stayed the night, firstly on the settee in the bedroom, but he kept asking me to get into bed.

I did and he kept trying to cuddle me but we did nothing.

SEVERAL DAYS LATER: Over the entire weekend we never ventured out of the flat. It was the first time we'd made love.

He was really aggressive – so strong and forceful, but I only give him five out of ten.

When we made love his nose got in the way, but he didn't care.

He's not bothered about the size of his nose.

I asked him whether he thought I should have a boob job and he said he hated anything plastic.

He said: 'Look at my nose. Some people think I should have a nose job but I don't see why.'

Vitamins

After we made love he said: 'Please stroke my nose.' It's furry like fungus and that made me laugh and then he got annoyed.

LATER THAT MONTH: I went over to see Ralph, we stayed in and he showed me his videos of him on TV's The Money Programme. He started to kiss me, then lifted my dress up and had sex.

A few days later Ralph called for me to go round. We had sex lots of times. Score: Eight out of ten.

FEBRUARY 1986: Fiona reveals that at the beginning of their affair she called him either The Burton Man, Ralphie, and even at one point Mr X. She writes:

I was working for Mr X, as he now tells me to call him, on a job for Top Shop – which he owns – wearing swimwear and fashion. I was paid £600.

Mr X came to the studio and told me to take off my gold jewellery because it looked cheap.

He made me try his large gold Rolex watch on and said he would buy me one soon.

He liked being an important person.

But Sir Ralph also revealed to her his secret fears – that his position could make him the target of terrorist or kidnap attacks.

He told her he was a member of a gun club and kept guns by his bed to protect himself. She reveals:

I thought he took it all to extremes.

He was so security conscious he would drive the few dozen yards to return a video with his three bodyguards.

A FEW DAYS LATER: Ralph and me sat in front of the fire eating sunflower seeds, going through the newspapers.

He says the seeds give him energy and are good for his sex life.

He's a real baby about keeping young and healthy.

He takes about 40 vitamin pills a day, some in the morning and some before he goes to bed. He rattles with pills at the end of the day.

But it doesn't stop him getting colds. He's always getting them.

Then he spends hours in the bathroom with all his ointments and sprays and things, and makes me take them too, even if I'm not ill.

He's worried after we make love that I'll pass his germs back to him. He's paranoid about germs.

I saw a picture of Selina Scott so I asked him what he thought of her. He just smirked and said: 'Let's go to bed.'

He read me his astrology book. Suddenly he radioed down to his bodyguards who were waiting outside and asked: 'Is everything in order, chaps?'

Then he got out of bed and from behind his large cabinet he produced a rifle with a long lens on top.

He stood behind his long curtains, then he strolled naked through to the living room and stood with his back to the wall.

With his other hand he moved the curtains and stood there for several minutes.

Eventually he saw me standing staring at him and said: 'Time for bed, sweetie.'

I asked him what he was doing and was he involved with the Mafia.

He looked at me and said: 'You never ask a Mafia man if he's involved with the Mafia, do you, otherwise you know what happens?'

He told me never to tell anyone about his gun, or to touch it.

We made love but he kept stopping to radio down to his men. I think he was talking in code.

He kept saying: 'Jasper got the carrot?' I asked him what he was talking about and he said it was a video he had forgotten to take back.

We made love five or six times altogether.

In the morning he changed into his gym clothes and his bodyguards accompanied us downstairs.

We arrived at his headquarters and worked out in the gym. I felt uncomfortable because Ralph's gym instructor was staring at me constantly.

After the strenuous workout, we went on a pulse rate machine. His rate was 44 and mine was 87.

We then went in the lift with his bodyguards still at hand. Then we went into his shower, which was through the secretary's office.

We made love in the shower, even though it was really uncomfortable for me. I pretended it wasn't. We then had sex again on the carpet in front of the mirror.

Afterwards we had breakfast on his desk.

Dizzy

He then ordered his car to take me home so he could rehearse a speech and plan his working schedule.

TWO DAYS LATER: Ralph was supposed to pick me up at 7.30 p.m. but he called and cancelled because he had to read a speech at a private function in Knightsbridge.

THE FOLLOWING WEEK: We went to Tramp night-club but for some reason Ralph wouldn't sign the register.

I had four pina coladas and felt really dizzy.

I sat there thinking to myself: 'I hope he doesn't ask me to dance in front of all these people.' But he did.

Madonna's record came on and he pulled me on to the dance floor.

I wore a tight yellow mini with black shoes and belt, he wore coffee coloured trousers and a cream top.

I was really surprised because he dances quite trendily, in fact too trendily for his age, I thought.

THE NEXT WEEK: I saw Ralph. We had sex non-stop.

We did it in front of the fire first, then as we were unpacking the shopping from Marks and Spencer he lifted me on to the kitchen unit.

He got a banana and used it on me before unzipping it and scoffing it down at the crucial moment. I hated it all.

Then we were in the bathroom cleaning our teeth – he cleans his teeth at least six times a day – and he began making love to me.

After that he went to the bedroom and came back with his small bag that he keeps in his bedside cabinet and took out a large dildo.

It was cream-coloured with large nodules on it, about ten inches long.

We both got into bed and he gave me a cuddle, then he put two pillows down the middle of the bed because he said it kept out the draughts.

I hated it when he did that because it made me feel lonely.

I suppose he didn't want me to bother him in the night.

Then he took his asthma spray, rubbed Vick into his chest, then put a liquid on to his forehead to stop his hairline receding any further.

Boasting

He woke me up at 4.30 a.m. and made love to me and told me to say: 'There's no one better than you.'

We got up at 6.45 a.m., got dressed then went downstairs with his bodyguards and got into the car.

While we were on the way to the office the driver gave Ralph a gun catalogue.

Ralph said there was one similar to theirs and all three men produced their black guns.

Ralph told me never to tell anyone what I'd just seen, but I got the impression he was boasting.

APRIL: Me and Ralph prepared dinner for a couple of friends of his. It was smoked salmon salad and awful.

After that he played a filthy porn video. I told him to turn it off, so he did – and replaced it with a Madonna tape.

MAY: I only saw Ralph about five times this month. I think probably because he has got quite paranoid.

On one Tuesday Ralph was supposed to call round at six o'clock but he was three hours late and I had to spend the time making sure that no one came into the flat.

I kept him informed on his portable phone that the flat was still empty until he arrived.

His three bodyguards patrolled, one outside the flat, one down the street and the other outside the car. It was ridiculous.

We only talked for a few moments when the bell rang.

I panicked, nearly pulling my hair out. I told him to hide. But he just stood there and smiled.

It was only my flatmate Jacqui Bell, and I told her to walk down the road until Ralph left.

When I came back into the flat Ralph was looking under the telephone, under the TV and in the wardrobe.

He made me feel uncomfortable. I told him to get out because she would be back in a few minutes.

Nasty

We were on the way to the car when one of the neighbours said: 'Hello Fiona, who've you got with you, the Mafia?'

Back at the flat in Hampstead he grabbed my arm really hard and forced me down on to the kitchen floor.

We had sex straight away and while he was doing it he was looking at me really nastily.

He was really rough, and scowling at me and for the first time I was frightened.

I told him to get off me and he hit me across the face.

I kicked his thigh with my heel and he shouted: 'Keep still, you little bitch!' He was really hurting me.

I told him I hated him and he ordered his men to take me home.

SEPTEMBER: Halpern thought he was being threatened by me and the newspapers.

I think he's a schizophrenic.

Judy McGuire and Greg Miskiw, News of the World, 24 July 1988.

....

The Battle of the Quality Sunday Giants

Pamella Bordes, Andrew Neil and Donald Trelford

In 1989, Pamella Bordes, a former Miss India, managed to embroil several British Sunday newspaper editors in a storm in a tea cup. In the late eighties, she moved to London and gained the attention of Donald Trelford, the editor of The Observer, *and Andrew Neil, editor of* The Sunday Times. *According to a semi-official account of her exploits published in* The Daily Mail, *she was often sent to entertain prominent arms dealers or politicians. After her affairs were publicised, Peregrine Worsthorne, who briefly edited* The Sunday Telegraph, *denounced Neil in print for his predilection for the company of attractive young women rather than Oxford high tables. Neil sued Worsthorne for defamation and won the case, although the damages awarded were paltry. The following extract about Miss Bordes' life appeared in a lengthy series published in* The Daily Mail.

Conducting a Duel Between the Editors

'When I whispered in *The Sunday Times* chief's ear, my words hit him like a bomb.'

PAMELLA BORDES 'picked up' Andrew Neil, the editor of *The Sunday Times*, in the London night-club Tramp.

She is very proud of how she did it. 'He was in a group arguing passionately about politics,' she says. 'His companion was a Sri Lankan girl. I thought: "That's interesting. He's with an Eastern woman."'

Pamella waited. 'Sooner or later she'll go to the loo. Then I'll move,' she calculated. When the woman left the table Pamella crossed the room, slid into her chair and whispered in Neil's ear: 'I find you very attractive.'

'I think it hit him like a bomb,' she says. 'This beautiful girl coming over and telling him that. He really believes that he has no looks. He believes he's ugly. But to me he had the look of power. He looks like Nero and I was madly attracted to him.'

Fateful

The problem was to get her phone number to him. Because at that moment the Sri Lankan girl returned. Introductions were made and Pamella discovered she and the girl, whose name was Renuka, had a friend in common.

'What a small world,' said Pamella. 'Look, I've just done a Cordon Bleu course. I'm going to have a dinner party and you must come.' Renuka pointed to Neil and said: 'He'll have to come with me.' Pamella thought to herself: 'Got him.'

She wrote her telephone number on a piece of paper. Immediately Neil snatched it, saying: 'I'll take that.'

Some time after that fateful meeting Pamella received a long-distance phone call. 'Hello,' said the voice with its distinctive Scots brogue. 'Do you remember me? It's Andrew Neil.' He said he had been skiing in Aspen, Colorado, and wondered whether she'd like to meet him for lunch on his return.

Pamella laughingly accepted. 'You sound American,' she told him. 'No, just transatlantic,' said Neil, who when working in the US had acquired a reverence for that nation's classless energy.

'He loved me thinking he was American,' says Pamella. 'The truth is he'd rather be American than Scottish.' A date was arranged for the following Sunday. Delighted at her catch, Pamella rushed to tell her friend Carlo Colombotti her news.

It was, after all, a moment of considerable triumph. True, she'd known powerful men in the past but that had mostly been for money or business.

This was different. Here was the editor of one of the world's most powerful newspapers asking her for a date. An eminently brilliant man who was, it was said, soon to head his employer Rupert Murdoch's entire European TV operation, he had entrée to the most powerful corridors in the land.

At 39 he was a leading member, not of the Establishment he despised, but of the new consensus-hating meritocracy forging a modern Britain. Best of all, he was unmarried.

For the girl who had clawed and whored her way from obscurity in India the possibilities for social advancement and respectability were dizzying.

That Sunday, Pamella dressed carefully, choosing a tailored black suit. 'Stick to classics,' she thought. At 1 p.m. Neil's Jaguar drew up outside Carlo's home.

He was very much the supreme five-star editor, she says. Over the weekend a major story had broken and all the way to the restaurant Neil was barking orders to executives over the carphone. A cynic might have wondered why, however, as his paper wasn't coming out for another six days by which time the news would be distinctly old.

'Get so and so on the next plane to Milan,' she heard him order. A call came through from Beirut. 'I was terribly impressed,' says Pamella. 'It was all sheer power.'

Pictures

At Pontevecchio in Earls Court, a restaurant Neil uses a lot, they ordered pasta and talked about Aspen and New York.

As the white wine flowed they started holding hands. He asked her to go to the ballet with him the following Thursday. But could she go back to his flat nearby just to check his diary?

She remembers thinking what a mess his flat in Onslow Gardens, South Kensington, was. There were books all over the place and plants in the wrong location. The loo walls were plastered with pictures of girls.

'This guy's on an ego trip,' Pamella remembers thinking.

The couple went for a walk, arm in arm, through St James's Park. Then he dropped her off in Park Lane where she met a girlfriend.

'Wow,' said the friend when Pamella told her about Neil. 'You've really hit the jackpot this time.'

On Monday Pamella made up a bouquet during her flower-arranging class at Moyses Stevens and decided to send it to Neil. Later she heard how he had shown the flowers to colleagues at work and boasted about this crazy girl who sent them. To her he was to confess: 'It was the flowers that did it.'

That Thursday they went to see Swan Lake at Covent Garden. All the editors of the so-called quality papers were there.

Neil had made it clear that he wanted Pamella to look stunning and she had chosen an orange suit by Ungaro – a gift from an Arab boyfriend – and got her hairdresser to plait her hair in a single braid down her back.

At the drinks party beforehand a small man hurried over to Pamella. 'Hello,' he said. 'Haven't we met before?'

Pamella smiled. It was the corniest line in the book. He told her he was the editor of *The Observer* newspaper. She remembers thinking: 'This man thinks he's so dashing but he's really just a little pixie.'

Donald Trelford's wife, she noted, was 'quite impressive. A very strong, majestic woman'.

After the ballet the editors went to a restaurant in Covent Garden.

Trelford, who was seated to Pamella's left with Neil opposite, started talking to her in a rather obvious way. 'The moment you walked into the room,' she claims he said, 'I thought "My God, what a striking woman."'

Pamella was self-obsessed enough to think Trelford was falling completely for her but cynical enough to think he might be behaving so outrageously to annoy or enrage Neil. She looked across at her escort, read his face and knew at once that Trelford was succeeding. For amusement she began to encourage him.

Trelford told her about his recent trip to Russia and about the book by the chess master Gary Kasparov he'd bought for *The Observer*. Kasparov was coming to Britain and Trelford said he'd introduce him to Pamella. The couple openly exchanged telephone numbers.

After all, Pamella thought, Andrew and she weren't lovers. But when Neil saw what was happening, she says, he almost choked on his food.

Lovely

Outside the restaurant he and Pamella had a furious row. She says he screamed: 'How dare you talk to Donald Trelford? He's going to try and use you against me.'

They rowed all the way back to Neil's flat but once there they made up. He suggested she stay the night and in the early hours of the morning, says Pamella, they became lovers.

It was the start of what was to be a passionate, turbulent affair.

Over the ensuing weeks the relationship intensified. She was frequently in his flat, cooking, tidying, manicuring his nails every Sunday and washing the stains from his pillowcases which she says were caused by the Australian hair restorer he used. He would video films from the TV for her. Once he said: 'I've taped *Bhowani Junction*. Ava Gardner is in it and she reminds me of you.'

Both seemed to have been very happy at this time. Although one is inclined to smile cynically when Pamella Bordes talks of love, she certainly was having a lovely time with Neil.

If not actually in love with him, she was certainly in love with the idea of being the girlfriend of a great national newspaper editor with all the amazing fringe benefits. And they certainly began to plan marriage.

Furthermore, Neil was delighted with her. She looked wonderful, had a stunning wardrobe, she was the perfect accessory. He really liked her, she says ruefully today.

He clearly did. Neil was kind and generous, buying her gifts and paying for her elocution lessons. He was solicitous to her comfort and did anything he could to make life better for her.

'It was all because he was really in love with me,' she says. 'He told me he loved me. We used to wake each morning and say "I love you . . . I love you."'

They went to David Frost's annual party. The US Ambassador was there, along with millionaire race horse owner Robert Sangster, TV presenter Robin Day and composer Andrew Lloyd Webber.

SDP leader David Owen was there too. She says he told her: 'I've heard all about you. You're much prettier than Andrew told me.'

The girl from nowhere had really arrived.

Before going to parties – there was a constant round of them – she says Neil would tell her what to wear. He also told her: 'I want you to refer to me always as "My boyfriend Andrew Neil". Always say that,' he said, 'And I'll call you my girlfriend Pamella Bordes.'

'He insisted we do that,' says Pamella. 'He said I wasn't acknowledging him enough. Every few minutes he'd ask: "Tell me you love me." He was so insecure.'

All this time Trelford, the rival editor, was still paying court and Pamella could not resist encouraging him.

Neither editor had any idea about Pamella's past. Both accepted her story that she was a well-connected Indian socialite from an important family. Neither journalistic instinct nor natural curiosity led them to make any critical examination of these claims.

Uneasy

Like any new lovers, Neil and Pamella spent hours exploring each other's past. But while he told her all about his ordinary Scottish background, his grammar school education and family's joy at their son getting to university, he seemed more interested in probing his own history for her than finding out about hers.

Perhaps he was uneasy about the talk of servants, large houses and a string of polo ponies which she conjured up for him. But his talk of his past gave her a very good insight into his weaknesses and insecurities.

With Trelford it was different. He talked about himself and his journalistic coups. But he also probed again and again about Neil, his newspaper rival.

Pamella swiftly weighed up the mechanics of both men's egos. Neil, she says, was the senior editor, running a big and successful newspaper and destined for even bigger things when Sky TV was launched.

'He was supremely confident professionally but very insecure socially,' she says.

Dapper

Trelford, she noted, was exactly the opposite. Dapper and self confident in any social gathering, he nevertheless was envious of Neil's professional success. 'He realised Andrew was the bigger editor,' she says.

Since in any relationship she always seeks to dominate, she played the weakness of each man against the other. She told Neil how suave and sophisticated Trelford was. 'Andrew wore cheapish looking suits without style and I told him so,' she recalls.

She says she made a mutual agreement with Neil. She would improve his social graces and give him more confidence in high society while he would seek to broaden her intellectual outlook so she could meet important men on equal terms.

At the same time, she says, she told Trelford how fast Neil's career was progressing upward. 'He really is going to be one of the top men in Britain,' she told him.

This, she admits, is something Trelford did not really want to hear. Both men helped move Pamella into the top strata of London life.

All the people she met she set out to make an impression on. She put their names and numbers into her book and called on some of them subsequently to aid her social climbing.

Trelford enjoyed the game. A snooker devotee, he sent Pamella a book on the sport inscribed 'To Pamella, who has snookered us all.' There was a book on chess too. The inscription: 'To Pamella, a queen amongst pawns.'

Frequent phone calls, she says, were followed by flowers and gifts – a gold pen, a bangle. These she had no hesitation in showing to Neil. 'Look what Donald has given me,' she said. 'He's adorable but so silly.' Sternly, Neil would demand she send them back.

Trelford flaunted Pamella, taking her to parties in such media watering holes as the Garrick Club and the American Bar at the Savoy.

'He made sure we were seen,' she says. 'He used to say: "Neil will hear about this within 24 hours."' Not surprisingly, there were ferocious rows between Neil and Pamella. He once screamed at her that he could forgive her anything but going out with Trelford.

Despite, or maybe because of, Trelford's attentions the relationship between Pamella and Neil flourished. More importantly, through Neil, she was meeting some of the most prominent names in Britain.

He took her to dinner at the home of a prominent religious figure. Lord Sainsbury was there too but it was Neil, she says, who dominated the conversation.

'Everywhere he goes he takes over,' says Pamella. 'He's a brilliant conversationalist in public but so insecure in private.'

Khashoggi's world seemed a million years away.

Neil took her to meet Rupert and Anna Murdoch at a restaurant in Jermyn Street. He took her to Arianna Stassinopoulos's publishing party at Lord Weidenfeld's.

'Andrew sneered about Arianna: "She is one of those girls famous for being famous." Then Arianna came over and said to Andrew: "I don't usually say this but my husband has asked me to tell you your girlfriend is one of the most beautiful women he has ever seen."'

Neil, says Pamella, was in seventh heaven.

Ballet

The way Pamella tells it, it was about this time they started talking about marriage and children. Neil had great plans for a child. He wanted it to be born in America, the country he worshipped, so it would have automatic citizenship.

At this point, however, something happened which provides another glimpse into the disturbed Bordes psyche. She discovered she was pregnant by a previous lover, a ballet dancer.

Without telling Neil, she had an abortion one Saturday.

That night she went out with him to the restaurant Rue St Jacques to celebrate his birthday.

A few days later he had a birthday party. Murdoch was there, so were Robin Day, TV presenter Melvyn Bragg, film director Michael Winner and his actress girlfriend Jenny Seagrove.

The rows over Pamella's friendship with Trelford were by now becoming almost daily events.

At Neil's flat one day, while he was at work, Pamella activated his answering machine. From the messages she concluded he had started seeing another woman.

In a scene of sublime irony the woman whose life had been devoted to duplicity went, in her own words, 'crazy with jealousy'.

'I rang him and screamed down the phone: "You're two-timing me. I'm going to teach you a lesson you'll never forget." I scribbled messages all over his mirrors in lipstick, four-letter words. I chopped up his suits. I smashed his crockery. I took his scotch and poured it down the sink.'

Later came the first of many reconciliations. But from that day on Neil never left her alone in the flat.

He continued her social education, taking her to the Cartier polo tournament and Wimbledon. He helped her start a cookery business, paying for ads in the magazines *Vogue* and *Harpers*, and arranged for her to prepare an office lunch. He also helped her find a flat in Pimlico.

'He'd pick me up around 8 on his way home from work,' she recalls. 'He'd often come early while I was in the bath and go through my letters. He was so jealous.'

Neil, of course, had every reason to be jealous. For the self-destruct button in Pamella had been pushed once again.

Awesomely scheming and shrewd, she is also capable of self-lacerating stupidity. Despite the cachet and security Neil could offer her she risked everything by spending two secret weekends in Paris.

The first was with a Brazilian who had been an earlier lover.

For the second trip, last August, she says, she booked herself into the Plaza-Athenee where she 'just happened to bump into' her former flame Ahmed Gadaff Al Diam.

Pamella justifies these two weekends this way: 'I wanted to play a little psychological game with Andrew. It always adds an element of mystery. It's important to have that with men and keep them intrigued and interested.'

Window

On the other hand, it may simply have been work. She was running short of funds.

When she got back on the Monday, she says, Neil's first words to her were: 'How was Paris?'

'I thought "God, I've been caught." I said: "How do you know?" He said: "I know everything about you."'

It was to be the final period between them of screaming rows and tearful reconciliations.

Today, Pamella says almost triumphantly: 'I made him cry a few times. I could always do that. But he made me cry too. We're both very emotional.'

Last September, after yet another violent row, she threw bricks through Neil's flat window.

The relationship between them had reached the point of no return and on November 7 she received a letter from his solicitors. In matter-of-fact language, it documented how she had destroyed £2,000 worth of his clothes, twice threw bricks through his windows, made death threats, circulated stories to damage his reputation and delivered 'by hand' dog excrement in a package. It said an injunction would be served against her if she made any further contact.

The letter was a fittingly squalid epitaph to a six-month affair.

If anything, the passionate affair between the editor and the call girl proves the formidable, primeval force of sexuality. It also shows how thin the veneer of success and sophistication is and how near Pamella came to destroying a seemingly shrewd, eminent and clever man.

Heart

Today, delivering her best actress lines, she says: 'I feel betrayed, cheated and humiliated. I'd given him my love from the bottom of my heart.'

Her words reveal more than anything her supreme ability to deceive herself. Blessed or damned by a total lack of insight into herself, she accuses almost everybody of having betrayed her when in fact she has betrayed herself.

As a tangential footnote, it is worth recording that Pamella says her relationship with Trelford became even stronger after the break-up with Neil.

Just before Christmas he took her for dinner at La Tante Claire. He gave her a Cartier handbag. She gave him some brass shirt-stiffeners from Turnbull and Asser.

'We were never lovers,' she says. 'We just used each other in our own ways to manipulate Andrew.

'It's funny. When Donald and I meet we do nothing but talk about Andrew. We're both obsessed with him.'

The Daily Mail, 21 April 1989.

The Henry Higgins of Capitol Hill

Congressman Barney Frank's involvement with a male prostitute

Barney Frank, the Democratic Congressman from Massachusetts, thought he could survive politically by making a clean breast of his involvement with a male prostitute. He was later censured by the House of Representatives Ethics Committee after allegations that he had fixed 33 parking fines for his former aide and also wrote a misleading memorandum in order to shorten his probation for other sex and drug offences. He was forced to resign the following year, to chants of 'Out the door, Barney!'.

Rep. Barney Frank (D-Mass.), one of the House's leading liberals, said yesterday he had privately hired a male prostitute with a criminal record as a personal aide, housekeeper, and driver and fired him about 18 months later in mid-1987 after learning that the man had used his Capitol Hill apartment for prostitution.

Frank, who is homosexual, said he had employed the man out of his personal funds in the hope that he could lead him away from prostitution and to a better life. It was an effort that the five-term lawmaker said was fuelled by his desire to prove himself a liberal who cared about a 'particular individual' as much as 'humanity in general'.

'I thought I was Henry Higgins ...,' said Frank, likening himself to the fabled English linguistic scientist in George Bernard Shaw's *Pygmalion* who attempts to transform a cockney waif into a member of English society. But Frank said he was instead 'victimised'.

'I was a loser. I lost money, and I was embarrassed,' Frank said. His statement, at a news conference in the Boston suburb of Newton, followed publication of reports in *The Washington Times* that detailed the former aide's relationship with the congressman and the principal of the Chevy Chase Elementary School in Montgomery County.

Republicans in Massachusetts called for Frank's resignation, citing what they termed his poor judgement; Democrats said the issue could threaten the 49-year-old congressman's career.

At the news conference in his district and in interviews yesterday, Frank identified the former aide as Steve Gobie, 32, a man who had been convicted of three felonies, including oral sodomy and possession of cocaine, in Alexandria Circuit Court in 1982. Gobie told *The Times* that Frank paid him $80 for their first sexual encounter in his 8th Street SE apartment after the congressman answered his want ad in a gay newspaper. Frank did not dispute this account.

The congressman conceded that the disclosures may hurt him politically and said that his fractious relationship with Gobie was a key factor in his decision to state publicly in the spring of 1987 that he is gay. That announcement apparently was made about the same time Frank fired Gobie, an action the lawmaker took after his landlord complained a second time about activities in the congressman's apartment while he was out of town.

Frank said he knew Gobie was still a prostitute when he hired him as a personal aide and that he did not expect him to 'go cold turkey' and stop the practice immediately. But Frank said he hoped that Gobie's prostitution would 'diminish' as he underwent therapy ordered by an Alexandria judge after he was convicted of contributing to the delinquency of a minor.

The congressman agreed with *The Times'* account that he initially paid Gobie for sex but said that relationship terminated 'a month or two' later when Gobie agreed to work for him. Frank disputed the newspaper's description of Gobie as his lover. 'I would not have had a sexual relationship with someone who was working for me,' Frank said.

'We never spent the night in my apartment,' Frank said. He said their relationship consisted of 'a couple of casual meetings with him, and then I said: "Look, I'd like to be your friend and I'd like to help you out."'

Although Frank said their relationship was short-lived, he said his friendship for Gobie was not. He said the friendship led him to disbelieve his landlord's initial complaints that Gobie and a woman were engaged in prostitution when Frank was away.

Gobie was paid about $20,000 a year to work as his aide, housekeeper and driver, the congressman said. In addition to the pay, Frank said he had hired a Northern Virginia lawyer for Gobie, paid for some of Gobie's court-ordered psychological counselling and written letters to court officials on his congressional letterhead stating that he had hired Gobie.

'... He was just taking advantage of me,' Frank said. '... I'll tell you how I explain it. The guy had a perfect set-up. He was in charge of keeping my house clean, he had keys to my house, you know ... He would know when I was leaving town and would drive me to the airport. He would know when I was coming back. He had absolute security.'

Frank declined to discuss whether he had used other prostitutes. He said that even at the time of his relationship with Gobie he was aware of the dangers of AIDS and was 'very careful'. He said he has since settled into 'a long-term relationship with someone whom I'd like to believe is monogamous'.

Frank has survived serious political threats before, but he and his supporters said yesterday that the latest disclosures pose a far more severe test.

An outspoken liberal, Frank was first elected to Congress in 1980 after eight years in the Massachusetts Legislature. In his freshman term in the House, political enemies in the legislature, most of them conservative Democrats who regarded Frank as a brash interloper, redrew the lines of his district to throw him into a battle with veteran Rep. Margaret M. Heckler (R-Mass.). Though he started as an underdog, Frank defeated Heckler, winning reelection in 1982 with 60 percent of the vote in one of the most expensive congressional contests in Massachusetts history.

Since then, he has solidified his grip on the gerrymandered district, which stretches from the liberal Boston suburbs of Newton and Brookline through some affluent commuter towns and down to Fall River, an old textile city with lingering economic problems. In 1988, the first election after Frank said publicly that he is gay, he won with 70 percent of the vote, receiving only 3,000 fewer votes than he had in 1984, when he had faced only token opposition.

In the House, Frank has been in the forefront of battles over housing legislation, civil rights and immigration laws and has waded into debates on defence and fiscal policy, where his quick wit delighted even Republicans with diametrically opposite views.

But yesterday, Alexander Tennant, the Massachusetts Republican Party's executive director, lost no time in calling a news conference to demand that Frank resign or be ousted from the Democratic-controlled House.

Tennant argued that the lawmaker 'showed profound lack of judgement ... lied about the situation ... [and] violated the law' in buying sex from a convicted prostitute, allowing him the use of Frank's apartment and interceding for him with probation officials by writing letters on House stationery.

'It's hard to believe Barney Frank is that naive,' Tennant said. 'If he does not have the decency to resign, the House should investigate him and remove him from office.'

House Speaker Thomas S. Foley (D-Wash.) said in a statement: 'There is no more able, articulate and effective member of the House of Representatives than Barney Frank. He has provided outstanding service to his constituency and the nation, and I'm absolutely confident he will continue to do so long after this matter has been forgotten.'

Rep. Chester G. Atkins (D- Mass.), chairman of the Massachusetts Democratic Party, issued a statement calling Frank one of 'the most gifted and talented legislators' on Capitol Hill and expressing confidence that his constituents 'know what an able representative and advocate he is for their interests.'

'This is obviously a difficult personal time for Barney,' Atkins said, 'but his personal life has nothing to do with the way he performs his public duties.'

Other prominent state and national Democrats were publicly silent on the incident, but privately many Massachusetts politicians said the unsavory elements of the relationship could imperil Frank's hold on the district.

Several Democrats pointed out that Rep. Gerry E. Studds (D-Mass.), who is openly gay, has continued to be reelected from a neighboring legislative district since being disciplined by the House in 1983 for his relationship with a congressional page. But one veteran Bay State campaign manager said, 'This is a different climate today ... The press is much tougher on personal stuff like this. We've learned that once a scandal like this gets on people's radar screens, the survival rate is practically zero.'

Bill McAllister and David S. Broder, *The Washington Post*, 26 August 1989.

The Feminist Geisha

Japanese Prime Minister Sosuke Uno and the geisha

Prime Minister Sosuke Uno was the first Japanese leader to resign (in 1989) because of his personal behaviour towards a woman. A month later, a cabinet minister in the new government of Prime Minister Kaifu was obliged to resign after it was revealed that he had paid another geisha $21,000 hush money.

Tokyo—The former geisha who has virtually wrecked the political career of Prime Minister Sosuke Uno smiles and bows demurely. 'My name,' she says, 'is Mitsuko Nakanishi.'

Nakanishi is wearing a white dress patterned with red flowers, clasped at the neck with a pearl pin. Forty years old, she possesses a delicate beauty, and it is not hard to imagine how Uno would have found her irresistibly alluring in the fall of 1985 when, by her account, they embarked on a five-month affair during which he paid her a total of about $21,000.

The woman who touched off this furore is, to say the least, a bundle of contradictions. On the one hand, Nakanishi manifests deep anger over what she says was Uno's callous disrespect toward her, and she laments that the status of Japanese women lags far behind that of their Western sisters.

In a soft voice laced with indignation, Nakanishi says she 'can't understand' Japanese women who send their husbands off on sex tours of Korea and Southeast Asia, inwardly hating the situation while at the same time fulfilling a wifely obligation by 'putting condoms in the husband's luggage'. On the issue of women's rights, she adds, 'I wish foreign countries would bash Japan.'

Among her sterner detractors are women. Kazuko Komiri, a salty 79-year-old film critic and television personality, was quoted in a magazine saying of Nakanishi: 'She sold her body for 300,000 yen a month, and then revealed it because her partner became famous. Such a woman is shameless.'

The youngest of nine children, Nakanishi became a geisha in an unconventional way: She had first married, borne a child, divorced her husband, gotten an office job – and only then entered the exotic world of 'flower and willow.'

Geisha traditionally are trained from girlhood, so that they can be properly schooled in the art of pampering and entertaining male clients. They learn the *samisen*, a guitarlike instrument, and traditional Japanese singing (*utai*) and dance. Although a geisha's relationship with a client doesn't always lead to sex, the temptations are obvious.

Nakanishi says her main reason for becoming a geisha was simply to make more money. She figured she could rake in several times the $900 monthly she had been earning as an 'office lady' in a law firm. 'My ex-husband had remarried and he wanted to raise my child,' she says. 'So I made up my mind to get up and do something.' Working as a geisha also appealed to her, she says, because she had studied the *samisen* and *utai* in her youth, and she liked the idea of deepening her appreciation of those traditional arts.

Asked whether it felt peculiar to adopt the servility required of a geisha, she replies, 'Yes. But I made up my mind that this was business.' Whatever sense of contradiction she felt with her modern instincts, she says, 'I made up my mind to just cut it from my thoughts.'

Only a month or so after she became a geisha in mid-1985, she says, Uno – then a prominent member of parliament – noticed her and arranged to meet her a few days later at a *ryotei*, an exclusive Japanese restaurant where geisha typically provide their services.

Precisely what happened between Uno and Nakanishi is obviously subject to doubt, especially since her veracity has recently come under a bit of a cloud. A Tokyo mass-circulation magazine published allegations – based on anonymous sources, and vigorously denied by Nakanishi – that she has lied in the past about her educational and artistic attainments.

But the basic elements of her story are widely regarded as credible because of the corroboration of the *okaasan*, or mother, of her geisha house, who told *Sunday Mainichi*: 'I understand a bit why she wanted to speak out. But a real geisha never talks.' (Uno has refused to discuss either her story or similar stories that have emerged recently about his relationships with other women.)

Nakanishi has recalled that when she and Uno sat together in a private *tatami* room at their first dinner in October 1985, Uno sought to impress her by showing her the about-the-author page of a history book he had written, which said he had served in a variety of posts, including minister of international trade and industry. Uno sang a few songs to relax her, but he eventually got down to business rather crudely, she says, advancing his offer of 300,000 yen per month by grabbing three of her fingers and demanding gruffly, 'How about this?'

She decided to accept his proposal to provide sex or social accompaniment whenever he called because, she told TBS, 'in the geisha world it's hard to say no,' and because 'I had just gotten divorced and I was not confident of myself.' But when he commanded her to 'lie down' right there on the straw *tatami* mat, she refused, she says.

They first had sex in late December, according to Nakanishi, who says Uno spoiled the occasion by harping on the fact that he was paying her, even though the sums he allegedly disbursed are widely regarded here as meagre by geisha standards.

In some respects, Nakanishi seems to have lost her perspective about what she should have expected from such an arrangement. For example, she recalls rushing to the bathroom in tears after receiving a phone call cancelling an assignation with Uno because his wife had come to Tokyo from his parliamentary district.

But her descriptions of Uno, which she imparts with a certain emotional intensity, suggest that his behaviour fell considerably short of the sensitive Alan Alda type. She recalls, for example, that at a small New Year's occasion, Uno humiliated her by gesturing derisively when he was asked by an older geisha if it was true that he and Nakanishi were carrying on a special relationship. Later, when the *okaasan* of her geisha house sought to entertain Uno by performing a special dance for him, the future prime minister made little attempt to disguise his scorn for the old woman's efforts.

According to Nakanishi, Uno would typically call her early in the morning – even though she worked late at night – to boast about his coverage in the newspapers and television. He promised her gifts, she says, but didn't come through. He didn't even provide a traditional parting gift when he broke off their affair in March 1986, she says; he merely claimed that he was subject to a *dokuta-stoppu* ('doctor-stop', or medical order) to refrain from sex.

Nakanishi has consistently maintained that it wasn't her wounded pride that prompted her to go public with her accusations against Uno. She says she believes that a man who treats women so shabbily shouldn't be allowed to lead a nation. Uno's behaviour 'goes to the fundamental question of relations between human beings,' she declares.

When Uno was elevated from foreign minister to prime minister early last month, 'everything which I had shut down inside myself suddenly burst,' she says. Although she says she dreaded the idea of becoming the centre of a scandal, she felt compelled 'to cut my flesh, and bleed myself' – figuratively speaking, of course – 'and by doing so, cut his bones.'

Nakanishi's tale has evoked a wide array of reactions. The Japanese public has long turned a blind eye toward the extramarital activities of politicians, and one oft-expressed opinion here is that Uno's main sin was not having a mistress, but rather failing to bestow the proper kindnesses. Holders of this view like to cite the late Bukichi Miki, a founder of the Liberal Democratic Party, who reputedly rebuffed a heckler by acknowledging that yes, he had several mistresses, 'but I take good care of all of them'.

Among those taking a less than harsh view – at least in public – is Uno's wife Chiyo, who in true Lee Hart fashion was quoted in a magazine as saying that she continues to trust her husband, and 'anyway this is a story of the past.' She also apologised on Uno's behalf because 'such trouble was caused' by the uproar . . .

Nakanishi may try to cash in on the controversy by writing a book, but in the meantime her notoriety has brought her mostly misery. No longer a geisha – she quit well before the scandal broke, and took an office job with a design firm – she has been unable to work because 'the yellow papers [tabloids and mass-circulation magazines] are constantly chasing me.'

Accordingly, she has gone into seclusion, undergoing Buddhist purification rites and trying to figure out what to do with her life. Leaning forward and putting her hand on her bosom, she says touchingly in English, 'My heart, broken.' Aha. Perhaps, then, this is really a story about unrequited love? 'No, no, no, no,' she retorts, again in English; she wasn't in love with Uno.

'There were so many things that happened, one after the other,' that angered her about Uno, she says, that she reached the point where she felt the urge to simply 'give back the money and say goodbye.'

But didn't she want Uno to love her?

'Well,' she replies, 'I am a woman. Such feelings are natural, I think.'

Paul Blustein, *The Washington Post*, 19 July 1989.

Prime Minister Uno's resignation was the first of many as each head of government was found to have some murky secret in their past.

....

Only the Little People Pay Taxes

New York hotelier Leona Helmsley's tax-dodging behaviour

Despite New York hotelier Leona Helmsley's pleas about her health, she was ultimately convicted and imprisoned in 1989 for several years on various tax-dodging charges, which is only appropriate for someone who once remarked that 'only the little people pay taxes'.

When we last left Leona Helmsley, the haughty hotel queen was running up outrageous bills for her $11-million mansion, firing people left and right and generally making her lawyer's description of her as a 'tough bitch' seem a tad on the mild side.

Now let us rejoin the sordid little tale unfolding at Manhattan federal court, where the latest evidence suggests that the bull-headed billionairess was charging her hotel empire for such items as a $58.49 wax job on her legs and a $12.99 girdle from Bloomingdale's. And stiffing a contractor for $600,000. And allegedly shaking down a champagne salesman. And buying almost as many shoes as Imelda Marcos.

In today's instalment, the obligatory embarrassment involves a memo to all servants at Helmsley's Greenwich, Conn., estate on proper preparations for the Queen's arrival: 'The pantry area must contain tea cosies, tea strainers and loose tea; as well as a martini mixer and pearl onions for drink garnish. It is imperative and mandatory that EVERYTHING must have a place. Whether it be a towel, or a needle, or a hairpin, or a dish pattern – each must be in a place.'

Following the tax-fraud trial, now in its seventh week, is not unlike rummaging through someone's underwear drawer. First you find the girdles (sneaking a look at the size), then the diary, then some other interesting objects until ... No more [Enough]. The thought of another piece of dirty laundry is enough to produce a state of nausea, the very feeling that one Helmsley ex-employee testified he had after each unpleasant session with the Queen.

But New Yorkers, possessed of a high tolerance for obnoxious behaviour, simply can't get enough.

'There is an inexhaustible appetite for information about her,' said Elaine Taylor-Gordon, an advertising executive whose firm just gave Helmsley the royal boot after handling her account for three years. 'She is a star. The sad thing about it is, she doesn't realize it. Whatever she has achieved, it has never been enough.'

Taylor-Gordon dropped the $5 million account after Helmsley casually mentioned she was unilaterally slashing the firm's fees by 60 percent. Partner Larry Aarons said Helmsley, who with her husband pays about $20 million a year in taxes, simply told him that 'she needed the money. That was her modus operandi. She would squeeze and squeeze.'

Even Harry Helmsley, the 80-year-old tycoon who is too ill to stand trial with his wife, had enough of her spendthrift ways at one point. When faced with mounting bills for his wife's $1 million pool enclosure at their country estate, according to one witness, Harry said: 'If you didn't order so many things, Lee, we wouldn't have this bill as big as it is.'

No less an authority on outrageous conduct than Mayor Edward Koch has joined the chorus, labelling Helmsley 'the Wicked Witch of the West' and castigating her for 'chintziness.'

Helmsley, 69, is accused of fraudulently billing her businesses for $4 million worth of renovations to her weekend estate, Dunnellen Hall, as well as personal items ranging from cosmetics to a $45,000 silver clock. She is also charged with extorting kickbacks from suppliers.

Witness after witness has described the Queen in less than flattering terms. Liquor distributor Lee West testified that he was forced to give Helmsley 40 percent of his commissions as a condition of selling champagne, whiskey and wine to her hotels. He said Helmsley's former aide and co-defendant, Frank Turco, told him to pay the kickbacks or 'we get somebody else to do the work' and that 'this money goes to Mrs Helmsley.'

West said he was later told his firm would have to rent a $55,000-a-year suite in Helmsley's Carlton House hotel to keep getting the liquor business. When he refused, West said, Turco told him: 'That's it [You're out].'

Milton Meckler, a former Helmsley vice president, told the jury a similar tale. When he ordered 600 RCA television sets for the hotels, Meckler said, Turco told him to demand three free TVs for Leona's birthday or RCA 'would lose the order'.

When Helmsley realized she had gotten the sets for free, Meckler said, she asked him: 'How many more can I get?' Meckler said he told her she was 'pushing it to the hilt.'

John Struck, another ex-aide, said Helmsley ordered him to refinish eight cherry wood doors leading to her mansion bedroom so they would match the light walnut floors. But when she returned early from a two-week vacation and the work was not done, he said, 'I knew that this was probably the end.' Struck was fired that day.

It was the bearded Struck who told the jury about Harry Helmsley objecting to the disputed pool-enclosure bills. He said that Leona Helmsley responded by screaming at her husband: 'You are getting sucked into this too. Can't you see they are trying to steal things from us? They are trying to rob us. We don't owe anything.'

The pool bill was never paid, Struck said.

And then there were the 10,000 evergreen plants for the mansion grounds – pachysandra, to be precise – that were charged to a Helmsley hotel in Connecticut.

Elaine Taylor-Gordon says Helmsley first granted her an audience in 1986, soon after the Queen had fired her previous agency, Beber-Distler (which is suing her for $1 million in unpaid fees). Taylor-Gordon was ushered into the royal penthouse suite at the Park Lane Hotel.

'She was extremely opinionated,' Taylor-Gordon says. 'She didn't let us speak. We were not offered anything. She said, "Well, let's have it." I understood immediately I was going to be the lady-in-waiting and my partner the footman.'

Helmsley nixed some of her proposed themes because, Taylor-Gordon says, 'she didn't want to do them because they didn't involve her. She definitely wanted to be in the advertising ... She is a symbol, a logo. She is not too much different from Betty Crocker.'

After Helmsley was indicted last year, Taylor-Gordon gently suggested removing her smiling picture from the ads. 'Mrs Helmsley felt that her customer identified with her, recognized her face and that we had diminished it to a small enough size already,' she says.

'There is no personal relationship with Mrs Helmsley, none. In three years of working with Mrs Helmsley, I never had a drink with her or a cup of tea with her.'

Mary Ann Eboli, Helmsley's long-time secretary, told the jury she twice saw co-defendant Turco deliver envelopes, apparently stuffed with cash, to the Queen in her office at the Helmsley Palace.

'I'm going to make the old lady really happy today,' she quoted Turco as saying on one such occasion.

Howard Kurtz, The Washington Post, 15 August 1989.

....

The Greatest Electronic Evangelical Tent Show of the Eighties

The Jim Bakker sex and hush-money scandal

Jim Bakker, the televangelist, was sentenced to forty-five years' imprisonment in 1989 and fined half a million dollars for various offences related to his PTL ('Praise the Lord' Ministry). Haynes Johnson, the distinguished Washington journalist, commented that 'his sentence brings to an end the great electronic evangelical tent show of the eighties, a drama of seduction, fleeced sheep, temples turned to dross and rampant greed.' After receiving his sentence, Mr Bakker conceded that 'I have sinned. I have made mistakes.'

CHARLOTTE, N.C.—Still proclaiming his innocence almost $2\frac{1}{2}$ years after a sordid sex and hush money scandal drove him from his PTL pulpit, Jim Bakker is back, in federal court here for his coming judgement day on mail and wire fraud charges.

'Our faith is in God,' he declared today, climbing out of a black BMW sedan at 8:55 a.m. to walk a gauntlet of TV cameras.

It was the first day of jury selection for the defrocked televangelist, who stands accused of defrauding devotees by raising millions through television to fund heavenly pursuits at his ministry, then diverting the money to fuel a lavish earthly lifestyle and cover up his 15-minute frolic with a former church secretary, Jessica Hahn.

Flanked by daughter Tammy Sue Chapman, 21, and his white-haired attorney, George T. Davis, 82, Bakker smiled and held his head up as he stepped quickly toward the gray granite courthouse across the street from a converted strip joint now housing 800,000 ministry documents and videotapes that prosecutors have assembled as evidence.

Ignoring reporters' shouted questions, Bakker said only, 'I'm happy to have my daughter with me.' His wife, Tammy Faye, who is not charged with wrongdoing, remained in Florida to run their new TV ministry, which is struggling along on fewer than a dozen stations from its headquarters at a down-at-the-heels Orlando shopping mall.

On the air this morning, she exhorted listeners through tears to pray for her husband. 'We have such trouble [with] things going on in Charlotte, North Carolina, today,' she said. 'It's like a circus ... I don't know how possibly Jim can get a fair trial [there].' Then she blew a kiss at the TV camera, aimed at her husband. 'I love you, sweetheart,' she said. 'Don't you dare give up.'

She was just warming up.

'Not only is Jim on trial, people,' she declared, 'but the church we know is on trial. Everything that has to do with Christian television is on trial when Jim walks into that courtroom.'

She also pitched for contributions to a legal defence fund she hopes will collect $1 million. A spokesman for Jim and Tammy Ministries said viewers were responding, but declined to reveal how much money has come in. A source close to the case says Bakker's lawyers have yet to receive 'a penny'.

'If our case is tried on truth, we will win,' Tammy Bakker told one reporter the other day. 'I'm asking God that everyone will simply tell the truth ... I'm praying for all the men who are lying.'

Bakker, a short man who friends say has always been insecure about his height, was natty in a gray double-breasted, summer-weight suit as he held his smile for two dozen members of the media here for a trial that could last more than a month. He came closer; they pressed forward. 'Hold the line,' shouted a TV cameraman, appealing to rivals to stay clear of his shot.

The line held, and a loud cheer erupted from TV crews as Bakker disappeared inside the courtroom of US District Judge Robert Potter, 66, nicknamed 'Maximum Bob' for the stiff prison terms he metes out. Bakker, 49, stands charged with eight counts of mail fraud, 15 counts of wire fraud and one count of conspiracy to defraud donors. If convicted on all counts, he could face up to 120 years in prison and more than $5 million in fines.

Outside, there were neither fans nor protesters, save a lunch truck operator, Michael Williams, 22, a former PTL supporter who said he was there 'to get a little of my money back' by hustling coffee and breakfast biscuits to the press.

'It's Jim's day of reckoning,' said Sam Johnson, 50, pastor of Heritage Village Church, before services the other evening. Johnson took over Bakker's former flock and launched his own TV ministry recently with a congregation of 900 faithful. He's moved it several miles from Heritage USA, the sprawling 2,300 acres in Fort Mill, S.C., that Bakker carved from cow pastures to build his religious TV empire and Christian theme park.

Adds Johnson: 'It's time for a full disclosure ... The pathetic thing about this story is that Jim Bakker ... never 'fessed up ... There was never any true contriteness. Just think what a better world it would be if they'd just said, "I was wrong."'

Bakker was indicted last December after a 16-month grand jury probe, along with his former top aide, Richard Dortch. Together they were accused of diverting for their personal use more than $4 million of $158 million raised from various ministry 'partnership' donor programs.

But two weeks before he was scheduled to go on trial with Bakker, Dortch cut a deal with prosecutors, pleading guilty to three counts of fraud and one count of conspiracy to commit fraud, and promising to testify against his old boss to reduce his own punishment.

Come Friday, Dortch, 58, who still faces up to 10 years in prison and $500,000 in fines, will be sentenced by Judge Potter, along with Bakker's former top personal aide, David Taggart, 32, and Taggart's brother James, 35, the ministry's former $120,000-a-year interior decorator.

Both Taggarts were convicted of tax evasion and conspiracy two weeks ago for failing to report as income $1.1 million in PTL funds used to pay personal bills between 1984 and 1987. Each faces up to 25 years in jail and $1 million in fines.

Summoned to testify for David Taggart, Bakker took the Fifth Amendment and avoided Taggart's gaze.

'David was deeply hurt,' said a former PTL employee who says he told the grand jury he once accidentally walked in on the two men while they were engaged in sex in the Heritage Grand Hotel's Presidential Suite. Bakker denies any homosexual behavior, despite three former employees who say they told the grand jury under oath they either observed such behavior or engaged in it with Bakker. David Taggart, when asked last year in federal bankruptcy court if he'd ever had sex with Bakker, took the Fifth Amendment.

But this trial is expected to focus on money, not sex. Perhaps offering a preview, government prosecutors at the Taggart trial served up a smorgasbord of financial excess, as a parade of witnesses testified that the Taggarts lavished such gifts as fur coats on themselves and others. On New York shopping sprees, they snapped up $96,000 rings, $75,000 bracelets and $3,750 cigarette lighters at Cartier. They bought a Trump Towers condo, jetting there to unwind from their long hours at Bakker's ministry.

In a post-mortem, the Taggarts' Washington, D.C., lawyer, Ben Cotten, says items charged as ministry expenses on the Taggarts' personal American Express cards made jurors blanch. 'They bought shoes for $1,500 a pair,' says Cotten. 'I've never even bought a suit worth $1,500. You can imagine how jurors felt who had joint household incomes of $25,000 or less.'

So it has come to pass, another bizarre chapter in America's longest-running soap opera about God and Greed: a trial with all the ratings potential of 'Dallas' or 'Dynasty', a saga of Old Testament proportions. And such publicity that, even as Bakker's lawyers renewed their request for a change of venue, Judge Potter asked the jury pool today if anyone 'would be willing to have yourself convicted based on publicity. What I'm trying to do is get you to put yourself in the place of the defendant, who has had a lot of publicity.'

But who on earth hasn't heard of Jim and Tammy, or studied their parable for modern living, save perhaps some blind Tibetan monk meditating in a cave with no satellite TV? Is there any place where their every move hasn't been chronicled, from supermarket tabloids to the nightly news? And why wouldn't inquiring minds gobble up every morsel, even potential jurors?

There's sex – heterosexual and bisexual, purportedly; adultery; hush money and misspent millions; lust for political power and respect as Bakker was courted before his fall by Presidents Carter and Reagan and candidate Bush for his cheap access to millions of television viewers and voters.

There's revenge; alleged blackmail; claims that one minister threatened physical violence on behalf of Jessica Hahn; a host of Christian brothers, trashing one another to get ahead like some mob mutation – America's Spiritual Mafia. There were cries of rape; women scorned; an all-star cast that trekked through Bakker's ministry at one time or another: Jerry Falwell, Pat Boone (who considered stepping in), former PTL board members Rex Humbard, James Watt, Efrem Zimbalist Jr. Almost anyone could wind up on the stand at Bakker's judicial Armageddon.

America's Holy War has gone ballistic, as Jimmy Swaggart tries to recover from last year's confession of unspecified sin shortly after he was photographed with a $20 prostitute on New Orleans's seedy Airline Highway, as top TV ministries report the ongoing fallout of diminished donations from this last round of sex and money scandals, and as Jessica Hahn announces a career move: her plan to host a ladies' mud wrestling special on cable TV.

So, how juicy will it get? Assistant US Attorney Deborah Smith doubts Bakker's bedroom will be put into play. 'At this time, the government has no plans to call Jessica Hahn on what happened in Florida,' she said last month in court. She was referring to the brief sexual episode Bakker admitted with the former church secretary turned nude *Playboy* pinup, an encounter that cost him the kingdom after he allegedly forked over $265,000 in ministry funds in an unsuccessful effort to keep her quiet about it.

Nor has John Wesley Fletcher, the 49-year-old fallen evangelist who flew in Hahn at Bakker's request that fateful day in 1980, and found a subpoena on his doorstep 120 miles up the road in Durham, N.C., where he's living with family as he weathers a divorce from his wife of 18 years and bounces back from a suicide attempt.

'I've lost all that's dear and precious to me because I was loyal to [Bakker],' he says, groping for meaning as he plops into a recliner. 'If they call me to testify, I'll tell the truth.'

Don't rule out a trial with sex. Assistant US Attorney Smith, on the case with co-counsel Jerry Miller, 41, has said that while the government has no plans to ask Fletcher to testify about sex at PTL, she won't slam the door on the possibility of 'getting into' that area if trial strategy requires it.

'I can see 14 different ways where we might have to go into that,' she told the US magistrate in court, though she offered no scenarios.

Indeed, prosecutors remain tight-lipped about the case, as they face off against Charlotte attorney Harold Bender, 47, once a federal prosecutor, and San Francisco attorney Davis, who won a sentence reduction for German munitions kingpin Alfried Krupp after he was sentenced at Nuremberg in 1948, as well as a pardon for labor organiser Tom Mooney after he spent 23 years in prison under a death sentence for a 1916 San Francisco bombing.

'I don't think [Bakker's] a criminal,' Davis said shortly after taking the case. 'When you stop and think of all the operations he was running and funding and handling, and the need that he had for help, for assistance, he's really not a managerial type. He's a minister.'

'I was a pastor. A businessman I was not,' Bakker testified before a federal bankruptcy judge last year.

'My whole judgement of him is that he's a decent, honest man of his word,' Davis said. Does it give him pause that the world may not love his client? 'Almost every case I've ever handled has been for a defendant who at the time he crossed my threshold was considered a despicable guy. That part doesn't bother me at all.'

Armed with videotapes of Bakker soliciting funds, prosecutors apparently aim to show a pattern of on-air deceit and broken promises. They say Bakker persuaded more than 100,000 donors to mail in $158 million, guaranteeing that each 'partner' who 'invested' $1,000 would receive three free nights a year at Heritage USA hotels for life. But according to the portrayal in the indictments, Bakker was an unholy huckster, hustling lodging with the Lord when there was no more room at the inn.

The 'partners' began to complain. But Bakker kept selling, despite the indictments charge, funnelling funds he said were earmarked for building programs to cover high salaries, bonuses and huge operating expenses. One monument to his hype, the 21-story Towers annex, sits boarded up on the Heritage grounds, a $24 million project for which Bakker raised $70 million but spent only $12 million before he resigned in March 1987.

At the same time, the government charges, the PTL board of directors awarded Bakker $3.5 million in bonuses when he was bemoaning a ministry in financial crisis. There were Rolls-Royces, Mercedes-Benzes, Cadillac limousines, gold-plated fixtures and dressing room Jacuzzis. New extravagances may be revealed.

'I used to drop $100 on cinnamon rolls just to make their hotel suites smell good,' said Don Hardister, PTL's former security chief, reminiscing over a pepperoni pizza at his home in Tega Cay, S.C. 'Nobody ever ate them, but Jim loved the smell. It was part of my job.'

Now it can be told: Hardister also played architect for the infamous air-conditioned doghouse. 'I just got tired of Jim and Tammy calling me at 3 a.m. like it was high noon to check on those idiot dogs,' he said. So he installed climate control.

'We put the dogs inside there but they didn't like it. You're talking about a couple of St Bernards who can suffer a little cold.' As for Tammy's other little pooch, Snuffles, 'she liked staying in the guardhouse with us,' said Hardister.

'I have a lot of regrets, especially being so silent about how the money was spent.'

He is not alone. 'I feel badly about all the people who were hurt,' said Fletcher, who once pulled down upwards of $1.5 million a year in donations as a travelling preacher whose frequent appearances on Bakker's show made him a celebrity in the late 70s and early 80s before he was banished. 'I really left at the right time, before it blew up. I saw it coming . . . Jim was absolutely, unquestionably a little Caesar. But there was a time when I looked upon him as the voice of God.

'Jim used to tell me, "John Wesley, your face is worth a million dollars," ' reflected Fletcher. 'What he meant was that after I appeared on the show, contributions shot up by $1 million.'

In two separate trips before the federal grand jury here, Fletcher says, he related his own three sexual encounters with the boss; how he once found Bakker and Taggart in bed in a Bermuda hotel room; and how Bakker asked him to procure a woman, any woman, to make Tammy jealous when their marriage hit the rocks in 1980.

As for Hahn, he remembers how elated she appeared after her famous trip to Florida. 'She only got mad and wanted money after she heard Bakker had called her a "New York bimbo" later,' says Fletcher, who disputes her version of ravaged innocence. He admits sleeping with her after his boss that day, but says it was her wish.

'She was brushing her hair when I got back to the room,' he said. 'She started telling me what a wimp Jim Bakker had been, how uncaring and unthoughtful he was. I said, "Jessica, I'm sorry it turned out that way. I told you he's having trouble with Tammy." We sat down on the bed. One thing led to another.'

Hahn has claimed she was raped. 'If she was raped, why didn't she run into the hall and scream, "Rape"? There was plenty of security. If I'd thought for a minute she was upset, I'd have stayed with her all night.'

In fact, Fletcher claims, they'd already slept together after her birthday dinner in February 1980 at the New York Sheraton – almost a year before she met Bakker. 'One way to look at it is I was sharing my girlfriend with my boss,' he said. Hahn has conceded the birthday dinner, but denied the aftermath. 'She was a gospel groupie who had been dying to meet Jim Bakker. She watched him on TV all the time.' Naturally, Fletcher didn't think there would be a problem.

If Hahn is called by the government, might Bakker's lawyers summon Fletcher to assail her credibility? Could it get down to two government witnesses, both under grants of immunity, thrashing each other's pseudo-romance?

Or might Bakker's sex life be used by prosecutors to show motive, explain why he paid top aides like David Taggart more than $300,000 a year? Was it to hide ministry secrets? Two former PTL employees who say they told the grand jury of Bakker's alleged bisexual conduct appeared on a list of witnesses filed with the court Monday.

'When I was forced out, Taggart told me, "John Wesley, I'd never let them do that to me. I know too much,"' said Fletcher. Taggart could not be reached for comment. Ben Cotten, Taggart's attorney, declined to delve into his client's sex life, saying, 'There's no indication that will come up' at Bakker's trial.

But Hahn, who hasn't been subpoenaed either, could become a factor should prosecutors assail Bakker's veracity, say sources close to the case. Former Bakker bodyguard Hardister says he was quizzed two weeks ago by prosecutors about Bakker and Hahn. 'They asked me, "When did Jim Bakker tell Tammy about Jessica Hahn?"'

When he resigned in March 1987, Bakker wept that he'd confessed the dalliance years before. But Hardister says he didn't tell Tammy until that month, right before handing PTL to Jerry Falwell and slipping into an exile calculated to restore him to his empire.

'Tammy was going around the house flipping through magazines, asking David [Taggart] what Jessica Hahn looked like,' Hardister said. 'She was asking, "Am I prettier than Jessica?" It was kind of sad.'

Prosecutors are also counting on Dortch to counter any Bakker claim that he had no knowledge of the $265,000 Hahn hush money, which was advanced by PTL builder Roe Messner, then reimbursed with a phoney invoice, the indictment says. If asked whether Bakker blessed the hush money, Dortch is expected to say that Bakker instructed him 'not to pay her a penny more than you have to,' according to one source close to the case. Dortch and Taggart played ministry go-betweens with Hahn. Dortch declined to comment.

Long ago, he was just a travelling tent preacher who hooked himself to high technology to build a religious TV empire that put the 'Jim and Tammy Show' into 13 million homes, rakes in $129 million a year in tax-exempt charitable donations and drew 6 million visitors annually to PTL's Christian theme park just down the interstate in Fort Mill, S.C.

It was quite a dream: a crime-free family resort for non-smoking, non-drinking born-agains hooked on Bakker's feel-good, 'you can make it' gospel. After prepping with Pat Robertson at his Christian Broadcasting Network in the late 60s, Bakker wound up launching his show from a converted furniture store here: the PTL Club, which stands for Praise the Lord or People That Love or more recently, among critics, Pass the Loot.

As money poured in, Jim and Tammy became born-again royalty to their charismatic Christian fans, laying out their troubles on the air, connecting with weary souls and spending like there was no tomorrow: a parsonage by the lake, with a miniature water slide for their children, a ministry jet, jewels, face lifts, breast surgery, trips to Europe.

All of it was paid for easily as contributions poured in. But Bakker was devoting so much time to his dream, friends say, that Tammy felt neglected, fell for a Nashville producer, Gary Paxton, who admits strong feelings but denies an affair. Paxton soon found himself banished.

'When you don't have godly wisdom about money and power, you can lose sight of reality,' Paxton said in a recent phone interview. 'I know a guy went to Bible school with Jim Jones, said he was a totally serious young man then, and look how he wound up.'

Soon, Fletcher was summoned by Dortch, his Illinois superintendent in the Assemblies of God, and defrocked. Drinking was the official reason, but Dortch held a letter accusing him of sexual misconduct to keep him muzzled about Hahn, Fletcher says.

'Remember the name Jessica Hahn,' Fletcher says he told Dortch. Then, in 1982, as Jim and Tammy boosted their market share, Dortch took a lucrative job running Bakker's ministry.

Tammy's heavy makeup and giddy persona and Jim's melodrama for the Lord drew crowds, ratings and theological ire from ambitious rivals like Swaggart, who attacked Jim Bakker's theme-park religion on PTL network airwaves that carried Swaggart's show for a fee. Heritage USA was 'a cancer', he said. Soon Swaggart was bumped from the PTL network, and upon hearing rumours of Hahn, pressed his attack for Bakker to come clean, according to Dortch. Bakker allegedly had peculiar tastes for a preacher, spending cash on kinky curios, including X-rated movies and sex toys his former bodyguard says he was ordered to buy. 'I spent about $250 on them once,' said Hardister, who remembers his boss popping one tape into his dressing room VCR. 'It didn't do a whole lot for me, but Jim seemed kind of fascinated. He said, "This is for Tammy and me." '

By 1984, letters were arriving from Hahn, demanding money, a settlement. She threatened a $12 million lawsuit; hush money and the rest is
history.

As Heritage USA fast became a Christian Disneyland, there was trouble
in paradise. In early 1987, Bakker slipped away to Palm Springs, Calif.,
where Tammy was fighting her addiction to prescription drugs at the Berry
Ford Center.

By then, Swaggart was pressing the Hahn episode with a passion, even
as he fended off his own accuser down on the Louisiana bayou: Marvin
Gorman, a budding televangelist and Bakker friend whom Swaggart had
charged with sexual misconduct, driving him off the airwaves and into
bankruptcy. Now he had caught Swaggart at a no-tell motel with a $20
hooker and there was hell to pay. For Swaggart, it was holy war on two
fronts.

Suddenly, that March, Bakker resigned, turning the ministry over to
Jerry Falwell as a caretaker. Confessing to a brief sexual encounter, he
plotted his return.

But he didn't count on the Assemblies of God defrocking him for
adultery with Hahn and 'alleged bisexual' activity or on Falwell lieutenants
like Jerry Nims, a savvy multimillionaire entrepreneur from Atlanta,
putting their noses into the files. 'My first impression of Jim was that
he was a nice guy, but it soon became obvious something was badly
wrong,' said Nims, the former president of the Moral Majority, last
week.

'The biggest shock was finding cancelled checks paid to Jim and Tammy
for hundreds of thousands of dollars when the place was busted ... You
had $160 million in building done on a no-bid basis with no invoices. I
kept asking for the invoices for nails and cement, but they were never
produced.'

And the oversold properties struck Nims as not only possible fraud, but
also violation of securities laws. He turned it over to the US attorney and
later, fretting at the lack of progress, flew to Washington to meet an
assistant attorney general. 'I used an analogy,' said Nims, 54. 'I said, "I'm
a citizen. I just witnessed a bank robbery. I've seen the guys who robbed
the bank. You're the policeman. Here's the information." '

Rather than return the ministry to those he viewed as Bakker surrogates,
Falwell delivered PTL into bankruptcy court. Toronto businessman
Stephen Mernick snapped it up for $65 million last year, but a Sept. 30
deadline to close the deal appears in jeopardy because of a title dispute
involving the Catawba Indians, who are claiming rights to 144,000 acres

in York County, S.C., that includes PTL. Landowners and Indians will appear before a federal judge Sept. 27.

With business dramatically down and the Heritage Grand Hotel running at 20 percent occupancy last weekend, Jim and Tammy's once-pristine paradise has fallen into disrepair. The hotel's paint is chipping; the roof leaks.

At Victor's Music Shop on the mall at Heritage USA, Jim and Tammy souvenirs are marked way down. *I Gotta Be Me*, a Tammy paperback, a bargain at 98 cents. Albums, mugs, slashed to the bone. Stacks of glossy coffee-table books with Jim and Tammy on the cover, once offered for a $100 donation, are moving well at $5 a piece, says Flora Sult, a cashier. 'Some people are still very fond of them,' she says.

Once jammed, Jim and Tammyland is a virtual ghost town. 'I hate to see it all so run down,' says Ray Mullis, a PTL supporter who drove seven hours from Eastman, Ga., with two sons, Jason, 11, and Jonathan, 8, and aims to keep coming back. They are browsing in the toy store in the mall.

'My boys love the water park,' he says. 'Jim Bakker had a vision –' Suddenly, toyshop owner Marjie Walters cuts him short.

'But he's never repented. He's never said, "I'm sorry." If they hadn't raped this place, just think what they could have done, how many more people they could have helped ... The homeless ... I don't mind a man of God making a good salary, but if you work for God, you don't need a tremendous salary.'

Indeed, the trials weigh heavily on many who have come to see the light.

'After the Taggart trial,' says Hardister, who publicly broke with his boss two years ago, 'a lot of Bakker people came up to me and said, "Don, will you please forgive us? We didn't believe it until we heard it in a court of law." I said, "I know how you feel. I didn't believe it until I saw the books." '

It's time to pray. Sam Johnson, pancaked with makeup, waits to take the stage at the new Heritage Village Church, where the TV cameras are rolling at Friday night Camp Meeting. Only 19 worshipers appeared that night, but most Sundays the sanctuary fills to its full capacity of 900, with former PTL employees and new members.

'It's almost as if there's been a tremendous war and the smoke is clearing,' Johnson reflects. 'There's been bombing, strafing, then suddenly out walks this remnant of soldiers. We are bedraggled, black and blue, tattered, but not without spirit. We're ready to climb the next hill, face the next onslaught.'

Art Harris, *The Washington Post*, 22 August 1989.

Bakker was released from prison on parole in late 1994. His statement to the press, after five years' imprisonment, merely announced that he 'looks forward to rebuilding his life, and being of useful service to others.' As for Tammy Faye, she divorced her husband in 1992 and married her former husband's contractor of choice. According to a friend, Tammy felt 'it could never work again with Jim . . . She had helped build three ministries and she said Jim had lost all of them.' Jessica Hahn, the 'church secretary' who claimed Bakker paid her hush money to keep her from talking about their relationship, had cosmetic surgery after the case was over. She posed again for Playboy *magazine and then became involved in an obscure syndicated television programme.*

....

No Way to Treat a Lady

The scandalous behaviour of Baroness de Stempel

The behaviour of Baroness de Stempel towards her aunt gripped the British public during her trial in 1990. The following account was the only one in which the baroness spoke to the press before her imprisonment.

On 20 April, Susan de Stempel was sentenced to seven years for forging the will of her aunt, Lady Illingworth, and for stealing more than £500,000. Michael de Stempel, her second husband, was given four years and her children, Sophia and Marcus Wilberforce, 30 and 18 months respectively, after being found guilty of conspiracy to steal. Susan doesn't think she'll take parole. 'It's not freedom in my view. I'd rather have all or nothing. I think that's a Wilberforce feeling coming out in me.'

Even in gaol, the Baroness is determined to put a distance between herself 'and the rest'. 'As soon as I started to talk to the police,' she says, 'I knew they wouldn't understand a word I said. They simply don't speak the same language. How can they? They don't know my sort of people. All families take bits of furniture from each other – it's the only way to save paying tax. I didn't defraud my aunt. Michael is as innocent as I am. And I didn't murder Simon Dale.'

Baroness Susan de Stempel (née Wilberforce) was tried in August 1989 for the murder of her first husband, Simon Dale. He was found battered to death with a crowbar in the kitchen of their Jacobean mansion from which she had tried to evict him for 14 years. At the end of an 11-day trial, she was found not guilty. But while investigating the crime, West Mercia police discovered 'bank accounts that were previously barely in credit had suddenly swollen beyond recognition'.

'We couldn't understand,' said Detective Inspector Cowley, 'why a woman living in a semi-detached farm-worker's cottage which she insisted on calling Forresters Hall could say she had no means of support, no assets, no money, but could float around in some very nice vehicles and live in a cottage jam-packed with lovely furniture.'

They understood why after they followed a trail that led back from bank accounts in the Channel Islands, auction houses throughout England, and property in Spain to an 86-year-old peeress, Margaret Lady Illingworth, Susan's aunt, who had died in a state nursing home in Shropshire. It transpired that this one-time society aristocrat, who had lived in the last privately-owned house in Grosvenor Square, had been lured by Susan de Stempel to Susan's cottage in Shropshire. Here, a prisoner of her senility, she was also a virtual prisoner of the family before she was off-loaded into a nursing home to die £8,000 in debt, while her niece Susan, aided by two of her five children – Marcus, 28 and Sophia, 27 – drained away part of her £1 million fortune.

Baroness de Stempel and Margaret Lady Illingworth, also known as Aunt Puss, had both grown up in the same house – Markington Hall in Yorkshire, the family home of the Wilberforces, whose most famous member was the 19th-century anti-slaver, William Wilberforce. The Wilberforces may have been grand, but one thing they didn't have was money. Locals still speculate that this was the reason why in 1931 Susan's aunt Margaret Wilberforce at the age of 31 married Lord Illingworth, the Postmaster-General who, at 66, was very much her senior.

Lord Illingworth died in 1942, but his wife embarked on a metropolitan and hedonistic lifestyle. She lived at No. 44 Grosvenor Square, which by the 60s was the last privately-owned house in the square, wintered in Monte Carlo and Switzerland and punctuated the rest of her calendar with the grandest parties. Lady Illingworth and her 30-room mansion (which had underground tunnels for the servants) were fixtures in the gossip columns. Every possible occasion was celebrated, while every meal was eaten off silver plate because as she remarked to one diarist: 'It saves the crested china, you know.'

In 1968, despite a vigorous campaign, the house with its William Kent mural in the dining-room and a temple in the garden, was pulled down to make way for the Britannia Hotel. Lady Illingworth's last appearance in the papers was as a dislodged grandee trying to decide whether to live at Claridge's or at the Connaught. When she moved out, there were 47 vans of valuable furniture, paintings, and other household equipment (including three crates of scrubbing soap, five packing cases of old Christmas cards and one crate of Elizabeth Arden Blue Grass scent – the smell of which Susan described as 'quite awful') which were all shunted off into store while she looked for a flat. In the end she went to live with her elderly cousin, Irene and her housekeeper in a large Kensington mansion block – York House off Kensington Church Street.

Lady Illingworth's society lifestyle was one for which Susan had also been groomed. Her childhood was much like any other uppercrust childhood: nannies, day nurseries, night nurseries, little contact with her parents, boarding school at five – a much earlier age than usual due to her father's army life. She went to a leading Catholic convent, St Mary's, Ascot. In 1957 she met Simon Dale, a tall, half-blind architect, at a party. They married in London that year, she aged 23 and he was 38. At the time of her wedding her parents had raised a storm of snobbish protest. In 1959, Susan Dale bought Heath House, a fine red brick house with classic Jacobean proportions for only £2,000 as it was severely dilapidated with only three habitable rooms.

There were five children born in six years and within a short time of moving to Heath House, the marriage was disintegrating. It was Susan's dwindling funds that supported them, her aunt's money that paid the school fees, while Simon Dale occupied himself with his own bizarre obsession that Heath House was located on the actual site of Camelot. 'He didn't have fairies at the bottom of his garden,' said a local Shropshire farmer. 'He had the whole of the court of King Arthur.' Marital conflict turned anger to physical violence. In 1973 Susan obtained a divorce from Simon Dale on the grounds of unreasonable behaviour, and reverted to the family name of Wilberforce, and settled down to life at Forresters Hall cottage. For 14 years, Susan Wilberforce fought to get Dale out.

It became a titanic struggle. Even when Susan put the house on the market at a low price, Dale put potential buyers off by waving a shot gun.

By 1980, the mental state of Lady Illingworth, a once pretty and well-liked woman, had deteriorated with the onset of Alzheimer's disease. A part-time secretary, Anne Greig-Smith, revealed: 'I had to put my finger exactly on the part of the cheque she had to sign.' Lady Illingworth did, however, make intermittent trips to her old home Markington, to which she had asked the younger generation if she might return to live. These visits were sometimes spontaneous. On one occasion she hailed a cab in Kensington High Street which she then took home to Yorkshire. However, she wasn't welcome as four days later, the Markington Wilberforces drove her home. 'When will you get it into your head,' said her housekeeper at York House, 'they don't want you.'

But it was to Forresters Hall that she was destined to make her last family visit. Accompanied by Sophia Wilberforce, this now muddled old lady came to stay in February, 1984 – ostensibly for a short holiday, but she was never to return to London. Susan had not kept in close contact with Lady Illingworth. Indeed in 1982 she said to Michael that she had not seen Aunt Puss for eight years, so it was doubly curious that she should suddenly invite an old lady into a cottage that was already bursting at the seams with herself and three children. It was fortunate that on his visits Michael eased the accommodation crisis by sleeping in a blue tent in the garden 'which was very cold. I had to wear two Guernseys.'

It was during Lady Illingworth's stay at the small, cramped Forresters Hall that her forged will was drawn up by Susan (on thin paper so that it was easier to trace Lady Illingworth's signature) and a Jesuit priest, Father Dooley – who had been imported from Stonyhurst College – was duped into being a witness. The new will left Lady Illingworth's whole estate to Susan (with a nod of £25,000 in the direction of Susan's brother Wilberforce and £10,000 to a cousin, Lord Richard Wilberforce, 'for having added lustre to the family name'). It was in direct contradiction to her first will in which Susan was not even mentioned.

Then the ruthless onslaught on money, goods, stocks and shares began. For days a fascinated public in the Birmingham Crown Court heard details of forged cheques, shared bank accounts, the sale of valuable antiques. It was as if a tap was suddenly turned on which gushed forth money – mostly withdrawn from cashpoint machines – which bought cars (two Peugeot 205s and a Peugeot estate), foreign holidays (Spain, New York and Japan), some earrings from Aspreys (£5,000) and a curiously tasteless flat on the Spanish coast. In the midst of her spending spree, Susan Wilberforce married Michael de Stempel on 11 September 1984 in Jersey.

But meanwhile what happened to Lady Illingworth? In December 1984 she was admitted to Hereford General Hospital after she threw a hammer at her bedroom window. 'She was,' said a hospital health worker, Pamela Luke, 'apparently abandoned by her niece in casualty. She said that the old lady was a sex maniac with a passion for hitchhiking and that no man was safe. I had to persuade her to even go and see her aunt when she came to the ward to bring a bag of clothes.' From there Lady Illingworth was taken to Langford House, a council-run old people's home, after Susan had assured the health authorities that her aunt had no money other than her pension. According to staff, she spent the days telling people she should be somewhere else – Yorkshire or London – and her nights wandering around, puzzled as to why the servants were still awake. Eventually she died in November 1986 – a destitute woman – and on the instruction of Susan de Stempel was given a pauper's cremation, despite her wish to be buried alongside her husband. Two months after her death, Susan informed the rest of the family.

The turbulent marriage of the de Stempels officially ended in 1986. For Susan the sale of Heath House became the only way out. Again and again she pleaded for a quick legal way to get Simon Dale out. He remained obdurate; the only shift in his life was that apart from King Arthur and Camelot in the garden, he now thought there was an early Armenian settlement in the basement. Then came the murder at Heath House. One wet September evening, 11 September 1987, someone was admitted through the kitchen door who then bludgeoned the 6ft 3in, 17-stone ex-architect to death.

His body was not found for two days, but because the Aga had been on full blast, it was difficult to establish an exact time of death other than sometime around supper – as the toad-in-the-hole he had prepared for himself was found roasted to cinders in the oven, while half-prepared vegetables lay on the table alongside some used sherry glasses.

Susan de Stempel and her children had been working on the exterior of the house on the Friday it happened. Three months later Susan was arrested along with Sophia and Marcus. Charges were dropped against them, but in July 1989 the Baroness stood trial for murder. Throughout the 11-day trial in sweltering heat she preserved the same frozen immobility. Questioned about this she referred to her childhood training, being forced to sit unblinking for 10 minutes at a time. Her *sang-froid* remained intact even when the jury left to consider its verdict. At the 'Not Guilty' all the Baroness did was put her hands in her pockets and smile.

The police now argue that but for the murder (the file remains open), the fraud would never have been found out. 'It was a family affair and though they might have been much surprised at the contents of the new will, no one would have fought it,' said Detective Inspector Cowley. The day Michael was sentenced, he said: 'Susan is a very evil and manipulative woman. She sacrificed me and the children because she couldn't get her own way.'

From Risley Remand Centre, Susan reflects on the case. 'Everyone keeps saying our family is straight out of *Brideshead* – but in *Brideshead* no one went to prison.'

Lucinda Bredin and Kate Wharton, *ES Magazine*,
Evening Standard, May 1990.

....

Recruit Scandal

Japanese financial corruption

Japanese financial scandals are virtually impenetrable for an outsider but as they can involve billions of yen, it is worth including this one from 1990 as a case study.

TOKYO—Hisashi Shinto, once one of Japan's most powerful business figures, was convicted of accepting bribes today in the first big court case to emerge from a scandal that rocked Japan's political world.

In a brief hearing this morning at Tokyo's District Court, Mr Shinto, the 80-year-old former chairman of the Nippon Telegraph and Telephone Company, the world's largest company, was sentenced to two years in prison and fined $170,000 for his part in the Recruit scandal, the stock and influence-peddling case that shook Japan for more than a year. The prison term, however, was suspended because of his age and what the court termed his 'past contribution to the business world'.

Mr Shinto was the best-known and most powerful member of the Japanese establishment indicted in the scandal, which ultimately forced the resignation of Noboru Takeshita, the former Prime Minister. As the scandal unravelled, it revealed a web of illegal dealings between part of the nation's business community and the ruling Liberal Democratic Party, but all the political leaders involved escaped indictment.

Villain and Victim

Mr Shinto's conviction marks the beginning of the end of the most embarrassing and far-reaching scandal in Japan since the Lockheed scandal of the mid-1970s, which involved payments to officials by Lockheed to promote sales of its aircraft.

So far, virtually none of the political reforms the ruling party promised in the midst of the Recruit scandal have been enacted, and with the conviction of Mr Shinto it seems increasingly unlikely that many will be.

In the Japanese press and in conversations among business leaders, Mr Shinto, a close ally of former Prime Minister Yasuhiro Nakasone, has been by turns portrayed as a villain and as a victim of a system rife with corruption. Many consider him a scapegoat, sacrificed by political leaders to avoid further disaster for the ruling party.

Still, Mr Shinto's conviction was a big victory for prosecutors. It marked the first time that a court concluded that shares in a real estate firm called Recruit Cosmos that were sprinkled among prominent business executives, bureaucrats and politicians were intended as bribes.

That, legal experts said, should undercut the defenses offered by 10 other defendants now standing trial on related charges, including Takao Fujinami, Mr Nakasone's former Chief Cabinet Secretary, and Hiromase Ezoe, the former chairman of the Recruit Corporation, which controlled Recruit Cosmos. Another politician charged with taking bribes is Katsuya Ikeda, a former member of the lower house of the parliament.

Mr Takeshita's chief fund-raiser, Ihei Aoki, who was also implicated, committed suicide in April 1989.

A Titan of Industry

During his 20-month trial before a three-judge panel, Mr Shinto denied that the shares, which he received before Recruit Cosmos went public and their value soared, were intended as bribes. The court's rejection of that argument 'reminds us that the same excuses were made by those political leaders who cleverly escaped from being brought to justice despite purchases of Recruit Cosmos shares by their secretaries or family members', said *The Japan Times*, a leading English-language daily, in an editorial tonight.

The presiding judge in the trial, Ken Toyota, said today that Mr Shinto 'bears heavy responsibility' for the scandal for accepting shares that were then funnelled into two secret political slush funds run by N.T.T., which runs Japan's domestic telephone network.

Mr Shinto was a titan of Japanese industry for precisely the reason that he was attractive to Recruit: He had access to influential politicians and could arrange entrée to Japan's clubby business community. It was under his stewardship that N.T.T. was changed from a Government-owned monopoly to a private firm, a transition that required strong political connections to ward off regulators who wanted to break up the company and new competitors who wanted to compete for its most lucrative businesses.

In 1986, Mr Shinto met with Mr Ezoe, the former Recruit chairman, on several occasions and arranged for N.T.T. to help the small company in two business deals. The first involved getting Recruit into the lucrative business of reselling special telephone circuits to businesses. The second involved obtaining for Recruit two supercomputers made by an American company, Cray Research Inc. N.T.T. purchased the supercomputers and resold them to Recruit.

At the same time, Mr Ezoe gave Mr Shinto about 10,000 Recruit Cosmos shares. For months, Mr Shinto insisted that he had no knowledge of the transactions and that an assistant had been responsible. But the court concluded today that he had lied and that the shares were used for direct contributions to prominent politicians and to buy tickets to fund-raising parties.

The fine is roughly equal to the profits that Mr Shinto realized when he sold the Recruit Cosmos shares. But the court concluded that he had not used the shares for his own personal gain, a mitigating circumstance that contributed to the suspended jail sentence.

In Japan, which does not have jury trials, it is normal to announce a verdict and sentencing at the same time.

N.T.T. Shares Falling

Since Mr Shinto's departure, N.T.T.'s fortunes have been mixed. It has derailed, at least for the time being, a Government proposal to break up the company. But its stock price has plummeted. At one point under Mr Shinto, it reached 2.5 million yen a share, or $18,500 at current exchange rates.

But scandal, slow business and a declining stock market have taken their toll. The stock closed today at 791,000 yen, or $5,860, less than a third of its high. The Japanese Government has postponed indefinitely its planned sale of additional Government-held shares in the company, for fear that it would not raise enough money.

'We will make our utmost efforts to restore public trust in response to the court's ruling,' Masashi Kojima, N.T.T.'s president, said today.

David E. Sanger, *The New York Times*, 10 October 1990.

Milken Gets Ten Years (on Paper at Least)

Junk-bond supremo Michael Milken goes to prison

Junk-bond supremo Michael Milken was released after serving less than two years of his 1990 sentence and is now advising the likes of pop star Michael Jackson as part of his community service requirement.

Michael R. Milken, the once-powerful financier who came to symbolize a decade of excess, was sentenced to 10 years in prison yesterday for violating Federal securities laws and committing other crimes.

The sentence, handed down by Federal District Judge Kimba M. Wood in Manhattan, was the longest received by any executive caught up in the Wall Street scandals that began to unfold in 1986, and many legal experts and people on Wall Street expressed surprise at its severity.

But Judge Wood left open the possibility that Mr Milken could be eligible for parole at any time during his sentence and that his sentence could be reduced if he co-operated in future investigations. Some legal experts said they did not expect him to be paroled until he had served at least a third of the prison term.

Three Years of Probation

After Mr Milken serves his term he faces a three-year period of probation. Mr Milken, who paid $600 million in fines and restitution when he pleaded guilty to the violations, will also be required to perform 1,800 hours of community service during each of three years of probation, or a total of 5,400 hours.

Judge Wood said the former financier had to be sentenced to a long jail term to send a message to the financial community, and also because he chose to break the law despite his advantages of position and intelligence.

'When a man of your power in the financial world, at the head of the most important department of one of the most important investment banking houses in this country, repeatedly conspires to violate, and violates, securities and tax laws in order to achieve more power and wealth for himself and his wealthy clients, and commits financial crimes that are particularly hard to detect, a significant prison term is required,' she said.

A Lengthy Investigation

The sentencing of Mr Milken closes the most significant chapter of the longest investigation ever of crime on Wall Street. Over four years, numerous top Wall Street executives confessed to criminal activities and testified for the Government. But Mr Milken did not cooperate with the inquiry and admitted his guilt only last April.

As head of the 'junk bond' operations of Drexel Burnham Lambert Inc., which collapsed earlier this year, Mr Milken financed some of the largest corporate takeovers in the 1980s. He pioneered the use of high-yield, high-risk junk bonds as instruments for corporate warfare, successfully convincing investors that the bonds' high returns more than compensated for the risk that the issuers would default.

The sentence came at the end of a highly emotional hearing, in which Mr Milken frequently broke into tears as he listened to one of his lawyers plead for leniency.

Dressed in a gray suit and red tie, Mr Milken made only one comment during the proceeding, tearfully telling Judge Wood: 'What I did violated not just the law but all of my principles and values. I deeply regret it, and will for the rest of my life. I am truly sorry.'

Mr Milken stood ramrod straight and did not flinch when the sentence was handed down. His lawyers and family, as well as the others in the courtroom, seemed momentarily stunned by the sentence.

When the hearing ended, Mr Milken's wife, Lori, and other family members came to his side. They quickly left the courtroom, and cries of sorrow were heard inside the court after the door closed behind them.

One Lawyer's Reaction

Lawyers and legal experts also expressed surprise. 'This is an incredibly long sentence,' said Michael Feldberg, a partner at Shea & Gould. 'If there is a message to be gained from this experience, it is, at least for this judge, co-operation is enormously important.'

In his settlement, Mr Milken had agreed to respond truthfully to any questions asked him by the Government after he is sentenced. Judge Wood said that if that testimony proves to be valuable in future investigations, she would consider reducing the sentence. Mr Milken's lawyers have 120 days in which to make a motion for a reduction of sentence, lawyers said.

A number of the lawyers who expressed surprise at the sentence noted that Judge Wood had discounted many of the most important charges made by the Government against Mr Milken in a pre-sentencing hearing held last month.

Judge Wood said yesterday that although she did not accept that Mr Milken committed insider trading or manipulated a particular security, as the Government tried to prove, she believed that the former financier had tried to prevent investigators from uncovering his crimes by suggesting to subordinates that they dispose of important documents. She also said she believed that Mr Milken had misled a client.

Some See Vindication

Government officials indicated that the sentence was a vindication of the four-year inquiry into Mr Milken's practices in the financial markets.

'This sentence should send the message that criminal misconduct in our financial markets will not be tolerated, regardless of one's wealth or power,' said Richard C. Breeden, the chairman of the Securities and Exchange Commission.

Mr Milken agreed to plead guilty in April to six felonies. He admitted to a conspiracy between himself and two clients, Ivan F. Boesky and David Solomon, the manager of an investment fund. Mr Milken pleaded guilty to hiding stock for Mr Boesky to allow the speculator to file false information with the Government, and at another time to allow him to avoid minimum capital requirements for a stock-trading firm.

Mr Milken also agreed to make up any losses that Mr Boesky might suffer from buying stock from a Drexel client who was trying to unload the securities, without recording the promise on Drexel's books.

With Mr Solomon, Mr Milken reached an agreement to charge the money manager's fund a fraction of a point more on certain purchases he made to recoup the 1 percent commission paid to Drexel salesmen. He also engaged in trades with Mr Solomon that allowed the money manager to illegally claim false losses on his income-tax returns.

28 Years Was Possible

Mr Milken had faced a maximum of 28 years in prison, but few legal experts were estimating that his sentence would exceed 8 years. He was ordered to report to Federal custody on March 4, 1991. A prison was not designated.

Mr Milken's lawyer, Arthur L. Liman, spoke first at the proceeding yesterday, asking Judge Wood to sentence his client only to a term of community service, saying the crimes were 'deviations' by Mr Milken.

Mr Liman repeatedly stressed that his client was not a criminal on a par with Mr Boesky, the stock speculator whose settlement of insider trading charges in 1986 and subsequent co-operation with the Government helped expose the Wall Street scandals.

'Two conflicting pictures have been presented of Michael Milken,' Mr Liman said. 'The Government, which has not spent time with him, tries to cast him in the Boesky mold, but I would say to Your Honor that that template does not fit.'

Mr Boesky, who pleaded guilty to filing a false statement with the Securities and Exchange Commission, was sentenced in 1987 to three years in prison. He was released on parole this year. ...

Immediately before sentencing Mr Milken, Judge Wood praised him for his generous nature, adding that she hoped he would continue on that path.

'You are unquestionably a man of talent and industry and you have consistently shown a dedication to those less fortunate than you,' the judge said. 'It it my hope that the rest of your life you will fulfil the promise shown early in your career.'

Kurt Eichenwald, *The New York Times*, 22 November 1990.

....

Saying the Unsayable about the Germans

Nicholas Ridley's Spectator *interview*

This 1990 interview by the editor of The Spectator *was one of the two most influential articles published during the Thatcher Government in the sense that it brought about the immediate resignation of one of Mrs Thatcher's closest allies (the other being the interview with Sarah Keays). The Conservatives claimed Mr Ridley's comments were off the record. This was categorically denied by Dominic Lawson.*

In modern political life there is no more brutal practitioner of the home truth. Not even Mrs Thatcher – whose own views owe much to his – is more averse to hiding the hard facts behind a patina of sympathy or politician's charm. In a mirror world Mr Nicholas Ridley would be Mr Cecil Parkinson.

Even knowing this, I was still taken aback by the vehemence of Mr Ridley's views on the matter of Europe, and in particular the role of Germany. It had seemed a topical way to engage his thoughts, since the day after we met, Herr Klaus-Otto Pohl, the president of the Bundesbank, was visiting England to preach the joys of a joint European monetary policy.

'This is all a German racket designed to take over the whole of Europe. It has to be thwarted. This rushed take-over by the Germans on the worst possible bases, with the French behaving like poodles to the Germans, is absolutely intolerable.'

'Excuse me, but in what way are moves toward monetary union, "the Germans trying to take over the whole of Europe"?'

'The Deutschmark is always going to be the strongest currency, *because of their habits*.'

'But Mr Ridley, it's surely not axiomatic that the German currency will always be the strongest . . . ?'

'It's because of the *Germans*.'

'But the European Community is not just the Germans.'

Mr Ridley turned his fire – he was, as usual, smoking heavily – onto the organisation as a whole.

'When I look at the institutions to which it is proposed that sovereignty is to be handed over, I'm aghast. Seventeen unelected reject politicians – that includes you, Sir Leon – with no accountability to anybody, who are not responsible for raising taxes, just spending money, who are pandered to by a supine parliament which also is not responsible for raising taxes, already behaving with an arrogance I find breathtaking – the idea that one says, "OK, we'll give this lot our sovereignty," is unacceptable to me. I'm not against giving up sovereignty in principle, but not to this lot. You might just as well give it to Adolf Hitler, frankly.'

We were back to Germany again, and I was still the devil's – if not Hitler's – advocate:

'But Hitler was elected.'

'Well he was, at least *he* was . . . but I didn't agree with him – but that's another matter.'

'But surely Herr Kohl is preferable to Herr Hitler. He's not going to bomb us, after all.'

'I'm not sure I wouldn't rather have ...' – I thought for one giddy moment, as Mr Ridley paused to stub out his nth cigarette, that he would mention the name of the last Chancellor of a united Germany – 'er ... the shelters and the chance to fight back, than simply be taken over by ... *economics*. He'll soon be coming *here* and trying to say that this is what we should do on the banking front and this is what our taxes should be. I mean, he'll soon be trying to take over *everything*.'

Somehow I imagined (and I admit it, because Mr Ridley is for ever accusing journalists of making things up) that I could hear a woman's voice with the very faintest hint of Lincolnshire, saying 'Yes, Nick, that's right, they *are* trying to take over everything.' I can at least recall, with no recourse to imagination, the account of one of the Prime Minister's former advisers, of how he arrived for a meeting with Mrs Thatcher in a German car. 'What is that *foreign* car?' she glowered.

'It's a Volkswagen,' he replied, helpful as ever.

'Don't *ever* park something like that here again.'

The point is, Mr Ridley's confidence in expressing his views on the German threat owe a little something to the knowledge that they are not significantly different from those of the Prime Minister, who originally opposed German reunification, even though in public she is required not to be so indelicate as to draw comparisons between Herren Kohl and Hitler.

What the Prime Minister and Mr Ridley also have in common, which they do not share with many of their Cabinet colleagues, is that they are over 60. Next question, therefore, to Mr Ridley: 'Aren't your views coloured by the fact that you can remember the Second World War?' I could have sworn I saw a spasm of emotion cross Mr Ridley's face. At any rate he answered the question while twisting his head to stare out of the window:

'Jolly good thing too. About time somebody said that. It was pretty nasty. Only two months ago I was in Auschwitz, Poland. Next week I'm in Czechoslovakia. You ask them what they think about the Second World War. It's useful to remember.' It is also useful to know that Mr Ridley's trips to Poland and Czechoslovakia are efforts, in the company of some of Britain's leading businessmen, to persuade the East Europeans of the virtues of doing business with Britain. How very annoying to see the large towels of Mr Kohl and his businessmen already covering those Eastern beaches.

But, hold on a minute, how relevant to us, now, is what Germany did to Eastern Europe in the war? Mr Ridley reverted to the sort of arguments he must have inhaled with his smokes when he was a Minister of State at the Foreign Office:

'We've always played the balance of power in Europe. It has always been Britain's role to keep these various powers balanced, and never has it been more necessary than now, with Germany so uppity.'

'But suppose we don't have the balance of power; would the German economy run Europe?'

'I don't know about the German economy. It's the German *people*. They're already running most of the Community. I mean they pay half of the countries. Ireland gets 6 per cent of their Gross Domestic Product this way. When's Ireland going to stand up to the Germans?'

The strange thing about Mr Ridley's hostility to the Bundesbank and all its works, is that, if he had ever been Chancellor of the Exchequer – a job he admitted to me he had once coveted, but no longer – then he would probably have matched the Germans in his remorseless aversion to inflation. But as he pointed out, 'I don't think that's relevant. The point is that when it comes to "Shall we apply more squeeze to the economy or shall we let up a bit?" this is essentially about political accountability. The way I put it is this: can you imagine me going to Jarrow in 1930 and saying, "Look boys, there's a general election coming up, I know half of you are unemployed and starving and the soup kitchen's down the road. But we're not going to talk about those things, because they're for Herr Pohl and the Bundesbank. It's his fault; he controls that; if you want to protest about that, you'd better get on to Herr Pohl"?'

There might be more financial discipline in a British economy run under the influence of men like Herr Pohl, Mr Ridley agreed. But, he added, suddenly looking up at me through his bifocals, 'There could also be a bloody revolution. You can't change the British people for the better by saying, "Herr Pohl says you can't do that." They'd say, "You know what you can do with your bloody Herr Pohl." I mean, you don't understand the British people if you don't understand this point about them. They can be dared; they can be moved. But being bossed by a German – it would cause absolute mayhem in this country, and rightly, I think.'

The rumbustious tone of Mr Ridley's remarks and the fact that our conversation was post-prandial may give the misleading impression that the politician was relaxing, and not choosing his words too carefully. Far from it. Mr Ridley had the smallest glass of wine with his lunch, and then answered all my questions with a fierce frown of concentration, one hand helping to provide frequent supplies of nicotine.

Dominic Lawson, *The Spectator*, 14 July 1990.

Winnie Mandela

Nelson Mandela's wife sentenced for violent kidnapping

Winnie Mandela, the estranged wife of South African President Nelson Mandela, was long considered to be a saint in the anti-apartheid cause until the killing of a youth at her house caused an outcry. Gavin Evans, the senior political reporter for The Weekly Mail, *an anti-apartheid South African newspaper, explains why the ANC's unquestioning support for Mandela's behaviour was a bad mistake. Winnie Mandela was later sentenced to six years' imprisonment for the kidnapping and beating of six young men but has so far managed to avoid going to prison.*

Her image plummeted further when intimate letters to her alleged lover were published in a South African newspaper. Nelson Mandela separated from her in 1991 but she still managed to maintain a position on the ANC national council.

JOHANNESBURG—One of the many sad truths about the trial of Winnie Mandela is that the African National Congress has put its reputation in the dock, too.

South Africa's first-lady-in-waiting is likely to walk out of court a free woman without having to defend herself against kidnapping and assault charges. The state had a case until one witness disappeared and two others feared they would be killed if they testified against her.

But as the likelihood of a successful prosecution fades, so the distaste for the African National Congress's handling of the affair grows. The strongest criticism is coming not from the white state but from within sections of the anti-apartheid movement. The growing accusations against the ANC include complicity in the kidnapping of a state witness, bullying behaviour outside the court, a selective attitude toward press freedom and an unwillingness to risk the possibility of Mrs Mandela's conviction.

The organisation has long had an uncomfortable relationship with Mrs Mandela. She was admired for her immense courage against extreme repression but despised for her excesses. Things really soured after April 1986, when she advocated the barbaric 'necklace' method of killing the enemy. Soon after, her bodyguards launched a reign of terror in Soweto that ended with the beatings of several boys and the killing of one.

The United Democratic Front, operating as the ANC's internal political arm, condemned Mrs Mandela. The congress, then in exile, was more cautious, but kept its distance when the bodyguards' leader was convicted of the murder. The judge found that Mrs Mandela had been present during the assaults, and public pressure forced the state to charge her 18 months after the event.

In two years, South Africa's Eva Peron, revered by her followers, had been transformed into its Imelda Marcos. At first, Nelson Mandela and the ANC stressed that justice must take its course. Then things changed. Insiders said that to move up in the organisation it was wise to get close to Mr Mandela, and to do that you had to support his wife.

So it was that the leadership made the astounding decision of making her head of their welfare department at a time when she was facing charges of assaulting a 14-year-old. Several ANC branches protested, as did a group of the congress's social workers, but to no avail. Next she was 'elected' to a regional committee – there was no secret ballot – and made president of the congress's Women's League. Her rehabilitation was complete. ANC officials denounced a 'trial by media' and reprimanded some journalists.

Mr Mandela began speaking of his wife's trial as part of a harassment campaign against her. It is true that the courts are creatures of apartheid, but no evidence suggests that the state has been out to give Mrs Mandela anything other than a fair trial. If anything, the state has been lacklustre in conducting the case. The feeling in Government circles seems to be that it would be better to leave her alone; no one wants to sour relations with Mr Mandela or reduce his impact in the ANC.

Within the anti-apartheid movement open criticism of Mrs Mandela has effectively been gagged. An unhealthy ethos has emerged in which some who praise her in public express concern and opposition when the microphones are off. Others talk of disillusionment, even of resigning from the congress.

The effect of this on the struggle for a non-racial and democratic South Africa is hard to gauge. If, as expected, the trial collapses, the most optimistic hope is that the criticism of Mrs Mandela and the ANC will jolt the movement into realising it can't get away with this kind of behaviour. But there seems little inclination to learn the obvious lessons.

As one congress leader, who didn't want his name used, put it: 'If this is how we behave before winning power then things can only get worse once we're in government.'

Gavin Evans, *The New York Times*, 1 March 1991.

A World-Class Shopper

Imelda Marcos's New York trial

Imelda Marcos, former beauty queen, shoe collector and wife of Ferdinand Marcos, the late Philippino dictator, was renowned for her skills in spending money. In the unlikely venue of New York, she and her friend Adnan Khashoggi were tried and acquitted in 1990 of looting hundreds of millions of dollars from her government's coffers. One witness told the trial that Mrs Marcos had begged her husband to purchase a skyscraper for her in New York, which he dutifully did. She reportedly wept with gratitude.

New York—One day on a trip to Moscow in 1982, Imelda Marcos spent $7,842.31 on scarves and chocolates. On another day she spent $1,332 on macadamia nuts, and she apparently lost $1,000 in an airborne poker game. On a single day in September of that year, she spent almost $190,000 on jewellery and $62,000 on artwork in Manhattan. And on July 25, 1983, she made a $1 million down-payment on a Michelangelo painting.

These expenditures were recorded over five years in six spiral-bound stenographer's notebooks that were introduced late Tuesday by Federal prosecutors, who have portrayed Mrs Marcos as a voracious and unrestrained spender during her overseas travels as the First Lady of the Philippines.

The notebooks became evidence in the second week of Mrs Marcos's racketeering trial in Federal District Court in Manhattan. Earlier this week, a former Philippine bank official, Oscar Carino, testified that the New York branch of the Philippine National Bank often delivered $100,000 in cash to Mrs Marcos's personal secretary, Fe Roa Jiminez, at Mrs Marcos's hotel suite in New York. By 1983, Mr Carino said, about $22 million had been withdrawn and most of it was not repaid.

Mrs Marcos's lawyer, Gerry Spence, has contended that the cash was used to pay for Mrs Marcos's travelling party, including hotel bills and security staff. He also said that a lot of the money went for gifts that Mrs Marcos took back to Manila.

Gift-Giving as a Way of Life

The notebooks, which were kept by Ms Jiminez from 1979 to 1984, in part support Mr Spence's contention. They show that several hundred thousand dollars went to hotel bills and security staff, and while they indicate that Mrs Marcos bought several luxury items, it is not clear whether the purchases were for herself or others.

Mr Spence has said repeatedly in interviews and at the trial that gift-giving is a normal way of life in the Philippines and a normal way of conducting state business. He has also argued that, given the difficulty in using the Philippine pesos in most places around the world, it was customary for Mrs Marcos to have with her large amounts of dollars to pay expenses.

Ms Jiminez made the notations in hand-written entries, designating Mrs Marcos as 'FL' for First Lady and using 'PFM' for President Ferdinand Marcos. Mr Marcos died last September.

The entries are sometimes for major items and sometimes for the trivial, like the time in Los Angeles when Mrs Marcos spent $59.23 on McDonald's hamburgers and fish fillets for her entourage of 16 people. On July 12 to 13, 1979, while in Morocco, Mrs Marcos's party spent $2,350 in tips, one entry says. On July 17, there is a $10,000 entry for dresses for 'FL and children'. On Sept. 14, 1982, Mrs Marcos spent $200 for 'disco and boogie records'. And on Sept. 15, 1982, while visiting Moscow, Mrs Marcos spent $6,281.88 on caviar.

Few days match Sept. 25, 1982, when Mrs Marcos's expenditures in Manhattan included $133,500 for jewellery by Fred Leighton, $52,000 for jewellery from Cartier and $62,000 for portraits by Ralph W. Cowan.

Often, it seemed Mrs Marcos spent spontaneously, buying items at airports. She spent $744.50 while waiting for a flight in Amsterdam on Nov. 16, 1982. Later that month, there are listings for $10,000 spent for 'Bloomingdale's shopping' and a $30,000 entry, with the notation, '60 envelopes of $500 for entertainers'. And from 1983 to 1984, the notebook lists thousands of dollars spent for dinners and shopping, and $104.90 for two Cabbage Patch dolls.

Craig Wolff, *The New York Times*, 20 April 1990.

Labour Party MP in Sex Scandal

Ron Brown smashes up his mistress's flat

This story provided welcome relief from the contention that while Conservative politicians were invariably involved in sex scandals, Labour Party MPs tended to be found guilty of financial improprieties.

MP 'stole ex-lover's jewellery and knickers'

LABOUR MP Ron Brown stole his ex-lover's jewellery and two pairs of her knickers after smashing up her flat when she refused to return to him, a court was told yesterday.

As Nonna Longden walked out with her new boyfriend, the 47-year-old Left-winger – wielding a bottle – broke nearly everything made of glass in her home, it was alleged.

Mirrors were smashed in the bedroom and bathroom, windows shattered and the top of a record player broken. When four pieces of one mirror which had been written on were later put together, they were found 'rather pathetically' to spell the word love, said Mr Camden Pratt, prosecuting. 'It may well be, say the Crown, that it was that which was behind this incident,' he told Lewes Crown Court, East Sussex. Mrs Longden denied the row flared because she refused to give 'politically sensitive' tape recordings back to Brown – using them as a bargaining counter for continued financial support from him. And she dismissed a suggestion that she gave the MP the knickers – one black pair, one white – to wrap around a cassette player. For three years, Brown, MP for Edinburgh Leith, led a double life with the 39-year-old brunette, it was alleged. He shared a London flat with her from Monday to Friday while attending the Commons, then returned home at weekends to his wife, May, in Edinburgh. Mrs Longden would spend weekends at her flat in St Leonards, Sussex.

Mrs Brown sat in the public gallery as Mr Pratt told how Mrs Longden – who was married but separated – met Brown four years ago at the Commons. Their relationship lasted about three years, ending in March last year when she became involved with another man, Dermot Redmond. After the break-up, Mrs Longden thought she and Brown remained friends.

The MP once paid for opera tickets for her and Mr Redmond and took them to lunch in the Commons.

But, said Mr Pratt, 'it is clear there were emotions running rather higher than those of just good friends.' Mrs Longden told the jury that trouble flared on April 25 last year, after Brown turned up at her flat saying he had been to a conference in nearby Eastbourne and thought he would call in.

She told him she had to meet Mr Redmond at the station, and the MP gave her £5 to buy a bottle of wine. Mr Redmond's train was late and she went back to the flat but found Brown had gone.

Mr Redmond arrived at 6.30 p.m. and the MP came back about five minutes later to find Mr Redmond consoling her at the bedside.

Upset

She explained that she had been shocked and upset by Brown's unexpected visit. 'Mr Brown walked into the bedroom and just threw down his coat on the floor. I think Mr Redmond said something to the effect that it was quite obvious he had been drinking and that he thought he ought to leave. Mr Brown said: "Where's the drink?" – meaning the drink for which he had given me the money. I said it was on the hall table and he left for a minute and came back with the bottle of wine and three glasses. He said: "Let's have a drink and sober up." '

He asked for 15 minutes alone with her. She agreed, but the conversation last only five minutes because his speech was slurred and incomprehensible. 'He said would I leave in an hour and go back to London with him because there was a new flat, to be in Dolphin Square, and would I go with him and start a new life in a new flat?' She refused.

'I said the best thing to do was to leave him there to sleep it off, and that we would go out. We did just that.' As she and Mr Redmond left, a glass was thrown. Then, as they crossed the road, a bottle of wine came crashing through a front window. They went to a phone box and called the police.

Brown was arrested at the local railway station. Wrapped in his raincoat, Mr Pratt said, was a photograph of Mrs Longden as a girl. In his pockets were the two pairs of knickers, a gold brooch, china earrings and a wristwatch Brown had given her as a present. There was also a cassette player which belonged to Brown or his staff. The MP denies stealing the property and also denies causing £778 worth of damage at the flat. Mr Pratt said Brown told police he had gone to the flat to get back some of his personal belongings, and Mrs Longden had refused to let him take them. 'He said Mr Redmond had thrown things at him and had gone for him.'

The MP claimed the damage was caused when he ducked some of the things which Mr Redmond was throwing at him. Mrs Longden agreed with Mr Edward Rees, defending, that her relationship with Brown had been 'fizzling out' and had become public knowledge with allegations made in newspapers. She agreed that when they broke up, she took a tape recorder – but she denied she had taken some tapes. Mr Rees said: 'I suggest you did, and that essentially is what the argument was that night. They were politically-sensitive tapes and you were using them as a bargaining counter for some continuing financial support at the end of the relationship.' Mrs Longden replied: 'There were no tapes.'

She said it had never occurred to her to make money by selling her story to the Press, although she had been offered cash. Mrs Longden agreed she had received financial help from Brown, including payments of one month's mortgage and payment for dental work.

When the relationship ended, her position was not financially secure. She said she did not know Brown had received settlement of a libel action involving *The Daily Telegraph*.

Earlier, she had agreed that on one occasion House of Commons security staff found her waiting for the MP in his office and she had said she was his wife. They said they knew Mrs Brown and 'they asked would I go along with them, which I did, and that was the end of it.' The hearing was adjourned until today.

Paul Harris, *The Daily Mail*, 3 January 1991.

Ron Brown was found not guilty of theft but guilty of criminal damage and was fined £1,000 and made to pay prosecution costs of £2,500. Mr Brown claimed the verdict was 'a moral victory'. He was deselected by the Edinburgh Leith Labour Party but fought the 1992 election there as an Independent Labour candidate, without success.

Never Paint a Gift Horse

Australian horse-racing scandal – the Fine Cotton affair

Horse racing in Australia is akin to a religion, with a public holiday declared on the day of the Melbourne Cup. The following incident not only caused problems for the perpetrators but managed to end the careers of Australia's most prominent bookmakers.

SYDNEY—On the night before the most notorious scandal in Australian racing history, a team of conspirators was painting a racehorse. The three men wore dishwashing gloves and, under the dim light of a stable, they drenched a talented horse named Bold Personality with hair dye. The next day, at Eagle Farm Race Course in Brisbane, they were planning to substitute him for Fine Cotton, a horse with a dismal record.

They drank until the wee hours, toasting their handiwork, talking about the money they would win from bookmakers across the continent. But the next morning, when they looked at the horse in daylight, they saw they had turned him red; not chestnut, but a bright, gleaming red.

This whole plot had been a comedy of errors, and the scene at Eagle Farm that afternoon was a farce. But the consequences would be anything but laughable. Not only did the conspirators go to jail, but the two most prominent racing families in Sydney had their lives permanently affected by a connection to the scandal. Their legal battles are still raging, and the Fine Cotton affair is still making headlines six years later.

John Gillespie, a former used-car salesman and a smooth-talking con man, had plenty of time to conceive and plan this ringer coup while he was serving a sentence in Brisbane's Boggo Road Jail. There he met a jockey, Pat Haitana, and he was most interested to learn that the rider's brother was a trainer. The con man already had selected the key personnel for his betting coup, but the trainer was a last, essential part of the team.

Almost as soon as Gillespie was released from jail, he contacted Hayden Haitana and outlined his scheme. Then, with financial backing from sources presumably from Australia's underworld he bought a nondescript horse with a mediocre record and sent it to Haitana. This was Fine Cotton.

He told the trainer to start running the horse and losing races as badly as possible. He later bought a similar-looking, but far more talented animal,

Dashing Solitaire, the intended ringer, and sent him to the trainer, with instructions to prepare him for an upcoming distance race. But Dashing Solitaire ran through a barbed-wire fence and injured a leg. Gillespie was unperturbed. The scheduled coup now was only a few days away, so he hurriedly bought Bold Personality, even though the animal bore no resemblance to Fine Cotton.

When Bold Personality came out looking more like a fire engine, the men shampooed him back to his original colour. The horse would have to run without looking at all like Fine Cotton. Gillespie assured his collaborators this didn't matter.

'I've got some of the stewards on my side,' he said. 'They'll all be betting on Fine Cotton. They'll all make sure they're looking the wrong way. And the same goes for the cops. They'll be backing the horse too.'

It is uncertain how much of this was truth and how much was bluster, but the word on Fine Cotton was leaking out around the country. The ringleaders of the coup had found a shrewd gambler to put down $40,000 in bets for them, and the gambler asked bookmaker Robbie Waterhouse for aid in doing it.

Waterhouse suggested a Melbourne businessman who would be an ideal front man to make the wager. He was such a high-roller that a $40,000 bet from him wouldn't attract unusual attention from bookmakers. Waterhouse proceeded to make his own bets on Fine Cotton through his own agents.

And thus did the wagering on Fine Cotton snowball. Gillespie had told other people to bet the horse, and they told others, until the snowball turned into an avalanche on Saturday afternoon.

After opening at 33–1, Fine Cotton's odds plummeted to 7–2. Bettors scrambled to bet the hot horse.

Fine Cotton (Bold Personality) fought head-and-head through the stretch with Harbour Gold, and the track announcer's call was broadcast to rapt gamblers across the country: 'Harbour Gold, Fine Cotton! Oh, Fine Cotton is going to hold on by a nose. He may have held on by a nose. The bookmakers won't be able to pay...'

Gillespie was accepting congratulations from policemen who had backed the winner when his joy was interrupted by a chant from the vicinity of the winner's circle. 'Wrong horse! Wrong horse!' a group of bookmakers' clerks were shouting in unison. 'Wake up stewards! Official inquiry! Official inquiry!'

Racing officials rushed into the winner's enclosure and inspected Fine Cotton. The chief steward summoned Haitana and inquired: 'Doesn't this horse look a bit lighter in colour than the last time you raced it?'

Fifteen minutes after the race, Harbour Gold was declared the winner.

The gamblers had lost their money – and much more. Haitana went to jail for a year. Gillespie, after absconding on bail, was found hiding in the cupboard of a house in Victoria and was jailed for four years. Many others had their licenses revoked.

But the people who lost the most were ones with seemingly peripheral connections to the scandal. Robbie Waterhouse was barred from racing, and so was his father, Bill, who had been the world's biggest bookmaker.

Andrew Beyer, *The Washington Post*, 2 February 1991.

The Mistress Hits Back

Jilly Cooper and her husband's mistress

Over the years, columnist and romantic novelist Jilly Cooper published hundreds of column inches about her blissful marriage to military publisher Leo Cooper. One day, over a salade pastorale façon Joel Robuchon *at Le Manoir à Quatre Saisons, she told a gossip columnist that there had once been a 'marital hiccup' in the household. Alerted by this, a second gossip columnist invited Jilly Cooper to yet another lunch, where she told all about the 'dalliance'. She said once her suspicions were confirmed, she felt shattered: 'Suddenly I started to feel like a character out of one of my own books ... I was so jealous. I wanted to be loved the best.'*

The mistress, who was not a dim bimbo, but a publisher's assistant, decided also to speak publicly about her equally traumatic time because of the affair. What gave the story added impact was that it did not appear in a trashy tabloid paper, but in The Guardian, *the British liberal's mouthpiece.*

I am the 'dalliance' referred to in *Today*'s story on Leo and Jilly Cooper's marriage (though I don't see how the word can cover an eight-year relationship). As *Guardian* readers are unlikely to have seen it, suffice it to say the double-page feature was only the latest in which Mrs Cooper has talked about my love affair with Leo, claiming I was 'energetically pursuing' her husband. As she seems intent on prolonging my pain, I feel I can no longer remain silent.

Tales abound in the tabloids of newsworthy husbands' infidelities and in most cases the erring husband and his long-suffering and forgiving wife present a united front, belittling the 'other woman' involved. But what of her, this third person in an often complex situation, who has little redress when everything falls apart? How does she cope? Should she decide to enter the fray and publicly defend herself, it will be seen as either an act of revenge (hell hath no fury) or a bid for financial gain. Much better that she creeps quietly away into a corner, licks her wounds and keeps her mouth shut.

Of course the knowledge of her husband's infidelity will be painful to the wife, but her husband's presence and public support will surely be some compensation, while what is the mistress left with? Most likely she will have made her lover her whole life. Such a situation will have demanded it. I am such a mistress and my desperate attempts to come to terms without Leo, after eight years, are continually being sabotaged by articles in the press about his marriage. For this reason, and on behalf of those thousands of ill-used and discarded mistresses, without redress, I would like to tell my story.

I first came across Leo at the top of a publishing house staircase (which, as he later admitted, was the moment he set me in his sights) as I motioned him upwards for an appointment with my boss.

He made very little impression on me initially, but then began a relentless campaign (Leo is a military publisher) to persuade me to embark upon an affair with him, being very attentive whenever we met in the office, insisting on coming to my house in the presence of my children and boyfriend, begging me to have dinner with him. He was so persistent that I eventually agreed to the occasional dinner or opera, always, despite his passionate entreaties, keeping him at arm's length and being adamant that I would not become involved.

He kept up his campaign for two years, using all the force of his extremely strong personality. He is wonderfully adroit with words, often poetic, and above all full of wit and humour. I began to be convinced by his desperation – he was lonely, it was difficult being married to Jilly, always taking second place to her stardom – together with the flatteries and persuasive ways of a man determined to have his way.

I eventually gave in. We began to see more of each other and he assumed more and more importance in my thoughts until I became deeply attached to him. I had had a fairly difficult life, bringing up three children as a single parent, and this sudden gift of such incredible happiness from someone so reassuringly strong, protective and loving was a balm.

I don't want to make public the intimate details of a gloriously passionate relationship; suffice it to say that he became my life and we gave each other extraordinary happiness, joy, laughter and love. He was divine to my children and we managed a very full life – dinners, the opera, his professional functions, my friends.

This continued for six years, Leo often under the extreme pressure of his double life and my weekends alone made bearable by his frequent reassuring calls, often made with hilarious ingenuity, sometimes from his home and surrounding telephone boxes. He took enormous risks all the time, often running into people he knew, but somehow passing me off. As my dependence on Leo grew, it got more difficult to be engulfed by him during the week and abandoned for another at weekends, plus having to cope with the many articles about their idyllic marriage.

After one particularly difficult article, I broke and went down to their house, naively but honestly believing that if we all sat down and discussed it, something could be worked out.

Of course everyone was very upset, particularly Jilly who was in a state of shock, but she was extremely nice to me and we all did a lot of talking. Next morning I was bundled unceremoniously, quite understandably, back on the train and I retreated from work to bed for two weeks, unable to eat or sleep. Leo paid me a visit, reassuringly telling me that all would be back to normal once the dust had settled. A week later we had dinner, after which there were further dramas involving us all, bringing about what seemed a complete abandonment by Leo.

A friend sent me to recover at a health farm where Leo rang me, asking for a meeting on my return. He wanted everything to go on, but under conditions of the utmost discretion since Jilly would be highly suspicious. Loving him so desperately, I had no choice. It was as though my life had been given back to me. He told me that, no matter what, he would never leave me, always look after me. I believed him.

Things continued much as before for about nine months, at which point we were seen at the theatre and Leo, on being accused by his eldest daughter of still seeing me, came and asked me what he should do; would I save him and his marriage? Several nightmarish weeks followed; our families were badly affected and there were emotional meetings, threats, entreaties. We were all in a desperate state. I continued to see him occasionally for a drink when he said he loved me and that he would look after me. But then he decided that his best interests lay with Jilly; he loved her and they had been married for so long.

So he took the necessary steps to prove to her that it was all over, calling the police in front of his secretary to escort me from his office where I had gone to beg him not to abandon me after so much and so long. I was made to attend a meeting with his friend and eldest daughter where I said that I accepted that it was over but asked to be treated with kindness and consideration.

I could not cope with the loss coupled with what seemed to be such extreme and selfish cruelty when it seemed to me that my only sin was loving him. However, the next thing was a lawyer's letter threatening me with an injunction if I did not completely let go. I was forced to take legal advice and advised to write saying I would have no further contact. Several months later we met (those months had been so lonely) and we have had many meetings since, but I loved him so much and not being able to show him has made me behave badly at these meetings and he has again cut himself off.

They say time heals everything but I don't believe it. The intensity of my love for Leo is as great as ever, and the pain of life without him insurmountable. I have spent money I don't have on psychiatrists, pills, psychologists, all to no avail. Nothing seems to alter one's mood of total despair and hopelessness, and the feeling that the price is unjustly high for simply having loved a man at his behest. There are no distractions in a life that had become necessarily empty during the years with Leo. My mistake was that I took everything he told me at face value – that he would always look after me, never leave me. And even the knowledge that this is not the case does not stop my love. Perhaps Leo feels guilt for the suffering he has caused two women. Then again, perhaps he is enjoying being in the limelight on his own account for once and can assuage that guilt by basking in the knowledge that he's once again faithful and true.

I feel, in all honesty, that my suffering has been and will be the greatest, but that it's of little importance to anyone. I do object, though, to Mrs Cooper continuing to rub salt in the wound by her everlasting undressing in public. So how do other women cope in similar situations? Are they made of sterner stuff, more intelligent and realistic about the situation? Do they find it within themselves to forgive and forget? Am I bitter, self-pitying, weak and obsessed? Perhaps so, but I don't know how to come to terms with this. Does anyone else?

The Guardian, 30 August 1990.

From the Files of the LAPD

Racist patrol-car conversations of Los Angeles Police

The following communications are all from patrol-car computers of members of the Los Angeles Police Department, four of whose members beat up a black motorist Rodney G. King while being filmed by an amateur video camera enthusiast. After the officers were acquitted, Los Angeles suffered the worst race riots in its history and a Commission of Inquiry was created, which uncovered the following taped messages. Police Chief Daryl F. Gates, a strong proponent of law and order, defended his officers, saying that the offending messages were in fact 'less than one-half of one percent of all transmissions audited'.

On Beatings, Shootings and Pursuit

'Capture him, beat him and treat him like dirt...'

'Sounds like a job for the dynamic duo ... after I beat him what do I book him for and do I have to do a use of force [report]?'

'Wakeup ... the susp on our perimeter got caught, but he got beat by a BB bat.'

'Tell [an officer] to use a baton next time...'

'No problemmm ... We R hungry ... we got a little physical w/a [name omitted] on Columbus ... it was fun ... we had to teach him a little respect ... for the police ... hahahahaha ... we had fun ... no stick time though.'

'Did U arrest the 85 yr old lady of [or] just beat her up?'

'We just slapped her around a bit ... she's getting m/t [medical treatment] right now.'

'We prond him straight out of his Jaguar...'

'He is crying like a baby.'

'Did U educate him?'

'Take 1 handcuff off and slap him around.'

'He is crying too hard and there is 4 detectives here.'

'Well don't seatbelt him in and slam on the brakes a couple times on the way to the sta...'

'I hope there is enough units to set up a pow-wow around the susp so he can get a good spanking and nobody c it...'

'I'm going to kill this guy.'

'Haaaaaa ... you're so bad ... u cutie u ... I'll be back I'm going to do it.'

'I obviously didn't beat this guy enough. He got right back up and is still being obnoxious.'

'Juvi says U hit him with flashlight ... I didn't see U do that.'

'Smile. I'm against viol.'

'I would just beat and release that fat slob in the red suit named ... Homey Claus ... and I heard reindeers real good eating ... hohoho mofo ...'

'The last load went to a family of illegals living in the brush along side the pas frwy ... I thought the woman was going to cry ... so I hit her with my baton.'

'It was fun ... but no chance to bust heads ... sorry.'

'Oh well ... maybe next time.'

'So are you going to take that call.'

'After the beating.'

'They give me a stick they give me a gun they pay me 50Gs to have some fun.'

'I'm gonna bk my pursuit susp. Hope he gets ugly so I can vent my hate. Hrr hrr ... A-H.'

'Standby we feel pretty food, we may have another foot pursuit here soon ... ha ha ha ha.'

On Minorities

'Well ... I'm back over here in the projects, pissing off the natives.'

'I would love to drive down Slauson with a flame thrower ... we would have a barbecue.'

'Sounds like monkey slapping time.'

'Hi ... just got m'exercise for the night.'

'Okay people ... pls. ... don't transfer me any Orientals ... I had two already.'

On Gender Bias

'U wont believe this ... that female call again said susp returned ... I'll check it out then I'm going to stick my baton in her.'

On Sexual Orientation

'No. 1600 how many homosexuals did you give orals to today?'

'That's a touchy subject ... not fit for [Mobile Digital Terminals] ...'

The Washington Post, 10 July 1991.

'The Largest Bank Fraud in World History'

The collapse of BCCI

The Bank of England was criticized for not acting quickly enough to alert the outside world to the activities of the Third World Bank, the BCCI.

The scandal surrounding the Bank of Credit and Commerce International (BCCI) exploded yesterday into a furious, embarrassing international political firestorm, with the actions of the British government and the Bank of England in the eye of a hurricane. Presenting the most detailed investigation to date of the long-festering BCCI affair, based on more than two years of exhaustive inquiries, Democratic Senator John Kerry of Massachusetts described 'a grotesque network of greed and influence' which spanned the globe.

Governments, central banks, international financial institutions, intelligence agencies, auditors, public relations firms and lobbyists, and highly-placed current and former politicians are all accused of incompetence, negligence, or outright criminality. Referring in particular to the involvement of the British government and the Bank of England in a scandal which cost depositors at least $10 billion, the committee recommended legislation allowing 'more aggressive US action against nations who permit their privacy and confidentiality laws to protect criminals'. The Bank of England's regulatory procedures had proven 'wholly inadequate', it said.

The 800-page report, published by Mr Kerry's Senate sub-committee on terrorism, narcotics and international operations, stated that 'the April 1990 agreement among Price Waterhouse UK (BCCI's auditors), Abu Dhabi (BCCI's principal shareholder), BCCI, and the Bank of England (the regulator with principal responsibility), resulted in Price Waterhouse UK certifying the financial picture presented in its audit as "true and fair".' This agreement meant that 'huge losses' incurred by BCCI were not 'adequately' described.

The joint Bank of England-brokered agreement to reorganise BCCI, 'rather than to advise the public of what they knew, caused substantial injury' to innocent depositors and customers of BCCI who continued to do business with an institution which each of the above parties knew had engaged in fraud. The report said: 'From April 1990, the Bank of England relied on British bank secrecy and confidentiality laws to reduce the risk of BCCI's collapse if word of its improprieties leaked out ...

'Despite its knowledge of some of BCCI's past frauds, and its own understanding that consolidation into a single entity is essential for regulating a bank, in late 1990 and early 1991 the Bank of England tentatively agreed with BCCI and its Abu Dhabi owners to permit BCCI to restructure as three 'separate' institutions in London, Abu Dhabi and Hong Kong. This tentative decision represented very poor judgement on the part of the Bank of England [and] was reversed abruptly when the Bank of England suddenly decided to close BCCI instead in late June 1991.

'The decision by the Bank of England in April 1990 to permit BCCI to move its headquarters, offices, and records out of British jurisdiction to Abu Dhabi had had profound negative consequences for investigations of BCCI around the world.

'As a result of this decision, essential records and witnesses regarding what took place were removed from the control of the British government and placed under the control of the government of Abu Dhabi, which has to date withheld them from criminal investigators in the US and the UK.

'This decision constituted a costly, and likely irretrievable error on the part of the Bank of England. Investigations of BCCI to date remain incomplete and many leads cannot be followed up as the result of documents being withheld from US investigators by the British government.'

The government of Abu Dhabi was also harshly criticised for alleged obstructionism by Senator Kerry and his Republican counterpart on the committee, Senator Hank Brown. 'Abu Dhabi's involvement in BCCI's affairs was far more central than it has acknowledged, involving in some cases nominee relations and no-risk transactions that Abu Dhabi is today covering up through hiding witnesses and documents,' the report said. Also sharply criticised was the auditing firm, Price Waterhouse UK, which as early as 'the end of 1987, given its knowledge about the inadequacies of BCCI's records, had ample reason to recognise that there could be no adequate basis for certifying ... that its picture of those records was indeed a "true and fair view" of BCCI's financial state.'

The report went on: 'Prior to 1990, Price Waterhouse UK knew of gross irregularities in BCCI's handling of loans to CCAH, the holding company of First American Bank shares, was told of violations of US banking laws by BCCI and its borrowers in connection with CCAH/First American, and failed to advise the partners of its US affiliate or any US regulator.' The Bank of England's action in finally shutting down BCCI came in the context of revelations in Washington about BCCI's secret and illegal acquisition of First American, Washington's biggest bank, using Arab frontmen and US-born nominees. First American's two top executives, Clark Clifford and Robert Altman, denied knowledge of this covert takeover and currently face criminal charges. In the same period of summer 1991, BCCI's penetration of other US banks also began to become clear. They included banks and savings institutions in Georgia, Florida and California, which were owned, run by, or linked with other leading US political figures or fund-raisers such as Bert Lance, a former Carter administration official. But the report also levels similar questions at the US Justice Department which appeared, in a 1990 memo, to suggest to Florida state regulators that a 1988 case brought against BCCI in Tampa should be concluded with a plea agreement (as it eventually was), rather than pursued through a nation-wide BCCI investigation or the closure of BCCI operations in the US. The department's intervention created an 'appearance of impropriety', the report said, also charging that the department under then attorney-general, Richard Thornburgh, effectively delayed BCCI-related investigations and, by failing to co-operate, obstructed the inquiries of the Manhattan district attorney, Robert Morgenthau. It was Mr Morgenthau who eventually succeeded last year in bringing the first criminal indictments in the affair, against BCCI principals Agha Hasan Abedi, Swaleh Naqvi, Ghaith Pharaon, and Faisal Saud al-Fulajj, and subsequently against Mr Clifford and Mr Altman. Political influence-peddling in the US, UK and elsewhere formed a major area of investigation. 'BCCI systematically bribed world leaders and political figures throughout the world. BCCI had relationships that ranged from the questionable, to the improper, to the fully corrupt in countries [from] Argentina [to] the United Kingdom and the US.'

One of the most prominent figures to be named in this context by the report was President Jimmy Carter. 'BCCI styled itself as the Third World's bank,' the report said, and 'courted' Mr Carter after he left office.

'It exploited the president's reputation and access by providing large amounts of funding to his charitable organisations. In turn, the President became an unwitting pawn of BCCI, failing to acknowledge, even when it became obvious, that the bank was a criminal institution.' It was Mr Carter who introduced former Prime Minister, James Callaghan, to Mr Abedi. As part of his recommendations for better regulation and less banking secrecy, Mr Kerry and his committee are now seeking closer scrutiny of foreign investors, institutions and foreign auditors doing business in the US. Chillingly, perhaps, for the Bank of England and others, the committee also demanded that the 'CIA and the State Department target foreign financial institutions as subjects for intelligence gathering and analysis'.

Simon Tisdall, *The Guardian*, 30 July 1991.

....

Captain Phillips's Gentleman's Agreement

Captain Mark Phillips faces paternity claim

Captain Mark Phillips, the former husband of Princess Anne, the Princess Royal, has never had a very good relationship with the press. After the release of the following story in The Daily Express *in 1991, it is doubtful whether there is much hope of a reconciliation in the future.*

Captain Mark Phillips, estranged husband of Princess Anne, is facing a paternity claim over a five-year-old child.

Lawyers for horsewoman Heather Tonkin are to begin proceedings this week. She says she spent a night in his hotel room and he is the father of her daughter.

Captain Phillips, 42, has never accepted that he is the father.

But under what his business agent calls a 'gentleman's agreement', Miss Tonkin has been receiving quarterly payments through the agent's company since her baby, Felicity, was born.

Payments

There is a dispute over the future of the arrangement now that Felicity (whose pet name is Bunny) has reached school age. So far, a total of £40,000 has been paid into Miss Tonkin's home-town bank account in Auckland, New Zealand. The payments are described as fees for acting as 'a consultant on equestrian matters'. Miss Tonkin, 37, a former art teacher, says that no such services have ever been sought or offered. She calls it 'hush money'.

'I am doing what I am doing for my child,' she says. 'I just hope and pray Mark will do the right thing and make a proper and legally-binding settlement on her.

'I wish I could wake up one morning in the knowledge that the record had been put straight and I don't have to worry any more.

'Nothing can compensate for the tears I have cried while trying to plan for Bunny's future, when at any moment I could find myself penniless.

'Bunny throws her arms around me to comfort me, asking why I am sad. But I have never been able to tell her.

'My ambition is to get Mark's public acceptance of her and to be able to enter his name on her birth certificate.

'She thinks her father is dead. She is entitled to know the truth.'

Miss Tonkin was upset by a magazine article that claimed Captain Phillips would enjoy a £1 million settlement when his marriage ended. Her lawyers instructed her to tape-record a series of phone discussions she was having last year with the Captain's go-between, Mr James Erskine, regional managing director of the celebrity agency, International Management Group. It was Mr Erskine who arranged the 'equestrian consultancy' payments. Now the tapes record him telling her: 'If you want to have a barney, he's just going to deny it . . . I will make life a bloody misery for you . . . I know who's going to win because I know where the clout is. The clout is with him.'

Miss Tonkin sent Mr Erskine photographs of Felicity and asked him to show them to the globe-trotting Captain.

Later, Mr Erskine told her: 'He's seen the photographs and all that jazz. And he hasn't come to any conclusion what he's prepared to do or what he's not prepared to do.

'He just said, "Look, at the moment carry on with what you're doing." And then he and I have got to talk about it.

'He's certainly not in a position to pay out large sums of money. He's more than willing to carry on helping in some shape or form but it's just a matter of quantifying that.'

It was 1986 when Mr Erskine flew to New Zealand to see Miss Tonkin after she had phoned Captain Phillips at the Gatcombe Park home he shared with Princess Anne, now 40. The royal couple were not then estranged, although his business as the world's best-known equestrian and her presidency of the Save The Children Fund meant they were often apart.

They did not officially announce their separation until November, 1989,

16 years after their Westminster Abbey wedding. Mr Erskine, who told Miss Tonkin he was Captain Phillips's 'very, very good friend', arranged in 1986 for her to receive £7,400 a year to be paid quarterly.

A formal letter from him to her states that the payments are fees for acting as a 'consultant on equestrian matters for the International Management Group in New Zealand'.

The letter, on May 13, 1986, back-dated payments to August, 1985, when the baby was born.

Miss Tonkin's first meeting with Captain Phillips was when she paid £60 to attend his New Zealand riding clinic in November 1983. He was 36. She was 31, the daughter of respected members of the Auckland medical community. According to her account, a year later they met again when he was in the country for a party to honour a local Olympic rider.

She says she was flattered and excited when Captain Phillips asked her for her phone number.

'Next day he rang to invite me to his hotel to what I thought was a small party for his friends,' she says.

She arrived at his room to find him alone. She says they spent the night together. She left at six in the morning.

'I was infatuated,' she says. 'I did not object in the least.' Her diary for that night, November 19/20, 1984, shows kisses in the shape of a horseshoe.

On December 18 she took a pregnancy test at a family planning clinic. It was positive. Her baby was born on August 10 next year. The birth certificate leaves blank the space for the father's name.

Miss Tonkin's lawyers have a certificate from the Auckland University department of obstetrics and gynaecology stating that conception would have taken place between 16 and 27 November. She says that three days after the test she phoned Captain Phillips at Gatcombe Park to tell him she was pregnant. It was four days before Christmas, and the family was on its way to join the Queen at Windsor Castle.

'At first Mark sounded pleased to hear from me but there was a stony silence when I broke the news.

'He repeated over and over again, "You mustn't have this child."

'He said he needed time to think and would ring back from Windsor when he had thought about it. He was obviously in shock.

'Two days later he rang me and again tried to talk me out of having the child. The call didn't last long when I insisted I was going ahead with it.'

She went on: 'I told him not to worry. I would get through it without bothering him. I was so naive. I really thought I would be able to manage on my own with welfare benefit.

'At that time I didn't know that benefit would be withheld unless I named the father so that the state could claim from him.'

When the baby was born she christened her Felicity Bridget but began calling her Bunny 'because her face was like a little rabbit'. Eighteen days after the birth came the first meeting between Captain Phillips and Miss Tonkin since their night together at Auckland's Town House Hotel.

He happened to be in New Zealand to speak at a dinner. She waited until he was alone. Then she went over and told him that the child had been born.

'He seemed stunned, very on edge and just wanting to get away. His eyes were darting around.'

By the time Felicity was seven months old, Miss Tonkin was 'exhausted and desperate'. She could not get a teaching job.

She rang Captain Phillips again at Gatcombe Park, this time asking his help. 'He said he would arrange for a friend to call me and make arrangements.'

Five days later, Mr Erskine contacted her from his office in Sydney, Australia. He rang again two days later to say he was flying to New Zealand on business and would discuss the problem with her.

They met at an hotel, and the arrangement to pay her for 'equestrian consultancy' was made. Miss Tonkin says now that it provides her daughter with no security. She is worried that the money could be stopped at any time. And she has asked for a lump sum to be invested for the child.

'If anything happened to me,' she says, 'what would happen to Felicity?'

Mr Erskine's tape-recorded responses to Miss Tonkin include the following statements:

- 'Mark does not have a million dollars. His net worth is half or less than that. He doesn't own his house. It's owned by the Queen.'
- 'Quite frankly, I said why bother paying a lump sum, why not pay it over a period of time, because it is less likely you are going to go back on your word.'
- 'How do we know you are not going to take the money and put it on a horse?'
- 'You know you've got some leverage over use because we don't want ... Mark doesn't want ... to have a scandal.'
- 'I'll say Mark virtually knew nothing about it. It will be on my own back to stop a scandal, because we're being blackmailed.'
- 'There's one thing you should realise. When this thing hits the fan, your daughter's life will be ruined...'

Miss Tonkin's lawyer, Kevin Ryan, says: 'I am confident that with the evidence, the taped conversations and the fact that he has paid up for five years, I can win this case.'

No Response from Captain Phillips

Captain Phillips has been made fully aware of the account Miss Tonkin has given *The Daily Express*. His personal secretary, Margaret Hammond, said: 'Captain Phillips has not chosen to respond.'

Yesterday he was staying with friends in California. His agent James Erskine said: 'I am sure that if Mark wanted to talk to anyone he would. If he didn't he wouldn't.

'My understanding is that Mark does not want to talk to anybody.' Mr Erskine described Miss Tonkin's story as 'strange' and 'interesting'.

Of the paternity action, he said: 'Fine, fine. These days, a DNA test is the only accurate measure of a father's responsibility. If I were her I would probably make a paternity claim.'

Buckingham Palace said that Captain Phillips is now a private person as far as it is concerned and it had no comment to make.

Norman Luck, *The Daily Express*, 21 March 1991.

....

Diana's Brother: 'The Affair that Almost Destroyed My Marriage'

Viscount Althorp and Sally Ann Lasson

Viscount Althorp (the current Earl Spencer) had his marital problems voluntarily broadcast to the world by gossip writer Nigel Dempster of The Daily Mail. *Lord Spencer thought that because the story was about to run in a rival paper by one of his former lovers it was best to pre-empt it with his own account. This approach may have been the wrong one as the rival paper later admitted that it was reluctant to proceed with the story in the absence of any corroboration. Miss Sally Ann Lasson, an occasional contributor to the glossy magazine* Tatler, *sold her story because she claimed she needed £5,000 to pay for a repair bill to her house.*

The Princess of Wales's brother told last night of the affair with an old flame which threatened to wreck his marriage to a beautiful model. Viscount Althorp revealed he slept with writer and cartoonist Sally Ann Lasson last March after his relationship with wife Victoria hit a rocky patch. The couple had been married only six months at the time. Althorp, 26, said he had told his wife – who gave birth to their first child in December – everything about the affair and they had put it behind them.

But he decided to give *The Daily Mail* his side of the story when he learned 32-year-old Miss Lasson had sold her account of the relationship to a Sunday newspaper for £5,000 after he refused to help her out of financial difficulties.

'I have caused my wife more grief than I would wish her to have in a lifetime with me and I accept full responsibility for the folly of my actions,' he said.

'Now, a month after the birth of our baby, we are deeply in love and our marriage is the most important thing in our lives. Victoria is profoundly upset but has asked me to say that our marriage will not be destroyed by a woman who belonged to our unhappy past.'

Althorp, a British-based TV reporter with America's NBC network, said he had a 'one-night stand' with Miss Lasson, a columnist of the magazine *Tatler*, in September 1986. After that, he claimed, she phoned him several times. They met again in May 1989, shortly before the whirlwind romance which led to his engagement to Victoria Lockwood.

'She was extremely jealous when I married Victoria,' he said. 'She made it clear that she had always wanted to be my wife.'

Knowing her marriage to songwriter Dominic King had ended in divorce, it was to Miss Lasson that Althorp turned nearly a year ago when his relationship with Victoria, 25, entered what he called an 'extremely unpleasant patch'.

He added: 'It was a foolish move in retrospect. But with a failed marriage behind her, I thought she was in a position to give advice. One afternoon last March, when I sincerely thought my marriage was over, I asked her to come to Paris with me and we had our second one-night stand. The experience so sickened me that I did not stay a second night and returned to London.'

Althorp said Miss Lasson began phoning him after he got back and they met in Mayfair in July. She was 'furious', he claimed, when he told her his marriage was becoming increasingly happy, 'demanding' he make her his mistress.

'After that there were more calls but from mid-August until December I did not hear from her.'

In December Miss Lasson told Althorp some workmen had run off with her money.

'She was desperate for £5,000 immediately,' he said. 'She wondered if I could help raise it. I was totally unreceptive to the idea. Early last month she told me she was suicidal because her father was ill and she had financial problems. I heard nothing more until Thursday when she informed me she had sold her story about me.'

Althorp is adamant he slept with Miss Lasson on only two occasions four years apart. And he says he will take legal action if any claims of a relationship beyond that appear in print. Miss Lasson did not answer the phone at her Knightsbridge flat yesterday and is thought to be abroad.

Nigel Dempster, *The Daily Mail*, 2 February 1991.

....

Long Dong Silver

Judge Clarence Thomas accused of sexual harassment

The most publicised case of sexual harassment in the United States ultimately ended in victory for the accused – Clarence Thomas, who had been nominated as an American Supreme Court judge. During Senate hearings to confirm his appointment, he was charged by Anita Hill, a former legal employee. According to her, the alleged offences were committed when he was chairman of the Equal Employment Opportunity Commission in 1982. What added interest to the case was that both were individuals from poor black backgrounds who later became graduates of Yale Law School. Professor Hill spoke in detail about her allegation that Judge Thomas turned office conversations to sexual matters.

'One of the oddest episodes I remember was an occasion in which Thomas was drinking a Coke in his office,' she said. 'He got up from the table at which we were working, went over to his desk to get the Coke, looked at the can and said, "Who has put pubic hair on my Coke?" On other occasions he referred to the size of his own penis as being larger than normal, and he also spoke on some occasions of the pleasures he had given to women with oral sex.' Another time, she said, he talked about a movie called *Long Dong Silver*.

Clarence Thomas responded to the allegations which had remained unmentioned for 10 years, in his opening statement to the Senate Committee on the Judiciary.

'Senator, I would like to start by saying unequivocally, uncategorically, that I deny each and every single allegation against me today that suggested in any way that I had conversations of a sexual nature or about pornographic material with Anita Hill, that I ever attempted to date her, that I ever had any personal sexual interest in her, or that I in any way ever harassed her.

The second and I think more important point, I think that this today is a travesty. I think that it is disgusting. I think that this hearing should never occur in America. This is a case in which this sleaze, this dirt was searched for by staffers of members of this committee, was then leaked to the media, and this committee and this body validated it and displayed it at prime time over our entire nation.

How would any member of this committee, any person in this room, or any person in this country like sleaze said about him or her in this fashion? Or this dirt dredged up and this gossip and these lies displayed in this manner. How would any person like it?

The Supreme Court is not worth it. No job is worth it. I am not here for that. I am here for my name, my family, my life, and my integrity. I think something is dreadfully wrong with this country when any person, any person in this free country would be subjected to this.

This is not a closed room. There was an FBI investigation. This is not an opportunity to talk about difficult matters privately or in a closed environment. This is a circus. It's a national disgrace.

And from my standpoint, as a black American, it is a high-tech lynching for uppity blacks who in any way deign to think for themselves, to do for themselves, to have different ideas, and it is a message that unless you kow-tow to an old order, this is what will happen to you. You will be lynched, destroyed, caricatured by a committee of the US Senate rather than hung from a tree.'

Excerpts from Clarence Thomas Senate Hearings of the
Committee of the Judiciary, October 1991.

After 107 days of hearings before the Senate, Clarence Thomas was confirmed by one of the narrowest margins ever – fifty-two votes to forty-eight.

....

Too Big to Fail

The Savings and Loans scandal in the US

The lesson of the Savings and Loans scandal in the United States is that you are assured of being bailed out providing your losses are so enormous that they threaten the entire financial structure of the country.

In its closing hours yesterday [November 1991] Congress finally approved the spending of $95 billion to cover mounting losses from a wave of bank and savings and loan failures, by far the largest sum the government has ever had to lay out to protect the nation's financial system.

Congress agreed to provide $25 billion to cover losses for the next four months as S&Ls are closed and to restructure the cleanup operation in ways that make the White House more directly accountable for its progress.

In separate banking legislation, it also agreed to lend the Federal Deposit Insurance Corp. $70 billion to shore up its nearly bankrupt deposit insurance fund and to toughen some bank regulatory rules. Both measures fell far short of the Bush administration's original goals.

The administration had sought initially to bring new powers and sweeping changes to the nation's battered banking industry, and it had asked for $80 billion to complete the S&L cleanup.

Regulators and administration officials warned repeatedly over the past several weeks that a refusal by Congress to spend the money would damage faith in the government's Depression-era promise to insure depositor accounts, sending shock waves through the nation's already shaky economy. Nevertheless, there was widespread unwillingness to vote for the massive spending measures – especially among Republicans – and the vote was stalled until just before Congress adjourned for Thanksgiving.

While the administration was relieved to get the funds it did, Treasury Secretary Nicholas F. Brady called the bank bill 'a pale shadow' of the strong reform the industry needs. 'Unfortunately, it is the taxpayer who may have to pay for Congress's inaction,' he said.

The loan to the FDIC is supposed to be repaid by the banks over the next 15 years, but if they cannot make the payments, the taxpayers will have to absorb the loss.

Since 1988, when the S&L crisis began, the government has spent a total of $104 billion to cover losses. That does not include interest costs on that money or \$92 million in working capital. That total, and the bank and thrift spending approved yesterday, dwarfs any previous municipal or industry bailout by the government. Lockheed Corp. received \$250 million in loan guarantees from the government, for example; Chrysler Corp. \$1.5 billion; and New York City, a \$4.5 billion long-term financing package.

In fact, the entire foreign debt of the Soviet Union roughly equals the loan to the FDIC approved yesterday.

By April, the RTC will be seeking another \$55 billion to continue funding the S&L cleanup, and some regulators believe the FDIC will be back for more help to cover the losses from banks now failing in record numbers.

The FDIC has argued that in most cases it's cheaper for the government to transfer all of a failed bank's accounts to another bank than to pay them off and some banks are 'too big to fail' because their collapse would endanger the financial system.

Susan Schmidt and Jerry Knight, *The Washington Post*, 28 November 1991.

....

A Life of Scandal

Obituary of Lord Moynihan

The Daily Telegraph *obituary for Lord Moynihan was one of its best ever on the life of a scandal-ridden peer.*

The 3rd Lord Moynihan, who has died in Manila, aged 55, provided, through his character and career, ample ammunition for critics of the hereditary principle. His chief occupations were bongo-drummer, confidence trickster, brothel-keeper, drug-smuggler and police informer, but 'Tony' Moynihan also claimed other areas of expertise – as 'professional negotiator', 'international diplomatic courier', 'currency manipulator' and 'authority on rock and roll'.

If there was a guiding principle to Moynihan's life, it was to be found on the wall of his office in Manila, where a brass plaque bore the legend, 'Of the 36 ways of avoiding disaster, running away is the best.'

Moynihan learnt this lesson at an early stage. The first time he ran away was in 1956, to Australia. There were two reasons for his flight. The first was to elude his father's fury over a liaison with a Soho night-club waitress. The second was to escape his wife, an actress and sometime nude model; they had married secretly the previous year, and she had now taken out a summons against him for assault. Her father had made a similar complaint – 'I regret to say I gave him a swift right upper cut,' Moynihan had announced from Australia. The idea was that he should work on his uncle's sheep farm in the bush, but after five days he ran away to Sydney, where he made his debut as a banjo-player and met the Malayan fire-eater's assistant who was to become his second wife. The next year he returned to London, where he effected a reconciliation with his first wife and found a job as manager of the Condor, a Soho night-club. This job did not last, and in 1958 he married the former fire-eater's assistant, by now a belly dancer working under his management.

'Of course,' Moynihan explained, 'it means I shall have to become a Mohammed first.' To this end, at dusk each day he kneeled to the setting sun with a cloth draped over his head. His father was displeased by the marriage, but Moynihan was unabashed. 'Actually,' he confided to a journalist, 'I only see the old man when I'm a bit short.'

Soon after the wedding he made his first court appearance, accused of the larceny of two bedsheets. He was found not guilty, but as he walked from the court he was presented with another summons, this one over a lease. It was time to run away again.

With his new bride, Moynihan moved to Ibiza to set up a night-club; when this failed he left his partner to pick up the pieces and fled to the mainland, before returning home once more. His next venture was a coffee bar called El Toro, with a Spanish bull-fighting theme, at premises at Beckenham, Kent. But that, too, failed, so Moynihan set off with his wife on a belly-dancing tour of Europe and the Far East. In 1961 the two of them converted to the Persian faith of Baha'ism: 'It propagates Oneness of Mankind,' Moynihan explained. On their travels he occasionally challenged people to duels, but nothing came of these. An Italian declined to fight: 'Moynihan's behaviour is founded on exhibitionism. It has nothing to do with gentlemanly conduct.'

In Tokyo he challenged an American journalist who had disparaged his wife's dancing: the critic elected martinis or cold noodles as weapons. In 1960s London Moynihan cut a rather ridiculous figure in kaftans, and worked for a time for Peter Rachman, the slum landlord, driving his maroon Rolls-Royce.

'I didn't really understand what I was involved in in those days,' recalled

Moynihan. 'It was quite cruel. They had this big Alsatian dog that had been taught to soil the tenant's beds.' Moynihan later claimed that three years after Rachman was reported dead he met him at an hotel in Izmir, Turkey, where they had a drink together and reminisced about old times.

After he succeeded his father in the peerage in 1965 Moynihan took the Liberal Whip in the House of Lords, where he was principally concerned in arguing that Gibraltar be given to Spain. The House was not impressed. In 1968 Lord Boothby interrupted one of Moynihan's speeches: 'My Lords, the noble Lord has bored us stiff for nearly three-quarters of an hour. I beg to move that he no longer be heard.'

Moynihan's business career and personal finances had meanwhile given rise to a number of misunderstandings. By 1970 he faced 57 charges – among them fraudulent trading, false pretences, fraud against a gaming casino and the purchase of a Rolls-Royce motor-car with a worthless cheque. To avoid disaster he fled once more, this time to Spain. 'I knew of my impending arrest 48 hours in advance,' he claimed. 'I'd been approached by a CID man who told me that for £50,000 the case against me would be dropped. Because I believe in God and England I told him to get stuffed.' His extradition was sought from Spain, but he disappeared, to resurface the next year in the Philippines. In 1968 he had married for a third time – another belly-dancer, this one a Filipino – and the new Lady Moynihan's family had a chain of massage parlours in Manila, where Moynihan remained for much of the rest of his life. At the Old Bailey in 1971 he was named in his absence as 'the evil genius' behind a series of frauds. 'This is a case of Hamlet without the Prince of Denmark,' declared the judge. 'The prince figuring behind all these offences is Lord Moynihan.'

As the 1970s wore on Moynihan found employment in the narcotics trade, as well as in fraud and prostitution. The first hint of this came in 1980, when he was named by an Australian Royal Commission as an associate of Sydney's 'Double Bay Mob', engaged in the import of heroin from Manila. No charges were brought, however, and Moynihan continued his life as a Filipino pimp under the patronage of President Marcos – 'my drinking chum', as he called him. Marcos apparently shielded him from prosecution over the murder of a night-club owner (who had married one of Moynihan's ex-wives). At one stage he ran a brothel within 100 yards of the British Ambassador's residence.

After the coup against Marcos in 1986, Moynihan's position became exposed, and the next year he was forbidden to leave the Philippines pending investigations of his links with drugs and prostitution. Moynihan was thus vulnerable to pressure from Scotland Yard and the American

Drugs Enforcement Agency to help them catch Howard Marks, a Balliol man who at that time controlled an estimated sixth of the global market in marijuana, and with whom he was already on friendly terms. He approached Marks with a bogus offer to sell him an island in the Philippines, on which he could grow marijuana; and in return for his own immunity agreed to wear a secret tape-recorder to ensnare his friend. Marks was duly convicted in Florida, with Moynihan as chief witness for the prosecution. The DEA gave him refuge and protection in the United States for a time, and hailed him as 'a hero, one of the good guys'. Marks saw things differently. 'I feel terribly betrayed,' he said. 'He's a first-class bastard.' Perhaps the most charitable judgement of Moynihan was one offered by a friend: 'Tony could never see wrong in himself, only in others. He thought he was just having harmless fun.'

Anthony Patrick Andrew Cairne Berkeley Moynihan was born on Feb. 2, 1936, the elder son of Patrick Moynihan, a barrister and stock-broker who succeeded to the Barony later that year. Patrick's father, Sir Berkeley Moynihan, an eminent surgeon who introduced surgical rubber gloves to Britain from America, had been created a baronet during Lloyd George's final administration, and then a peer in 1929. Young Tony was educated at Stowe and did his National Service with the Coldstream Guards; it was the last contact with respectability, and he was inclined to reminisce over it in his cups. His father, the 2nd Lord Moynihan, died in 1965, financially embarrassed and facing charges of homosexual importuning. He had been chairman of the Liberal Party executive from 1949 to 1950 but resigned from the party in 1963; his decision was announced by the Freedom Group, in which he was associated with Edward Martell. Colin Moynihan, Conservative MP for Lewisham East and currently Minister for Energy, is the son of his second marriage and thus the half-brother of the 3rd Lord Moynihan. The two were never close, but in 1985 they fell out when Tony Moynihan announced that he intended to sell the Victoria Cross won in 1855 by their great-grandfather, Sgt (later Capt.) Andrew Moynihan. Colin Moynihan is said to have raised £22,000 to pay off his errant half-brother.

In Manila, to which he returned after his sojourn in America, Moynihan lived in the suburbs in a heavily fortified house with a swimming pool, and had as his base in the city a brothel named the Yellow Brick Road. 'I just sit back and collect the money,' he said. 'The girls do all the work.'

He frequently spoke of returning to England – 'to clear my name,' as he put it. 'I miss things like decent roast beef and good newspapers, the civilised way of life.'

In 1988 he claimed to have travelled on a false passport to London, and to have sat in a car outside Lord's, listening to cricket on the radio. More recently he claimed to have secured immunity from police prosecution, and announced that he looked forward to taking his seat on the Labour benches of the House of Lords. Giving evidence at Marks's trial in 1989, Moynihan told the court that he had been appointed to the Order of Don Quixote by General Franco, whom he much admired. The court seems to have believed him, but no such order exists. In *Who's Who* his recreation was listed as 'dog breeding', but when pressed on this matter he strenuously denied it: 'As for breeding dogs, I can tell you I don't. Like every Englishman I like dogs, but that's where it ends.'

Moynihan is reported to have been married five times, and to have fathered various children. The heir to the Barony appears to be his son Daniel, born in February this year.

The Daily Telegraph, 26 November 1991.

Since the obituary appeared, there has been considerable debate about the legitimacy of the claim to the Barony by Daniel. Apart from a rival half-Philippine heir, the brother of Lord Moynihan, Colin Moynihan, the former British Minister for Sport, has also made a formal claim for the title to pass to him and his descendants.

....

Sir Joh: Unmasking a Self-Made Knight

Sir Joh Bjelke-Petersen is charged with corruption

Sir Johannes Bjelke-Petersen, Premier of the deep north Australian state of Queensland for nearly two decades, faced charges of corruption and perjury. The case was abandoned after it was revealed that the foreman of the jury was a paid-up member of Bjelke-Petersen's political party. Several of his closest political colleagues were imprisoned on corruption charges including one of his police commissioners. At the time, Queensland enjoyed the dubious reputation of being the most corrupt state of Australia.

'No politician is two-faced,' Boston mayor Jim Curley remarked, 'if he was, he'd wear the other.' Just so; Sir Joh wore three. There was the articulate, mild-mannered, apparently rather female-dominated little man; there was the cunning and ruthless man; and there was the bumbling old yokel who couldn't seem to put two coherent words together.

The last, we may suspect, was at once a mask to cover the face of the cunning man and a technique to exhaust the film in a television camera (and, latterly, the questions of probing lawyers). At bottom, it may have reflected a massive contempt for the audience.

The source of aspects of Bjelke-Petersen's character may lie in Hugh Lunn's account of his early years.

He was born in New Zealand on Friday, January 13, 1911, came to Australia in 1913, and left school in 1924. The little boat person was thus the victim (but later the beneficiary) of a cult of ignorance that went back to the days of the Labor hegemony.

He lived alone in a cow bail from the age of 13 until he was 28, his only companion a bread box, a Coolgardie safe, and presumably a Bible, and he hacked at impenetrable jungle vine scrub from before dawn until 11 p.m.

He entered Parliament, in the Country Party interest, in 1947. In 1952, then 41, he married Florence Gilmour, 31, a secretary in the bureaucracy. It was a marriage made in heaven: Flo played the organ; Joh sang the hymns.

Labor, in office more or less since 1915, retired hurt in 1957. Two years later, Bjelke-Petersen procured for £2 an authority to prospect for oil from Mines Minister Ernie Evans, and within a month sold 51 per cent of the piece of paper for £12,650. He did not see how the profit could be part of his taxable income. The tax people did, and so did the High Court.

Premier from August 1968, his career should have ended abruptly in October 1970 when a faction sought to unhorse him as leader. He remained in office by producing what he claimed was the proxy of Neville Hewitt, who was overseas: since he had not been able to reach Hewitt, he figured no one else had either.

Bjelke-Petersen was the great master of the politics of paranoia and provincial narcissism. During the Springbok rugby tour of 1971, he learned that firmness in the face of dissent and perceived anarchy would play in the hinterland; for the three years of the Whitlam Labor government, he relentlessly played the 'southern socialists' (code for communists) card.

He adroitly thwarted a highly dubious plan by the then Labor attorney-general, Lionel Murphy, to gain an extra Senate seat by 'persuading' Democratic Labor Party senator Vince Gair to quit the Senate to become the Ambassador to Ireland and the Holy See. Malcolm Fraser thus had the numbers to block supply.

With Labor's departure, a reversion to local law and order politics was required for the 1977 elections. Bjelke-Petersen also had a dream: to make Queensland a country separate from Australia with its own seat on the United Nations; it might become necessary to close the border.

However, police commissioner Ray Whitrod was seen as soft on dissent and perhaps of too independent a mind; a more compliant commissioner was required – one who would permit his troops to break a few heads in the cause of law and order and street theatre for the television cameras.

Bjelke-Petersen thus had one agenda, an inspector, Terry Lewis, who had been ingratiating himself with Bjelke-Petersen by mail from Charleville, perhaps had another. Their interests converged: in November 1976, Bjelke-Petersen pushed Inspector Terry Lewis through Cabinet as first assistant commissioner.

Whitrod says he told the police minister, Tom Newbery: 'This is pretty shattering to me; it's widely known in the force that Lewis was one of Frank Bischof's bagmen. (Bischof, commissioner from 1958 to 1969, was demonstrably corrupt; a bagperson is a collector of bribes.) That was when he was a sergeant.'

Newbery, perhaps amazingly, replied: 'He wouldn't do that sort of thing now.'

Whitrod asked if that was Cabinet's thinking. Newbery said it was. Whitrod asked to address Cabinet; Bjelke-Petersen refused. Whitrod resigned and Cabinet appointed Lewis as commissioner on November 22, 1976. In the circumstances, such an appointment may appear to have the potential for a scandal of atomic proportions, and so it did: 'Sir' Terry Lewis is now doing 14 years for corruption.

Meanwhile, the law and order campaign was a huge success. A change in the law made Lewis, rather than a magistrate, the final arbiter on permits to march in the streets; roused from apathy, the chattering classes obliged by tumbling into the street. So did the police, now virtually Bjelke-Petersen's private army; cameras whirred. The famous Harry Akers, a dentist, got knocked back for a permit to march with his dog, Jaffa, at 2.45 a.m. for 100 metres down a No Through road outside Bundaberg. Harry marched anyway and was observed by a car load of detectives but they had sense enough not to arrest the offending man and dog.

A Bjelke-Petersen family company, Ciasom, bought a property, Ten Mile, in 1982 for about $1.5 million. To discharge a loan and get working capital, Ciasom sought a $3 million loan in Swiss francs from the Singapore-based Asian bank. On December 8, 1982, the bank's man in Sydney, E. Vogt, saw Bjelke-Petersen in his office and sent a telex to head office urging that the loan be made. If not, 'we believe it would affect negatively our business in this State.' Bjelke-Petersen said he did not do business that way.

In 1983, some members of his coalition partners – the Liberals – perhaps for obvious reasons pressed for a parliamentary accounts committee, and some crossed the floor to vote with Labor on a motion to that effect. Bjelke-Petersen split with the Liberals and won government in his own right on the basis of a campaign that the Liberals had voted with the 'socialists'.

He advised Her Majesty in 1984 to grant him a knighthood at the exalted level of KCMG, and in 1985 Bob Katter Snr began the process of having him elevated to the British peerage. This eventually came to nothing, although he got a knighthood for Lewis in 1985.

Ciasom's loan in Swiss francs started to go bad in January 1985 when the dollar began falling. In October that year, he put it on Perth entrepreneur Alan Bond for $1 million to pay out a defamation action but eventually settled for $400,000. In April 1989, the Australian Broadcasting Tribunal found – on a standard of proof higher than the balance of probabilities – that Bond believed Bjelke-Petersen had subjected him to 'commercial blackmail' in demanding the payout.

Bjelke-Petersen's election win, against the run of play, in 1986 seemed to have adversely affected his political judgement. Subject to incessant flattery by dubious types who wore white shoes like a badge, he came to the view that the rest of Australia was pining for his brand of politics. He decided to become prime minister at the head of a non-existent party but managed only to split the federal Coalition and so help secure the return of the Hawke Government in 1987.

His national adventure, however, had the fortunate effect for Queensland that deputy premier Bill Gunn was running the State when the balloon finally went up on corruption; Gunn asked the Hon. Gerald Fitzgerald QC to conduct an inquiry. Bjelke-Petersen tried to reassert his authority over the local National Party but kept on making political mistakes. His colleagues got rid of him in December 1987.

It is said that Bjelke-Petersen 'did a lot for Queensland' but the verdict of history will surely be that in his time, every institution of the State was thoroughly debauched. The stench of corruption hanging over his party caused a swing of 15.5 per cent against it in 1989 and Labor returned to office for the first time since 1957.

Meanwhile, the special prosecutor's decision presumably means that he will not have to return his KCMG to Her Majesty.

Evan Whitton, *The Australian*, 30 October 1990.

....

Right Out of a Romance Novel

William Kennedy Smith on trial for rape

William Kennedy Smith, the nephew of President Kennedy, was acquitted of rape and battery charges against a girl he met in a Palm Beach bar while out having a late-night drink with his other famous uncle, Senator Edward Kennedy. This was the most widely covered rape trial of the year, if not of the past decade, and led to charges of impropriety against The New York Times, *after they named and printed a lengthy profile on the alleged rape victim. In the summing-up, Kennedy Smith's counsel claimed that rather than a rape, their close encounter was 'right out of a romance novel'.*

WEST PALM BEACH, FLA., Dec. 11—William Kennedy Smith, breaking 255 days of public silence in the rape case against him, testified today that he was 'picked up' at a bar by his accuser, who initiated sex and then lied to police when she said a crime had occurred.

Even though the woman acted 'disoriented', calling him 'Michael' and asking to see his driver's license, Smith told the jury, he complied when she 'playfully' encouraged him to have sex with her on the lawn of the Kennedy compound March 30.

Smith's five-hour appearance today also was highlighted by clashes between Judge Mary E. Lupo and prosecutor Moira K. Lasch, who was rebuffed in her attempts to introduce testimony about other sexual misconduct allegations against Smith.

Smith, 31, testified that, during intercourse, he wrongly called the woman 'Cathie', adding, 'The minute I said it, I knew it was a mistake.'

Turning to face the jurors, Smith said, 'She sort of snapped and told me to get the hell off of her.' After slapping him, he said, she appeared 'very upset'. He said she again asked him for his identification and was 'shaking and crying'.

Smith's sometimes angry account, in which he said his medical career has been threatened and his family harmed by a 'real nut', differed radically from the alleged victim's testimony about the alleged rape.

The woman, 30, testified tearfully last week that Smith forced her to have sex against her will so violently that her rib, shoulder and leg were bruised.

Smith, composed and often speaking slowly and deliberately, seldom appeared nervous today during a 40-minute recitation for defense attorney Roy E. Black of the disputed events at the Kennedy estate.

But when he raised his hand for the oath, it shook. When his testimony was over, he sat back down at the defense table, closed his eyes and rested his head in his hands.

Under four hours of cross-examination by Lasch, Smith sometimes rocked in the witness chair as she asked him repeatedly to describe in graphic and minute detail how he and the woman had sex.

Before Smith took the stand at 9 a.m., Lasch had lost an important legal battle. Lupo ruled that, unless Smith referred to himself in testimony as non-violent or to his relations with women in general, Lasch could not question him about three women who have said in sworn depositions that Smith attacked them in the 1980s.

Lasch told Lupo forcefully that Smith's attorneys had 'already opened the door' to the women's testimony and that, if their testimony were barred, Smith would be 'home free' when he testified.

Constrained, Lasch used most of her cross-examination to insinuate that Smith had fabricated his account of consensual sex with his accuser and deviously aligned it with testimony from his uncle Sen. Edward M. Kennedy (D-Mass.), and his cousin Patrick Kennedy, both of whom were at the estate at the time.

'If you are implying that my family is lying to protect me, you are dead wrong,' Smith said in his most impassioned response to Lasch.

Sen. Kennedy has testified that, about midnight on Good Friday March 29, he roused Smith and Patrick Kennedy, 24, from bed after the two had returned from a bar called LuLu's and gone to sleep. Smith and Patrick Kennedy dressed and accompanied the senator to Au Bar, the night-club where Smith met the accuser later that night, the senator said.

Today, however, Lasch called as a rebuttal witness an undercover police officer who testified that she saw Smith at LuLu's at 1:15 a.m. March 30. Lasch tried to use the 75-minute discrepancy to show that Smith and his uncle and cousin tried to corroborate each other's testimony. She asked

Smith at least 15 times to specify the time of night various parts of his account occurred. Smith responded to each question, saying he could not remember.

'You got to Au Bar at 2 a.m.,' Lasch declared, sarcastically asking him whether he wanted the court to believe that, in the one hour before the night-club closed, the woman 'was overcome with your animal magnetism.'

'I never said anything about my animal magnetism,' he said, unable to suppress a smile.

Later, after describing graphically two separate sexual encounters with the woman on the beach and on the lawn, Lasch asked Smith whether, physically, 'this is possible' and added, 'What are you, some kind of sex machine?'

'It is the truth, Ms Lasch,' he responded.

Throughout Smith's lengthy appearance, his cousin Robert F. Kennedy Jr, 37, a New York attorney, sat in the first row, leaning forward intently.

At times, Smith spoke so softly that everyone in court appeared to be straining to hear him. His long-awaited account of the alleged rape that has been publicized around the world drew spectators shortly after midnight Monday seeking one of 16 visitors' seats in the tiny courtroom.

Rita Naron, 36, a legal assistant for a law firm in Boca Raton, said she planned a day off and arrived in the middle of the night to secure a seat. As Smith testified, she said, she studied his face intently.

'I don't believe him,' she said. 'I didn't think he's telling the truth. There are discrepancies in her story and in his story. He just answered a little too coolly and calmly. He appeared as though he had been coached.'

However, Joyce Armoogam, 58, who sat in the same row as Naron, said that she had believed Smith's accuser but that his testimony changed her mind. 'He sounded very believable,' she said. 'He hesitated a little bit with some of his answers. It didn't seem like it was a script. Sometimes, his voice cracked with emotion. I tend to believe him now.'

Describing under Black's questioning the hours before he went to Au Bar, Smith said he played parlor games with family and friends and talked about 'comparative literature' and Harvard University graduate students with his sister, Amanda, a student there. Then, the medical resident said, he went to LuLu's at the urging of friends and, tired from an exhaustive schedule on hospital rotation, he went to bed.

After Sen. Kennedy came into his bedroom and suggested a drink at Au Bar, Smith said, he dressed and went with him and Patrick. There, Smith said, the alleged victim 'brushed up' against him when he went to get a drink at the bar.

Smith testified that he believed that the woman was aware that he had come in with Sen. Kennedy and that she set out to meet him.

'The impression is, I got picked up,' Smith said. While they danced, he said they kissed. 'We were mutually attracted,' he said. 'Things developed along a sexual way very quickly.'

When Smith saw his uncle and cousin leaving and contemplated catching up with them, he said, the woman offered him a ride to the Kennedy estate.

By contrast, the woman testified that she never kissed Smith at Au Bar and that he asked her to drive him to the estate, saying the Kennedys had departed.

The woman also testified that neither she nor Smith said anything 'suggestive' and that their conversation at Au Bar centred largely on her child, then 1, who had been born prematurely.

Today, Smith said no such conversation occurred. 'Absolutely not,' he said when Black asked him whether he had known that night that she had a child. 'If she did mention her daughter, I would have asked her about her husband,' Smith said. The woman has never been married.

The defense has hammered repeatedly at the woman's inability to remember when and where she took off her pantyhose March 30. They were found later by a friend on the passenger seat of her car. Today, Smith said that, in the car, the two kissed and discussed going swimming at the estate, she said, 'Give me a minute' and apparently took off the pantyhose while he waited in the parking lot.

She testified that, while in the car, he never mentioned going swimming and that she went to the house only for a quick tour of the home she described as a 'landmark'.

When the two dangled their feet in the backyard pool, Smith said, the woman became 'confused' and called him 'Michael' and asked for his driver's license.

Smith said she asked him, 'Have you ever been ashamed of your family?'

He said his 'recollection is she said, "My grandfather was head of a tire company, and he did some terrible things and he was a terrible person and you might do anything to get away, you might change your name, you might do all sorts of things. Do you know what I'm talking about?"'

Smith said that he thought she was temporarily 'disoriented' but that he accompanied her when she said, 'Let's go to the ocean.' After walking there 'arm-in-arm' and kissing, he said, they sat on a towel and 'started to neck ... she unbuttoned my pants. I took her panties off with her help.'

Telling Black that he was embarrassed, Smith paused. At Black's urging, he added that he 'could feel her ... She was excited.' But because the two had no means of birth control, he said, she simply 'massaged him,' and he ejaculated. Told that she did not want to go swimming, he said, he went alone for '10 to 15 minutes'.

When he returned, he said, she had left the beach and, with just a towel around his body, he climbed stairs to the backyard and saw her standing there. He said that he told her that he wanted to go to bed but that she 'pulled' off his towel, took off her underpants and, with her hand, forced him inside her.

Because he had no condom, he said, his plan was to avoid ejaculating inside her, but he became excited and, holding her tightly, told her to stop moving. He testified that he said 'stop it, and I called her Cathie,' the name of a long-time girlfriend.

Asked by Lasch if he understood the word 'no', Smith said, 'She never lost her right to say "no" to sex with me. When she did say, "Get off me," that's exactly what I did.'

He said he could not say why a doctor found that the woman had a bruised rib and the imprint of five fingers on her arm later that day. 'I do know she did not get them from me,' Smith said.

Mary Jordan, The Washington Post, 11 December 1991.

A jury acquitted Smith of all the charges.

....

Tailhook Scandal

Sexual hijinks at US Navy convention in Las Vegas

In September 1991, more than 4,000 American Marine Corps and Navy aviation officers attended the annual Tailhook Symposium in Las Vegas. It was soon reported in the press that hundreds of the men ran riot through the hotel, with drunken parties involving public sex plus numerous assaults on females in hotel corridors. The behaviour of the servicemen was so outlandish that more than 140 officers were referred for court-martial and disciplinary action. Four admirals were forced to resign and eventually Lawrence Garrett III, the United States Navy

Secretary, had to hand in his resignation when it was revealed that he had witnessed many of the indecent assaults at the Convention but had done nothing about it. Three years later, Paula Coughlin, a former Navy Lieutenant, who was the first woman to complain about sexual harassment at the convention, was awarded $1.65 million damages against the Las Vegas Hilton.

A new word entered the American language after Tailhook '91 – 'ballwalking', which referred to the exposure of a male's testicles while strolling.

The official inquiry gave detailed accounts of the goings-on in various hospitality rooms, with the 'Rhino' suite providing the most sensational behaviour.

The VMFP-3 suite was called the 'Rhino' room or suite, as the rhinoceros was the squadron mascot. In addition, we were told that former squadron members in attendance at Tailhook '91 could be identified as such as they wore headgear in the form of a rhinoceros horn at various times throughout the weekend.

By most accounts, the suite was organized and administered as an entertainment suite. Although the VMFP-s squadron was deactivated in 1990, former squadron members sponsored the suite at Tailhook '91. Since the squadron had been deactivated, no squadron commander or XO was present at the convention. However, the former CO and XO (both active duty) did attend Tailhook '91. They told us they participated in the planning of the hospitality suite and visited the suite throughout the weekend of the convention. Suite activities centered around a hand-painted mural of a rhinoceros (approximately 5' x 8') to which was affixed a dildo rigged by squadron members for use as a drinks-dispensing mechanism. The dildo dispensed an alcoholic-based liquid referred to as 'Rhino Spunk' by attendees. A squadron member acted as bartender and operated the dispensing machine. By way of background, witnesses told us that the original 'Rhino' mascot was made of papier-mâché and was displayed by the squadron at the 1989 and 1990 Tailhook conventions. The original 'Rhino' also had a large phallus device from which drinks were dispensed. Women received a drink by kissing the papier-mâché 'Rhino' on the lips.

As the original 'Rhino' had been given to a bar in Pensacola, FL, after the Tailhook '90 convention, a decision was made by a number of former senior and junior officers to create a new mascot (the mural) for Tailhook '91. During Tailhook '91, some women would kiss, suck, or stroke the dildo to obtain a drink.

A number of aviators told us that while in the suite they observed a 'deep throat' contest during which women would simulate performing oral sex on the dildo. The crowd would chant, 'Beat the line ... beat the line.' The chant referred to a line that was placed on the dildo to indicate how much of the dildo the previous woman was able to take in her mouth. Former squadron members stated that women were not forced, coerced, or intimidated in any way to drink from the dildo. However, many witnesses informed us that women were certainly encouraged to drink from the 'Rhino' and various organized chants were used to accomplish that, such as 'Kiss the Rhino,' 'Do the Rhino,' or 'Suck the Rhino'. Women's names were also used in the chants. If a woman drank from the 'Rhino' or refused to drink, she would be cheered or booed accordingly by the crowd. A number of women told us they found the behaviour to be unnerving.

During the course of our investigation, five women told us that on entering the suite, they were physically restrained from leaving. During one of those incidents, a woman noticed that an unknown individual was behind the mural. The individual removed the dildo and replaced it with his exposed penis. Another woman explained that she was escorted through the suite to the mural and as the crowd started to chant her name she was surrounded. An individual whom she believed to be an aviator grabbed her arms. She perceived that she would be prevented from leaving until she drank from the rhinoceros's penis.

Other activities reported to have taken place in the suite included women exposing their breasts to obtain squadron T-shirts. Additional incidents that were detailed by witnesses included 'mooning', consensual sex, and one episode in which a former squadron member had his pants pulled down by two women visitors to the suite. Reportedly, men who were wearing 'Rhino' horns and believed to be aviators were 'butting' women with their horns in the third-floor hallway on Saturday evening.

Office of the Inspector General, The Tailhook Report,
Department of Defense, 1993, pp. 136–8.

'A Game of "Gotcha"'

Bill and Hillary Clinton interviewed on US television about Gennifer Flowers

President Bill Clinton was nearly out of the presidential race in January 1992 when allegations oozed out through supermarket tabloids that he had had a long-standing affair with Gennifer Flowers, a former part-time cabaret singer, who had once made a fleeting appearance on a television variety show called 'Hee Haw'. In a brilliant counter-move, Governor Clinton and Hillary were interviewed by Steve Kroft on the CBS TV show '60 Minutes' immediately after the broadcasting of the Superbowl, which probably guaranteed him the largest audience of the year.

(The President ran into further difficulties when it emerged that he had a nodding acquaintance with marijuana. However, public opinion was mollified when it transpired that he had not inhaled but merely rested the joint in his lips.)

Kroft: Who is Gennifer Flowers? You know her?

Bill Clinton: Oh, yes.

Kroft: How do you know her? How would you describe your relationship?

Bill Clinton: Very limited, but until this, you know, friendly but limited.

Kroft: Was she a friend, an acquaintance? Does your wife know her?

Hillary Clinton: Oh, sure.

Bill Clinton: Yes. She was an acquaintance, I would say a friendly acquaintance...

Kroft: She is alleging and has described in some detail in the supermarket tabloid what she calls a 12-year affair with you.

Bill Clinton: That allegation is false.

Hillary Clinton: When this woman first got caught up in these charges, I felt as I've felt about all of these women: that they ... had just been minding their own business and they got hit by a meteor ... I felt terrible about what was happening to them. Bill talked to this woman every time she called, distraught, saying her life was going to be ruined, and ... he'd get off the phone and tell me that she said sort of wacky things, which we thought were attributable to the fact that she was terrified.

Bill Clinton: It was only when money came out, when the tabloid went down there offering people money to say that they had been involved with me, that she changed her story. There's a recession on.

Kroft: I'm assuming from your answer that you're categorically denying that you ever had an affair with Gennifer Flowers.

Bill Clinton: I said that before. And so has she.

Kroft: You've said that your marriage has had problems, that you've had difficulties. What do you mean by that? What does that mean? Is that some kind of – help us break the code. I mean, does that mean that you were separated? Does that mean that you had communication problems? Does that mean you contemplated divorce? Does it mean adultery?

Bill Clinton: I think the American people, at least people that have been married for a long time, know what it means and know the whole range of things it can mean.

Kroft: You've been saying all week that you've got to put this issue behind you. Are you prepared tonight to say that you've never had an extramarital affair?

Bill Clinton: I'm not prepared tonight to say that any married couple should ever discuss that with anyone but themselves. I'm not prepared to say that about anybody. I think that the...

Kroft: ... That's what you've been saying essentially for the last couple of months.

Bill Clinton: You go back and listen to what I've said. You know, I have acknowledged wrongdoing. I have acknowledged causing pain in my marriage. I have said things to you tonight and to the American people from the beginning that no American politician ever has.

I think most Americans who are watching this tonight, they'll know what we're saying; they'll get it, and they'll feel that we have been more candid. And I think what the press has to decide is: Are we going to engage in a game of 'gotcha'? ... I can remember a time when a divorced person couldn't run for president, and that time, thank goodness, has passed. Nobody's prejudiced against anybody because they're divorced. Are we going to take the reverse position now that if people have problems in their marriage and there are things in their past which they don't want to discuss which are painful to them, that they can't run?

Kroft: You're trying to put this issue behind you, and the problem with the answer is it's not a denial. And people are sitting out there – voters – and they're saying, 'Look, it's really pretty simple. If he's never had an extramarital affair, why doesn't [he] say so?'

Bill Clinton: That may be what they're saying. You know what I think they're saying? I think they're saying, 'Here's a guy who's leveling with us.' ... I've told the American [people] more than any other candidate for president. The result of that has been everybody going to my state and spending more time trying to play 'gotcha'.

Hillary Clinton: There isn't a person watching this who would feel comfortable sitting on this couch detailing everything that ever went on in their life or their marriage. And I think it's real dangerous in this country if we don't have some zone of privacy for everybody...

Kroft: I agree with you that everyone wants to put this behind you. And the reason the problem has not gone away is because your answer is not a denial...

Bill Clinton: Of course it's not. And let's take it from your point of view, that won't make it go away. I mean if you deny, then you have a whole other horde of people going down there offering more money and trying to prove that you lied. And if you say yes, then you have just what I have already said by being open and telling you that we have had problems. You have, 'Oh good, now we can go play "gotcha" and find out who it is.'

Now, no matter what I say, to pretend that the press will then let this die, then we are kidding ourselves. I mean, you know, this has become a virtual cottage industry. The only way to put it behind us, I think, is for all of us to agree that this guy has told us about all we need to know. Anybody who is listening gets the drift of it and let's go on and get back to the real problems of this country...

Kroft: [The] question of marital infidelity is an issue with a sizable portion of the electorate. According to the latest CBS News poll ... 14 percent of the registered voters in America wouldn't vote for a candidate who's had an extramarital affair.

Bill Clinton: I know it's an issue, but what does that mean? That means that 86 percent of the American people either don't think it's relevant to presidential performance or look at whether a person, looking at all the facts, is the best to serve.

Kroft: I think most Americans would agree that it's very admirable that you've stayed together – that you've worked your problems out and that you've seemed to reach some sort of understanding and arrangement.

Bill Clinton: Wait a minute, wait a minute, wait a minute. You're looking at two people who love each other. This is not an arrangement or an understanding. This is a marriage. That's a very different thing.

Hillary Clinton: You know, I'm not sitting here – some little woman standing by my man like Tammy Wynette. I'm sitting here because I love him, and I respect him, and I honor what he's been through and what we've been through together. And you know, if that's not enough for people, then heck, don't vote for him.

Kroft: One of your campaign advisers told us the other day, 'Bill Clinton has got to level with the American people tonight, otherwise his candidacy is dead.' You feel like you've leveled with the American people?

Bill Clinton: I have absolutely leveled with the American people.

Kroft: You came here tonight to try to put it behind you ... Do you think you've succeeded?

Bill Clinton: That's up to the American people and to some extent up to the press. This will test the character of the press. It is not only my character that has been tested.

The Washington Post, 27 January 1992.

The Other Sunny Husband: Prince Alfred von Auersperg

Obituary of the first husband of 'Sunny' von Bulow

Another Daily Telegraph *obituary – this time the first husband of 'Sunny' von Bulow.*

PRINCE Alfred von Auersperg, the first husband of 'Sunny' von Bulow, who has died aged 57, spent his last years in an irreversible coma in a hospital following a motor-car accident. His last years echoed those of his first wife, who is now into her second decade of coma in a New York hospital.

'Alfie' von Auersperg was a peripheral participant in the much-publicised drama of the von Bulow case and, as he lay in his coma, his character was portrayed in a Hollywood film about the von Bulow case, *Reversal of Fortune.*

The relentless exploitation of this saga by the media is now to bear fruit in a television documentary scheduled for later this summer.

Prince Alfred Eduard Friedrich Vincenz Martin Maria von Auersperg was born in 1935 into an impoverished Catholic princely family seated in Prague.

The Auerspergs originated in Carniola in the 13th century, became Counts in 1630, and Princes of the Austrian Empire in 1653; all members of the family have been styled Prince since 1791.

In recent years the family has been dogged by scandal. Prince Alfred's brother Louis and his brother-in-law, Arndt Krupp von Bohlen (a member of the Essen cannon dynasty), both succumbed to the bottle.

Prince Alfred's mother, Countess Henriette Larisch, was a kinswoman of Maris Larisch, a central figure in the Mayerling tragedy in which Crown Prince Rudolf of Austria and his mistress Marie Vetsera died.

His father, Prince Alios, was a member of the diplomatic service, who served at the German Legation in Berne.

Young 'Alfie' – a pleasant youth of simple mind, boyish good looks and slick golden hair – led an easier life, his inclinations veering to the sportive. He was a keen skier, and might well have made it to the Olympic team but for an ill-timed broken leg.

He was employed by the energetic Baroness Pantz as a tennis professional at the Mitterzill Club in Austria, where his powerful service attracted the attention of the American heiress Sunny Crawford, taken there on holiday by her mother and future stepfather, Russell Aitken.

On the rebound from a romance with a more erudite prince, Miss Crawford married Prince Alfred in 1957. They had a son, Alexander, born in 1959, and a daughter, Annie Laure, born in 1958, both of whom featured prominently in the trial of their mother's later husband, Claus von Bulow.

At first Alfie and Sunny von Auersperg lived in Munich, where he and his father were involved in a publishing venture which floundered. The Prince's alleged *affaire* with the Italian actress Gina Lollobrigida attracted wide publicity.

Subsequently the Prince became a white hunter in East Africa, though this career came to an ignominious end when one of his clients, Gunther Sachs's brother, confronted by a wild animal at close quarters, panicked and ran into the line of fire. He was permanently lamed.

Later the Prince embarked on a safari deal with the self-proclaimed Emperor Bokassa in the Central African Empire. The Prince had just moved in with his trucks and tents when an anti-Bokassa coup was effected. The Prince beat a hasty retreat in a light aircraft.

The Prince's marriage to Sunny Crawford was dissolved in 1965. 'You can't hate Alfie,' his former wife would say, before she too fell into a coma. 'It would be like hating trees or grass.'

She had given him $1 million at the time of the wedding and on their divorce presented him with a house in Kitzbühel and a further $250,000 in settlement.

The Prince then married Hanne-Lore Auer, a Tyrolean night-club singer, who left him for a crooner. After their divorce he married thirdly, Princess Bea, a jeweller in Marbella, Spain.

Von Auersperg suffered his fatal injury while driving with his son, who escaped uninjured.

The Daily Telegraph, 1992.

....

Charity Begins at the Office

'Lady' Rose Aberdour steals £3 million from London hospital charity

'Lady' Rosemary Aberdour managed to steal nearly £3 million from the London hospital charity where she worked in order to live a parody of a glossy magazine lifestyle. It all went well until a puzzled Earl of Morton read a newspaper story that the five-foot-three-inch, fourteen-stone secretary was passing herself off as his daughter. His enquiries led to her demise. After fleeing to Brazil, 'Lady' Rosemary returned to face the music, which ended with a four-year prison sentence.

The morning Rosemary Aberdour turned up for work in a £57,000 Bentley Turbo, a chauffeur at the wheel and a bodyguard at his side, the head of the hospital charity that employed her could scarcely believe his eyes.

'You might have thought the Queen was arriving, the way she held out her hand and said "good morning",' said Mr John Young, chairman of the trustees of the National Hospital Development Foundation.

Coolly, Aberdour told him: 'You must understand that, having inherited £20 million, I have to have a minder because I might be kidnapped.'

Mr Young recalled that at the time it seemed a plausible tale. What he did not know then was that the foundation was paying for the car, the chauffeur, the bodyguard and the £8,900 personalised number plates H1 RUA. The three letters stood for her full name, Rosemary Una Aberdour. She purported to be Lady Rosemary, daughter of the Earl of Morton.

But her aristocratic pedigree existed only in the fantasy world she created with the help of more than £2.7 million stolen from the charity. It financed a spending spree of spectacular proportions. The self-styled Lady Rosemary's extravagances ranged from having her black Labrador, Jeeves, chauffeur-driven to Scotland for a walk in the hills, to splashing out £780,000 on a series of £49-a-bottle champagne parties at expensive venues.

One party at the 13th-century Thornton Watlass Hall in North Yorkshire continued, with changing guests, for a fortnight. A fleet of rented vintage cars ferried guests to York races and other attractions. Nightly revels included a Halloween party with 'live' bodies leaping from coffins and the fortnight's end was marked by one of the biggest fireworks and laser displays seen in the country.

Aberdour hired a helicopter to fly her secretary as a birthday treat to Conway Castle, North Wales. Trumpeters greeted them on the battlements and two knights-in-armour vied for their attentions before they were led to two thrones and serenaded. At the Battersea penthouse she rented, again with the charity's money, she threw a St Valentine's Day party with drag queens from a West End cabaret providing the entertainment. The apartment was decorated as a beach front for a 'Caribbean thrash' and guests fished for lobsters and crayfish to barbecue. Mr Stephen Moore, director of Bojollys, the party designers, now owed £11,000 by Aberdour, said: 'No one spent more on parties than her.'

She used his firm for a £65,000 funfair party with dodgems and a ghost train in London's Docklands. For her 29th birthday celebration at the Savoy, Bojollys turned the Abraham Lincoln Room into a Chinese temple at a cost of £50,000. Another of the party organisers was Mr Peregrine Armstrong-Jones, the Earl of Snowden's half brother, whose firm is being sued by the charity for the recovery of £428,000 spent by Aberdour. Lawyers have served writs on Mr Armstrong-Jones, 31, an Old Etonian, his wife Caroline and their company, Bentley's Entertainments Ltd. Mr Armstrong-Jones declined to comment. Unknown to him, the bills she settled were paid with stolen money. His company was the largest creditor, owed a total of £109,000, when Aberdour was declared bankrupt in December.

In February last year, Aberdour invited a dozen friends to join her on a hired yacht, the *Jamaica Bay*, to sail around St Lucia in the West Indies for a fortnight at £29,000 a week. On another occasion, she flew friends to St Lucia in a hired jumbo jet. Mauritius was another favoured destination and £106,000 was spent with one holiday firm alone. She also travelled in style on land. As well as the Bentley Turbo, she drove a £70,000 Mercedes sports car.

And she recruited five personal staff – the chauffeur and bodyguard, plus a female butler and two secretaries. But the total of £134,000 spent on 'staff wages' also included the salaries of two extra secretaries needed, she said, at the National Hospital to help with fund-raising.

Her first flat, in Queen's Gate in South Kensington, at an annual rent of £41,000, was not quite to her liking. In its place, she chose to spend £123,000-a-year on the Battersea apartment, overlooking the Thames at Waterside Point. Cheaper flats were taken in the area for members of her personal staff. More than £400,000 went on credit-card spending. The 37-page police inventory of contents seized from the four-bedroom, four-bathroom penthouse listed 320 bottles of champagne and fine wine.

Her pursuit of the high life was in extraordinary contrast to her background as the daughter of Mr Kenneth Aberdour, Essex radiologist, and his wife, Jean, once a secretary at the National Hospital. The trustees' chairman, Mr Young, head of the London brewery, was not alone in being taken in by Aberdour's explanation of her rise from a humdrum middle-class secretary to an extravagant world of champagne parties. Mr Young said: 'She was a brilliant actress. I'm not stupid and her change to a woman who had come into money seemed quite subtle.'

Aberdour joined the charity in 1986, and for her first two years worked hard raising cash for a new wing and medical equipment for the hospital, an internationally renowned centre for the treatment of multiple sclerosis. Parkinson's and Alzheimer's diseases, epilepsy and strokes. Mr Young credits her with helping to raise more than £1 million. The truth astounded him. He said: 'I was shocked and absolutely incredulous, especially after her devotion.'

One of her coups was to convince the trustees that the Queen's Square Ball, named after the hospital's Bloomsbury address, but little more than a staff party, could be revived as a lucrative fund-raising showpiece. She organised three balls, and assisted in many legitimate high society fund-raisers, some attended by the Princess of Wales, the charity's patron. Writing in a foundation brochure, she spoke of gaining 'great motivation from meeting patients who show immense courage in coping with their illnesses, often against incredible odds.' In reality she was lengthening the odds against patients by helping herself to their money.

The thefts began in 1988 but accelerated in 1990 and 1991. When she was exposed in June 1991, she had almost emptied the charity's coffers. In probably the most brazen action of the whole fraud, she promised in autumn 1990 to make five personal donations totalling £500,000 to the foundation. She gave £100,000 of stolen money as a first instalment. She insisted on anonymity, because she 'did not want to be seen to flaunt her wealth'. She knew that to be listed as a generous patron might well alert her parents. She was careful to hide her aristocratic pretensions from her family or old friends.

Her good luck held out when her appearance on the socialite circuit took her into the gossip columns. Still no one raised the alarm. Mr Young and other foundation staff do not believe she joined with theft in mind. He says she may have started to yearn for the glamorous life led by those who attended the events. Certainly, she was present at charity functions attended by the Princess of Wales or Princess Michael of Kent. Detectives believe the stealing habit grew when she found how easy it was after the first theft, the relatively small-scale transfer of £4,000 from the proceeds of a ball into one of her bank accounts.

Although Aberdour fled to Brazil when she was unmasked, she co-operated with police after her boyfriend went to Rio to persuade her to face the music.

At 5ft 3in, and weighing 14st, Rosemary Aberdour may have seen the charity money as a source of second hand glamour. Two of her personal staff were keep-fit experts to tone her up, a task not aided by her habit of eating biscuits by the boxful. She may also have wanted to buy friends. But the glamour and the friendship eluded her. Stone cold sober at one of her parties, with all around her drinking her champagne, she remarked as she left early: 'No one wants me. No one loves me at all. I'm off.'

John Steele and Colin Randall,
The Daily Telegraph, 29 March 1992.

....

The Whitewater Affair

The Clintons' shady business dealings

This story, which first appeared in The New York Times *in March 1992, did more damage to the Clinton candidacy and later his presidency, than any other. Very little has been added despite countless attempts to discover more details about the sorry affair.*

WASHINGTON, March 7—Bill Clinton and his wife were business partners with the owner of a failing savings and loan association that was subject to state regulation early in his tenure as Governor of Arkansas, records show.

The partnership, a real estate joint venture that was developing land in the Ozarks, involved the Clintons and James B. McDougal, a former Clinton aide turned developer. It started in 1978, and at times money from Mr McDougal's savings and loan was used to subsidize it. The corporation continues to this day, but does not appear to be active.

Mr McDougal gave a detailed account of his relationship in several interviews in the last two weeks. This account, along with an examination of related local, state and Federal records and interviews with dozens of others in Arkansas, found the following:

- Available records covering the most active period of the real estate corporation, called Whitewater Development, appear to show that Mr McDougal heavily subsidized it, ensuring that the Clintons were under little financial risk in what turned out to be an unsuccessful enterprise.

    The corporation bought 200 acres of Ozark Mountain vacation property and planned to sell it in lots. During this period, the Clintons appear to have invested little money, so stood to lose little if the venture failed, but might have cashed in on their 50 percent interest if it had done well.

- The Clintons and Mr McDougal disagree about what happened to Whitewater's records. Mr McDougal says that at Mr Clinton's request they were delivered to the Governor's mansion. The Clintons say many of them have disappeared. Many questions about the enterprise cannot be fully answered without the records.

- After Federal regulators found that Mr McDougal's savings institution, Madison Guaranty, was insolvent, meaning it faced possible closure by the state, Mr Clinton appointed a new state Securities Commissioner, who had been a lawyer in a firm that represented the savings and loan. Mr Clinton and the commissioner deny giving any preferential treatment. The new commissioner approved two novel proposals to help the savings and loan that were offered by Hillary Clinton, Governor Clinton's wife and a lawyer. She and her firm had been retained to represent the association.

- The Clintons improperly deducted at least $5,000 on their personal tax returns in 1984 and 1985 for interest paid on a portion of at least $30,000 in bank loan payments that Whitewater made for them. The deductions saved them about $1,000 in taxes, but since the error was more than three years ago, Internal Revenue Service regulations do not require the Clintons to pay.

The complicated relationship between Mr McDougal and the Clintons came to light in an investigation by *The New York Times* of the Clintons' tax records and business relationships. It raises questions of whether a governor should be involved in a business deal with the owner of a business regulated by the state and whether, having done so, the Governor's wife through her law firm should be receiving legal fees for work done for the business.

Confusion Is Cited

Asked about these matters, the Clintons retained two lawyers to answer questions. The lawyers said the improper tax deductions were honest errors, made because there was confusion over who really owned a certain piece of Whitewater property and who was responsible for the loan taken out to buy it, Whitewater or the Clintons.

The deed for the land and the loan papers are all in the Clintons' names.

The lawyers said they were not in a position to answer questions about where the money that went into Whitewater came from. But generally, they said, they thought neither the Clintons nor Mr McDougal had profited from the venture. They also said the Clintons were once liable for about $100,000 in bank loans that financed Whitewater's original purchase of land. But the lawyers have only been able to find original documents showing $5,000 that the Clintons paid.

Some questions about the relationship and the Clintons' role in it may be difficult to resolve because of differing accounts and the missing records.

The two lawyers representing the Clintons are Susan P. Thomases, a long-time friend, and Loretta Lynch, a campaign aide, who participated in several hours of interviews at Ms Thomases' Manhattan offices Thursday and Friday.

Payments on Debt

The records that are available, and Ms Thomases' account, show that Whitewater made payments between 1982 and 1985 on Mrs Clinton's $30,000 real estate debt, reducing the debt by about $16,000 while also paying at least $14,000 in interest. At least one of those checks was signed by Mr McDougal.

Mrs Clinton originally borrowed the $30,000 from a bank also controlled by Mr McDougal, Bank of Kingston, but 'Hillary took the loan on behalf of the corporation,' Ms Thomases said. That, she explained, is why Whitewater made the payments.

The Clintons' 1984 and 1985 tax returns show that they took deductions for interest payments of $2,811 and $2,322 that Whitewater had made.

'It clearly is an error,' Ms Thomases said. She noted that the tax returns for those years were prepared by accountants in Arkansas.

The Clintons' gross income in 1984, as reported on their tax returns, was about $111,000 and they paid $22,280 in Federal taxes. In 1985, their reported income was about $102,000, and they paid $18,791 in Federal taxes.

Long-time Friendship

Mr Clinton and Mr McDougal had been friends since the 1960s. When Mr Clinton became the nation's youngest Governor at 32 years old, he took Mr McDougal into his administration as an aide for economic development. It was at about this time that the men formed Whitewater.

A few years later Mr McDougal, having left government in 1979, bought control of a small savings and loan association, Madison Guaranty, and built it into one of the largest state-chartered associations in Arkansas.

But over time, the savings and loan got in trouble, like many others around the country. Finally Federal regulators took the savings and loan away from Mr McDougal, and a Federal grand jury charged him with fraud, though he was acquitted. The Clintons were not involved in those proceedings.

Mr McDougal began having personal problems. He was found to be suffering from manic-depressive illness, though he was judged competent to stand trial. In the interviews, Mr McDougal appeared stable, careful and calm.

A year after the Clintons and McDougals bought the Ozark Mountain property and founded Whitewater Development in 1979, the corporation bought a modular house for about $22,000 and placed it on one of its lots.

That lot was then conveyed to Mrs Clinton, and the deed indicates that she paid nothing for it. Ms Thomases says this was an error by Whitewater. The deed, she said, should have shown the price and said that Mrs Clinton paid.

But the house was carried on the books as a Whitewater corporate asset and used as a model house to attract other buyers, according to Whitewater records produced by Ms Thomases. Because the records are incomplete, it is unclear exactly what happened. But about the same time, Mrs Clinton personally borrowed $30,000 from Mr McDougal's bank to pay for the house and the lot.

Ms Thomases said Mrs Clinton and the corporation regarded this as a corporate debt, though it was in Mrs Clinton's name. The corporation included no one but the Clintons and the McDougals. It was this debt that Whitewater made payments on until the end of 1985.

One year after acquiring the property, Mrs Clinton sold it for $27,500 with payments to be made over time, records show. It is not clear who received the buyer's down-payment of $3,000. But Ms Thomases said it was the corporation that took the loss on its books. A few years later, the buyer went bankrupt and stopped making payments, and then he died.

In 1988 Mrs Clinton bought back the house from the estate of the buyer. Records show that she paid $8,000 and then resold the property a short time later for about $23,000, after closing costs. The Clintons reported a capital gain that year of $1,640.

Ms Thomases explained that the capital gain was small because, as part of that transaction, Mrs Clinton had to pay off Whitewater's remaining $13,000 debt on the property, originally incurred by Mrs Clinton. The payments the previous owner had been making to Whitewater before he went bankrupt had been used to help pay off that debt.

Account Overdrawn

It was during the period when Whitewater was making the Clintons' loan payments that Madison Guaranty was putting money into Whitewater.

For example, Whitewater's check ledger shows that Whitewater's account at Madison was overdrawn in 1984, when the corporation was making payments on the Clintons' loan. Money was deposited to make up the shortage from Madison Marketing, an affiliate of the savings and loan that derived its revenues from the institution, records also show.

It was also in 1984 that Madison started getting into trouble. Federal examiners studied its books that year, found that it was violating Arkansas regulations and determined that correcting the books to adjust improperly inflated profits would 'result in an insolvent position', records of the 1984 examination show.

Arkansas regulators received the Federal report later that year, and under state law the Securities Commissioner was supposed to close any insolvent institution.

As the Governor is free to do at any time, Mr Clinton appointed a new Securities Commissioner in January 1985. He chose Beverly Basset Schaffer, a lawyer in one of the firms that had been representing Madison.

Fund-Raising Ideas

Ms Thomases, after talking to Mr Clinton this week, said the Governor chose her because they were friends, and because he wanted to appoint a well-qualified woman to an important post.

In interviews, Mrs Schaffer, now a Fayetteville lawyer, said she did not remember the Federal examination of Madison but added that in her view, the findings were not 'definitive proof of insolvency'.

In 1985, Mrs Clinton and her Little Rock law firm, the Rose firm, twice applied to the Securities Commission on behalf of Madison, asking that the savings and loan be allowed to try two novel plans to raise money.

Mrs Schaffer wrote to Mrs Clinton and another lawyer at the firm approving the ideas. 'I never gave anybody special treatment,' she said.

Madison was not able to raise additional capital. And by 1986 Federal regulators, who insured Madison's deposits, took control of the institution and ousted Mr McDougal. Mrs Schaffer supported the action.

Jeff Gerth, *The New York Times*, 8 March 1992.

Mike Tyson

Boxing champion convicted of rape

Despite his lisping voice and gentle demeanour, Mike Tyson, the former heavy-weight boxing champion, was unable to convince a jury that his midnight sex session with an eighteen-year-old beauty pageant contestant was an innocent fling.

INDIANAPOLIS, Mar. 26 [1992]—Mike Tyson's life as a free man ended today as an Indiana judge rejected pleas for leniency and sent the former heavyweight boxing champion to prison for six years for raping an 18-year-old beauty pageant contestant last July.

Judge Patricia J. Gifford, saying Tyson was capable of raping again and had not expressed sufficient remorse for the crime, sentenced him to 10 years on each of three felony convictions, then suspended four years for 'mitigating' circumstances. The sentences must be served concurrently. It will be at least three years before he is eligible for parole.

Tyson, wearing a light gray suit and black and red tie, solemnly answered 'yes' when the judge asked if he understood the terms of his sentence. Then, with a wall of attorneys and boxing promoter Don King circling him, the 25-year-old millionaire prize-fighter was led from the hushed courtroom with a new identity: Indiana Department of Corrections inmate 922335.

'The guys in the ghetto still love you, Mike,' a man yelled as Tyson left through a rear exit. 'We love you, Mike,' a woman screamed as she burst out sobbing.

Handcuffed and taken into custody by the Marion County Sheriff's Department, Tyson was later to be transferred to the Department of Corrections, where he was to be processed like any other felon: He would exchange his suit and tie for the standard prison attire of white T-shirt and blue jeans and would undergo a strip search, de-lousing and a shower before being assigned to a two-man cell.

Special prosecutor J. Gregory Garrison said Tyson should be imprisoned immediately because he had shown 'an ongoing, practiced pattern of aggressive behavior toward women ... He is guilty, he has been convicted, he is to be remanded.'

Tyson, who gave a rambling 11-minute statement midway through the

$2\frac{1}{2}$-hour hearing, insisted he had not raped Desiree Washington, a Miss Black America pageant contestant, when he took her to his hotel room early in the morning of July 19.

'I have not raped anyone, I did not rape anyone by any means,' Tyson said in a quiet, hurried voice. 'I'm sorry to Miss Washington. I by no means meant to hurt her or do anything to her. I'm sorry Miss Washington took it personally. I'm sorry Miss Washington isn't here so I could apologize to her.'

Tyson conceded that his behavior toward women during the pageant had been 'kind of crass' and he accepted blame for 'saying some things that were horrible'.

'I got carried away and I got into a situation that got way out of hand,' he said, referring to lewd remarks and gestures he made to contestants at pageant activities.

During the 13-day trial that ended with Tyson's conviction Feb. 10, Washington testified that Tyson lured her to Room 606 of the Canterbury Hotel and raped her.

'We made an arrangement and the situation happened,' he said of his late-night encounter with a woman whom he characterized as 'sophisticated. It was incredible to believe that I could take her upstairs and do horrific things to her.'

Tyson said prosecutors and some witnesses portrayed him unfairly. 'I was devastated listening to people say how stupid I was,' he said. 'I kept reading things that weren't true, that were vindictive and ferocious, that weren't fair. Things that were said by the prosecutors were distasteful and disdainful.'

Often gesturing with his hands, Tyson said he had thought a lot about the case and was nervous and 'slightly afraid' to be in court because he was not guilty of committing a crime.

'I don't come here begging for mercy, ma'am,' he told Gifford. 'I expect the worst. I can't see anything good coming out of this. I've been crucified and humiliated world-wide. And socially with women. Rape is a bad thing, an extremely bad thing. The situation that occurred was not meant harmfully at all,' he said, adding that there were 'no black eyes, no bruises, no scars'.

He ended by telling Gifford: 'Ma'am, if you may, I'm prepared to deal with whatever you have to offer me.'

Washington, a freshman at Providence College in Rhode Island, was not in the courtroom. But she wrote a letter to Gifford and today county prosecutor Jeffrey Modisett read portions of it in court.

'In the place of what has been me for 18 years is now a cold and empty feeling,' the letter said. '... Although some days I cry when I see the pain in my own eyes, I am also able to pity my attacker. It has been and still is my wish that he be rehabilitated.'

Defense Attorney Fuller, a partner in the Washington firm of Williams & Connolly, asked the judge to suspend all of Tyson's sentence or place him in an alternative residential program where he could undergo counseling. He said that despite Tyson's impoverished background and lack of education, Tyson had shown determination by becoming a boxing success.

Fuller said the boxer's life was filled with people interested only in his career. Fuller singled out Tyson's boyhood trainer, Cus D'Amato – whose companion, Camille Ewald, was in the courtroom today – saying that 'Mr Tyson-the-man was secondary to Mr D'Amato's purpose.'

Gifford, who received hundreds of letters as well as thick pre-sentencing reports, acknowledged she struggled to reconcile disparate portraits of him. 'From everything I've read and heard so far, we're looking at two different Mike Tysons,' Gifford said before asking him several questions. 'It makes the court's decision even more difficult.'

Ultimately, the 53-year-old judge, a former sex crimes prosecutor, seemed to be swayed by the seriousness of the crime and Tyson's apparent failure to understand the magnitude of what he had done. 'You have been given many gifts ... Your background and what you have done with yourself is a mitigant,' she said. 'You are to be commended. You have done a lot.'

But as to whether Tyson was capable of raping again, Gifford said, 'Quite honestly I'm of the opinion that you are.' She added, 'Something needs to be done with that attitude that I hear from you, saying that somehow she [Washington] misunderstood.'

With that, Tyson was stripped of his life as a famous boxer, stripped of the houses, women, cars and jewels, and sent to the Spartan life in a prison cell.

Alison Muscatine, *The Washington Post*, 27 March 1992.

'A Great Lay, but a Little Heavy'

Jani Allan and Eugene Terre Blanch

Jani Allan, a South African gossip writer, was upset by a British television documentary that suggested that she had had a passionate affair with Eugene Terre Blanch, a failed South African white separatist. She lost her case in August 1992 and was left with a legal bill thought to approach half a million pounds. The following witness is believed to have damaged her case.

The knees and gnarled toes were definitely Jani Allan's. And peeping through the keyhole of the bedroom door, her flatmate Linda Shaw guessed the naked bottom belonged to Eugene Terre Blanche. Yesterday a jury in the High Court was asked to picture the South African scene as it considered Miss Allan's claim that she was libelled by Channel Four allegations that she had an adulterous affair with the Neo-Nazi leader of the right-wing AWB.

'It was a large bottom and it was on top of Jani rising up and down,' said Miss Shaw, 37. 'I assumed they were having sex.'

Wrexham-born Miss Shaw, who broke down in tears at the end of a two-hour, still unfinished session in the witness box, was asked by Mr George Carman QC: 'From what you could see of the physique and shape of the naked bottom how did it compare with the physique of Mr Terre Blanche as you have seen him clothed?'

'It looked about the same size and shape,' she replied. 'He was a fairly large man.' Miss Shaw told the jury how it was that she stumbled on the sex scene at 3 a.m. in the Johannesburg flat she shared with 40-year-old Miss Allan.

'I woke up and saw this huge man standing in my room undoing his shirt buttons,' she said. 'I asked him what he was doing. He said Jani said I liked sex very much and I was a whore and I would not mind if he came upstairs to have sex with me. Obviously I was terrified. I thought he was going to rape me. I said I was going to call the police, and I told him to get out. He called me a whore and various other things.'

He left her bedroom and she sat on the floor shaking and wondering what to do.

'Eventually I opened my bedroom door, crept halfway down the stairs and cried Jani's name very softly.'

She could hear talking, laughter and music from the lounge. Miss Allan did not respond to her call. 'I went back upstairs,' she said. 'I locked the door again and sat wondering what to do. Then I heard this stomping of feet past my bedroom door towards her bedroom.'

Miss Shaw said an 'incredible noise' came from the room, as if every piece of electrical equipment had been switched on. 'I was petrified. I thought maybe they were hurting Jani and using the noise to hide her screams.

'I crept along the passage and tried calling her name. I tried calling and there was no response. I turned the handle and the door was locked.'

Miss Shaw said she looked through the keyhole and saw Miss Allan's feet flat on the floor with the large white bottom in between them. She knew they were Miss Allan's feet because of the gnarled toes. Miss Allan thought they were ugly and was 'neurotic' about her feet.

Mr Carman said: 'You then said you saw what you called a bottom.' Miss Shaw agreed. 'Colour?' asked Mr Carman. 'White,' she replied. The QC asked her: 'Are you able to identify the sex or shape?'

Miss Shaw said: 'I did not see genitals. It was a large bottom and it was on top of Jani, rising up and down.' She could also see brown leather boots or shoes either side of Miss Allan's feet.

Mr Carman asked her: 'Was it a movement indicative of sexual activity?' 'Yes,' she replied.

Miss Shaw said the next day she told Miss Allan what she had seen. Her flatmate replied: 'Sweetie, you've had a nightmare. Nothing of that sort happened.'

Miss Shaw said that the incident led her eventually to move out of the flat, although the two, who had both worked together at the South African *Sunday Times*, remained friends.

On a later occasion Miss Shaw added, 'Jani had told me she was having sex with Terre Blanche. She said he was a great lay but a little heavy.'

Bill Mouland, *The Daily Mail*, 30 July 1992.

Escobar's Gin Palace

Pablo Escobar, Colombian billionaire drug-dealer

Pablo Escobar, the Colombian billionaire cocaine dealer, 'surrendered' to the authorities in 1991 in return for promises that he would be well looked after and treated leniently. Mr Escobar, who was suspected of exporting hundreds of tons of cocaine to the West and murdering hundreds of Colombians, decided to depart from prison when there was a threat that he was going to be moved to a military facility. His other concern was an American Supreme Court decision declaring that it was permissible for American law enforcers to kidnap foreigners abroad to bring them to justice in the US. Despite Escobar's impressive international reputation as a world-class villain, it now appears that an even more violent cocaine gang has taken over in Colombia. Escobar was discovered and shot by security forces in 1993.

ENVIGADO, Colombia, July 31—The image of Pablo Escobar lounging on his prison water bed while co-ordinating shipments of tons of cocaine to the United States on his cellular telephone is not quite accurate, say lawyers who visited the trafficker in his hillside jail here.

First of all, Colombia's wealthiest citizen had to make do with a foam mattress until his water bed was installed last year. Second, until he received his cellular phone he had only the rustic services of the 50 carrier pigeons in his personal prison aviary.

Finally, the lawyers say, the 42-year-old Mr Escobar was not one to work in bed, and presided over his business meetings at the head of a proper boardroom table. He also enjoyed the use of an office equipped with a computer linked by modem to a national computer network.

What about charges that Mr Escobar continued trafficking until he escaped from the jail on July 22?

'It was important to have him physically detained, but no one really thought he would stop trafficking,' said Juan Guillermo Sepulveda, a lawyer from nearby Medellín who, as local state prosecutor, helped negotiate Mr Escobar's surrender June 19, 1991.

In the wake of Mr Escobar's escape, formerly tight-lipped officials are coming forward with a flood of new information confirming long-held suspicions that the fenced-off complex overlooking this suburb was not the trafficker's jail but his fortress, a cage that he was able to gild to his liking and from which it appears he could have escaped whenever he wanted.

But there was little reason for Mr Escobar to want to leave, not until the Government began a crackdown last month to reassert control over the prison. With the state paying his security bill, Mr Escobar quickly developed the comforts of home in his prison compound.

For exercise, there was a soccer field and a personal gymnasium. He spruced up his personal living quarters with rugs, walk-in closets, a video cassette player, a stereo system, a bar, a refrigerator, a 60-inch color television and a whirlpool bath. The living quarters included a reception area with a wood-burning fireplace. The police also discovered large quantities of pornographic magazines and videos.

'Pablo Escobar's rooms looked like a wealthy bachelor's pad,' an official in the state prosecutor's office told the newspaper *El Tiempo* on Friday. 'It seems to have been designed by an interior decorator. The colors of the rugs, curtains and bedspreads match perfectly.' ... 'It's very difficult to predict the outcome,' Fernando Brito, director of Colombia's intelligence police, said in an interview in Bogotá. 'Escobar is a very wily man and he has very great economic power. We are confronting the world's most powerful criminal.'

Short of domestic servants in his luxurious prison, Mr Escobar impressed several of his guards to serve as bartenders and waiters during his parties, photographs confiscated at the prison indicate.

The police also found a large selection of women's underwear, leading them to conclude that the prisoners received frequent visits from prostitutes. But one photograph taken at a prison party shows a male trafficker dressed up in women's clothing.

'The whole spectacle is disgusting,' Colombia's Attorney General, Gustavo de Greiff, said after inspecting the prison and reviewing a series of party photographs. 'It is absolutely incredible that no one rang the alarm bell, that no one said anything.'

The authorities suspect that a food truck with a false bottom may have smuggled in the contraband items seized from lockers after Mr Escobar's escape: computers, pistols, tear-gas masks, radiotelephones, a cellular phone and bundles of United States currency.

But not all of Mr Escobar's comforts were obtained illicitly. Correspondence between officials and lawyers for Mr Escobar in the period leading up to his surrender to the authorities shows the lawyers won guarantees of Mr Escobar's freedom to choose his guards and to design his jail, nicknamed 'The Cathedral'.

Inside the jail, 17 members of the 28-man guard service were picked by Mr Escobar's allies in the municipal government of Envigado, his power base for two decades. Dressed in civilian clothes, these 17 guards patrolled the jail's innermost security ring, a report issued on Thursday by Colombia's National Association of Prison Guards said.

Their shift from prison guard to bodyguard became apparent during the army's recent early-morning assault to reassert control over Mr Escobar and his 14 fellow inmates. While guards from the federal service offered no resistance, seven of the Envigado guards fought back, and one was wounded.

'Look at the prison guards like a presidential guard,' Jose Salomon Lozano, one of Mr Escobar's lawyers, suggested in an interview in Medellín. 'They have to respond for the life of the President. They cannot allow an attack from the outside. Enemies can appear disguised as soldiers.'

The army assault was prompted in part by Mr Escobar's refusal to allow security changes at The Cathedral. According to a Government report made public last week, an engineering company inspected the jail last October and pronounced it 'very vulnerable' to escape.

In January, Fernando Carrillo Florez, then Colombia's Justice Minister, maintained that the prison 'does not fulfil the minimum requirements for a high-security jail.' He recommended a $4 million construction plan, including fencing off prisoners' free access to the eight-acre prison grounds and fortifying perimeters with concertina wire, land mines and electronic sensors.

But work progressed slowly. On June 8, it stopped entirely after 'two prisoners demanded that the contractors suspend work,' the Government report said. Unhappy with the changes, Mr Escobar summoned a crew of Envigado city workers, who started to tear down an offending stretch of electrified fence. Army officers ordered that the fence be put back up.

'As soon as work resumed, 10 prisoners intimidated and beat the construction foremen and, with death threats, demanded suspension of work,' the log reported for June 12. 'Work was suspended.'

To back up their threats, several prisoners photographed the construction workers and said they would be killed if they were ever seen again in Envigado.

Suspicious that Mr Escobar might have ordered the construction of an escape tunnel, Colombia's Defense Minister, Rafael Pardo, ordered the air force to take infrared photographs of the prison grounds, a technique that allows detection of tunnels. On June 27, an air force plane made a successful photo run, eluding fire from a prison antiaircraft battery. The photographs did not reveal tunnelling activity.

The antiaircraft battery had been installed in response to Mr Escobar's fear that his numerous enemies – drug rivals, relatives of murder victims, or the United States Government – would try to bomb the prison.

Indeed, on March 9 the police in El Salvador announced the arrest of nine people who allegedly had shipped three 500-pound bombs to Cali, Colombia. Arrested members of the Salvadoran Air Force said Cali's cocaine cartel intended to use the bombs to obliterate their Medellín rivals in prison here.

On Mr Escobar's orders, construction workers dug a rudimentary bomb shelter. Civil aviation authorities closed the airspace over the prison and guards had standing orders to douse the lights if a plane entered the area at night. The traffickers also controlled the prison's electrical system, an advantage they may have put to use when they escaped in the early hours of July 22 during a mysterious three-minute blackout.

Many people here believe that Mr Escobar had slipped out of jail on several previous occasions.

'Since September, my in-laws have been saying that Escobar has been seen around town,' an American woman living in Envigado said. 'I guess he was tired of being locked up and went out for joy rides.'

Mr Sepulveda, the lawyer, recalled that during a jail visit last year the trafficker told him, 'Here I have what I like – books, soccer and my family.'

During his 13-month jail stay, Mr Escobar refused to permit the police to take identity photographs. The only known photographs of Mr Escobar taken inside the jail, published this week in *Semana* magazine, show a heavy-set family man with a moustache surrounded by his wife, Victoria Eugenia Henao, his 15-year-old son, Juan Pablo, and his 4-year-old daughter, Manuela, who held a pet white rabbit.

'Daddy, I love you, and I send you Colombia's biggest kiss,' Manuela chirped in a radio message the day her father fled the jail.

James Brooke, *The New York Times*, 5 August 1992.

Fergie's Holiday Plans

*The Duchess of York and John Bryan's holiday
romp in the South of France*

*This story which was emblazoned on the front page and on many more inside
of* The Daily Mirror *in 1992, did more to destroy the credibility of the Duchess
of York than anything else.*

'LOVE BLOSSOMS AT THE LITTLE HOUSE IN THE PINES ... BUT IN THE
FOREST SOMETHING STIRRED'

Fergie's Texan pal last night failed in a dramatic last-ditch bid to stop
The Daily Mirror from publishing the snaps of his holiday romp with the
duchess.

Wealthy John Bryan's court action against *The Mirror* followed a frantic
international effort to ban the sensational pictures.

But Bryan's application for an injunction was refused by a High Court
judge after an hour-long hearing.

The poolside pictures, taken in the south of France last week, show the
couple kissing and cuddling as love blossomed in a romantic retreat
outside St Tropez.

In one intimate shot, Bryan is seen kissing the duchess's foot.

The snaps torpedo any claims that ... financial adviser.

And today the stage is set for a furious final showdown at Balmoral
Castle where the Duke and Duchess of York have joined the Queen and
other royals on holiday.

Fergie and daughters Bea and Eugenie yesterday moved OUT of their
apartments in the castle.

They moved IN to a former gamekeeper's lodge on the edge of the
50,000-acre estate. Prince Andrew is believed to have stayed behind at the
castle.

Only last weekend 37-year-old Bryan was telling journalists there was
every chance of a reconciliation.

But down in the forest on the French Riviera, something stirred. And
the pictures, a record of holiday bliss in the arms of another man, almost
certainly end any chance that the royal couple can mend their marriage.
The photos were taken by an Italian freelance. He shot his film from public
paths around the villa in the pines.

Yesterday, alerted that the snaps were about to be splashed all over the world, Bryan began an incredible hunt to find who had them – and get them banned. Bryan's lawyers sought an order preventing the magazine *Paris Match* from using the photos. The case was put on hold by the French courts when the magazine appeared WITHOUT the pictures. The action switched to Hamburg – then to the High Court in London. The charade of Fergie and her 'financial adviser' began after the royal bust-up in March.

It followed an earlier scandal when snaps of Fergie, her children and Texan oil tycoon Steve Wyatt were found in a London flat. With the marriage in deep trouble, Bryan stepped in as the honest broker, vowing friendship to both the duke and duchess. He said: 'I am a financial adviser to both.

'The Queen herself has insisted that I get involved in all aspects of the negotiation at all levels.'

Bryan pleaded for 'breathing space' to give the couple a chance of sorting out their problems.

'They have asked me to do what I can to help and I am happy to do so,' he said.

Fergie and John travelled together to the Far East, New York, Argentina and Paris – always insisting their relationship was purely professional. Then last week, Fergie flew to France to join Bryan at the villa in the millionaires' playground of St Tropez. The duchess would begin her day at the pool around 11 a.m. And when Beatrice, four, and Eugenie, two, were in the house or playing at the nearby seaside, Fergie would go topless. Either the multi-coloured bikini top came off or her one-piece swim suit was rolled down.

Fergie and John frequently kissed and caressed.

The pictures show them sharing a cigarette and embracing in the pool. At one point Bryan, in pink-flowered bathing shorts, massaged the duchess's legs before planting a tender kiss on the sole of her foot. Neither wore sun hats in the 86-degree heat. Fergie, worried that John might burn, patted sun cream on his bald patch. One witness said: 'They couldn't claim this is a spot the Texan could not reach himself.'

Fergie, lounging on a blue and white striped mattress, clearly felt she was still carrying too much weight on her legs and thighs. She would pinch her bulges, sometimes grimacing in dismay. In the afternoons she did exercises. And throughout the day she dived and swam to shouts of encouragement from Bryan: 'Go on. Carry on. Do more.'

Fergie drank Evian water – up to three litres a day. She and Bryan, absorbed in each other's company, did not read or listen to music. Friends sunbathed nearby – but the duchess had no hesitation in peeling off her top as long as the children weren't around. When alone, with a nearly-finished bottle of wine at their side, the couple would go into a passionate embrace. It would only break up when the girls returned. In the pool, John played with the little princesses, cuddling and talking quietly to them. There were squeals of laughter as they all played 'catch'. Fergie would urge John: 'Give me a ride on your shoulders.' And there would be more laughter when she toppled in the water. In quiet moments, Eugenie wanted to snuggle up to mum.

Fergie, in head scarf and dark glasses, flew in to the tiny local airstrip on Sunday, August 9.

A Mercedes, one of the two hired for the week for £3,000, took her the four miles to her holiday home. The pink villa, Le Mas de Pignerolle (House of the Little Pines). is owned by British businessman Charles Smallbone. Its magnificent scallop-edged pool is set in extensive gardens. There were no local police on hand for the VIP arrival. Just John Bryan – the man who time and time again has brushed aside suggestions that he and the duchess are lovers.

In SCOTLAND yesterday, Fergie stayed hidden at Balmoral while Princess Di took little Beatrice swimming.

In LONDON, Bryan made his last move. He went to the High Court at 6.30 p.m. to try to stop *The Mirror* from publishing the pictures. But Mr Justice Latham, sitting after normal hours, told the Texan's lawyers they had not made out a case for a ban. Later, Bryan said in a statement that 'my privacy and that of the Duchess of York has been grossly infringed.' Last night he arranged for a friend to pick up a copy of *The Mirror*. After seeing the photos, he muttered: 'Where are the topless ones?'

James Whitaker, Harry Arnold, Martin Phillips, Ron Ricketts,
Georgina Walsh and Frank Gilbride, *The Daily Mirror*, 20 August 1992.

....

Sex, Lies, Videotapes ... and Woody Allen

The Woody Allen/Mia Farrow saga

It is likely to be considerable time before there is anything approaching a last word on the Woody Allen/Mia Farrow saga. Court-appointed psychiatrists could find no evidence that Woody Allen had in fact abused his child but made strong recommendations that the parties concerned should undertake therapy.

NEW YORK, AUGUST 20, [1992]—The twisted psychodrama of Woody Allen and Mia Farrow reached a sordid new low today as her press agent revealed that Farrow had videotaped her 7-year-old daughter Dylan recounting alleged sexual abuse by Allen.

A copy of the videotape landed in the hands of producers at a local television station, who considered airing it but were stopped by lawyers representing both feuding parents, said John Springer, a spokesman for Farrow.

Both Allen and Farrow, through their representatives, profess to acting in the best interests of the children – 11 in all – brought up by the actress with help from her former companion and film director.

But the siblings in what once appeared a happy, if unconventional, family have been left in anguish and divided against one another, friends and relatives said. Farrow and her children have spent months in psychiatric care, one friend said, coping with the implications of Allen's admitted affair with one of Farrow's grown daughters and of Farrow's contention that he sexually abused Dylan. Allen has sued for custody of Dylan and two other children, Moses, 14, and Satchel, 4.

Dylan was adopted first by Farrow and then also by Allen. The Connecticut State Police are investigating the abuse charge and have already interviewed Farrow, the child and the doctor who examined Dylan, according to Farrow's lawyer, Alan Dershowitz. No charges have been brought.

In an extraordinary off-screen appearance Tuesday, Allen denied vehemently that he sexually abused any of his children. A vindictive Farrow concocted the charge, Allen said, in retaliation for his love affair with her daughter Soon-Yi Farrow Previn.

Allen said his lawsuit seeking custody of the three youngest children is a step he took only in response to Farrow's 'outrageous allegations . . . I felt that for the sake of all my three children I must try and remove them from an atmosphere so unhealthy it can surely leave irreparable scars.'

The war of words, pictures and videotape intensified today. Attorneys and representatives from each side, as is typical in a celebrity custody battle, charged that the opposing partner was responsible for making the dispute so public. Springer, Farrow's PR man, said he didn't know how the local Fox affiliate got the video of Dylan. But Leslee Dart, Allen's spokeswoman, said the tape must have come from either Farrow's attorneys or Connecticut police, the only ones who had copies. Police would not comment.

A statement from Channel Five said: 'The tape seemed to support Farrow's allegations of abuse. The child seemed nervous and visibly shaken. We can't show you that tape because attorneys for Allen, Farrow and a New York state judge have requested we not show it.'

Dershowitz, meanwhile, made the rounds of the morning talk shows today asserting, 'Woody Allen doesn't want custody of his children . . . He brought his child custody charges so that he could say the sexual abuse allegations were a card being played as part of the child custody dispute,' Dershowitz told Bryant Gumbel on the *Today* show. 'He just wants to deflect attention from the serious charges.'

Dart bristled at the suggestion that the custody suit is a smoke screen, saying, 'Mr Allen has never cared more about anything in his life.'

The videotape of young Dylan being questioned by her mother about sexual abuse could be a potentially explosive weapon for public relations purposes, lawyers commented today, but is unlikely to be admissible in a courtroom.

'Unless this tape is done by a court-appointed professional, I would find it to some extent reprehensible,' said Louis Newman, a seasoned divorce attorney here who is not involved in this case. 'Children are easily manipulable, as any judge knows.

'If the charges are based on thin air,' Newman added, 'this is something that can come back and haunt her [Farrow]' in a custody proceeding.

Farrow's children have been stepping forward to defend their mother against Allen's charges that she is an unfit parent. 'Any statement about her being an unfit mother is ridiculous,' Daisy Previn, 17, told reporters before ducking into a car.

'His [Allen's] accusation that she's an unfit mother is absurd,' said Fletcher Previn, also 17. 'Anyone who knows my mother knows that.'

As an infant, Daisy was airlifted out of Vietnam and adopted by Farrow and her then-husband, conductor André Previn. Fletcher is one of three biological children of Farrow and Previn.

Previn, conductor laureate of the London Symphony Orchestra beginning this fall, broke his silence today on the romance between his daughter Soon-Yi and Allen.

'As a father I don't think I have a colorful enough vocabulary to tell you what I think of the affair,' Previn, 63, told *The New York Post*. 'My opinion of [Allen] gets lower by the day.'

The relationship is 'an unspeakable breach of trust' that has 'caused a great deal of anguish in the family and caused there to be a real rift between Soon-Yi and her siblings,' Previn said. 'I haven't spoken to her recently. Her siblings have tried, but she seems not to want to have anything to do with them.'

Soon-Yi's liaison with Allen 'is a first-time experience for her. She only just got out of high school last year ... She's a kid. She doesn't know any better. It's just that she's come under the influence of an articulate older man.'

Allen is 56, Soon-Yi is said to be 21, but Farrow's defenders say adoption papers are not reliable, and Soon-Yi could be younger.

The New York Daily News Thursday reported that Farrow and her older children are searching for Soon-Yi, whom she hasn't seen in two weeks. 'Mia loves her, and she's very afraid for her,' a family insider told the newspaper. 'She wants very much to let her know she can come home.'

The Farrow faction contends that Soon-Yi was at a camp in Maine until two weeks ago, when she was taken away in a limousine. Members of the Allen camp, however, said that Farrow kicked Soon-Yi out of the house and had made no effort to contact her, according to *The Daily News*.

Maria Roach, a close friend of Farrow's and godmother to one of her children, said that Farrow's family reacted to Allen's affair with Soon-Yi with laments of, 'Daddy is sleeping with your sister!' The revelation sent the family into psychiatric care for several months, Roach told *The Los Angeles Times*.

A letter Roach said she received from Farrow revealed the actress' grief: 'Obviously, my vision has been unclear and I have spent more than a dozen years with a man who would destroy me and corrupt my daughter,' Farrow wrote, 'leading her into a betrayal of her mother and her principles, leaving her morally bankrupt with the bond between us demolished.

'I can think of no crueller way to lose a child or a lover,' she wrote.

Former lovers of both Allen and Farrow stepped into the picture today. Frank Sinatra, who was 50 when he wed Farrow, then 21, released a statement saying, 'I have known Mia Farrow for many years, and without exception she has always been warm, compassionate and caring. Mia is, quite simply, a good and loving person.'

Laurie Goodstein, *The Washington Post*, 20 August 1992.

....

'I am Exhausted. I'm so Knackered'

David Mellor and Antonia de Sancha

John Major's Minister for the Arts and Sport (or 'Fun' as the tabloid press described it), David Mellor, thought that he could survive the scandal in The People *exposing his adultery with a minor actress. Reality was somewhat different. One of the popular images in the story is of Mellor stripping down to a Chelsea football jumper before sleeping with the actress. Shortly afterwards, Mr Mellor resigned from the Cabinet for unrelated reasons, but he has remained a prominent media 'personality'. He has since separated from his wife.*

Cabinet Minister David Mellor's involvement with actress Antonia de Sancha has interfered with his work as the Secretary of State for National Heritage.

On one occasion, a liaison at a London flat left Mr Mellor too tired to write two important speeches.

He told her the following day: 'You have absolutely exhausted me. I feel seriously knackered. I had a wonderful time with you last night and I've felt really positive all day.

'I don't think I could have slept for more than an hour last night.

'I must get some sleep. I'm worried and apprehensive. I've got two big speeches to do tomorrow, neither of which I have prepared.'

That evening, the Conservative MP for Putney – nicknamed the Minister for Fun – left the House of Commons early, but the following morning confessed he still had not prepared the text of his speeches.

He asked Ms de Sancha: 'Where will you be, because I need some inspiration.'

In the General Election edition of his constituency newsletter, Mr Mellor was pictured having breakfast with his wife Judith and children, and described how important the local community was to him.

Secrecy

He was first introduced to Ms de Sancha at a friend's party. Subsequently the couple dined together at London's exclusive La Famiglia restaurant.

Ms de Sancha, who tells friends she was born in Spain, near Barcelona, was actually delivered in Queen Charlotte's Hospital, London.

Sometimes she has used the name Tania Sanka – she listed the phone at her flat in Chiswick, West London, in that name.

Despite being sworn to secrecy by Mr Mellor about their relationship, Ms de Sancha has told a number of friends she is seeing him.

The speeches Mr Mellor had difficulty preparing were for the inauguration of London's City Technology College for the Performing Arts and the re-opening, on Wednesday, July 8, of Hampton Court, which was attended by the Queen.

After his engagement at the College, Mr Mellor went on to Hampton Court which needed extensive refurbishment after it was gutted by fire.

Having written his speech only hours before, he arrived too late to take his place close to the Queen.

This month he provided two tickets for Ms de Sancha and a female friend to visit Wimbledon during the tennis championships. He has gone to extraordinary lengths to ensure their friendship remains secret, although he and Ms de Sancha speak to each other at least twice a day on the telephone – sometimes minutes before Cabinet meetings.

They arranged their secret meetings at a friend's apartment, tucked out of sight in a posh private mews near Oxford Street.

Mr Mellor asked Antonia to stay there last week when he began to suspect their relationship might become public.

He even called on one of his trusted lackeys, journalist Paul Halloran, to try to discover if news of it was leaking and, if so, how to ensure it did not reach the newspapers.

By his own admission, the MP's wife of 18 years is totally unaware of his relationship with Ms de Sancha.

Before she went into hiding, Antonia had been living at a friend's house in Chelsea.

Mellor stayed the night with her there and visited her there on at least three other occasions during two weeks when her friend was away.

The couple's last tryst at the one-bedroom flat was on Monday, July 6.

Measures

Mr Mellor arrived just before 11 p.m. and was photographed as he left at 7.55 the following morning.

Mellor believed his relationship with Antonia would never be unearthed because of the elaborate measures he had employed to keep it quiet.

The former Foreign Minister – who attacked Israel's treatment of Palestinians on the West Bank and is a close friend of top PLO man Jaweed al-Ghussein – even questioned Antonia about her background, to make sure she had no Israeli connections.

He feared an Israeli plot to expose him.

Mr Mellor gave Antonia detailed instructions about how to hoodwink reporters if quizzed about their relationship.

He told her: 'They might just come out with a straightforward accusation and say, "You're having an affair with David Mellor, aren't you. Admit it."

'Now remember the golden rule is nobody needs ever to have to have a conversation with a journalist. All you have to say is, "I'm amazed you've had the cheek to call me," or "I don't know what you're talking about, I'm not participating in this conversation," bang, put the phone down.'

And the Minister, a barrister, reminded her: 'Don't forget I'm trained in the assessment of evidence.'

But he confessed if he had been seen arriving at the house where Antonia was staying and observed leaving in the morning, that would be proof enough.

Alone

He added: 'By and large, if they caught me going in at half past ten and coming out at eight in the morning, they've got a story.'

In fact, *The People* can report that Mr Mellor entered the flat at 10.58 p.m. and left at 7.55 in the morning.

He continued: 'You see, what we choose to do when we're alone is a matter only for us and people can only blow us away if one of us betrays the situation or if we are caught in a situation so obvious and flagrant that no denial is possible.

'We have no need to tell anybody of our relationship.'

And he reassured Antonia: 'Keep your pecker up, my love. We can handle this. Just remember what you have to do if you are put to the test.'

Ms de Sancha replied: 'No. I know exactly what to do if I'm put to the test. I'm not stupid.'

Mr Mellor then bragged: 'They haven't got anything. They only get more if we are too ill-disciplined and give them more.'

Vowed

Despite the danger of impending discovery, Mr Mellor vowed to stand by his love.

He said: 'There are moments we have shared together of such special quality they can only come out of a genuine feeling and cannot be a betrayal.'

He cooed: 'I'm talking to you full of love and not in any sense recriminatory. I have nothing but respect for you and, you know, let's ride over this bump, OK?'

When asked by Antonia whether he still loved her, Mr Mellor replied, without hesitation: 'Of course I do.

'I want to see you again. We'll stay apart for a bit, then get back together. You know how much I want to see you.

'Do you think I want to lose you? Of course I don't.'

Following his consultations with New Zealand-born Halloran, Mr Mellor proudly reported to Antonia the investigative journalist's view that nothing would be published.

'In other words they have nothing that they can print at the moment,' he said. 'So I mean it's good news in the sense that they can't allege a sexual relationship or anything like that.'

But despite his confidence that the relationship would not come to light, Mr Mellor urged Antonia to leave the flat before it came under scrutiny.

Proof

He said: 'If you could find somewhere else to live, that would be more helpful because that place is going to be very exposed now.'

Following Halloran's report to him, the Minister ruled out the possibility that any newspaper might run the story. And he arrogantly informed Ms de Sancha that two newspapers, including *The People*, were 'too stupid' to obtain proof for a story.

He said: '*The People* are stupid enough to try and get into it, but they are stupid and crude, you know, and therefore too stupid probably to make a good job of this if we don't actually help them.'

The People, 19 July 1992.

....

'Being Economical with the *Actualité*'

Alan Clark is cross-examined during the Matrix Churchill inquiry

In 1991, Paul Henderson, the managing director of a small machine tools company called Matrix Churchill, faced a seven-year jail sentence for selling goods to Iraq that could be used for military purposes. This was technically in contravention of British government guidelines on the subject, but what was not taken into consideration was that for more than fifteen years, Henderson had been an invaluable operative for British intelligence services. Even more to the point, Alan Clark, a government minister, had suspected the purpose of the equipment, but in line with government thinking, did not object to providing an export licence.

Perhaps the most shocking aspect of the whole affair is that several government ministers, including Michael Heseltine, Kenneth Clarke, Malcolm Rifkind and Tristan Garel-Jones, signed orders preventing the court from seeing intelligence papers relating to the service of Mr Henderson on the specious grounds of 'national security'. However, the judge overturned the order after seeing how relevant the information was to Mr Henderson's case. Had this not occurred, it is quite likely that Mr Henderson may have been wrongly imprisoned. One other factor aided Henderson's case: the disarmingly frank evidence of Alan Clark, the iconoclastic Tory MP, as told here by Paul Henderson.

It was Wednesday 4 November when Alan Clark entered the witness-box. Under the prodding of Moses, he reviewed the minutes prepared by Anthony Steadman of the critical meeting with the machine-tool makers on 20 January 1988. They were, he maintained, 'completely accurate'.

When asked about the significance of the purpose of the machines when export licensing was considered, he said: 'Well, it was important that the specification should be of a nature that the peaceful use of tooling was the principal element in considering their eligibility.'

Moses questioned him about autumn 1989, when he had discussed relaxing restrictions on sales to Iraq with William Waldegrave and Lord Trefgarne.

'If you had known that machine tools were going to be exported with tooling, fixtures and part programmes to machine parts for fuses for military ordnance, what would your attitude have been then in relation to the granting of licences?' asked Moses.

'My attitude would have been that they would have fallen irredeemably within the guidelines, even though the guidelines had been relaxed.'

Judge Smedley interrupted to clarify the answer, asking: 'You mean their export would be a breach of the guidelines?'

'Yes, exactly,' replied Clark.

It was highly damaging evidence. Export licences for the Cardoen contract had been granted after the meeting of the ministers on 1 November 1989. Minutes after eliciting the statement he needed, Moses sat down. The examination of Clark had taken only an hour. Geoffrey Robertson's dismantling of him would go on considerably longer.

I cannot recall ever hearing Geoffrey say he was going to destroy a witness or take him apart. His strategy with Clark would not be to confront him at all.

'I am going to win him over to our side,' Geoffrey told me the night before Clark's appearance. 'I'll handle him with kid gloves and make him feel good. He'll want to help us by the time I ask the important questions.'

Clark had certain personality traits that the defence lawyers felt could be exploited.

He was a bit of a rogue, ostentatious in his lifestyle and willing to speak his mind. He was not a typical Establishment man, and he was intellectually aloof. Geoffrey's strategy was that the more he showed Clark, the more malleable he would become.

Throughout the evidence of the lower-ranking civil servants Geoffrey had set the scene for the appearances of Clark and then Lord Trefgarne. Men such as Anthony Steadman and Eric Beston had each given evidence under cross-examination that the ultimate decisions had been made by the ministers. Now, the jury would be poised for Clark and Trefgarne to give them the final answer. Did the government know about the real purpose of the Matrix Churchill machines?

Geoffrey started politely, asking general questions about the nature of the guidelines for sales to Iraq from 1987 to early 1989, when Clark left the DTI for the MoD. He probed the ways they had been eased after the end of the Iran–Iraq war in the summer of 1988.

Then he showed him a memo written by Stephen Lillie of the Foreign Office on 1 February 1989. It had supported the decision by the ministers to approve the licence for the ABA contract.

'Does it assist you to recall the basis for this decision?' asked the QC. 'Although they "may be used for munitions manufacture", the cease-fire had held for long enough to make that not a sufficient reason under the new guidelines to stop them?'

'Yes,' said Clark.

'The third reason you see is the attraction of allowing them to be sent "rather than losing an intelligence access" to the Iraqi procurement network that was in Matrix Churchill?'

'Yes,' said Clark. 'I think the anxiety by now had started to shift towards Iraq's nuclear and chemical capability, and this rather pedestrian technology was no longer a matter of very great concern to us.'

Clark had made a distinction of significance. The government was concerned with nuclear-weapons technology and similar weapons of mass destruction. But even the prosecution had never linked our machines to such matters.

By late afternoon Clark seemed tired of the process and eager to get out of the witness-box. Geoffrey had remained steadfastly polite and respectful. They had gone over the debate with Whitehall concerning Iraq policy and sales of defence goods to Saddam Hussein. Clark had admitted that he favoured sales. As Minister of Trade at the DTI, it was his job, he said, to 'maximise' trade. Whenever Clark's memory seemed to fail, he had been reminded gently with a document.

The following day, by the time Geoffrey brought up the meeting in January 1988 where I had argued for releasing the hold on our licences, he had Clark precisely where he wanted him.

'You knew by that stage, 20 January, that the exports had been frozen because of the discovery they were going to munitions factories?' he asked.

'Yes,' said Clark.

'Was the purpose of that meeting to consider whether they could be unfrozen?'

'Yes.'

'And do you recall congratulating them on getting the order?'

'I expect, I hope I would have done. It would be uncivil if I did not.'

Using the minutes prepared by Steadman and the set prepared by John Nosworthy for the MTTA, Geoffrey led Clark through the meeting ever so slowly and carefully. Sitting in the dock, I had a vision of my life boiling down to these few minutes.

The licence applications said the machines would be used for 'general engineering purposes'. But, asked Geoffrey, didn't Clark know at the time that they were for military purposes?

'I do not see that the fact that they are using them, they were using them for munitions, excludes them for general engineering purposes,' responded Clark.

'But, here, the writer of this minute is attributing to you a statement: "The Iraqis will be using the current order for general engineering purposes." Which cannot be correct to your knowledge?'

'Well,' said Clark with a thin smile, 'it's our old friend "being economical" isn't it?'

'With the truth?' Geoffrey asked.

'With the *actualité*,' said Clark. 'There was nothing misleading or dishonest to make a formal or introductory comment that the Iraqis would be using the current orders for "general engineering purposes". All I didn't say was "and for making munitions". If I thought that they were going to be doing that. It simply would not have been appropriate, at a meeting of this kind, to widen it any further than the rather stilted and formal language which I used.'

There it was. The admission. He knew they were for military purposes. Yet he had not said so in 1988 because it would have been 'inappropriate'. It was the 'nod and a wink' I had long been describing.

Geoffrey continued with his willing subject.

'You didn't want to let anyone know that, at this stage, these machines and their follow-up orders were going to munitions factories to make munitions?'

'No,' said Clark.

'And the emphasis on "peaceful purposes" and "general engineering" and so on would help keep the matter confidential?'

'I do not think it was principally a matter for public awareness. I think it was a matter for Whitehall cosmetics.'

'A matter for Whitehall cosmetics, to keep the records ambiguous?'

'Yes, yes.'

'So the signal you are sending to these people is, "I am the minister. I will help you get these orders and the follow-up orders through the rather loose guidelines and the rather Byzantine ways of Whitehall. Help me by keeping your mouth shut firmly about military use"?'

'I think that is too imaginative an interpretation. I think it was more at arm's length than that.'

'But in any event, it was how they would help you, by not making the Whitehall cosmetics run, rather by keeping quiet, stating "nothing military"?'

'Yes,' said Clark. 'I do not think they needed that advice from me but ...'

'But they got it?'

'Not quite in so many words. I do not think I said "nothing military".'

'They got it by implication?'

'Yes,' agreed Clark. 'By implication is different. By implication they got it.'

Geoffrey Robertson sat down. There was a silence, then a buzz of whispers as the court adjourned for a short while. As Judge Smedley left the bench he was overheard saying to a clerk: 'Can you believe what you have just heard?'

Paul Henderson, The Unlikely Spy (London, 1993), pp. 250–4.

The revelations in the case led directly to the setting up of the Scott Inquiry which has been looking into British trade with Iraq during the last decade. At the inquiry, Michael Heseltine was the only signatory to the banning order on Henderson's intelligence documents to express disquiet about the affair.

....

Camillagate!

Telephone conversation thought to be between Prince Charles and Camilla Parker-Bowles

These tapes, purporting to be a true record of a telephone conversation between Prince Charles and his friend Camilla Parker-Bowles, have never been authenticated. They first appeared in an Australian women's magazine called New Idea.

The full and shocking transcript shows just why Diana was so shattered. The sexy bedtime phone call – containing amazingly intimate details – between Prince Charles and Camilla Parker-Bowles can easily be seen as the final, precipitating event that led to Princess Diana pulling the plug on her sham of a marriage.

Camillagate

THIS IS THE ENTIRE TRANSCRIPT FROM THE CAMILLAGATE TAPE. THE RECORDING STARTS WHILE THE CONVERSATION IS IN PROGRESS.

CHARLES: ... he was a bit anxious actually.

CAMILLA: Was he?

CH: He thought he might have gone a bit far.

CAM: Ah well.

CH: Anyway you know, that's the sort of thing one has to beware of. And sort of feel one's way along with, if you know what I mean.

CAM: Mm. You're awfully good at feeling your way along.

CH: Oh stop! I want to feel my way along you, all over you and up and down you and in and out...

CAM: Oh.

CH: Particularly in and out.

CAM: Oh, that's just what I need at the moment.

(Scanner enthusiast who recorded conversation speaks over couple to record date – December 18)

CH: Is it?

CAM: I know it would revive me. I can't bear a Sunday night without you.

CH: Oh God.

CAM: It's like that programme "Start the Week". I can't start the week without you.

CH: I fill up your tank!

CAM: Yes you do!

CH: Then you can cope.

CAM: Then I'm all right.

CH: What about me? The trouble is I need you several times a week. All the time.

CAM: Oh, God, I'll just live inside your trousers or something. It would be much easier!

CAM: (laughs) What are you going to turn into, a pair of knickers? (both laugh). Oh, you're going to come back as a pair of knickers.

CH: Or, God forbid, a Tampax. Just my luck! (laughs)

CAM: You are a complete idiot! (laughs) Oh, what a wonderful idea.

CH: My luck to be chucked down a lavatory and go on and on forever swirling around on the top, never going down!

CAM: (laughing) Oh darling!

CH: Until the next one comes through.

CAM: Oh, perhaps you could just come back as a box.

CH: What sort of box?

CAM: A box of Tampax so you could just keep going.

CH: That's true.

CAM: Repeating yourself. (laughing) Oh, darling. Oh I just want you now.

CH: Do you?

CAM: Mmm.

CH: So do I.

CAM: Desperately, desperately, desperately. Oh, I thought of you so much at Yearly.

CH: Did you?

CAM: Simply mean we couldn't be there together.

CH: Desperate. If you could be here – I long to ask Nancy sometimes.

CAM: Why don't you?

CH: I daren't.

CAM: Because I think she's so in love with you.

CH: Mmm.

CAM: She'd do anything you asked.

CH: She'd tell all sorts of people.

CAM: No she wouldn't, because she'd be much too frightened of what you might say to her. I think you've got, I'm afraid it's a terrible thing to say, but I think, you know, those sort of people do feel very strongly about you. You've got such a great hold over her.

CH: Really?

CAM: Are you . . . I think as usual you're underestimating yourself.

CH: But she might be terribly jealous or something.

CAM: Oh! (laughs) Now that is a point! I wonder, she might be, I suppose.

CH: You never know, do you?

CAM: No. The little green-eyed monster might be lurking inside her. No. But I mean, the thing is you're so good when people are so flattered to be taken into your confidence, but I don't know they'd betray you. You know, real friends.

CH: Really?

CAM: I don't. (pause) Gone to sleep?

CH: No, I'm here.

CAM: Darling, listen, I talked to David tonight again. It might not be any good.

CH: Oh no!

CAM: I'll tell you why. He's got these children of one of those Crawley girls and their nanny staying. He's going, I'm going to ring him again tomorrow. He's going to try to put them off till Friday. But I thought as an alternative perhaps I might ring up Charlie.

CH: Yes.

CAM: And see if we could do it there. I know he's back on Thursday.

CH: It's quite a lot further away.

CAM: Oh, is it?

CH: Well, I'm just trying to think, coming from Newmarket.

CAM: Coming from Newmarket to me at that time of night, you could probably do it in two-and-three-quarters. It takes me three.

CH: What, to go to, um, Bowood?

CAM: Northmore.

CH: To go to Bowood?

CAM: To go to Bowood would be the same as me really, wouldn't it?

CH: I mean to say, you would suggest going to Bowood, uh?

CAM: No, not at all.

CH: Which Charlie then?

CAM: What Charlie do you think I was talking about?

CH: I didn't know, because I thought you meant...

CAM: I've got lots...

CH: Somebody else.

CAM: I've got lots of friends called Charlie.

CH: The other one. Patty's.

CAM: Oh! Oh there! Oh that is further away. They're not...

CH: They've gone...

CAM: I don't know, it's just, you know, just a thought I had, it fell through, the other place.

CH: Oh right. What do you do, go on the M25 then down the M4 is it?

CAM: Yes, you go, um, and sort of Royston, or M11, at that time of night.

CH: Yes. Well, that'll be just after, it will be after shooting anyway.

CAM: So it would be, um, you'd miss the worst of the traffic. Because I'll, er, you see the problem is I've got to be in London tomorrow night.

CH: Yes.

CAM: And Tuesday night A's coming home.

CH: No...

CAM: Would you believe it? Because, I don't know what he is doing, he's shooting down here or something. But darling, you wouldn't be able to ring me anyway, would you?

CH: I might just. I mean, tomorrow night I could have done.

CAM: Oh darling, I can't bear it. How could you have done tomorrow night?

CH: Because I'll be (yawns) working on the next speech.

CAM: Oh no, what's the next one?

CH: A Business in the Community one, rebuilding communities.

CAM: Oh no, when's that for?

CH: A rather important one for Wednesday.

CAM: Well, at least I'll be behind you.

CH: I know.

CAM: Can I have a copy of the one you've just done?

CH: Yes.

CAM: Can I? Um, I would like it.

CH: OK, I'll try and organise it . . .

CAM: Darling . . .

CH: But I, oh God, when am I going to speak to you?

CAM: I can't bear it. Um . . .

CH: Wednesday night?

CAM: Oh, certainly, Wednesday night. I'll be alone, um, Wednesday, you know, the evening. Or Tuesday. While you're rushing around doing things I'll be, you know, alone until it reappears. And early Wednesday morning, I mean, he'll be leaving at half-past eight, quarter-past eight. He won't be here Thursday, pray God. Um, that ambulance strike, it's a terrible thing to say this, I suppose it won't have come to an end by Thursday.

CH: It will have done?

CAM: Well, I mean, I hope for everybody's sake it will have done, but I hope for our sakes it's still going on.

CH: Why?

CAM: Well, because if it stops he'll come down here on Thursday night.

CH: Oh, no.

CAM: Yes, but I don't think it will stop, do you?

CH: No, neither do I. Just our luck.

CAM: It just would be our luck. I know.

CH: Then it's bound to.

CAM: No it won't. You mustn't think like that. You must think positive.

CH: I'm not very good at that.

CAM: Well I am going to. Because if I don't, I'd despair. (pause) Hm – gone to sleep?

CH: No. How maddening.

CAM: I know. Anyway, I mean, he's doing his best to change it, David, but I just thought, you know, I might just ask Charlie.

CH: Did he say anything?

CAM: No, I haven't talked to him.

CH: You haven't?

CAM: Well, I talked to him briefly, but you know, I just thought I – I just don't know whether he's got any children at home, that's the worry.

CH: Right.

CAM: Oh ... darling, I think I'll ...

CH: Pray, just pray.

CAM: It would be so wonderful to have just one night to set us on our way, wouldn't it?

CH: Wouldn't it? To wish you a happy Christmas.

CAM: (indistinct) Happy. Oh, don't let's think about Christmas. I can't bear it. (pause) Going to go to sleep? I think you'd better, don't you? Darling?

CH: (sleepy) Yes, darling?

CAM: I think you've exhausted yourself by all that hard work. You must go to sleep now. Darling?

CH: (sleepy) Yes, darling?

CAM: Will you ring me when you wake up?

CH: Yes I will.

CAM: Before I have these rampaging children around. It's Tom's birthday tomorrow. (pause) You all right?

CH: Mm. I'm all right.

CAM: Can I talk to you, I hope, before those rampaging children ...

CH: What time do they come in?

CAM: Well usually Tom never wakes up at all, but as it's his birthday tomorrow he might just stagger out of bed. It won't be before half-past eight. (pause) Night, night, my darling.

CH: ... Darling ...

CAM: I do love you.

CH: (sleepy) Before ...

CAM: Before about half-past eight.

CH: Try and ring?

CAM: Yeah, if you can. Love you darling.

CH: Love you too. I don't want to say goodbye.

CAM: Well done for doing that. You're a clever old thing. An awfully good brain lurking there, isn't there? Oh darling. I think you ought to give the brain a rest now. Night night.

CH: Night darling. God Bless.

CAM: I do love you and I am so proud of you.

CH: Oh, I'm so proud of you.

CAM: Don't be silly, I've never achieved anything.

CH: Yes you have.

CAM: No I haven't.

CH: Your great achievement is to love me.

CAM: Oh darling. Easier than falling off a chair.

CH: You suffer all these indignities and tortures and calumnies.

CAM: Oh darling, don't be so silly. I'd suffer anything for you. That's love. It's the strength of love. Night. Night.

CH: Night, darling. Sounds as though you're dragging an enormous piece of string behind you, with hundreds of tin pots and cans attached to it. I think it must be your telephone. Night night, before the battery goes. (blows kiss) Night.

CAM: Love you.

CH: Don't want to say goodbye.

CAM: Neither do I, but you must get some sleep. Bye.

CH: Bye, darling.

CAM: Love you.

CH: Bye.

CAM: Hopefully talk to you in the morning.

CH: Please.

CAM: Bye. I do love you.

CH: Night.

CAM: Night.

CH: Night.

CAM: Love you for ever.

CH: Night.

CAM: G'bye. Bye my darling.

CH: Night.

CAM: Night. Night.

CH: Night.

CAM: Bye bye.

CH: Going.

CAM: Bye.

CH: Going.

CAM: Gone.

CH: Night.

CAM: Bye. Press the button.

CH: Going to press the tit.

CAM: All right darling. I wish you were pressing mine.

CH: God I wish I was. Harder and harder.

CAM: Oh darling.

CH: Night.

CAM: Night.

CH: Love you.

CAM: (yawning) Love you. Press the tit.
CH: Adore you. Night.
CAM: Night.
CH: Night.
CAM: (blows a kiss)
CH: Night.
CAM: G'night my darling. Love you ...
Charles hangs up.

New Idea, 23 January 1993, pp. 22–5.

....

'Oh Squidgy, I Love You, Love You, Love You'

Telephone conversation thought to be between the Princess of Wales and James Gilbey

Prince Charles did not look quite so silly once another amateur scanner released the following transcript to the press. It purports to be an exchange between the Princess of Wales and James Gilbey, a used-car salesman, on a car telephone on New Year's Eve in 1989. There has been no confirmation or denial by any of the alleged parties.

MALE VOICE: And so darling, what other lows today?
FEMALE VOICE: So that was it, I was very bad at lunch. And I nearly started blubbing. I just felt really sad and empty, and I thought: 'Bloody hell, after all I've done for this f ...... family.'
M: You don't need to. Cos there are people out there – and I've said this before – who will replace emptiness. With all sorts of things.
F: I needn't ask horoscopes, but it is just so desperate. Always being innuendo, the fact that I'm going to do something dramatic because I can't stand the confines of this marriage.
M: I know.
F: But I know how much more than they because ...

M: Well, interestingly enough, that thing in *The People* didn't imply either one of you.

F: No.

M: So I wouldn't worry about that I think it's common knowledge, darling, and amongst most people, that you obviously don't have...

F: A rapport?

M: Yeah, I think that comes through loud and clear.

. . .

M: Darling, no sort of awful feelings or guilt or...

F: None at all.

M: Remorse?

F: None. None at all.

M: Good.

F: No, none at all. All's well.

M: OK then, Squidgy. I am sorry you have had low times ... try, darling, when you get these urges – you just try to replace them with anger like you did on Friday night, you know.

F: I know. But you know what's really quite un ... whatever the word is? His grandmother is always looking at me with a strange look in her eyes. It's not hatred, it's sort of interest and pity mixed in one. I am not quite sure. I don't understand it. Every time I look up, she's looking at me and then looks away and smiles.

M: Does she?

F: Yes. I don't know what's going on.

M: I should say to her one day: 'I can't help but ask you. You are always looking at me. What is it? What are you thinking?' You must, darling. And interestingly enough, one of the things you said to me today is that you are going to start standing up for yourself.

F: Yes.

M: Mmmm. We all know that you are very capable of that, old Bossy Boots.

F: I know, yes.

M: What have you had on today? What have you been wearing?

F: A pair of black jodhpur things on at the moment and a pink polo neck.

M: Really. Looking good?

F: Yes.

M: Are you?

F: Yes.

M: Dead good?

F: I think it's good.

M: You do?

F: Yes.

M: And what on your feet?

F: A pair of flat black pumps

M: Very chic.

F: Yes (pause in tape) The redhead is being actually quite supportive.

M: Is she?

F: Yes, she has. I don't know why.

M: Don't let the [?] down.

F: No, I won't. I just talk to her about that side of things.

M: You do? That's all I worry about. I just worry that you know she's sort of . . . she's desperately trying to get back in.

F: She keeps telling me.

M: She's trying to tag on to you [?]. She knows that your PR is so good, she's trying to tag on to that.

F: Jimmy Savile rang me up yesterday and he said: 'I'm just ringing up, my girl, to tell you that His Nibs has asked me to come and help out the redhead, and I'm just letting you know so that you don't find out through her or him. And I hope it's all right by you.'

And I said: 'Jimmy, you do what you like.'

M: What do you mean, help out the redhead, darling?

F: With her publicity.

M: Oh, has he?

F: Sort her out. He said: 'You can't change a lame duck, but I've got to talk to her, cos that's the boss's orders and I've got to carry them out. But I want you to know that you're my number-one girl and I'm not . . .

M: Oh darling, that's not fair, you're *my* number-one girl.

F: (voice much quieter in the background) Harry, it might be in my bathroom. (louder) What did you say? You didn't say anything about babies, did you?

M: No.

F: No.

M: Why darling?

F: (laughing) I thought you did.

M: Did you?

F: Yes.

M: Did you darling? You have got them on the brain.

F: Well, yeh, maybe I . . . well, actually, I don't think I am going to be able to for ages.

M: I think you've got bored with the idea, actually.

F: I'm going to . . .

M: You are, aren't you? It was sort of a hot flush you went through.

F: A very hot flush.

M: Darling, when he says His Nibs rang him up, does he mean your other half or PA rang him up?

F: Eh? My other half.

M: Your other half.

F: Yes.

            · · ·

M: Oh Squidgy, I love you, love you, love you.

F: You are the nicest person in the whole wide world.

M: Well darling, you are to me too. Sometimes.

F: (laughs) What do you mean, sometimes?

M: Darling, it's so nice being able to help you.

F: You do. You'll never know how much. You'll never know how much.

M: Oh I will darling. I just feel so close to you. So wrapped up in you. I'm wrapping you up, protecting.

F: Yes please, yes, please.

            · · ·

M: . . . Oh, Squidgy.

F: Mmmm.

M: Kiss me please (sound of kisses). Do you know what I'm going to be imagining I'm doing tonight, at about 12 o'clock. Just holding you so close to me. It'll have to be delayed action for 48 hours.

F: (giggles)

M: Fast forward.

F: Fast forward.

M: Gosh, I hope Ken doesn't say no.

F: I doubt he will.

M: Do you?

F: He's coming down on Tuesday and I'm going to tell him I've got to go back on Tuesday night. And I've got to leave and be back for lunch on Wednesday. But I can do that.

M: You can?

F: And I shall tell people I'm going for acupuncture and my back being done.

M: (hysterical laugh) Squidge, cover them footsteps.

F: I jolly well do.

Today, 24 August 1992.

A Bit of Reconstruction Can Go a Long Way

The extravagance of Jacques Attali

Jacques Attali, the intellectually challenging founder and president of the European Bank for Reconstruction and Development, was never very popular in London financial circles during his brief reign. A senior confidant of President Mitterrand, he was pegged to take the upper echelons of London financial society by storm. However, this austere socialist did not spend a great deal of time socialising out of hours. Part of his problem may have been a lack of invitations, especially after it was learned that even when he was invited to dine at private houses, he liked to send 'sweepers' in advance just to check if the house was bugged.

His future became even more uncertain when the Financial Times *investigated his substance rather than his style. Robert Peston won a journalistic award for his discovery that during the bank's first two years of existence, Attali spent more on decorating his offices and flying around in private jets than he actually disbursed to the troubled economies of Eastern Europe. Later, there was another revelation about some confusion regarding his private expenses. He resigned shortly afterwards and returned to France, blaming 'Les Anglo-Saxons' for his demise.*

The European Bank for Reconstruction and Development was set up in 1991 to help eastern Europe build on the ruins of communism with private investment. Two years later, as delegates attending next week's annual meeting in London will learn, the main beneficiaries of its largesse have been its staff, consultants, building contractors and aircraft leasing companies. It has provided considerably less in loans and investments to the former Soviet Union and eastern Europe than it has consumed in fitting out its London offices, paying salaries and meeting other overheads.

Here are the facts:

From April 15, 1991 to the end of last year its total running costs, mainly salaries, travel costs and general overheads, have been £128 million.

Its budget for 1993, which is denominated in European Currency Units, is Ecu 135m (£109m).

It spent £18m of UK government funds on equipping its previous office, which it occupied for less than two years before moving to its new office block at Number One Exchange Square in the City last December. It is in the process of spending a further £55.5m on fitting out this building.

By the end of last year it had disbursed only Ecu 126m (£101m) in loans and investments to eastern Europe and the former Soviet Union. This is just half what it allocated to its buildings and its running costs in the same period.

Some disparity between the costs of running the bank and the initial provision of finance to the region was inevitable. Start-up costs for any new institution are big and it was explicitly modelled on the World Bank, whose running costs are substantial.

But the bank's intellectually dynamic founder and president Mr Jacques Attali, who for much of the 1980s was the special adviser to the French President, Mr François Mitterrand, admits that 'disbursement [of loans and investments] is amazingly slow in terms of our [original] forecast.'

He adds, however: 'I would say it is a good thing, because it demonstrates that we are very cautious.' He says he would be facing considerable criticism from his shareholders – the leading industrial countries together with those of the former Eastern bloc – if the bank were being reckless in its investment policy.

The bank also points out that it has stayed within its administrative and building budgets, which have all been approved by these shareholders, including Mr Norman Lamont, the Chancellor of the Exchequer, who is one of the bank's governors.

Mr Attali's talents for designing grand schemes for the regeneration of eastern Europe and the former Soviet Union are not in doubt. But he is not by nature a financial controller or a chief executive. Two questions therefore suggest themselves concerning the execution of the bank's mission: should the investment policy of the bank be loosened to facilitate a more rapid disbursement of funds? Does the budget-making process put enough pressure on the bank to keep its expenditure in check?

Mr Attali appears to have inherited from Mr Mitterrand a passion for monumental architecture – the slabs of Carrara marble which frame the lifts in the lofty mirrored entrance may have been expensive, but the bank says they have great symbolic significance.

A different kind of marble, Travertine, was originally installed. According to Mr Pierre Pissaloux, a former high-flying French civil servant who is the bank's budget director, this marble was inappropriate. So it was replaced by Carrara statuary slabs in various stages of polish, at a cost of £750,000.

The point of the exercise, says Mr Pissaloux, was that the new marble represented what the EBRD was trying to do for people in eastern Europe –

'changing them from something rough into something polished'.

Mr Attali said he was not embarrassed by the bank's opulent offices. He said he had a 'duty to provide them [employees] with a very good environment' as compensation for the reduced pay they earn at the bank compared with what they could receive in the private sector.

He also set a condition that the building cost should be 'below the average cost' of comparable projects in the City. Both arguments in favour of the building are questionable.

Some of Mr Attali's colleagues came from the private sector, but most say they were lured by the challenge and excitement of changing the face of eastern Europe.

They could probably earn more if they returned. However, the average EBRD salary – including secretaries and lower-grade staff – is Ecu 58,300, high compared with most public-sector organisations but not by world bank standards.

EBRD employees do not pay UK taxes, thanks to the founding charter signed by the government. But the bank itself levies an 'income tax' averaging about 10 per cent which it uses to help finance its operations. The average salary is equivalent therefore to a UK gross salary of more than £65,000.

Mr Attali is the highest paid employee, with a 1992 salary of £150,000 after deduction of the internal tax.

Were he to pay UK taxes, this would be the equivalent of a gross salary of more than £240,000 – £75,000 more than the governor of the Bank of England received last year, £163,000 more than the Prime Minister and £40,000 less than the basic salary of the Chairman of National Westminster Bank.

Mr Attali has said he wants to waive the EBRD's general pay rise of 5.5 per cent for the current year.

The question of whether the £55.5m fitting-out cost is reasonable by City standards is more complicated. The UK government was desperate to attract the bank to London – it is the only leading international institution of its kind in the British capital – and provided £40m towards the costs of its offices. The Bank spent £18m of this on its offices in Leadenhall Street – which it occupied for 20 months – and the balance of £22m is being spent on the new headquarters. The bank received an additional £250,000 grant from the Corporation of London.

The building covers 403,000 sq ft in total. The cost of fitting out that space per sq ft is £138. Only 320,000 sq ft of that space is usable, however, which pushes the cost up to £173 per sq ft. Building consultants say that both figures are at the top end of normal fitting-out costs.

Mr Pissaloux disputed that judgement. The bank, he pointed out, had special needs, such as translation facilities for its annual meeting and conferences. If these special factors were excluded, he said, the cost per sq ft was £108. 'That is at the lower end of the City fit-out costs,' he said. 'I am at ease with that.'

Gleeds, the quantity surveyors, said that fitting-out costs for a large merchant bank's office would typically be about £70 per sq ft for gross space in a shell and core building (a building containing neither furnishings nor mechanical and electrical equipment).

Mr Pissaloux also said that part of the building's cost had been met from saving rent due on the Leadenhall offices and by striking an advantageous deal with the building developer, Rosehaugh Stanhope Developments.

By finishing work on its Exchange Square building ahead of schedule the bank was able to save six months' rental payments on Leadenhall. That rent saving was worth £6m, Mr Pissaloux said. In addition Rosehaugh Stanhope Developments, the building's developer, gave £9.5m towards the fitting-out costs, plus a rent-free period of two years and five months, which is worth £38m.

Property agents said, however, that the deal with Rosehaugh was in line with market conditions at the time. 'When the EBRD was looking, the market was dead,' said a surveyor. 'Property companies were falling over themselves to deal with it.'

Staff move to the new building just before Christmas and the move was celebrated with a party held at London's Grosvenor House Hotel. Mr Attali said the party's cost was 'very low'. In fact, it amounted to £52,000, £80 for each of the 650 employees or consultants who attended.

The bank also argued that Mr Attali's regular use of rented private air planes was value for money. Mr Attali said he used private jets on two sorts of occasions only: when he had to fit in a large number of meetings over a short period in many different countries (as happened quite frequently), or if his destination was not served by regular international flights (which was the case in many parts of the Soviet Union).

He spent £600,000 last year on private jets. Mr Pissaloux said that he had earmarked between £350,000 and £400,000 in this year's budget for between 15 and 18 trips by private jet – this comes to about £22,000 per flight. Mr Pissaloux stressed that all expenses were overseen by the bank's board of directors, who are government officials representing the 53 countries which are the bank's shareholders. Even the building costs had stayed within the special capital budget approved at the end of 1991.

The main responsibilities of these directors are to approve loans, investments and spending. A series of board committees scrutinise salaries (the

Remuneration Committee), the annual budgets (the Finance Committee) and the annual accounts (the Audit Committee). One director insisted that they were a tough independent force, whose aim was to ensure that the bank did not waste money. But, in the matter of their own remuneration, they were not independent from the EBRD.

As Mr Attali said: 'It's a very strange system – we pay for them but they are representing their governments.' The directors, who are typically secondees from the shareholders' civil services, receive EBRD salaries and EBRD tax breaks. 'It's enormous pay compared to a normal civil servant,' said Mr Attali.

In 1992 the 23 directors, their 23 alternates and 23 secretaries, who occupy two floors of the bank's head office, were paid an average salary before the 10 per cent tax of Ecu 87,000 each – equivalent to a UK gross salary of £100,000. It is arguable that if directors were paid directly by their governments they might exert tougher financial disciplines on the bank.

The experience of private-sector companies also suggests that any board as big as the EBRD's will rarely have the cohesion to put significant pressure on executives.

Robert Preston, The Financial Times, 13 April 1993.

....

Senator Packwood's Passion for Women

Senator Bob Packwood's pursuit of women

This story in The Washington Post *in December 1992 caused extreme aggravation for Senator Bob Packwood, an Oregon Republican. These allegations have never been proved.*

Ask those who have worked for Sen. Bob Packwood about his treatment of women, and two portraits emerge.

One is the Oregon Republican's record as a leading advocate of women's rights during his 24 years in the Senate and his much-admired history of hiring women, promoting them and supporting their careers even after they leave his office. Women currently hold the most powerful posts on his staff. The other is a side of Packwood, 60, that few who have experienced it or heard about it want to talk about. Since Packwood's earliest days on Capitol Hill, he has made uninvited sexual advances to women who have worked for him or with him, according to former staff members and lobbyists, including 10 women who, independently of each other, have given specific accounts of Packwood's behavior toward them.

The women, including six whose names and detailed allegations were given to Packwood by *The Washington Post*, said his approaches were unwelcome and unreciprocated. In some cases, they said, the behavior took place when he had been drinking. Several said he was abrupt, grabbing them without warning, kissing them forcefully and persisting until they made clear that they were not interested or had pushed him away. No one said Packwood punished her for rejecting him, but several decided to leave their jobs within months. Several pointed out that Packwood was married when he approached them; he and his wife divorced last year after 27 years of marriage.

None of the women complained formally; some said they feared no one would believe them and that their careers might suffer.

According to several former employees, Packwood's behavior created an undercurrent of tension and resentment among some in the office that appears to have been most pronounced in the late 1970s and early 1980s. Some female staff members said that more experienced employees told them to avoid working alone with the senator after hours.

Asked about these accounts days before his reelection to a fifth term earlier this month, Packwood said none of them was true. Later, he provided statements intended to cast doubt on the women's credibility.

On Friday, however, he said in a three-paragraph statement to *The Post*: 'I will not make an issue of any specific allegation.'

The statement also offered an apology: 'If any of my comments or actions have indeed been unwelcome or if I have conducted myself in any way that has caused any individual discomfort or embarrassment, for that I am sincerely sorry. My intentions were never to pressure, to offend, nor to make anyone feel uncomfortable, and I truly regret if that has occurred with anyone either on or off my staff.'

Jack Faust, a Portland lawyer and a close friend of Packwood's who has counseled him about how to handle the allegations, said Friday that Packwood 'is admitting to some human flaws ... You have armies of politicians trying to dodge this and that. He's accepting responsibility.'

With all the information presented to Packwood by *The Post*, 'denial is not credible,' Faust said. 'There's nothing to be gained in a denial. The best thing to do is accept it, not make an issue of it, and go back to work.'

. . .

Faust said it took several weeks for Packwood to accept what he was being told. 'His first stage was denial, then recognition,' Faust said.

One former colleague and close friend of Packwood's, who said he had discussed the allegations with the senator over the past several weeks, said Packwood now 'understands the importance and implications' of his behavior. I think at this point in time, he is saddened by it all. I think his ownership of the problem is real.'

Faust said that 'it would be totally inconsistent' for Packwood, given his standing as a long-time supporter of women's rights, to mount an aggressive attack on the women who had spoken up. Packwood has championed such issues as abortion rights, the Equal Rights Amendment and family leave. He has raised millions of dollars for his campaigns through nationwide appeals to women who supported his legislative efforts; feminist leader Gloria Steinem signed a fund-raising letter for his 1980 campaign.

The National Abortion Rights Action League has consistently endorsed him. 'We owe a great deal to him,' said Kate Michelman, NARAL's executive director.

Packwood was an early backer of the Capitol Hill Women's Political Caucus's policy on sexual harassment, signing soon after the document was circulated in spring 1991. The policy lists examples of sexual harassment, including unwanted physical contact, unsolicited flirtations and dirty jokes. Fifty-seven senators have signed it.

The Senate, along with the House of Representatives, has exempted itself from federal law prohibiting sexual harassment, although its rules broadly prohibit discrimination based on sex. A new Senate office on employment practices, which began operating this summer, would not disclose how many, if any, complaints of sexual harassment it has received. The office was established following sexual harassment allegations by Anita F. Hill against Clarence Thomas during Senate hearings on his Supreme Court nomination last year. The only previous avenue for complaint was the Senate Select Committee on Ethics.

Earlier this year, the committee declined to investigate allegations that Sen. Brock Adams (D) had committed sexual improprieties with eight women, saying no one had filed a complaint about Adams's conduct while he was a senator. The *Seattle Times* reported the women's accounts, but did not name them to Adams or in the newspaper. Adams, who said the allegations were untrue, later decided not to run for reelection.

The allegations about Packwood do not reflect the experiences of some other current and former Packwood employees, who said in interviews that they never saw him make any unwanted advances nor heard anyone complain that he had.

Mimi Weyforth Dawson, who worked as Packwood's press secretary and chief of staff between 1973 and 1981, said Packwood, more than anyone she has ever worked for, recognizes women as professionals and gives them opportunities that other employers do not. In an interview before Packwood's statement of apology, she called the allegations 'rubbish'.

Dawson is one of several women who went from Packwood's office to high-level posts elsewhere. President Ronald Reagan tapped her for a seat on the Federal Communications Commission in 1981, where she served for six years.

Her views were echoed by Henrietta S. Fielek, who served in top positions on Packwood's staff from the late 1970s to the late 1980s. Fielek, now director of public affairs at the Department of Education, said she had heard rumors about Packwood's conduct before joining his staff but saw nothing to substantiate them. Such rumors, she said, are 'cheap talk on Capitol Hill'.

The rumors had circulated in both Washington and in Oregon for years, but had not surfaced publicly. The Post's inquiry began in early October after Florence Graves, a freelance journalist, contacted the newspaper with information that she had gathered while reporting an article for another publication about sexual harassment on Capitol Hill in the wake of the Clarence Thomas hearings. Graves was hired on a contract basis to work with Post staff members on the story.

When first contacted by The Post, those who said Packwood had made sexual advances to them were reluctant to talk about their experiences for a newspaper article. Eventually, several agreed to allow their names to be used in the interviews with Packwood, and four consented to be identified in print if others agreed as well.

In addition to these women, three former staff members and a lobbyist decided not to be identified publicly or to Packwood because, they said, they were worried that they could suffer professionally or financially if they challenged the conduct of a senior senator or appeared disloyal in a city, Washington, that puts a premium on loyalty.

One of these former aides said she had warned Packwood years ago that his behavior would damage him some day. Another said she still was haunted enough by her decision to remain quiet after quitting the office that she wrote a letter to Anita Hill after the Thomas hearings.

The letter, a copy of which she provided to *The Post*, praised Hill for having more courage than the former Packwood aide. 'My disillusionment with a man and a position I had previously held in such high regard overwhelmed me,' she wrote. 'I suppose somehow I felt I did something wrong.' She did not identify Packwood by name in the letter.

Packwood was one of two Senate Republicans to vote against Thomas' confirmation. Packwood said at the time that he objected to the nominee's legal theories. He did not take a position on Hill's testimony.

Packwood separated from his wife, Georgie, in early 1990, and later cited irreconcilable differences in filing for divorce. Asked in late October about allegations of unwanted sexual advances by her former husband against female employees, Georgie Packwood said: 'I have been aware of these allegations for many years. It does not come as any surprise to me.'

She declined to amplify, saying only, 'I'm very regretful that this sort of thing will be in print, for our children's sake.'

Early Days in the Senate

The earliest account of Packwood's unwanted advances goes back to 1969, when he first arrived in Washington. Thirty-six years old, he was the youngest member of the U.S. Senate.

Julie Williamson was a 29-year-old legal secretary who had worked long hours during the 1968 campaign. After the election, Packwood hired her for his new Senate office in Portland, Ore. She was on the telephone there one afternoon in early 1969, she said in interviews this fall, when Packwood walked in and kissed her on the back of the neck. 'Don't you ever do that again,' she said she told him.

Williamson said Packwood then followed her into an adjoining room where he grabbed at her clothes, pulled on her ponytail and at one point, stood on her toes. 'He couldn't get the girdle off and I kept struggling and he just gave up,' said Williamson, now 53 and a Democratic political consultant who supported AuCoin this fall. 'I was really frightened.'

Williamson said she quit her job within weeks.

Asked in the Oct. 29 interview about Williamson's account, Packwood said it was totally untrue. 'I would have no reason to approach her,' he said. But in a subsequent interview, he said he had recalled that he and Williamson had discussed a 'continued warm personal relationship' during that period, but that the notion 'passed like a summer storm.'

Williamson recalled a conversation with Packwood after the incident, but said it involved only her effort to get the senator to explain 'why he came after me'.

Packwood provided a written statement from Ann Elias, a close friend who also knew Williamson and whose husband, James A. Elias, had run the 1968 Senate campaign. The statement said that Elias believed Williamson had wanted a romantic relationship with Packwood.

Elias's statement does not mention that Williamson, upset and agitated, came to Elias's apartment in 1969 to tell her that Packwood had made advances that day. Elias acknowledged the visit in an interview; she said she did not include it in her statement because she was not asked for any details.

Elias said she does not think Williamson did anything to invite Packwood's behavior. But, Elias said, Williamson's 'tone and demeanor' in subsequent conversations, though nothing Williamson explicitly said, left her with the impression that Williamson might entertain the idea of romance with Packwood.

Williamson's husband in 1969, Douglas C. Myers, said that an 'upset' Williamson told him about the incident hours after it happened. Two other Williamson friends confirmed in interviews that she told them of Packwood's advances at the time.

. . .

In early 1976, Paige Wagers was a 21-year-old college graduate with a new job as a mail clerk in Packwood's Washington office. At the bottom of the staff hierarchy, she was surprised when Packwood invited her into his office once to play bridge with two top aides, she recalled in recent interviews. Soon after, Packwood buzzed her on the interoffice phone and asked her to come to his office.

She said Packwood locked the door behind her and then embraced her, running his fingers through her hair and forcefully kissing her on the lips. She said he told her how much he liked her wholesome good looks. 'It was very clear that it was a sexual thing,' she said. 'It was very hard to get him to let go of me.'

Wagers said she pulled away and talked her way out of his office. After the incident, she said, a Packwood aide told her that such advances had occurred before and advised her not to go into his office alone. Wagers said she ignored two more invitations from Packwood to come to his office. Within a few months, she said, she took another Capitol Hill position.

Wagers, a Republican who admires Packwood's legislative record, said she had a second encounter with Packwood around 1981. She was working for the Labor Department and ran into Packwood in one of the Capitol's subterranean passageways. Packwood seemed interested in her work, and

Wagers said she felt proud that she now had a job that enabled her to talk about issues at a higher level with her old boss. But as they walked along a corridor, she said, Packwood abruptly opened a door and ushered her into an unmarked private office.

Packwood shut the door, immediately kissed her and reached out to push pillows off a sofa, she said. Wagers said she pulled away and 'I made it clear in the nicest way possible that I wasn't interested.'

Wagers said she felt betrayed by Packwood and stupid for allowing herself to be caught in the same situation a second time. She expressed frustration at how she was treated. 'You don't feel like you're going to be taken seriously,' she said. 'You are going to be given opportunities only because you're cute.'

In his initial interview with *The Post*, Packwood said he remembered Wagers, but 'there's no event with Paige', either in 1976 or 1981.

Five of Wagers' former colleagues and friends said they remembered Wagers telling them about one or the other of the two incidents close to the time they occurred.

Wagers said friends in Washington had advised her not to complain at the time, saying that she, rather than Packwood, would suffer. 'That's the way Washington is. You have to build, you can't have enemies, you can't be discredited from the time you come in,' said Wagers, who is now studying for a master's degree in social work and works part time as a dance instructor. But, she said, 'you know it happened to you ... and that it's right to say what happened. But because only the two of you were in the room, there is no way you can prove it. You're vulnerable. You're totally out on a limb.'

After-Hours Encounter

Former Packwood staff members said the senator worked hard, often beginning his workday at sunrise. They said he sometimes drank wine or beer by dinner time and some said he did not handle the alcohol well, losing his temper or becoming forward with women.

Packwood disagreed. 'I don't think my basic nature changes' with alcohol, he told *The Post*.

. . .

Conflicting Reactions

Over the past few weeks, as reports of *The Post*'s inquiries have circulated, some former Packwood staff members said they felt torn between the instinct to protect their old boss, a senator whose legislative record they respect, and a responsibility not to protect actions they could not condone.

'People who found his behavior objectionable also found compelling reasons to remain in his service,' said a man who has been both a friend and aide of Packwood's. 'They respected him on other levels and found the work important.'

But another former aide, who said she repeatedly had to rebuff Packwood, said his actions had jeopardized all he had stood for. This woman, who spoke on condition she not be identified, said she finally left the office because he did not curb his behavior.

'He couldn't seem to help himself,' she said. 'I cannot tell you how many people sat down with him and said, "You are going to come to a bad end. All your career's work on women's issues and on progressive issues is going to turn to dust."'

Florence Graves and Charles E. Shepard,
The Washington Post, 22 November 1992.

The Mother of Scandals

Financial scandals swamp Italy

Italy has been in turmoil since the early 1990s, following revelations of massive public corruption and the subsequent erosion of public confidence in the ruling Christian Democratic party. Even though Signor Silvio Berlusconi managed to form a government of business-technocrats, the purging process is far from over yet. During the height of the revelations in 1993, a number of prominent businessmen shot themselves rather than endure the humiliation of drawn-out investigations and imprisonment. The most senior of all the suicides was Raul Gardini.

ROME, July 23—One of Italy's best-known tycoons was found dead of a gunshot wound in his Milan apartment today as the country's huge and ever-broadening corruption investigation moved close to the core of his business dealings.

The police said they were treating the case as a suicide. The dead man is Raul Gardini, the 60-year-old former head of the Ferruzzi conglomerate. A man who epitomized the stylish life of Italy's super-rich, he was perhaps best known around the world as the chairman of the syndicate that owned *Il Moro di Venezia*, the Italian yacht that made it to the finals of the America's Cup, sailing's greatest prize, in 1992.

Mr Gardini was the second member of Italy's business elite said to have taken his own life this week. Gabriele Cagliari, head of the state energy corporation, Ente Nazionale Idrocarburi, was reported to have asphyxiated himself with a plastic bag in his cell on Tuesday after 133 days in San Vittore Prison in Milan.

Focus on Magistrates' Tactics

The deaths of men with the same high public profiles here as the heads, say, of General Motors or IBM in the United States stunned many Italians and fed an emotional debate over the tactics used by Milan's investigating magistrates to force confessions from leading businessmen and politicians.

'We have got to change the climate away from a witch hunt,' said Gerardo Bianco, a senior official of the Christian Democratic Party, which has been deeply tainted by the kickbacks scandal.

President Oscar Luigi Scalfaro, who has outraged the Milan investigators by suggesting that their techniques 'can sometimes kill', said today that Mr Gardini's death demonstrated a need for 'meditation and review' of investigating techniques.

It has become the Milan investigators' practice to hold top businessmen in jail under preventive detention laws until they identify purported co-conspirators and are then released on bail. Mr Cagliari was the first such detainee to commit suicide in jail.

Since February 1992, at least 2,500 businessmen and politicians have been investigated or arrested in connection with illicit payments, often in return for public works contracts, that have been at the center of the scandal.

Disgracing the Elite

The investigation has convulsed Italy, discrediting the political bosses who ran the country during the cold war and disgracing the entire political and business elite. Former Prime Ministers Giulio Andreotti and Bettino Craxi have both been implicated. Such has been its effect on the country's political life that some commentators have called it a revolution.

Like many other leading businessmen, Mr Gardini was told earlier this year that he was under investigation, but he had not been held in detention like Mr Cagliari and had refused to volunteer a confession as executives of other companies, notably Fiat and Olivetti, have done.

Then, last week, another former Ferruzzi boss, Giuseppe Garofano, returned from five months of self-imposed exile in London and Switzerland to face arrest and interrogation. According to investigators, Mr Garofano named Mr Gardini repeatedly in 14 hours of questioning.

According to police officials, Mr Gardini shot himself in the head with a pistol shortly after an employee brought breakfast to his bedroom, along with copies of morning newspapers reporting accusations by Mr Garofano that he had falsified company accounts and paid bribes to politicians. Police officials said he had left only a visiting card inscribed with the first names of his immediate family and the single word 'grazie'.

Mr Gardini was chairman of the family-owned Ferruzzi group from 1980 to 1991, when he was forced out in a family feud. In that period, he led the Ravenna-based company on a huge expansion drive that culminated in the 1987 acquisition of the Montedison chemicals giant, transforming a grain business into Italy's second-largest corporation, with holdings in the United States, France and Latin America.

What caught the public eye as much as his seeming financial success, though, was the glamor. Mr Gardini and his wife, Idina, cut elegant figures in the glittering Ravenna palazzo that was their home. He displayed extravagant tastes, racing yachts worth millions of dollars in prestige events, and made it to the America's Cup final in his first attempt before losing to *America 3*.

In his business dealings he personified the abrasive and frenetic mood of the 1980s, as much a time of rapidly amassed wealth in Italy as on Wall Street.

But the meteor began to dim in 1989, when Mr Gardini formed a short-lived merger with the chemicals division of ENI, the state energy group that Mr Cagliari took over in the same year. The joint company, called Enimont, foundered under accusations of mismanagement, and one of the strands of the investigation by the Milan magistrates concerns reported payments worth some $38 million to the then-dominant Christian Democrats and Socialists.

Losses Reportedly Hidden

In 1990, ENI paid Ferruzzi the equivalent of $2.8 billion to relinquish its 40 percent stake in Enimont. Investigators have questioned whether the sale was deliberately overvalued.

Mr Gardini was ousted from Ferruzzi in 1991 in a family dispute over how the company should be restructured. His wife sold her shares to other family members for some $400 million, and Mr Gardini went yacht racing in California before returning to Italy last year to start new business ventures in food and mineral water.

As recently as last month, he was conducting a spirited public defense of his tenure as head of Ferruzzi, saying its present indebtedness – totalling a staggering $20 billion – was not his fault.

According to Mr Garofano's leaked testimony, however, Mr Gardini falsified company balance sheets to hide losses totalling between $200 million and $300 million incurred in speculations on the Chicago futures market in 1989. He also accused Mr Gardini of having used real estate deals to build up covert slush funds.

Mr Garofano was chairman of Montedison from 1990 until January this year. He faces accusations of paying a $160,000 kickback in company funds to the Christian Democrats.

Investigators said Mr Gardini died shortly before he was due to be arrested along with three other high-ranking Ferruzzi figures. It was not clear whether he knew of his impending arrest. The three other men – Carlo Sama, Vittorio Giuliani Ricci and Sergio Cusani – were arrested later in the day.

The debacle sealed the collapse of Ferruzzi, whose shares dropped on the Milan exchange to 395 lira, on a par value of 1,000 lira, and whose affairs had already been placed in the hands of creditor banks because of the extent of its indebtedness.

Alan Cowell, *The New York Times*, 24 July 1993.

Manning Clark

The flaws of Professor Manning Clark, as revealed by his publisher

Manning Clark was the most famous Australian historian of the century. His six-volume History of Australia *remains the standard work on the subject. Peter Ryan, his publisher and editor for more than two decades at Melbourne University Press, caused a furore when he wrote the following piece about the great man. He was later accused of being a cannibal and scoundrel by the many admirers of Clark still in high positions in the Australian academic establishment.*

> '... the sorry tale of the frog
> who burst his belly with his own afflatus'
> James McAuley

This essay is an overdue axe laid to the stalk of a tall poppy. Never mind that Australians are accused of an envious bent for lopping the heads off achievers: any poppy grown into a lush and suffocating jungle must be pruned and cleared, to let in light and fresh air.

Manning Clark's *A History of Australia* was issued in six thick volumes over the quarter-century 1962–87. For many people, it has come almost to *be* Australian history, defining Australia much as the Old Testament defines Judaism. Long and troubled thought about this prodigy of my own times persuades me that Clark's *History* inflated itself progressively and relentlessly over the years, so that as its volume increased its density diminished. Born though it was of a weighty and even a noble vision, it achieved eventually the insubstantiality of thistledown. It became a construct spun from fairy floss, and much of that false.

Between 1947 and Manning Clark's death in 1991 I watched – so it seemed to me – a scholar transformed into the creature of his creation; into the prisoner of his own pen; into the puppet of the process he had himself begun with the hard, lonely labour and deep soul-searching that lay behind his *History*.

I had, in all conscience, opportunity enough for observation both of author and of book. I met Manning as his honours student in 1947, his second year of teaching what then was the outrageously newfangled subject of Australian history at Melbourne University. We very quickly became roistering companions, doing all the things that roisterers do.

Of the many things in my life upon which I must look back with shame, the chiefest is that of having been the publisher of Manning Clark's *A History of Australia* and of having given him that support and encouragement which an author expects of his publisher. As each succeeding volume got worse than its predecessor – and it did – I ought to have followed my instinct, and resigned from the press...

Why, near the end of my life, should I be setting all this out? It is a painful labour, performed without relish, and one certain to cost me friendships. Perhaps it amounts to no more than having a bad tooth extracted – one which has been nagging for years. I am not sure.

Since the editing of Volume I had been completed before my time at Melbourne University Press began, the manuscript of Volume II was my first experience of dealing with Manning's work 'from the egg'. I had never met such an egg in my life. Some authors – some of the greatest – have simply no talent for producing a manuscript which an editor could truthfully call 'a pleasure to work on'. With Manning, every technical blemish known to the editorial craft was strewn thick upon his pages. His efforts to expunge such faults rarely helped, since his handwriting, on his own confession, was about fifty per cent illegible.

The copy editing of a Clark manuscript was thus invariably tedious, prolonged and expensive, but I do not say this to complain. It cost MUP a great deal of money, but his sales earned a great deal more. Manning couldn't help it, and I confess to being myself far from able to produce an impeccable typescript. He was always pleasant to his editors in their interminable sessions together, and generous in his praise when their job was finished.

Of more concern than the technical faults were his eccentricities of style, his readiness to replace reasonable explanation with gnomic pronouncement, his tendency to let the narrative lift itself onto a level exalted beyond the requirements of commonsense, and above all his unreliability with mere facts.

The manuscript of Volume II saw my only serious effort to challenge the wisdom of trying to tell Australian history in the style of an Old Testament prophet, or of the chorus in a Greek tragedy. He could see no danger in the needless constant treading on the edge of bathos. I think he allowed me to delete a few of the more conspicuously repetitive 'fatal flaws' and such like, and to correct the attributions to the Bible of passages drawn from the Book of Common Prayer (odd, for a son of the vicarage); but that was it.

When for a third time I re-read the manuscript of Volume II as a whole,

I realised that a Manning Clark is a Manning Clark is a Manning Clark; as well try to remove the bubbles from a glass of ginger beer. The publisher had two possible courses: take him as he was, 'fatal flaws', blood-on-the-wattle and all, for another three to five volumes – the final size of the project not then having been decided; or break the contract and refuse to publish any further parts.

It was the hardest decision of my time at MUP. To discontinue would have required the agreement of my Boards of Management, and in this matter it is highly doubtful that they would have accepted the recommendation of their Director. But I consulted no-one, and decided alone to continue. I don't think Manning, whose intuitions were sometimes almost supernaturally keen, suspected any subterranean crisis. But I cursed that I was not working for some other publishing house, where my scruples would signify less, or not at all.

. . .

One observed the outward trappings of the Manning Clark *persona* being developed with almost as much care as was being lavished on the manuscript. I cannot remember the year the beard appeared, nor the heavy boots, nor the broad leather belt, the curious hat, the stout walking stick. Presuming on long intimacy, I jeered as each new costume item was added. He took my jibes with imperturbable good nature and witty ripostes, never denying that he was turning himself into 'a character'. He reported with delight upon a visit he made in the USA to the hatter who outfitted John Wayne. 'You got two feet of head there, Mr Clark,' said the bespoke supplier, after measuring the skull which would support the Clark handmade hat. Well before the launching of Volume IV in Canberra in 1978 Manning was an Australian icon, as instantly recognisable as Chesty Bond, or Rolf Harris.

. . .

Manning Clark's *A History of Australia* remains largely an imposition on Australian credulity – more plainly, a fraud; and the author himself was partly a mountebank. But he was intelligent, lively and a stimulating companion. Never to have known him would, in retrospect, have been an unthinkable deprivation. There were things in him to admire; to have beaten the grog was an achievement of character; after his 'wild days' passed, his devotion to his large family was touching; he stuck to his immense task of writing, even under the handicap of serious health problems; he could be sly, as some of his friends found, to their hurt surprise, yet his devotion (for example) to journalist and old university chum Ian Fitchett, in his long last illness, was a paragon of fidelity.

He suffered deep depression. Often of a Monday morning he would ring me, and ask to be cheered up. It was not difficult, for his spirits rose steadily in response to some piece of scandal, or a bawdy story I had collected for him over the weekend. Somehow, during those Monday morning phone calls, I felt as close to him as I ever got. Of all the people I have met, Manning's character is the most elusive, the most baffling to pin down and to describe. But though it was easy to like him, and to enjoy his company, it was impossible to give him my respect, or to respect any of his writings since the documents of 1955.

...

His *History* is made tedious by repeated sneers at the bourgeoisie, mostly trivial, irrelevant and embarrassingly juvenile – echoes of student Labour Club conferences in the 1940s. Fair play for the bourgeoisie is not expected, though taking them to task for a supposed taste for Brahms is a bit hard.

But who was sneering? A man who had never left the shelter of the bourgeois cocoon in his life; the vicar's son who went to Melbourne Grammar, to Melbourne University and on to Oxford, who taught at Geelong Grammar and moved on to tenured appointments in Australian universities; the professor who lived in a Robin Boyd house in the leafiest part of Canberra; the owner of several properties, the man who travelled the world in comfort, who was steeped and soaked and saturated in bourgeois culture and who, above all, profoundly understood it, loved it, and drew from it his heart's ease and his mind's refreshment. To kick down the ladder by which one mounted is one of mankind's widespread habits, but it is not attractive; and it is described by one short word: humbug.

His passion to be a public figure grew with the years, and though he could produce a *pronunciamento* about every issue of the day, his words were not invariably based on any special qualification or insight. A. D. Hope drew a bead on those who would be Australia's 'public wise men, even if they had to wear a funny hat as trademark'; Hope was aiming at Patrick White's tea-cosy and at the fur-felt millinery of Manning Clark. The *History* repetitively denounces 'grovellers' to the Crown, but how that form of servility differs from fawning on each successive Labor prime minister is hard to see, and he accepted from the Queen the Companionship of the Order of Australia. Manning was happy to be used by the Labor Party as an electoral asset, and in the days when Mr Keating was Treasurer (and strenuously white-anting Mr Hawke) Manning told me that he had formed a close personal relationship with Keating, whom he had discovered to be not the flint-hard politician of popular perception, but a man who was 'very warm and soft'.

Whether clad in their original crimson jackets or their new pictorial covers, thousands of six-volume sets of Manning Clark now stand in libraries or on private bookshelves. Are they dog-eared from constant consultation, or unread, coated with dust? . . . Alas, their limitations are conspicuous and disappointing.

There is no strong narrative thread to guide a reader firmly through the broad plot from 1788 to 1935, even though Australia's history is short, and not unduly complicated; Clark's original three filaments of Protestantism, Catholicism and the Enlightenment are certainly not spun successfully into such an articulating cord. As for individual themes, such as gold or wool, exploration or trade unions, it is very hard to follow what any of them signified, or what exactly happened.

. . .

Quite apart from the bad example set by his factual inaccuracy, parents and teachers sensitive to the needs of young minds will be reluctant to plunge them too deeply into Manning Clark, especially as other history books are now available. There is something depressing, morale-lowering, spirit sapping in the groans of 'unleavened bread' and 'kingdom of nothingness'. And they come oddly indeed from a man who did as well out of bourgeois life as Clark did.

If our history were really as black as Clark so wickedly paints it, children would just have to face it. But in fact, Australia's fortunes went up and went down; we won some and we lost some; history is simply life writ large. The great depressions of the 1890s and 1930s were painful times, but for all that we once enjoyed the highest standard of living on the globe, and amazed the rest of the world with our bold political and social progress. Few of the original convicts wanted to go back home, and today people queue up at Australian embassies the world over, seeking to migrate here. The Australian experience of life for ordinary people has not lacked its rough patches, but by the standards of comparison which the real world allows, it has been unrivalled in its spaciousness and freedom. And these are the people whom Clark portrays not merely as losers, but *destined* to be losers.

The six volumes are almost unbelievably prolix – the opinion of one who has read the entire work not merely once throughout, but three times, and some parts oftener. It is a vast cauldron of very thin verbal soup, in which swim morsels of nourishing meat, widely spaced. I have been told that a single-volume abridgement is in preparation. The scholar

preparing it can hardly find his commission a serious challenge. He need –
metaphorically – merely stick a pin in the mass and allow the gaseous
verbal excess to hiss its way out.

What, then, has preserved the existence, and even the influence, of this
immense and odd cultural artefact? Perhaps it survives as a relic, a product
of the sixties and seventies which an ageing generation still clutches as a
security blanket? Perhaps, deep in many an unconscious, it retains vague
but comforting associations with Woodstock and Vietnam protests and
nice Mr Whitlam who, on the very point of establishing the kingdom of
heaven upon earth, was 'crucified' by the 'forces of Mammon'? Perhaps
... who knows?

A mystery it remains – over a million printed English words, probably
unrivalled in their power to combine the *non sequitur* with the anticlimax,
and to wring the last drops from a series of foregone conclusions. It could
almost be claimed for Manning Clark's *A History of Australia* that it has
given longwindedness and self-pity a bad name.

Peter Ryan, *Quadrant*, 1993.

....

The Revealing Story of Lady Buck

Lady Bienvenida Buck and Sir Peter Harding

*Although it is widely assumed that politicians can survive a bit of publicity
about extramarital affairs, the same standards do not apply to Britain's senior
military figures. Sir Peter Harding, chief of Britain's armed forces, resigned a day
after this story appeared in the* News of the World.

The chief of Britain's armed forces has been bedding an ex-Tory defence
minister's Spanish wife. Married Sir Peter Harding, 60, is a trusted aide of
the Queen and John Major. Lady Bienvenida Buck, 32, is a sultry blonde
... Sir Peter abandoned his bodyguard and turned himself into a terrorist

target for a series of sex sessions. In torrid love notes he told her: 'You have the body of a young girl ... your breasts so petite. I long to envelop you in kisses.'

Gently caressing his lover's leg under the restaurant table, defence supremo Sir Peter Harding was the very picture of a man in love. Oblivious to the other diners in the relaxed luxury of the Meridian Hotel's Oak Room, the dashing RAF man stared deep into the Spanish eyes of his beautiful Bienvenida and sipped champagne. Then he glanced down at her tiny hand in his, caught sight of his wrist-watch ... and leapt to his feet in panic. 'My God,' he hissed. 'I'm late for my meeting with the PM!'

Suddenly he was gone, all thoughts of passion forgotten as he raced towards Number 10 to advise John Major on national security. But Bienvenida gradually came to accept the bizarre consequences of loving the top military man in Britain. For during their two and a half year affair, Sir Peter:

- Jumped naked from her bed, mumbling: 'Must go – top level conference on!'
- Confided his concern for young pilots facing death in the Gulf War, while he seduced Bienvenida over a romantic dinner for two.
- Kept his RAF driver waiting at the wheel for $2\frac{1}{2}$ hours while he helped his mistress feed ducks at Regent's Park.

The contradictions of their situation were not lost on Bienvenida. Like the time they shared a steamy sex session at a flat she had borrowed from a friend. 'Once we had made love,' she remembered, 'he said regretfully, "Sorry, I have to go – top level conference on!"'

'He got out of bed naked, showered, dressed and called a taxi. I thought it was ironic that minutes after leaving my bed, he was discussing high-level security issues.' They fell in love in February 1991 when the Gulf War was raging. Sir Peter, then 57, divided his time between manoeuvring his young mistress into bed ... and sending young men to death in the desert.

Bienvenida, then 34, had been married to Tory MP Sir Antony Buck for just 11 months. But after falling for Sir Peter at an official dinner, she readily agreed to see him at the Belvedere Restaurant in London's Holland Park. At the time, London restaurants were having a lean time, as customers fearing terror attacks inspired by Saddam Hussein stayed at home. But Sir Peter – a major target beyond the Iraqi tyrant's wildest dreams – was only too happy to eat, drink and be merry. 'I was surprised that he could find time for a romantic dinner with such pressure on him,' says Bienvenida. 'He was Chief of the Air Staff at the time, and the man directly responsible for those planes flying into Iraq. As far as I could tell, he came directly from his desk. RAF pilots had been shot down, some killed, and some captured and paraded bruised and injured on TV. I remember him saying how brave they were, how proud he was of them and how tragic to see young men coming back in coffins. But he had this incredible ability to switch off. We'd talk about the war, then he'd completely forget it and start ordering wine and flirting. I wondered how, even as his pilots were flying into danger, he could be romantic with me at such a time of national crisis.'

Throughout the Gulf War, the married defence boss continued to meet Bienvenida. 'Even though the war was still on,' she recalls, 'he always had time for lunch.' Before the last tanks had rolled out of Kuwait, they were lovers. From their very first night of sex in a borrowed flat in St John's Wood, Bienvenida was surprised by Sir Peter's unbridled passion. But she was shocked at his total disregard for his own safety. For despite his undisputed status as a top grade terrorist target, he would dismiss his bodyguard/driver, blab about his future movements and canoodle with her in public. Sir Peter soon raised the suspicions of his driver who reported to his MOD bosses. And they are believed to have called in MI5 to monitor the couple's love letters for breaches of security. A security expert said: 'If this woman had told the IRA or one of Europe's terror groups, it would have been easy to assassinate him.' And the affair was in clear contravention of the MOD's new code of conduct – banning adultery. As the man at the very top of the armed forces, Sir Peter knew that he had no choice but to quit when exposed. Once, as she dined with Sir Peter at the Meridian Hotel in Piccadilly, they spotted a senior Army officer with a much younger woman. As the other couple left, says Bienvenida, the officer approached Sir Peter and said: 'Look, old boy. I was never here. You never saw me in here at all, OK?' Sir Peter readily agreed. Later in the affair, after Sir Peter's promotion to Chief of Defence Staff, Bienvenida recalls him keeping his RAF driver waiting for hours ... while he picnicked with her in Regent's Park. As the minder waited in Sir Peter's official car for $2\frac{1}{2}$ hours, the lovers nibbled titbits, fed ducks and held hands. Bienvenida says: 'It was sunny, we picnicked and strolled in the park. But when it was time for him to go, he told me his car and driver were still waiting. I thought it was an incredible waste of money and manpower – not to mention the risk he was taking.'

News of the World, 13 March 1994.

Index